D0490004

Please return / renew by date shown.
You can renew at: **norlink.norfolk.gov.uk**
or by telephone: **0344 800 8006**
Please have your library card & PIN ready.

STEVE JOBS

insanely great

a graphic biography by jessie hartland

10 9 8 7 6 5 4 3 2 1

Virgin Books, an imprint of Ebury Publishing,
20 Vauxhall Bridge Road,
London SW1V 2SA

Virgin Books is part of the Penguin Random House group of companies whose
addresses can be found at global.penguinrandomhouse.com

Penguin
Random House
UK

First published by Virgin Books in 2015
First published in the United States by Schwartz & Wade Books in 2015

www.eburypublishing.co.uk

A CIP catalogue record for this book is available from the British Library

ISBN 9780753557020

Printed and bound by Clays Ltd, St Ives plc

Penguin Random House is committed to a sustainable future for our business, our
readers and our planet. This book is made from Forest Stewardship Council® certified
paper.

MIX
Paper from
responsible sources
FSC
www.fsc.org   FSC® C018179

This one's for
my son, Sam—
lover of apple pie
as well as those
other, nonedible
apple products.

Contents

Here's to the crazy ones. The misfits. The rebels. The troublemakers. The square pegs in the round holes. The ones who see things differently. Because the people who are crazy enough to think they can change the world are the ones who do.

— S.J.

Timeline

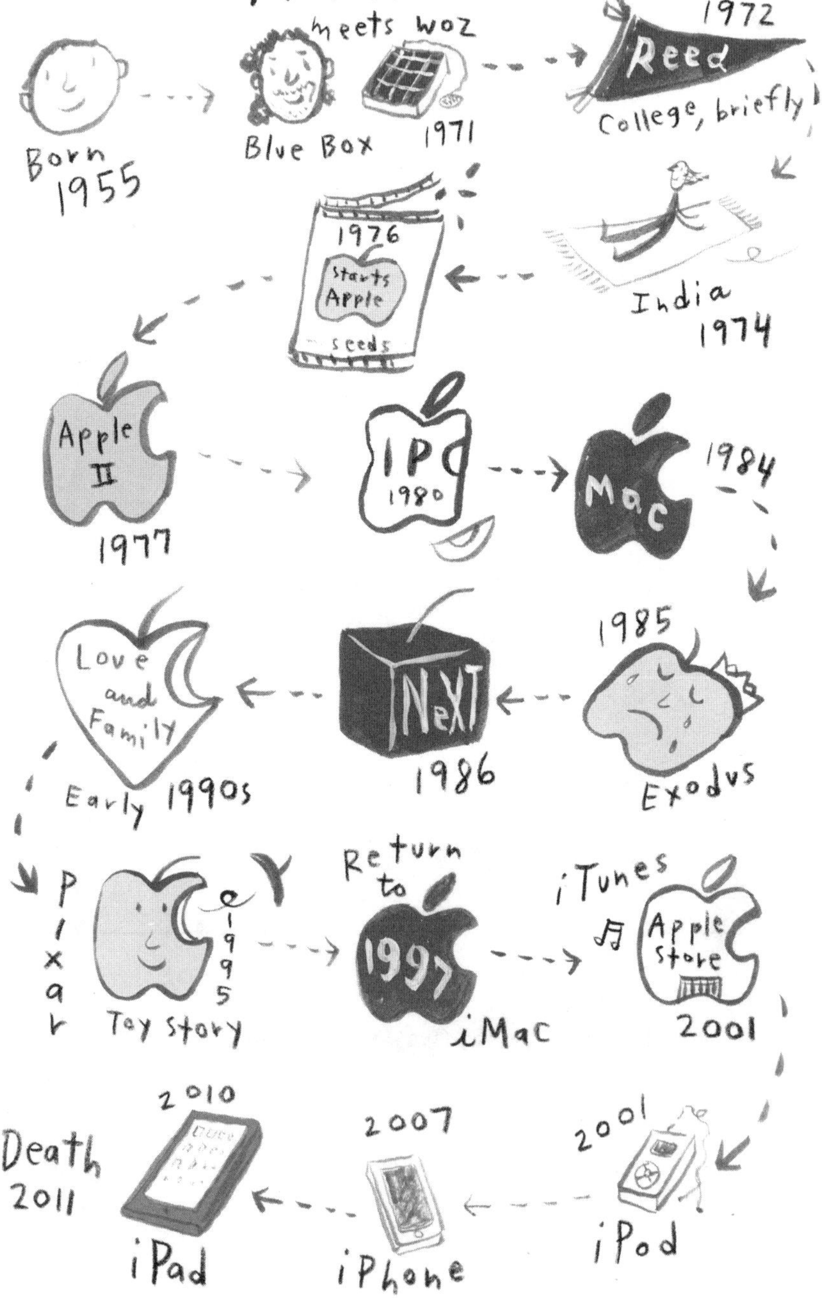

Born
1955
meets woz
Blue Box
1971
1972
Reed
College, briefly
India
1974
1976
Starts
Apple
seeds
Apple
II
1977
IPO
1980
Mac
1984
1985
Exodus
NeXT
1986
Love
and
Family
Early 1990s
Pixar
1995
Toy Story
Return to
1997
iMac
iTunes
Apple
Store
2001
2001
iPod
2007
iPhone
2010
iPad
Death
2011

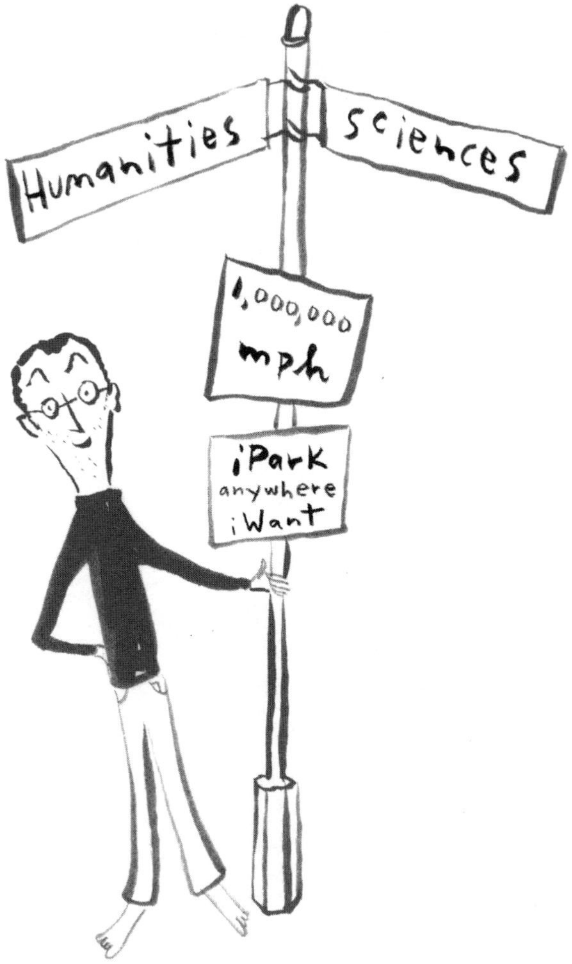
Humanities
sciences
1,000,000
mph
iPark
anywhere
iWant

the journey
is the reward

-S. J.

STEVE JOBS

He was a tinkerer. He was willful and rebellious and did NOT like to follow rules.

He dropped out of college after just one semester and took a calligraphy class.

He started Apple Computer in his parents' garage and it became the world's most valuable company.

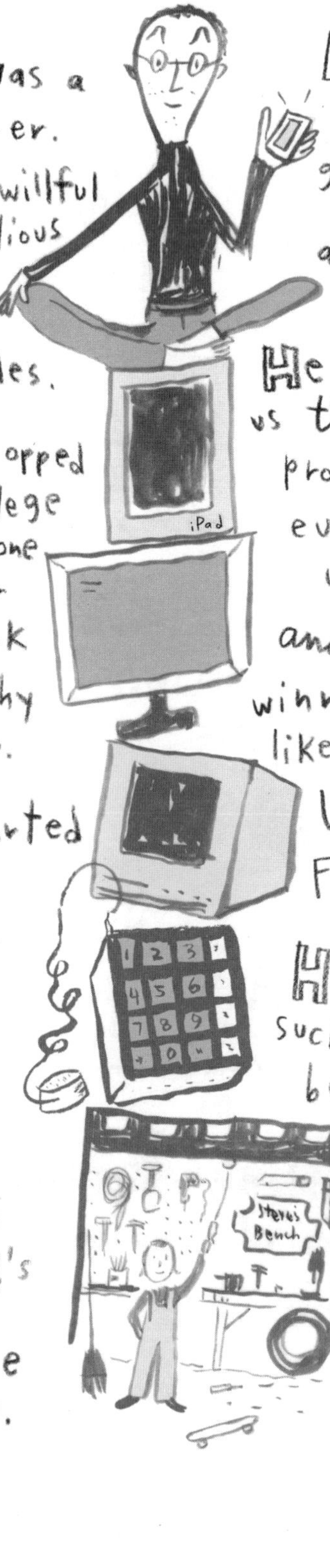
iPad
Steve's Bench

He was a techno-geek and an artist.

He brought us the COOL products everyone wants, and award-winning films like Toy Story, UP, and Finding Nemo.

How did such an iconoclast become the world's best businessman? This is the story.

chapter

1

The

Young Sprout

(1955 - 1965)

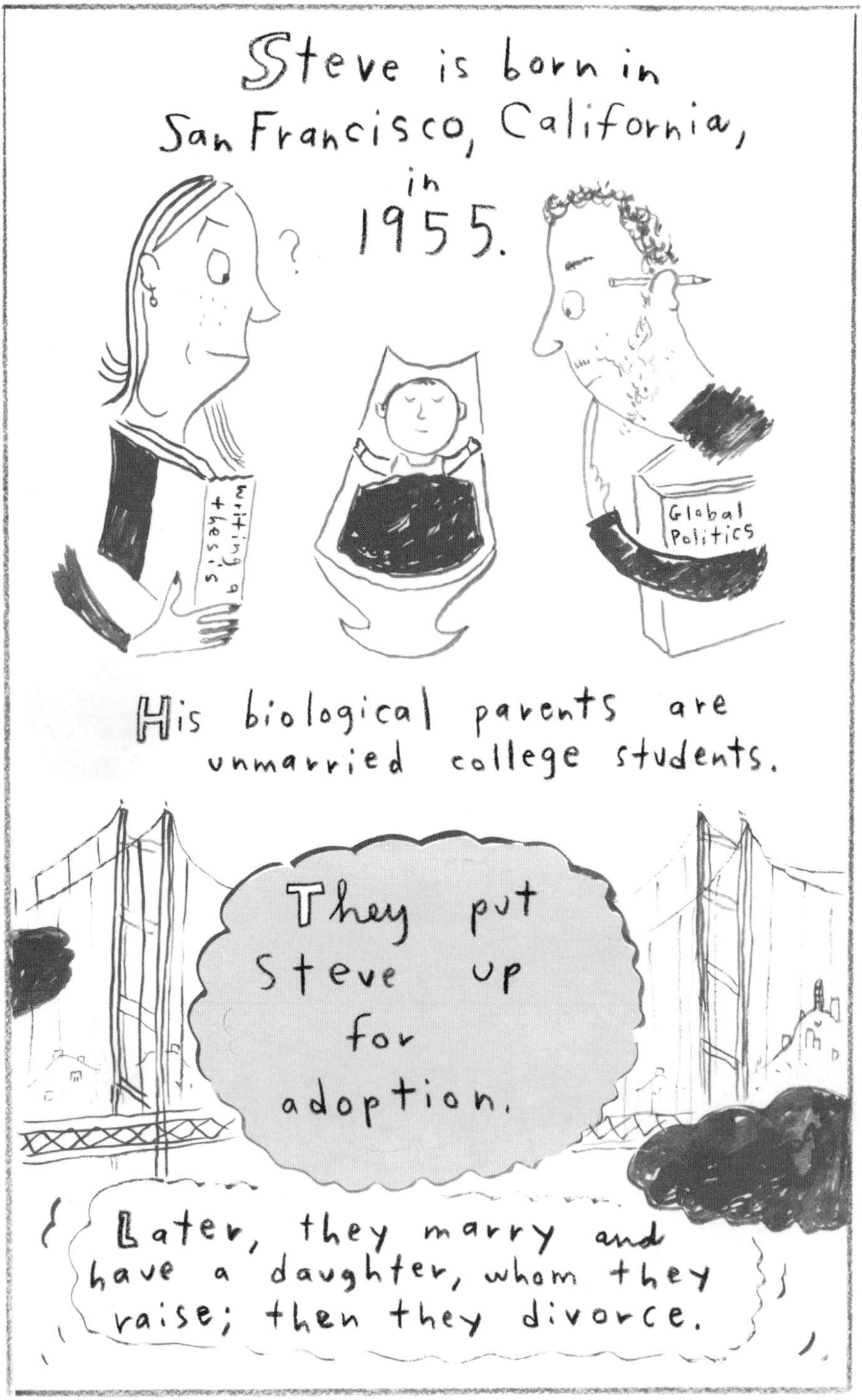
Steve is born in San Francisco, California, in 1955.
writing a thesis
Global Politics
His biological parents are unmarried college students.
They put Steve up for adoption.
Later, they marry and have a daughter, whom they raise; then they divorce.

Steve is adopted by Clara and Paul Jobs.

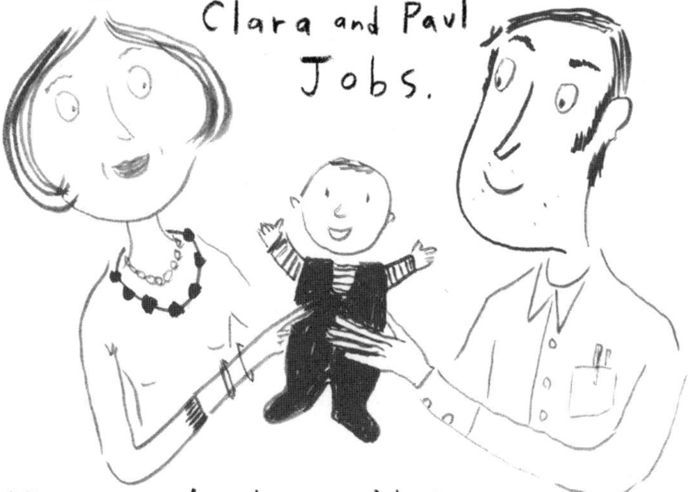

Unable to have their own baby, they are ecstatic. Two years later, they adopt a girl, Patty.

Steve grows up in the Santa Clara Valley (now Silicon* Valley), south of San Francisco.

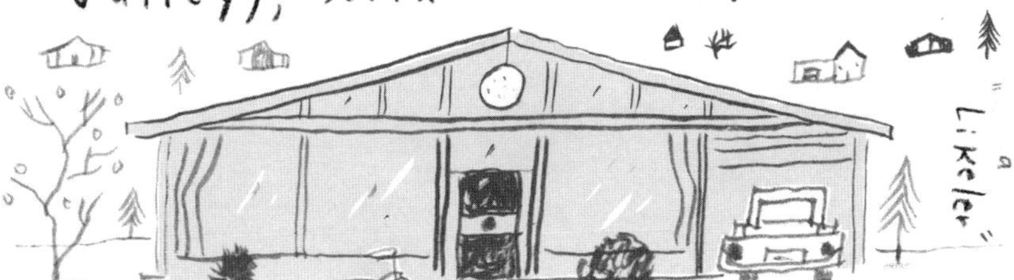
a "Likeler"

They live in a tract home inspired by the developer Joseph Eichler: simple, modern, suburban.

* a common element found in sand and glass, used in making high-tech devices

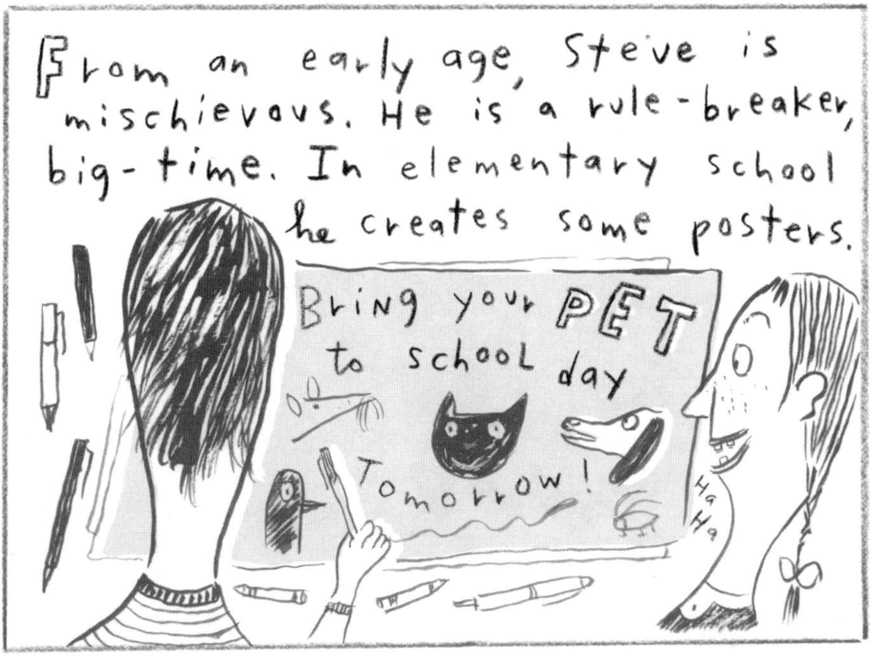
From an early age, Steve is mischievous. He is a rule-breaker, big-time. In elementary school he creates some posters.
Bring your PET to school day
Tomorrow!
Ha Ha

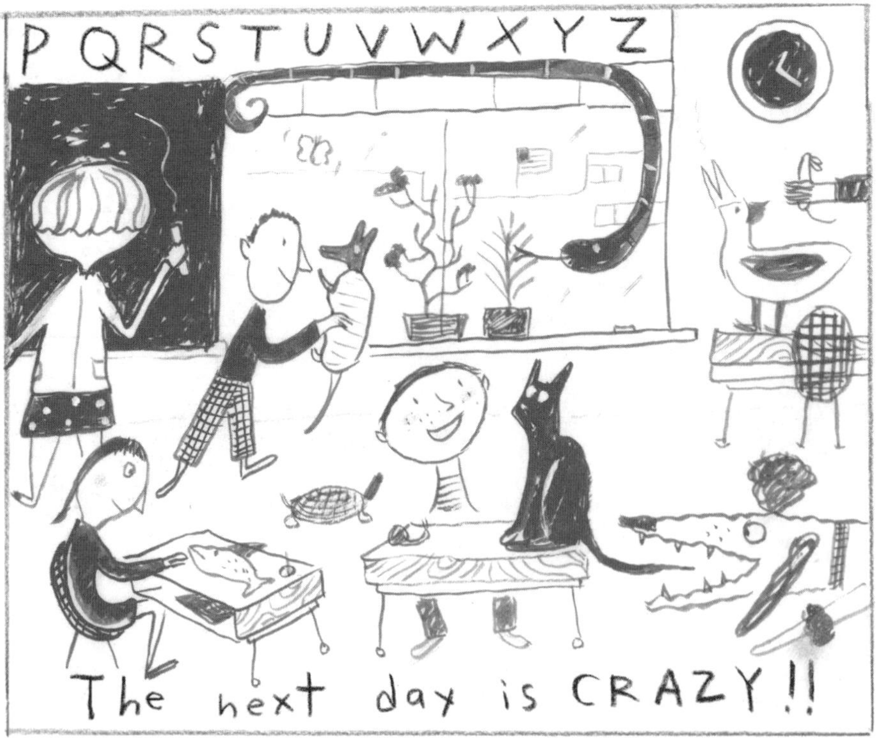
PQRSTUVWXYZ
The next day is CRAZY!!

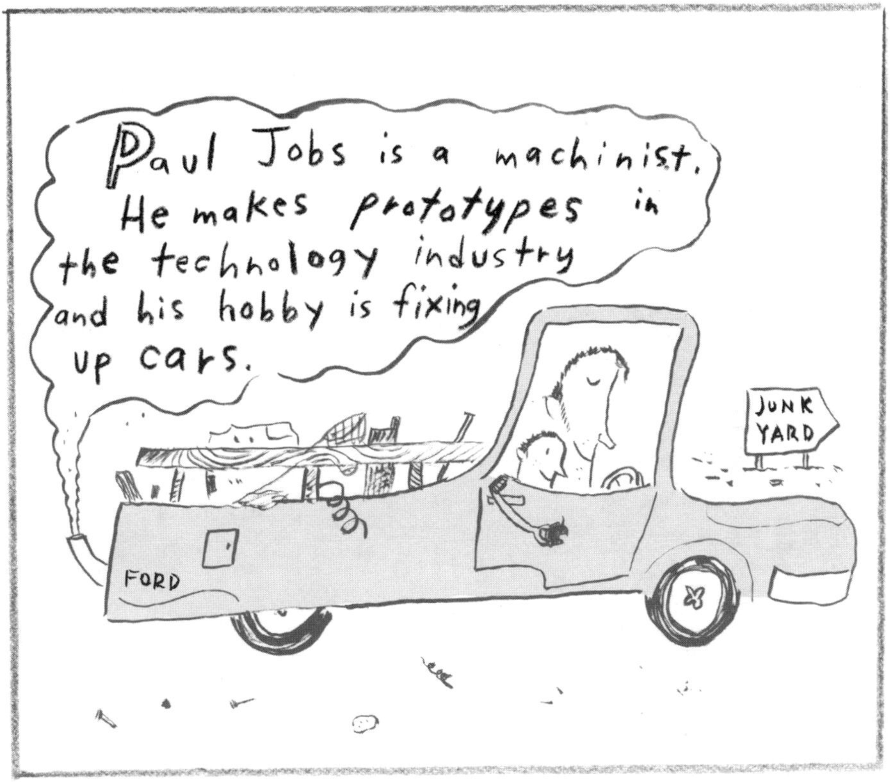
Paul Jobs is a machinist. He makes prototypes in the technology industry and his hobby is fixing up cars.
JUNK YARD
FORD

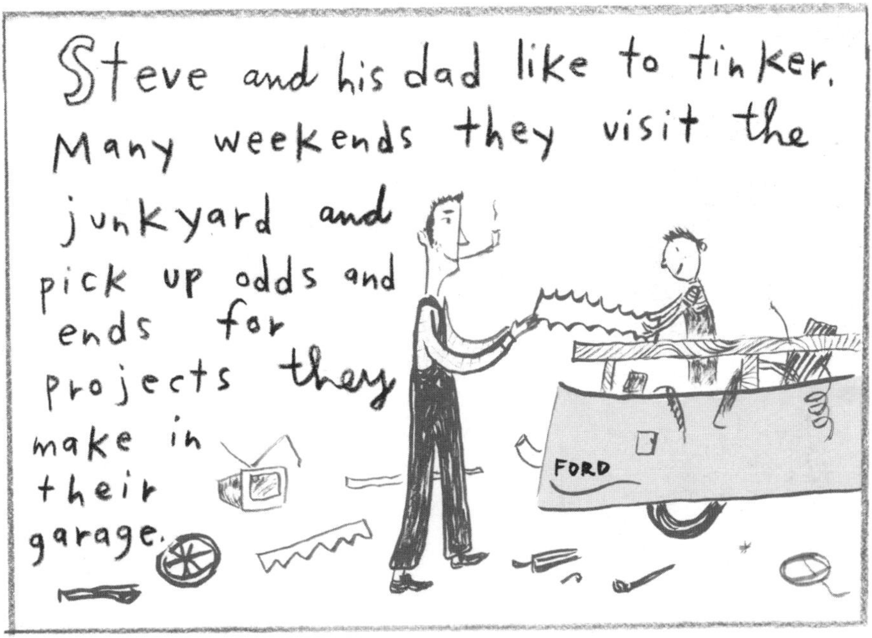
Steve and his dad like to tinker. Many weekends they visit the junkyard and pick up odds and ends for projects they make in their garage.
FORD

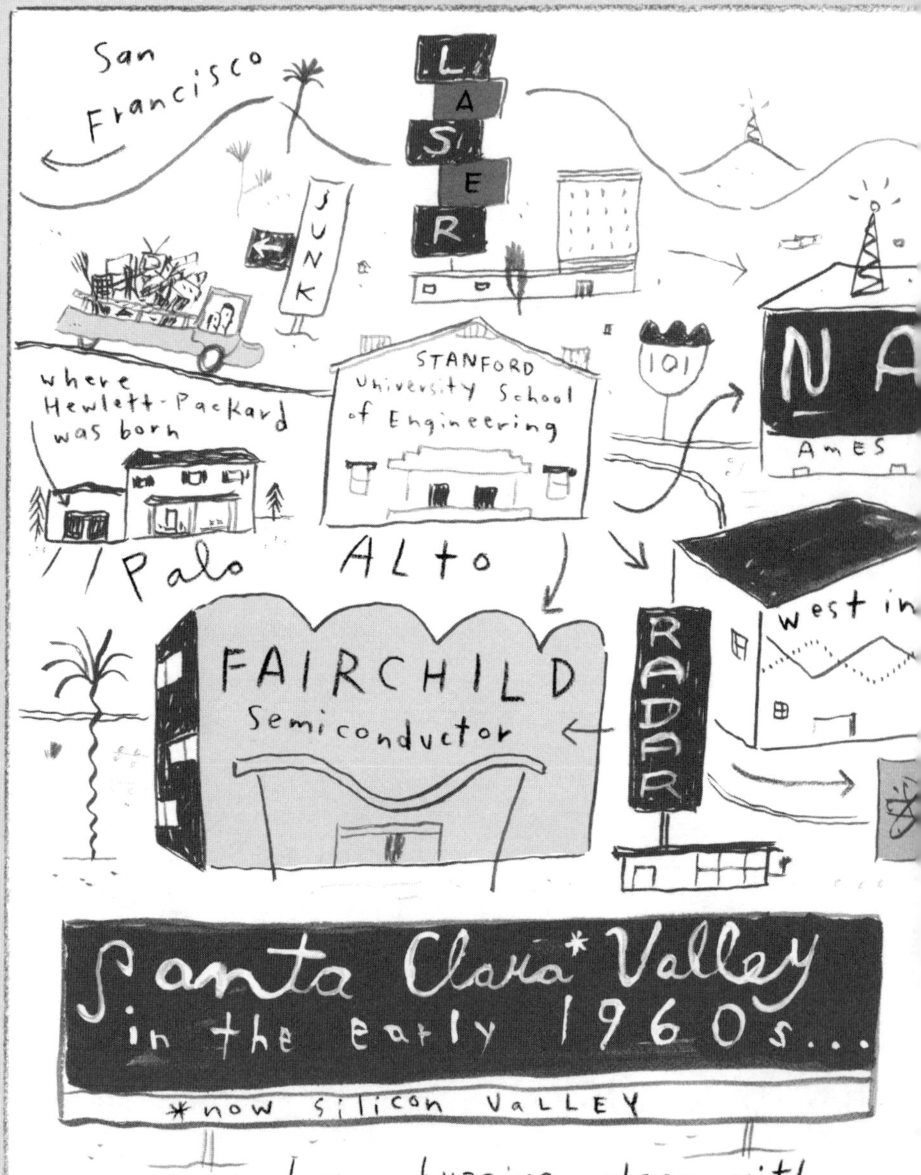
San Francisco
LASER
JUNK
STANFORD University School of Engineering
101
NA
AMES
where Hewlett-Packard was born
Palo Alto
FAIRCHILD Semiconductor
RADAR
west in
Santa Clara* Valley in the early 1960s...
*now Silicon Valley

...is a busy, buzzing place with hundreds of technology companies employing thousands of people. The United States is in a cold war and a space race with the Soviet Union. The Russians live in a communist society, considered a threat to US capitalism.

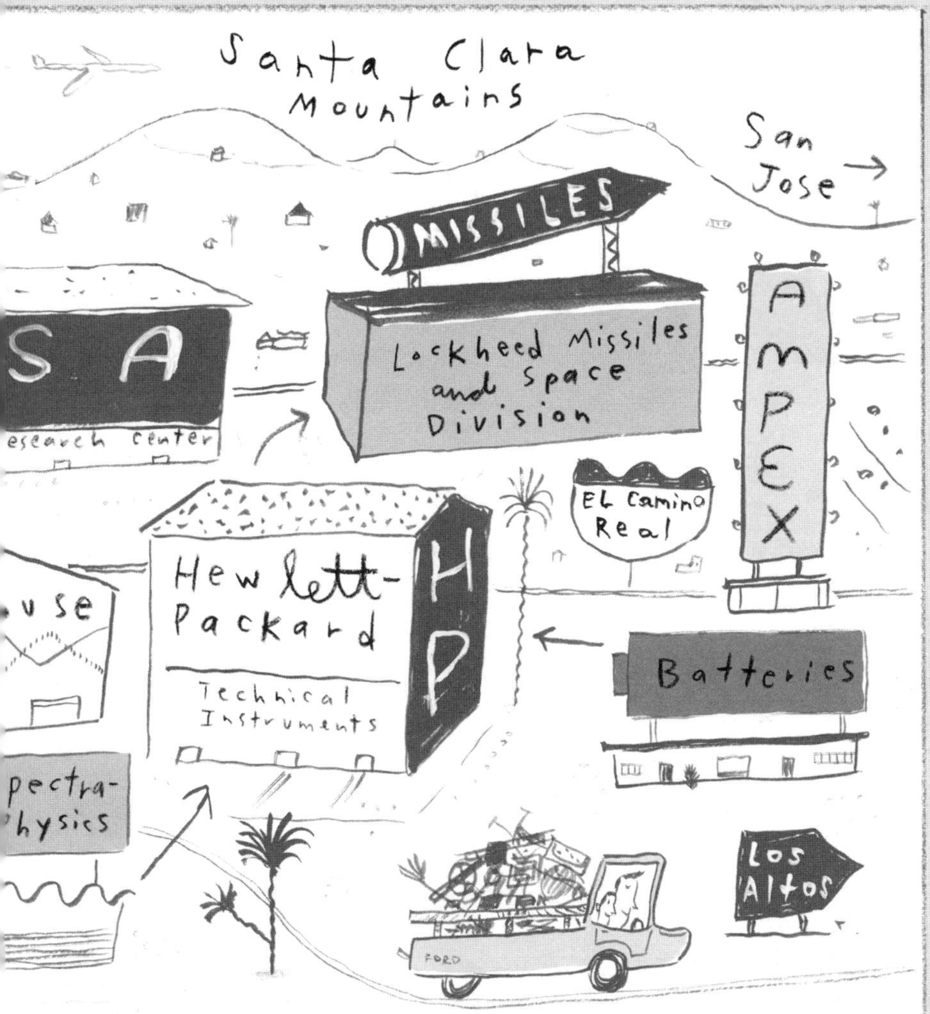
Santa Clara Mountains
San Jose
MISSILES
Lockheed Missiles and Space Division
AMPEX
SA
esearch center
EL Camino Real
Hewlett-Packard
Technical Instruments
HP
Batteries
use
pectra-
hysics
Los Altos
FORD

Having launched Sputnik, the first satellite, in 1957, the Soviets are winning the space race. Scrambling to catch up, the US government is funding oodles of defense contractors who are experimenting with new space and weapons technology. These Silicon Valley businesses are part of what's called the military-industrial complex.

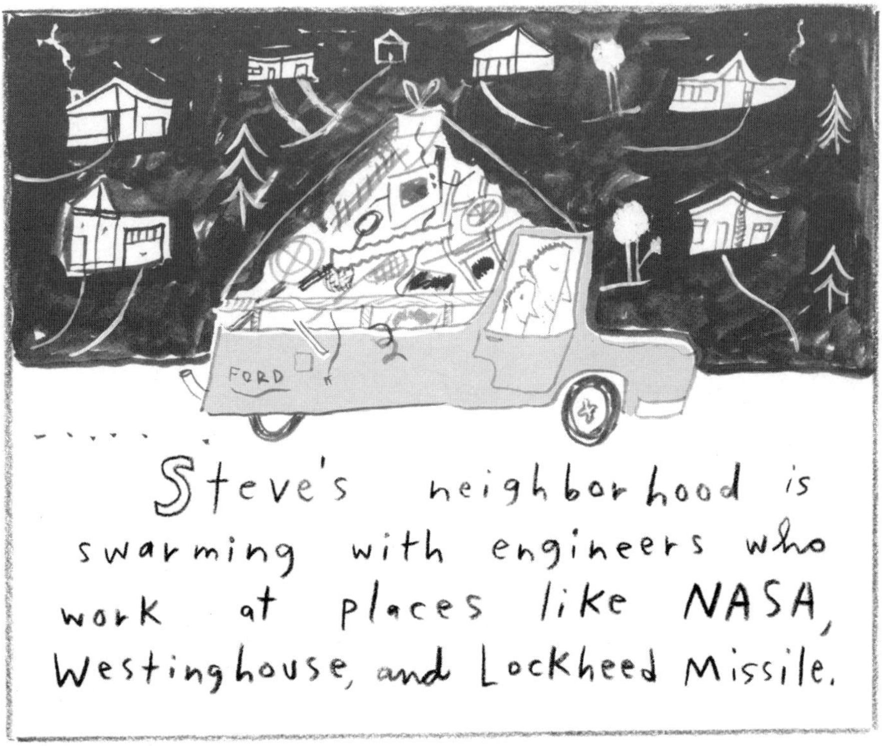
FORD
Steve's neighborhood is swarming with engineers who work at places like NASA, Westinghouse, and Lockheed Missile.

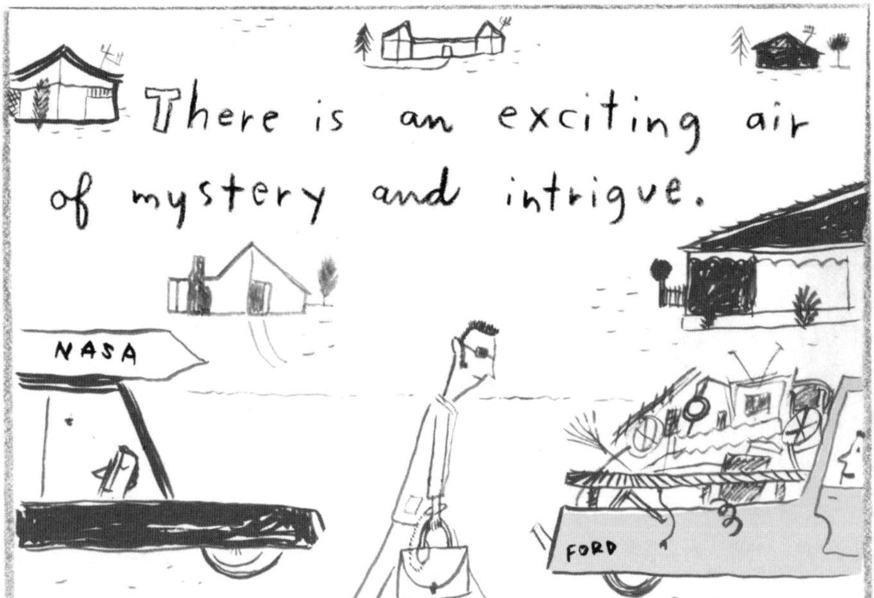
There is an exciting air of mystery and intrigue.
NASA
FORD

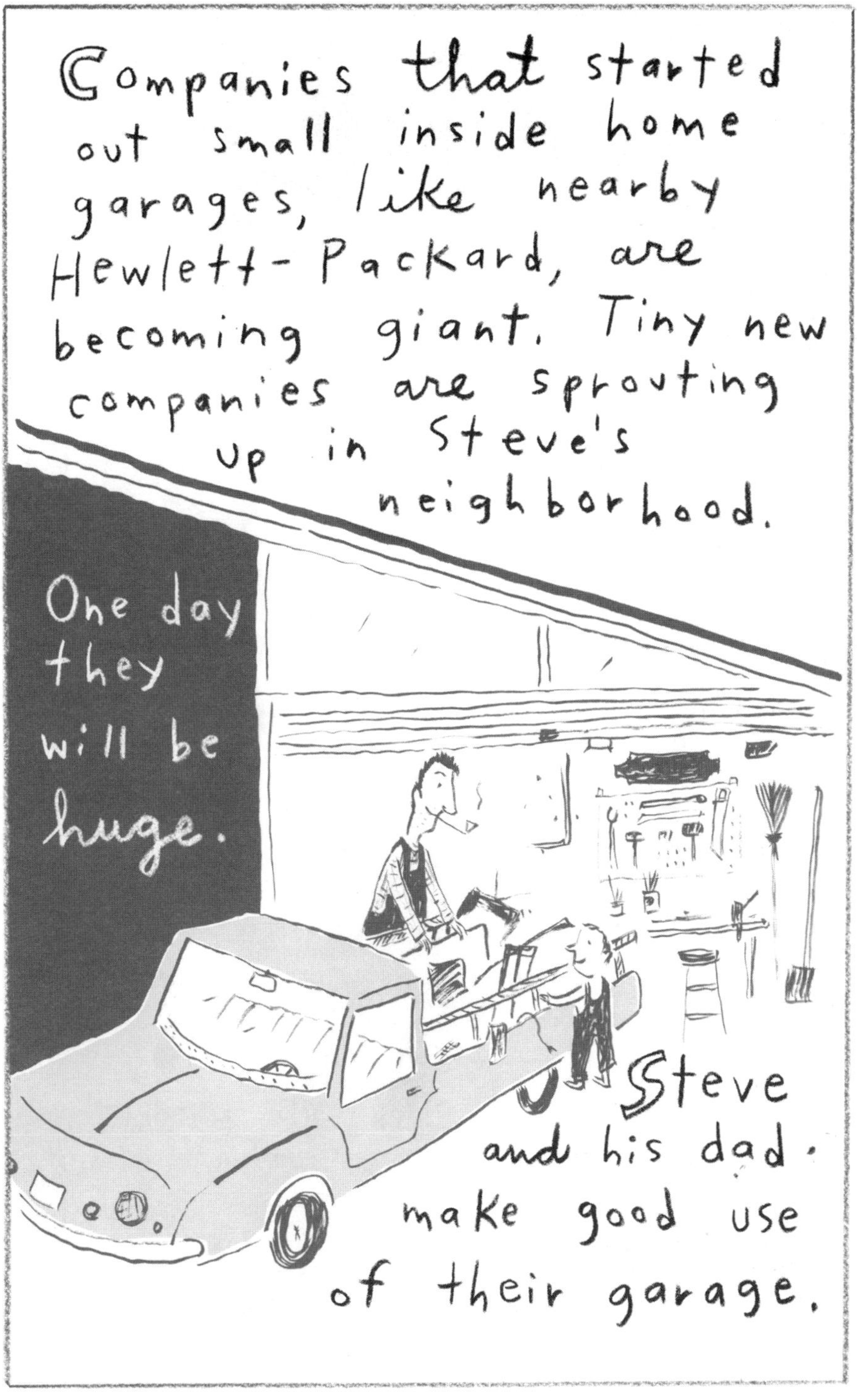
Companies that started out small inside home garages, like nearby Hewlett-Packard, are becoming giant. Tiny new companies are sprouting up in Steve's neighborhood.
One day they will be huge.
Steve and his dad make good use of their garage.

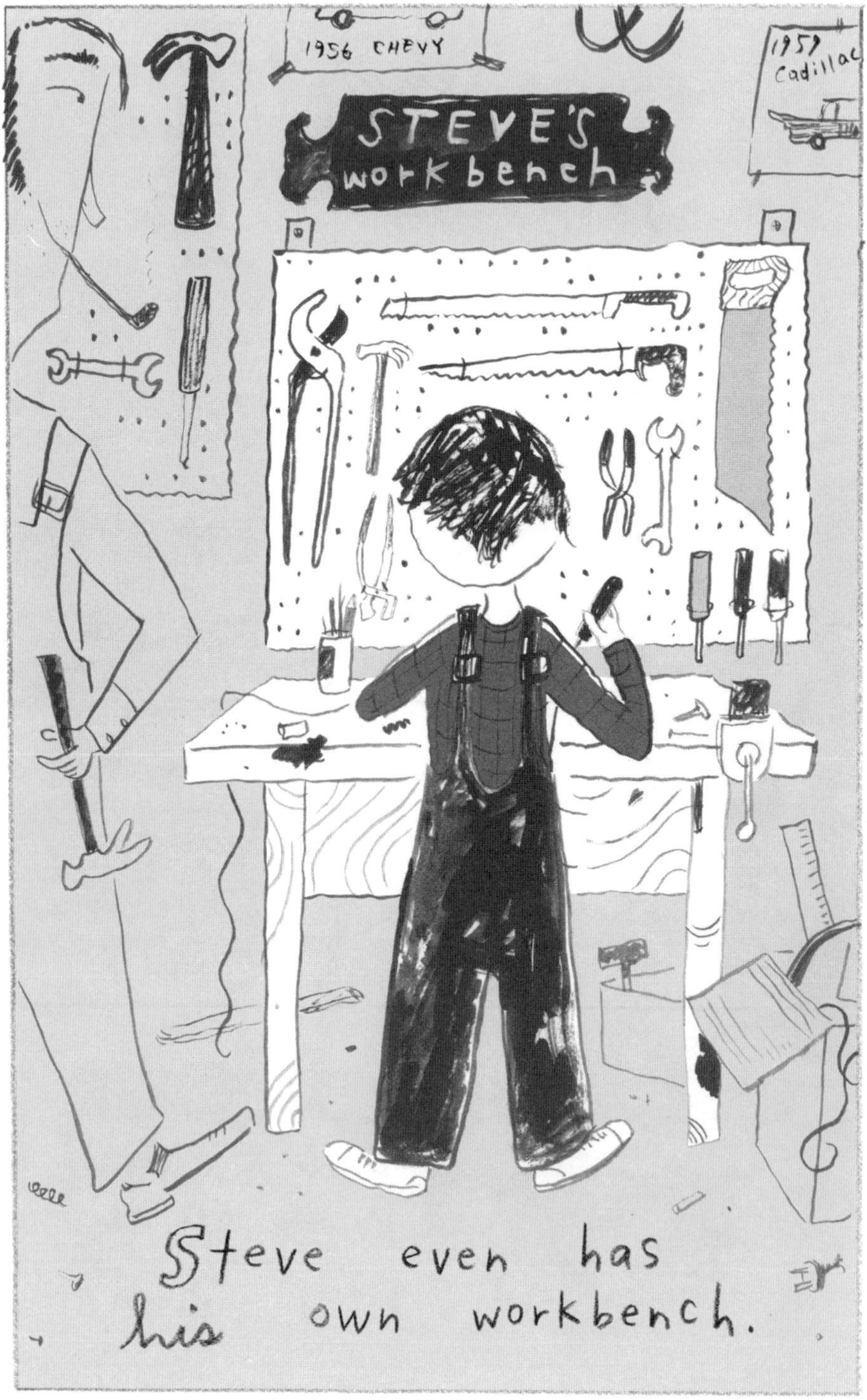
1956 CHEVY
1959 Cadillac
STEVE'S work bench
Steve even has his own workbench.

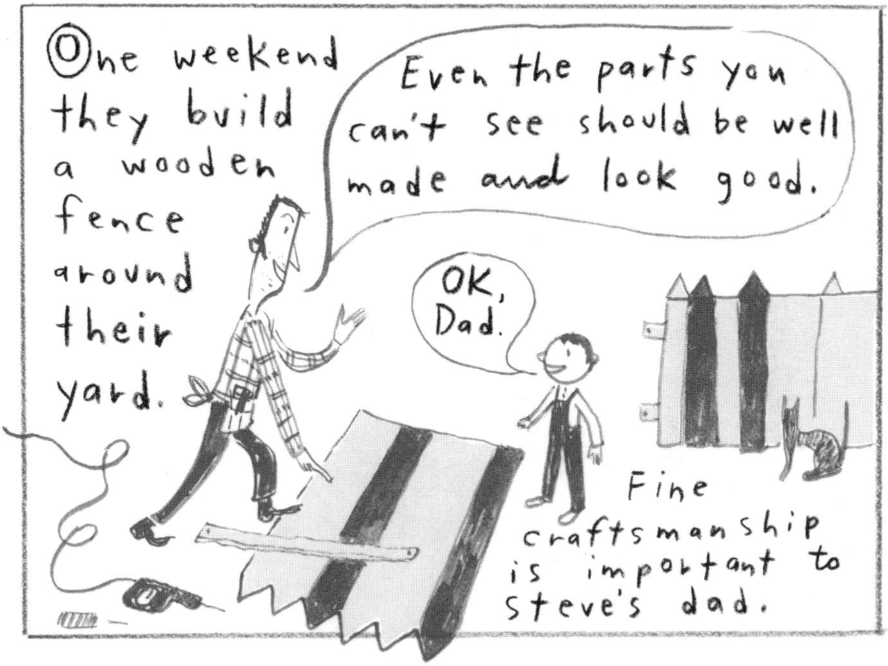
One weekend they build a wooden fence around their yard.
Even the parts you can't see should be well made ~~and~~ look good.
OK, Dad.
Fine craftsmanship is important to Steve's dad.

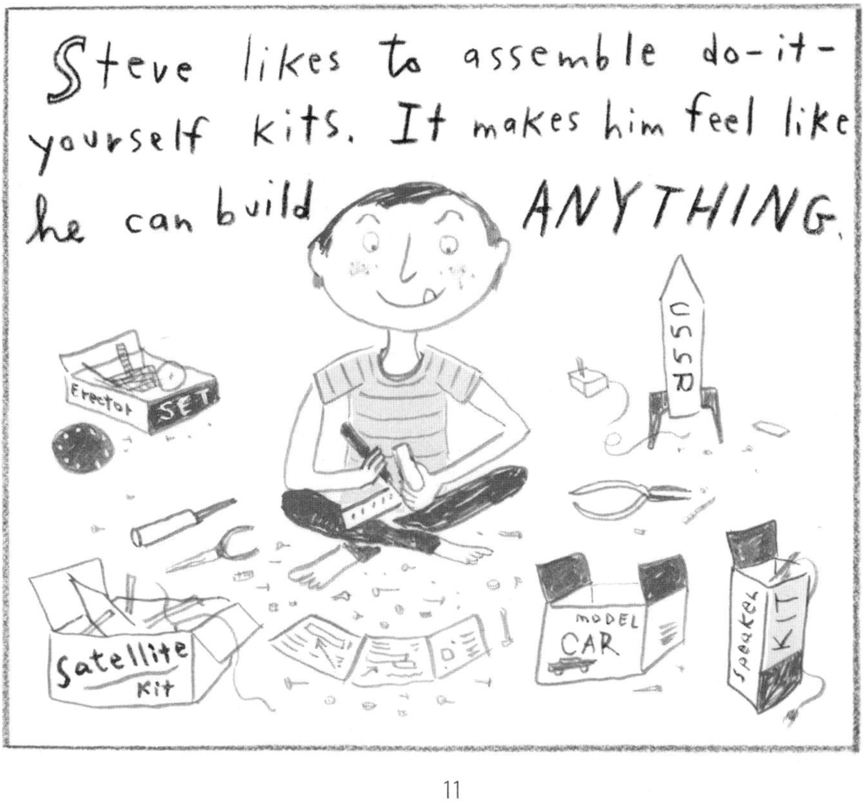
Steve likes to assemble do-it-yourself kits. It makes him feel like he can build ANYTHING.
Erector SET
USSR
Satellite Kit
MODEL CAR
Speaker KIT

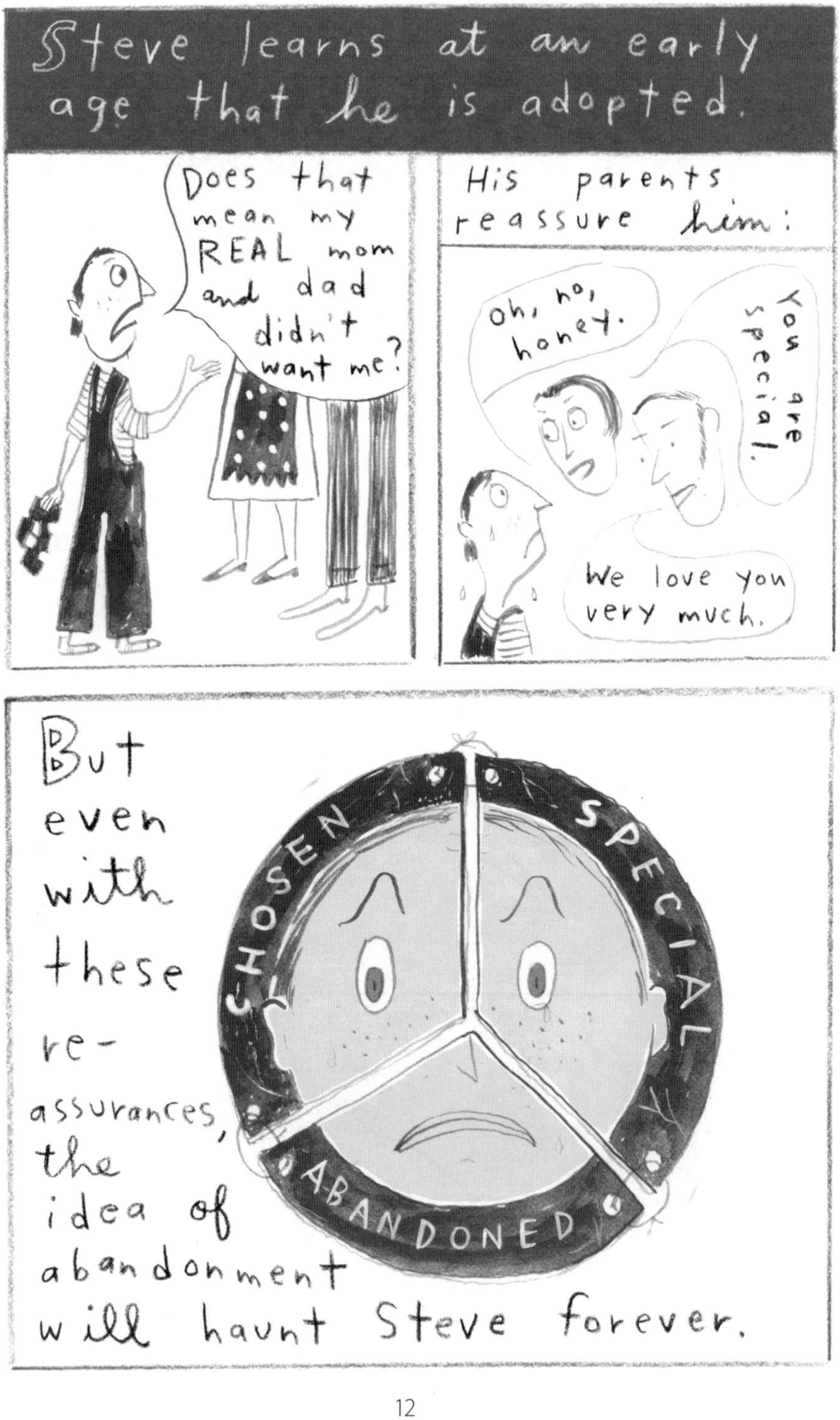
Steve learns at an early age that he is adopted.
Does that mean my REAL mom and dad didn't want me?
His parents reassure him:
Oh, no, honey.
You are special.
We love you very much.
But even with these re-assurances, the idea of abandonment will haunt Steve forever.
CHOSEN
SPECIAL
ABANDONED

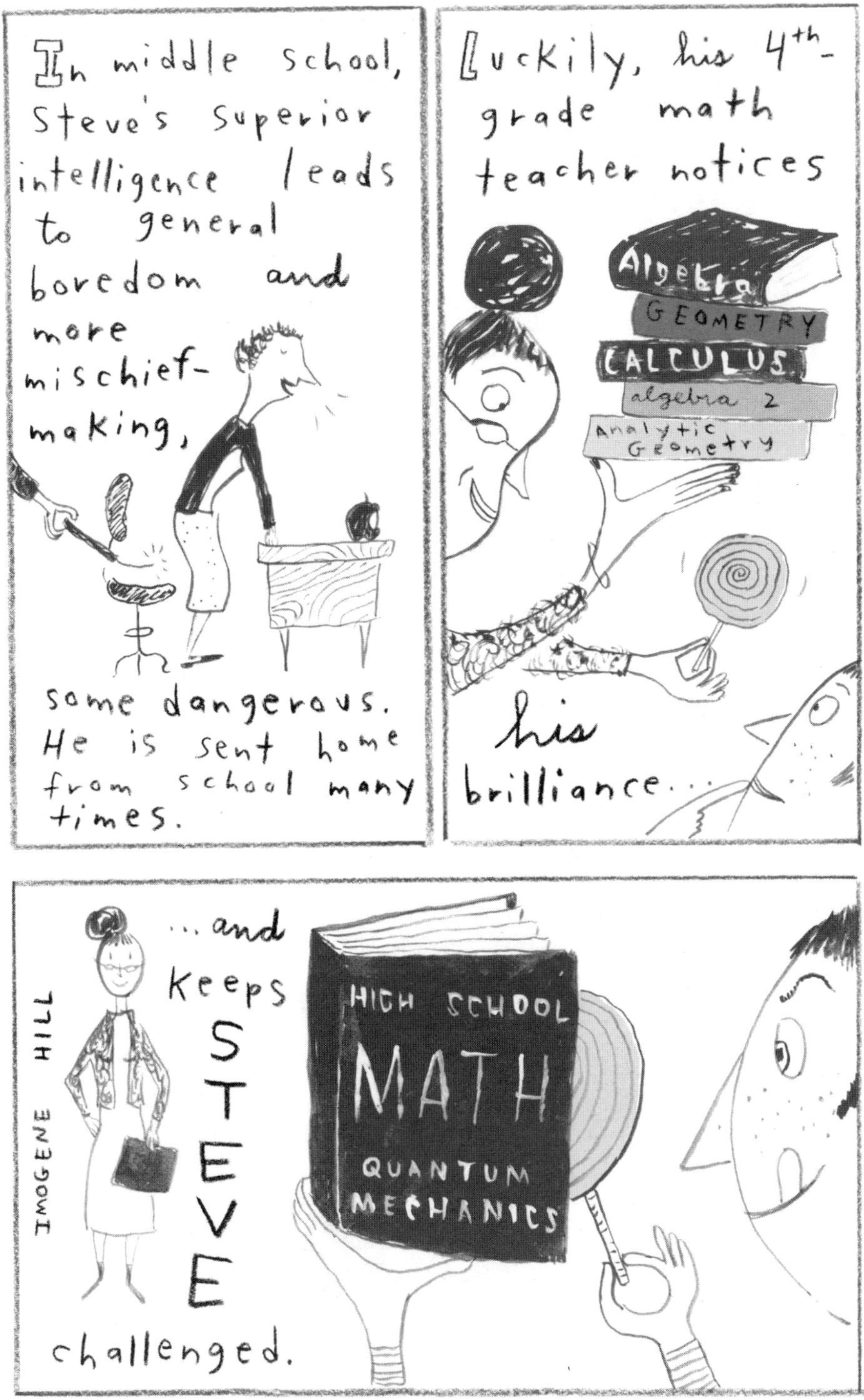
In middle school, Steve's superior intelligence leads to general boredom and more mischief-making,
some dangerous. He is sent home from school many times.
Luckily, his 4th-grade math teacher notices
Algebra
GEOMETRY
CALCULUS
algebra 2
Analytic Geometry
his brilliance...
IMOGENE HILL
...and keeps STEVE challenged.
HIGH SCHOOL
MATH
QUANTUM MECHANICS

Outgoing and always curious, Steve makes friends with some of the neighborhood engineers.
Steve, I'm glad you're here. Let me show you something.
COOL!
battery
carbon microphone
speaker
Hey, Dad! Mr. Lang can amplify using just a carbon mike, a battery, and a speaker!
No, son, that's not possible! You've got it wrong.
Gee whiz, my dad does not know every-thing.
See! I told you!
I'll be darned!
They don't come brighter than that, Paul.

chapter

2

Growing Up
(1965 – 1971)

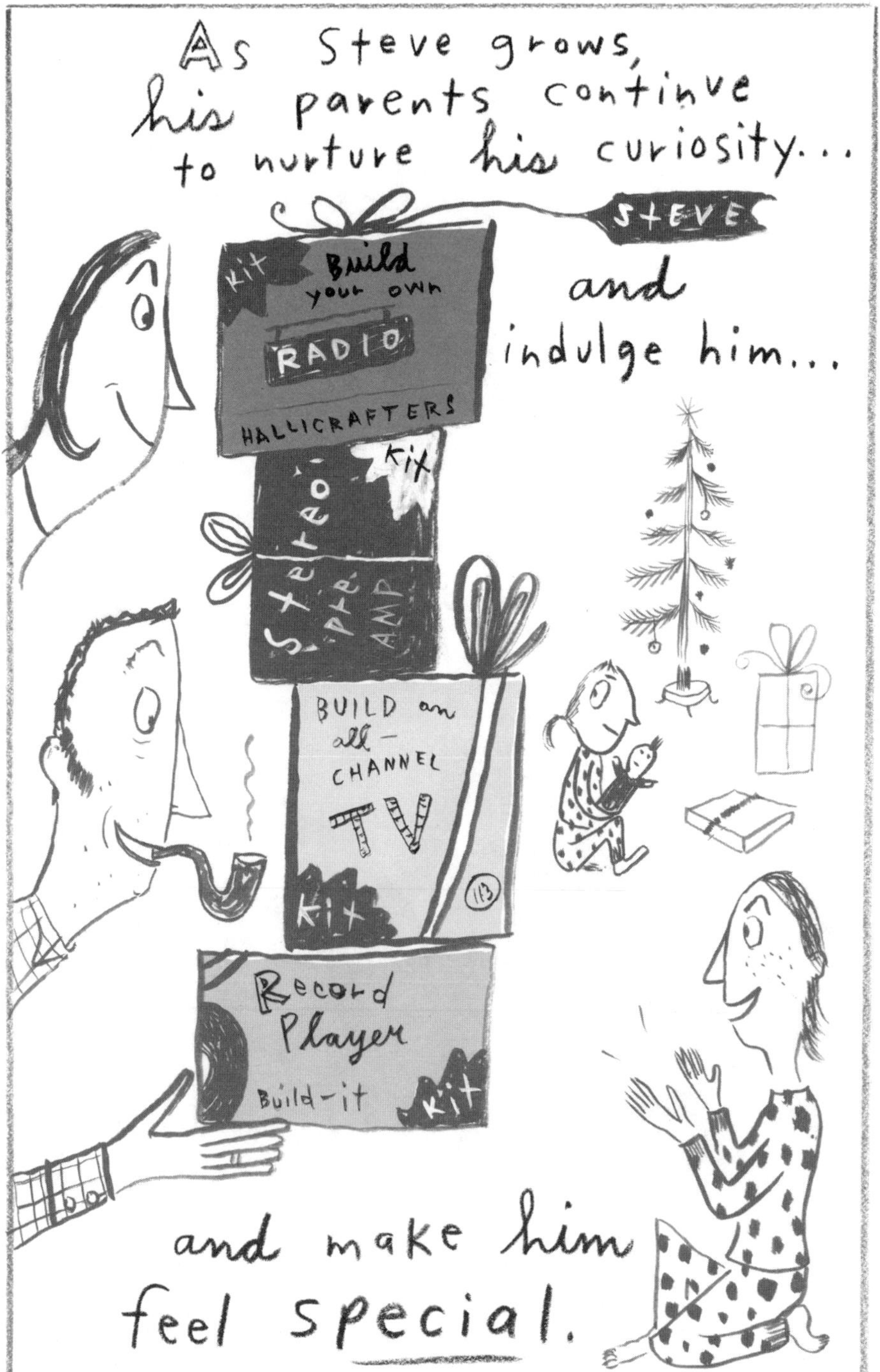
As Steve grows, his parents continue to nurture his curiosity...
STEVE
kit
Build your own
RADIO
HALLICRAFTERS
kit
Stereo
Stereo Pre AMP
and indulge him...
BUILD an all-CHANNEL TV
kit
Record Player
Build-it
kit
and make him feel special.

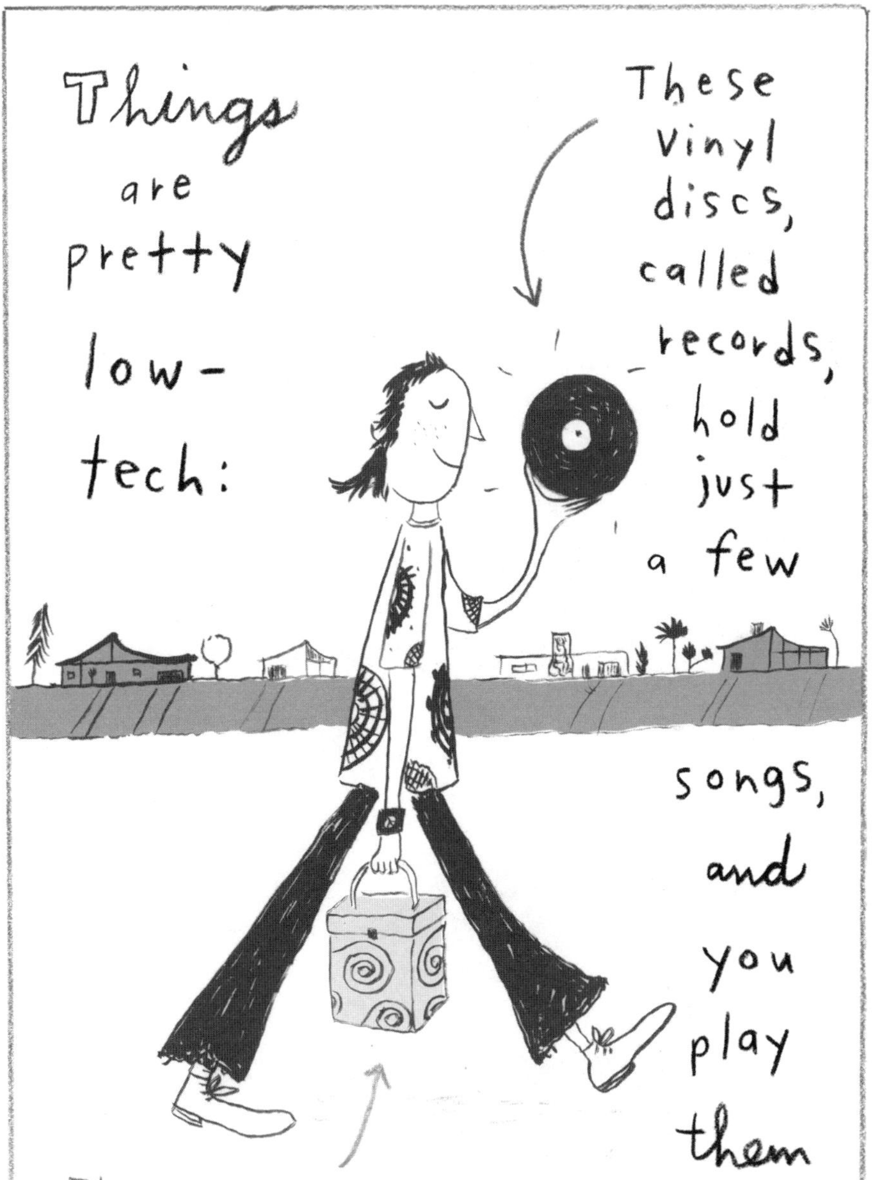
Things are pretty low-tech:
These vinyl discs, called records, hold just a few songs, and you play them on an electric...
The records are carried around in a case like this.

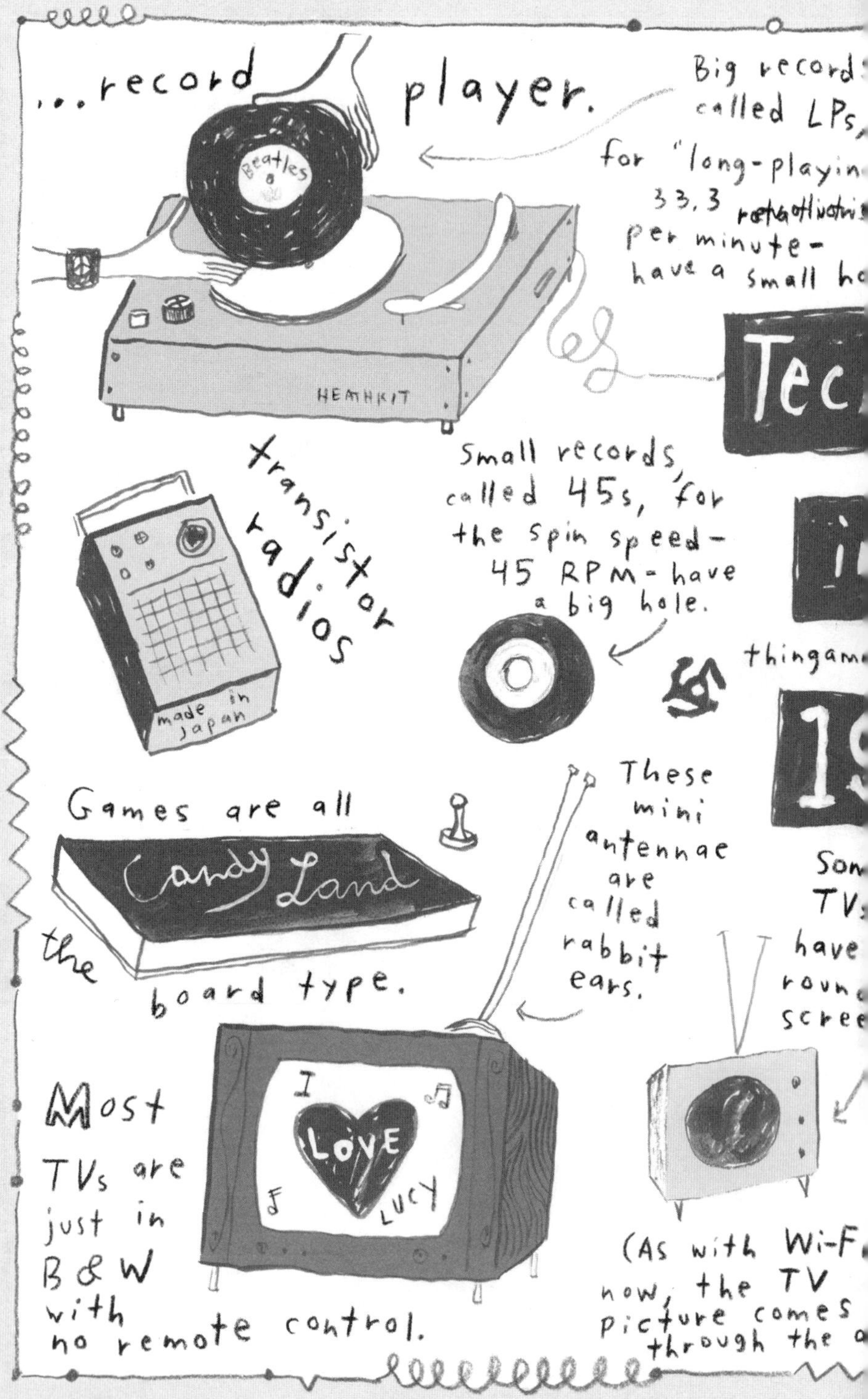
...record player.
Big records
called LPs,
for "long-playin
33.3
per minute-
have a small ho
Tec
i
19
Beatles
HEMHKIT
transistor radios
made in Japan
Small records, called 45s, for the spin speed-45 RPM-have a big hole.
thingam
Games are all Candy Land the board type.
These mini antennae are called rabbit ears.
Som
TVs
have
roun
scree
Most TVs are just in B&W with no remote control.
I LOVE LUCY
(As with Wi-F
now, the TV
picture comes
through the a

All phones are the rotary-dial type with cords.

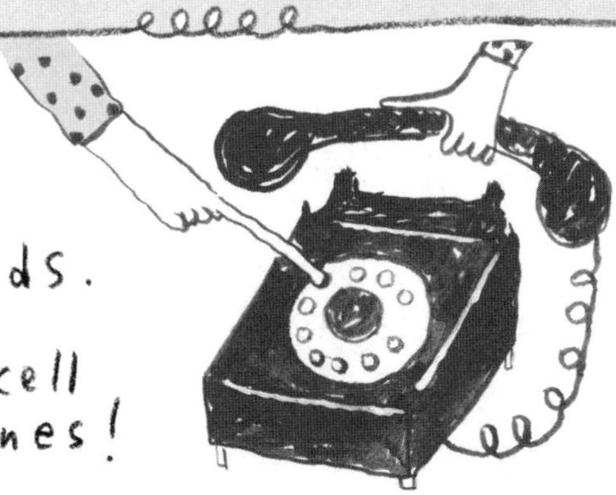

No cell phones!

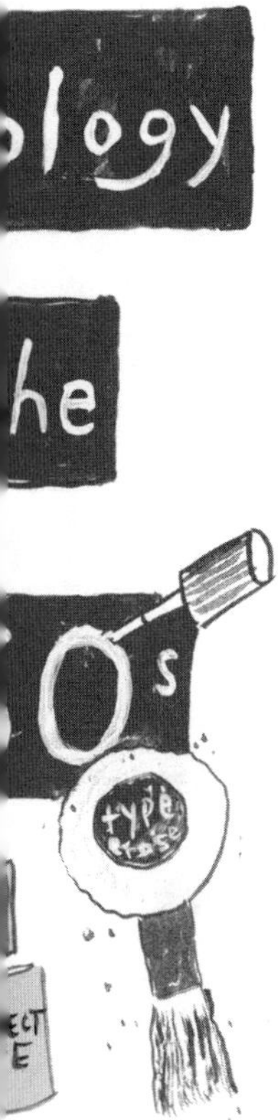
ology
he
Os
type erase

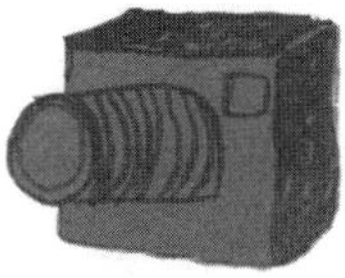

Cameras require film and developing.

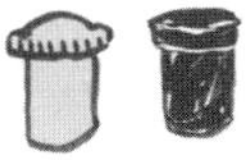

If you have to write something official, you use a typewriter.

To correct mistakes, you use a special kind of eraser or paint.

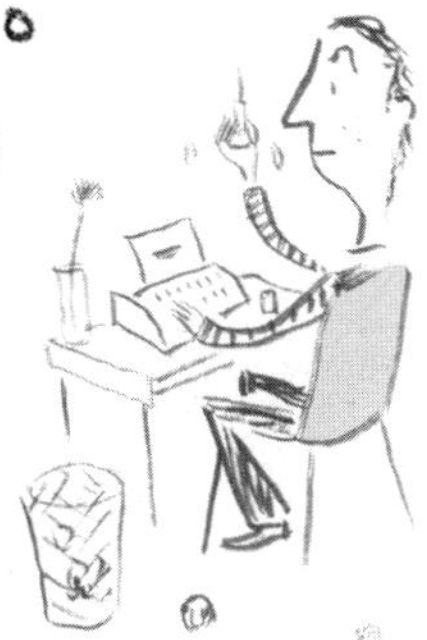

No ONE has a computer in their home.

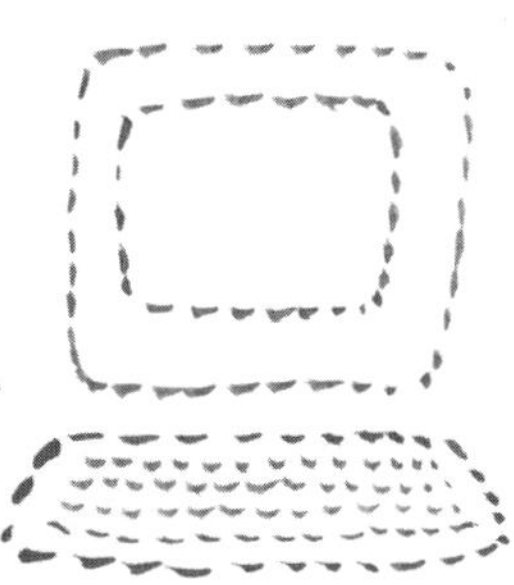

No Internet!

No Google.

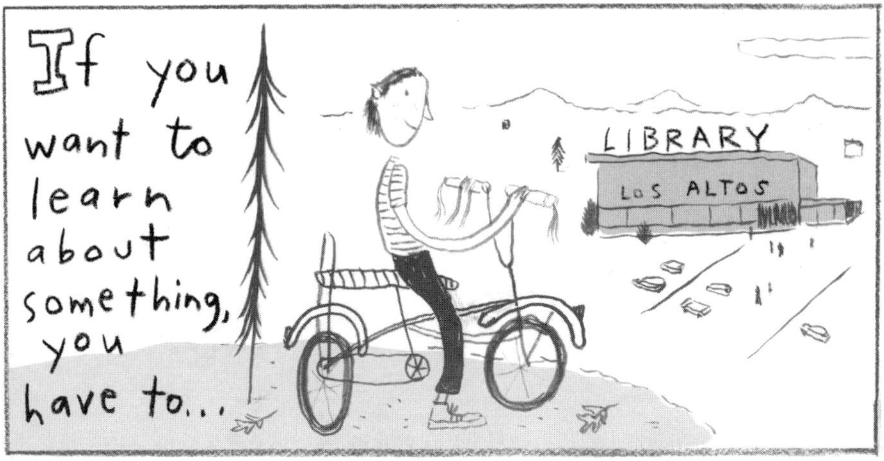
If you want to learn about something, you have to...
LIBRARY
LOS ALTOS

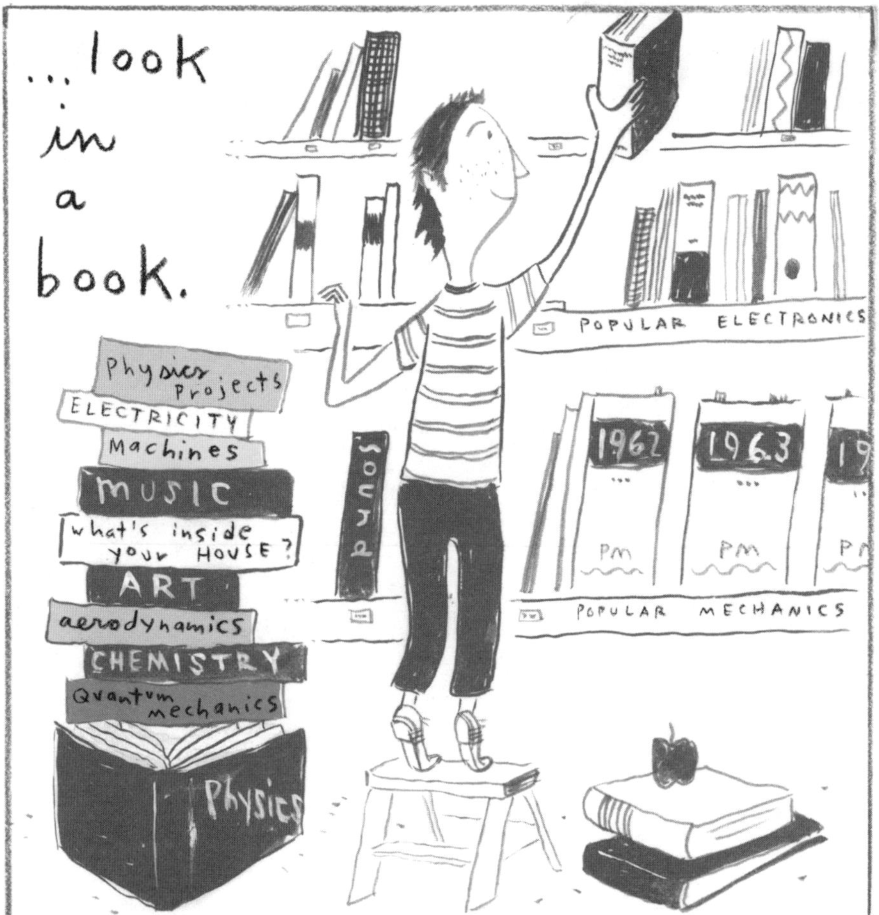
...look in a book.
POPULAR ELECTRONICS
physics projects
ELECTRICITY
Machines
MUSIC
what's inside your HOUSE?
ART
aerodynamics
CHEMISTRY
Quantum mechanics
PHYSICS
SOUND
1962
1963
PM
POPULAR MECHANICS

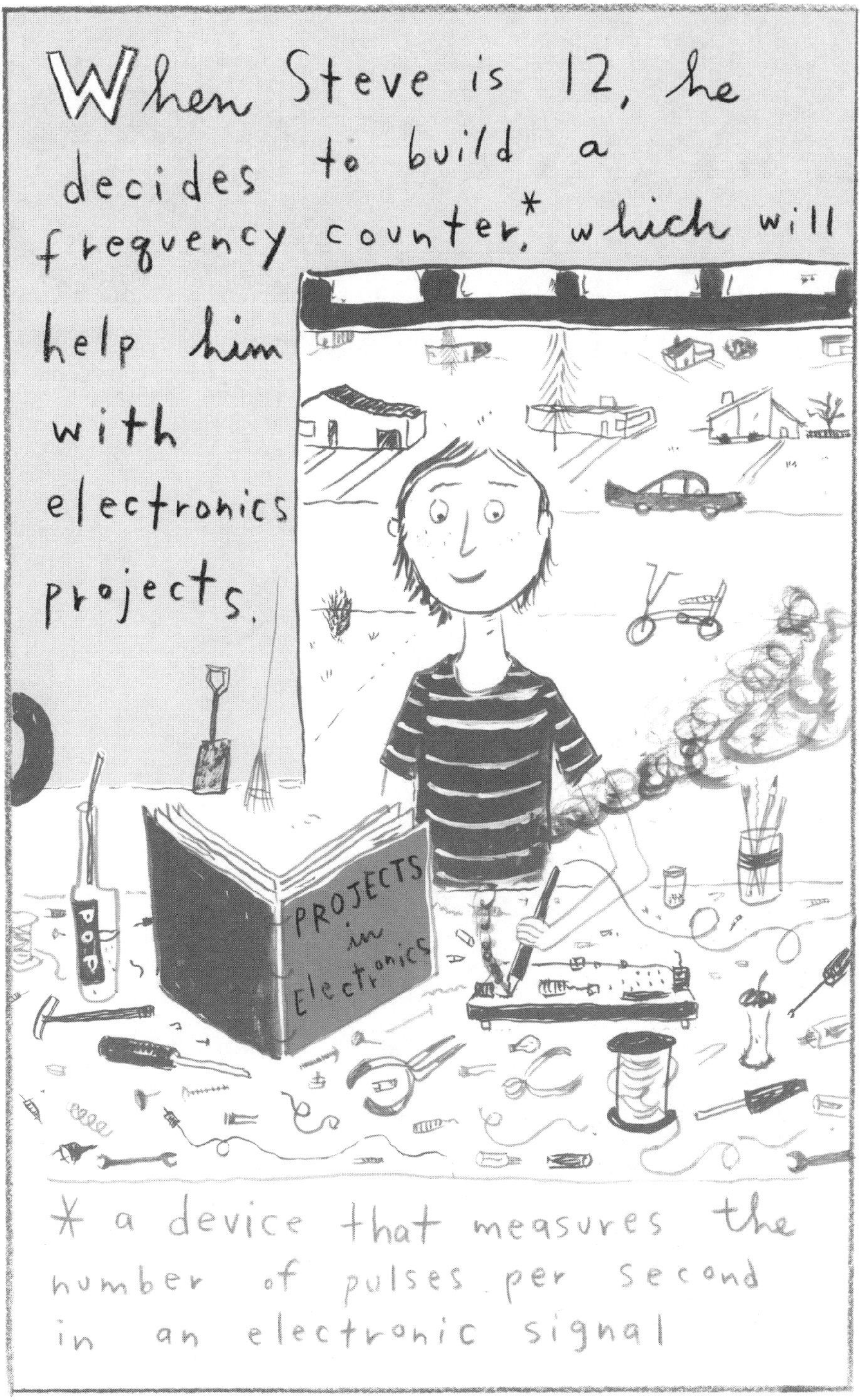
When Steve is 12, he decides to build a frequency counter,* which will help him with electronics projects.
PROJECTS in Electronics
POP
* a device that measures the number of pulses per second in an electronic signal

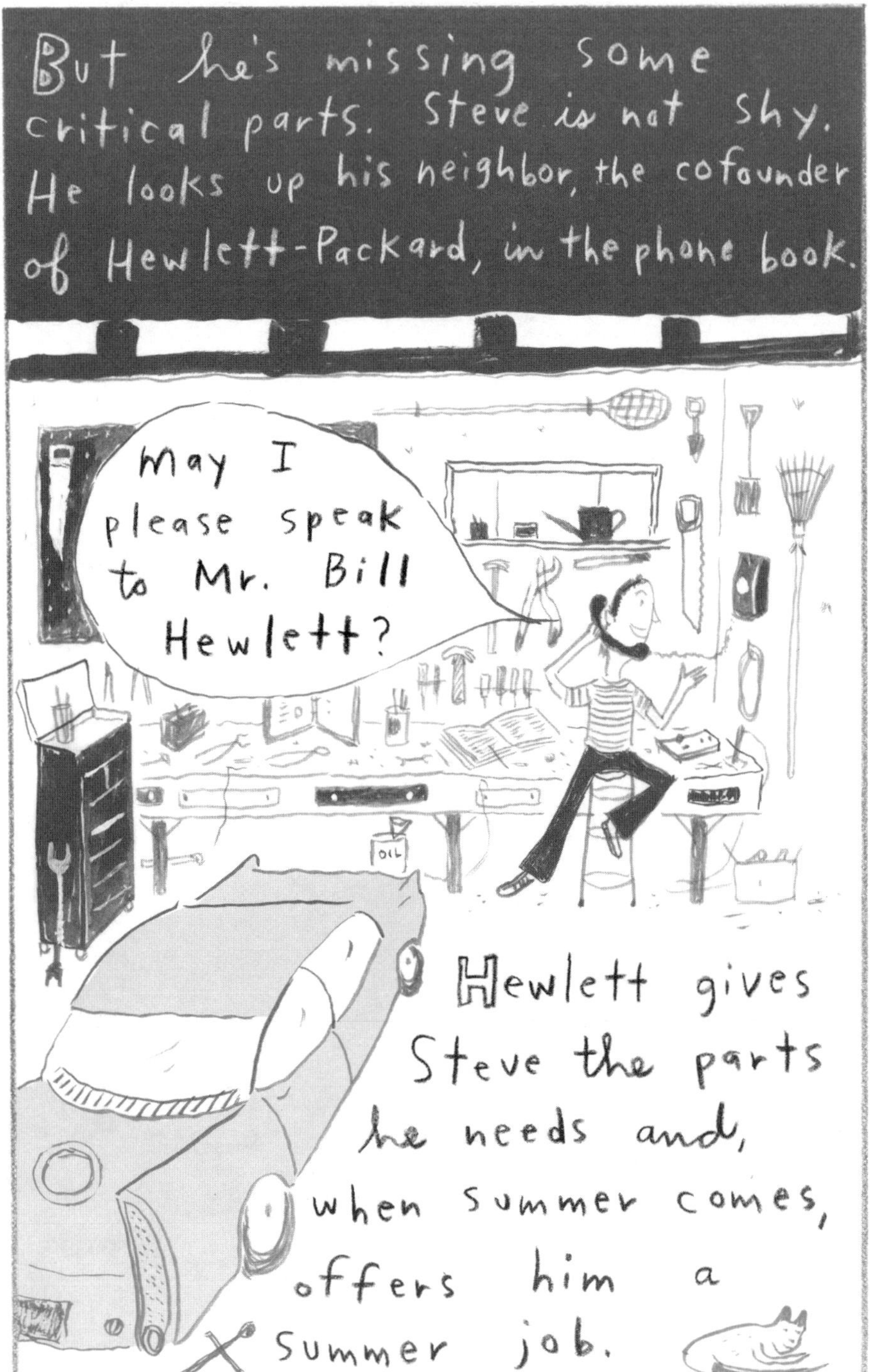
But he's missing some critical parts. Steve is not shy. He looks up his neighbor, the cofounder of Hewlett-Packard, in the phone book.
May I please speak to Mr. Bill Hewlett?
OIL
Hewlett gives Steve the parts he needs and, when summer comes, offers him a summer job.

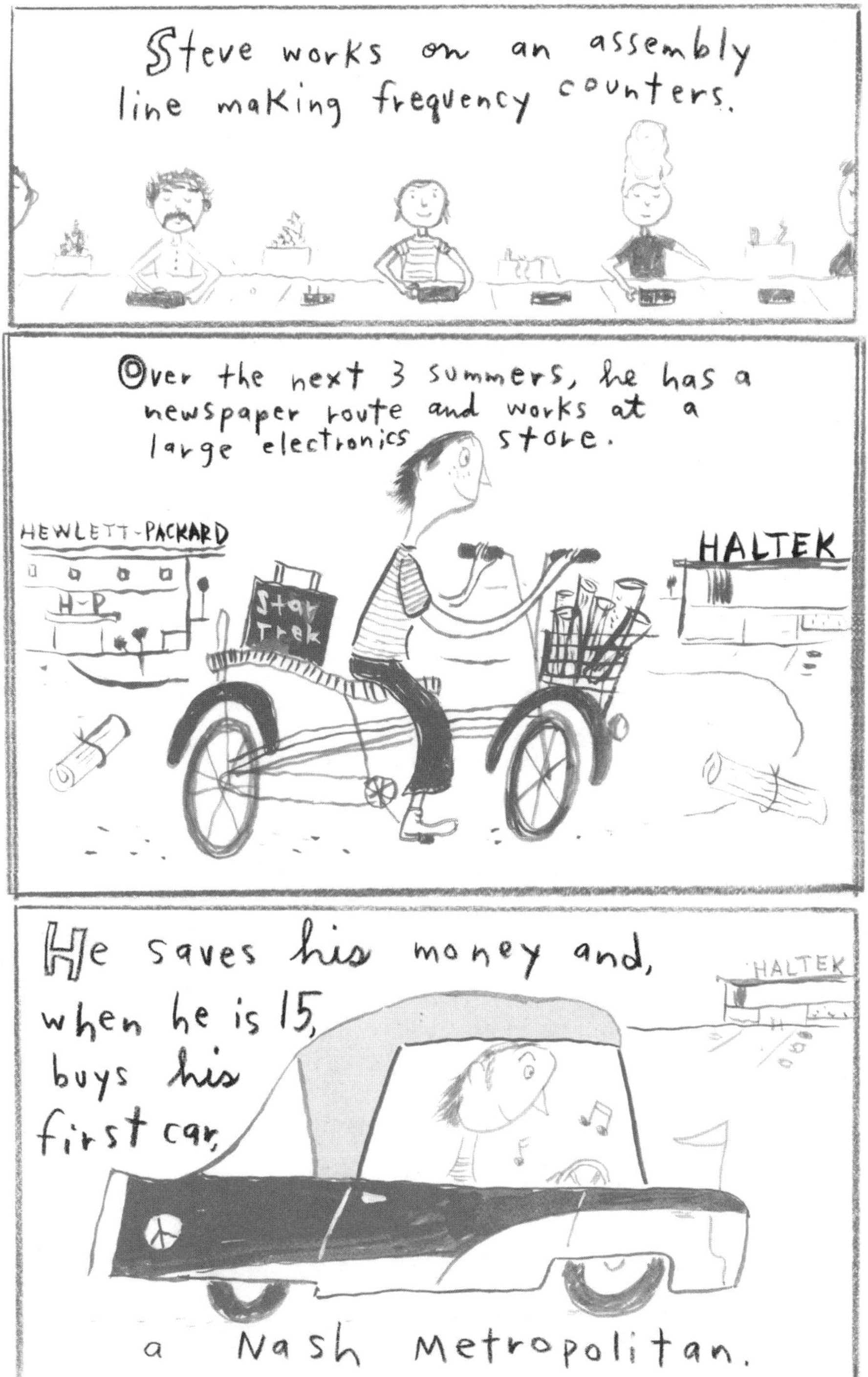
Steve works on an assembly line making frequency counters.
Over the next 3 summers, he has a newspaper route and works at a large electronics store.
HEWLETT-PACKARD
H-P
Star Trek
HALTEK
He saves his money and, when he is 15, buys his first car,
HALTEK
a Nash Metropolitan.

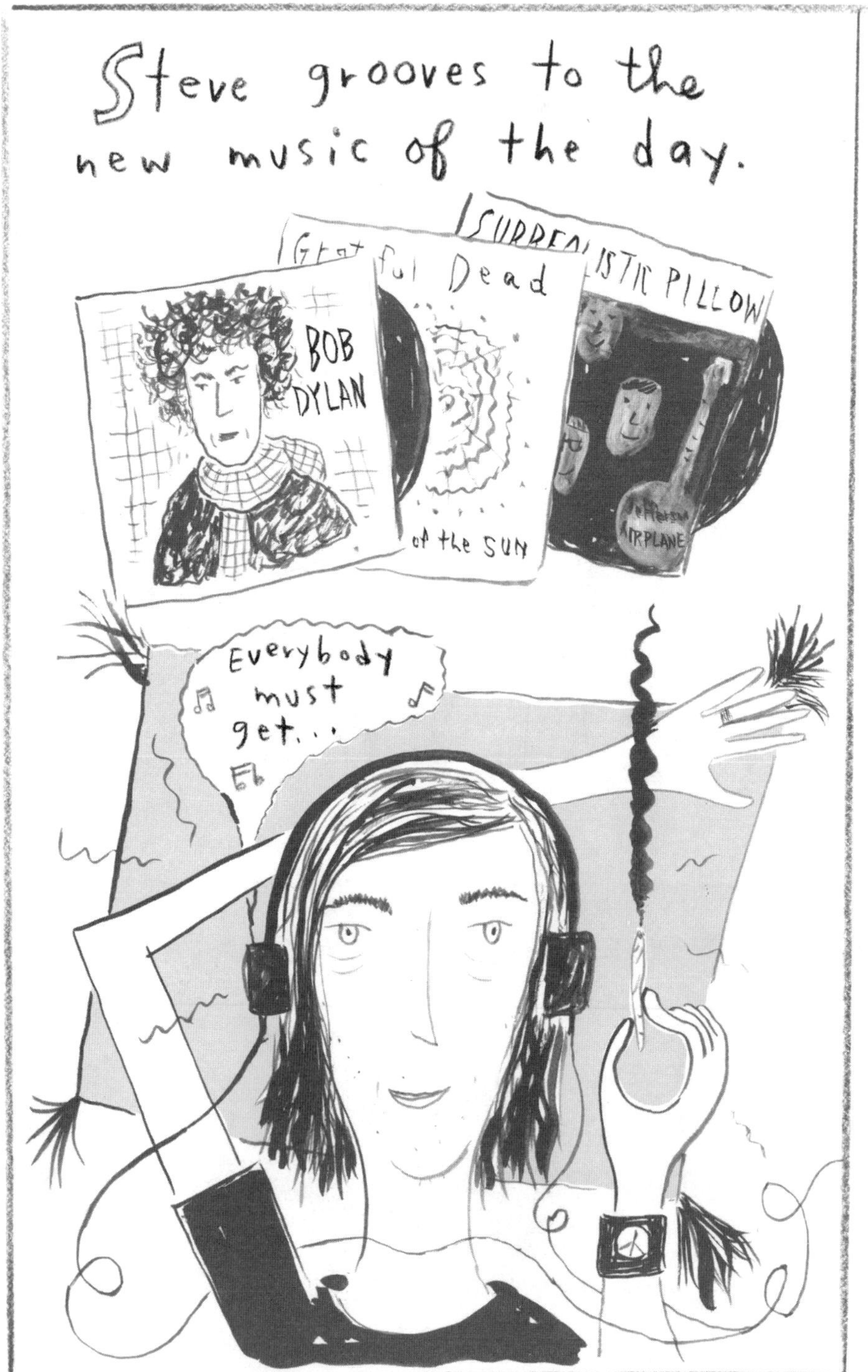
Steve grooves to the new music of the day.
BOB DYLAN
ful Dead
of the SUN
ISTIC PILLOW
AIRPLANE
Everybody must get...

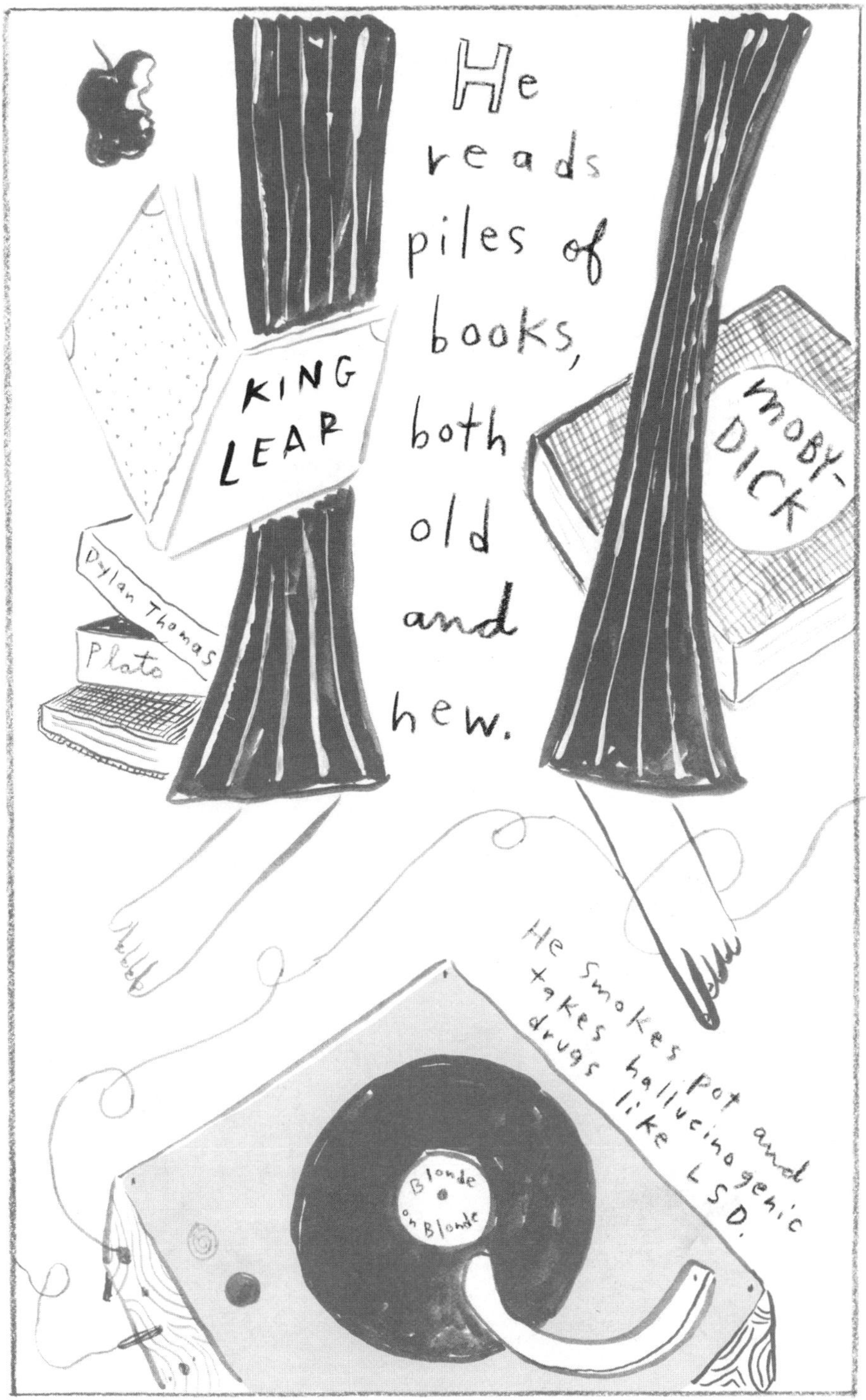
He reads piles of books, both old and new.
KING LEAR
MOBY-DICK
Dylan Thomas
Plato
He smokes pot and takes hallucinogenic drugs like LSD.
Blonde on Blonde

The high school electronics class is outta sight!

Steve learns how to create light shows using lasers—
Far out!
Totally cool!
Groovy!
Dylan
a big hit at parties!

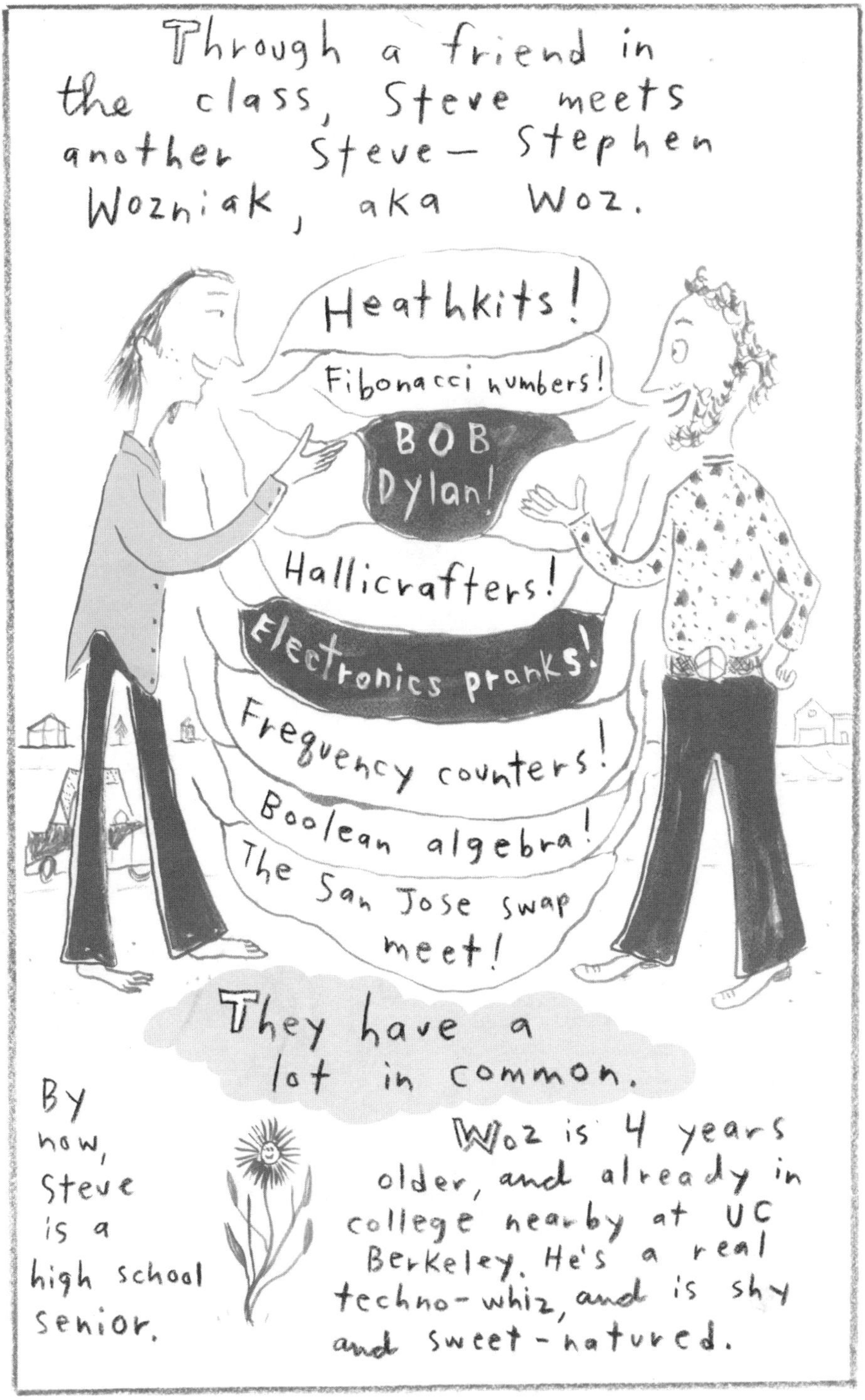
Through a friend in the class, Steve meets another Steve— Stephen Wozniak, aka Woz.
Heathkits!
Fibonacci numbers!
BOB Dylan!
Hallicrafters!
Electronics pranks!
Frequency counters!
Boolean algebra!
The San Jose swap meet!
They have a lot in common.
By now, Steve is a high school senior.
Woz is 4 years older, and already in college nearby at UC Berkeley. He's a real techno-whiz, and is shy and sweet-natured.

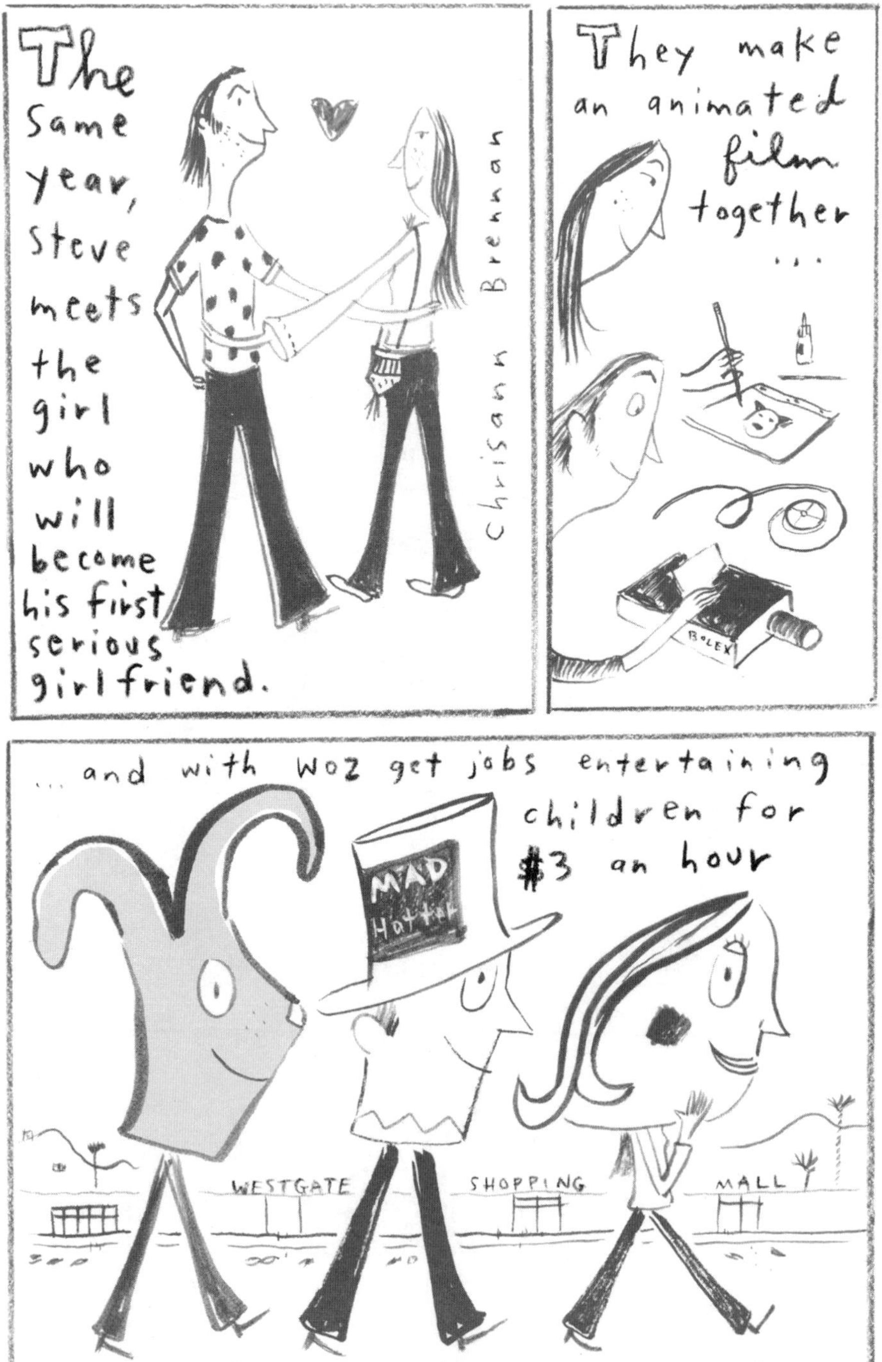
The same year, steve meets the girl who will become his first serious girlfriend.
Chrisann Brennan
They make an animated film together ...
BOLEX
... and with woz get jobs entertaining children for $3 an hour
MAD Hatter
WESTGATE SHOPPING MALL
at a local shopping mall.

Chapter 3

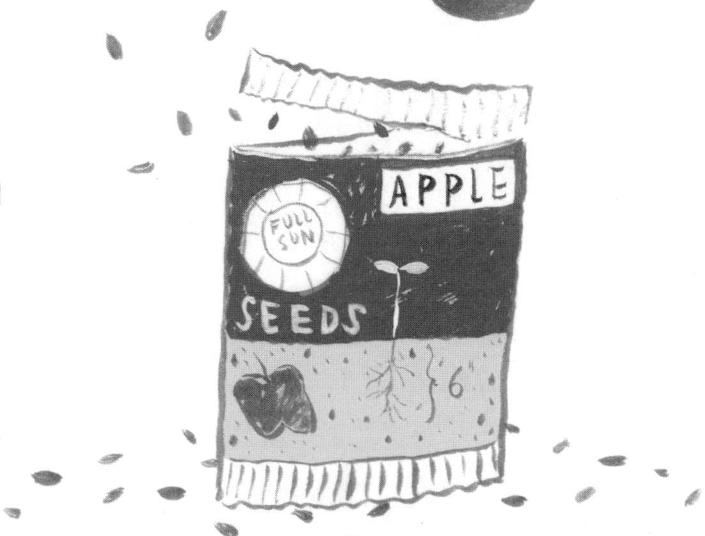
APPLE
FULL SUN
SEEDS
6

Steve and Woz Start Their First Business

(1971)

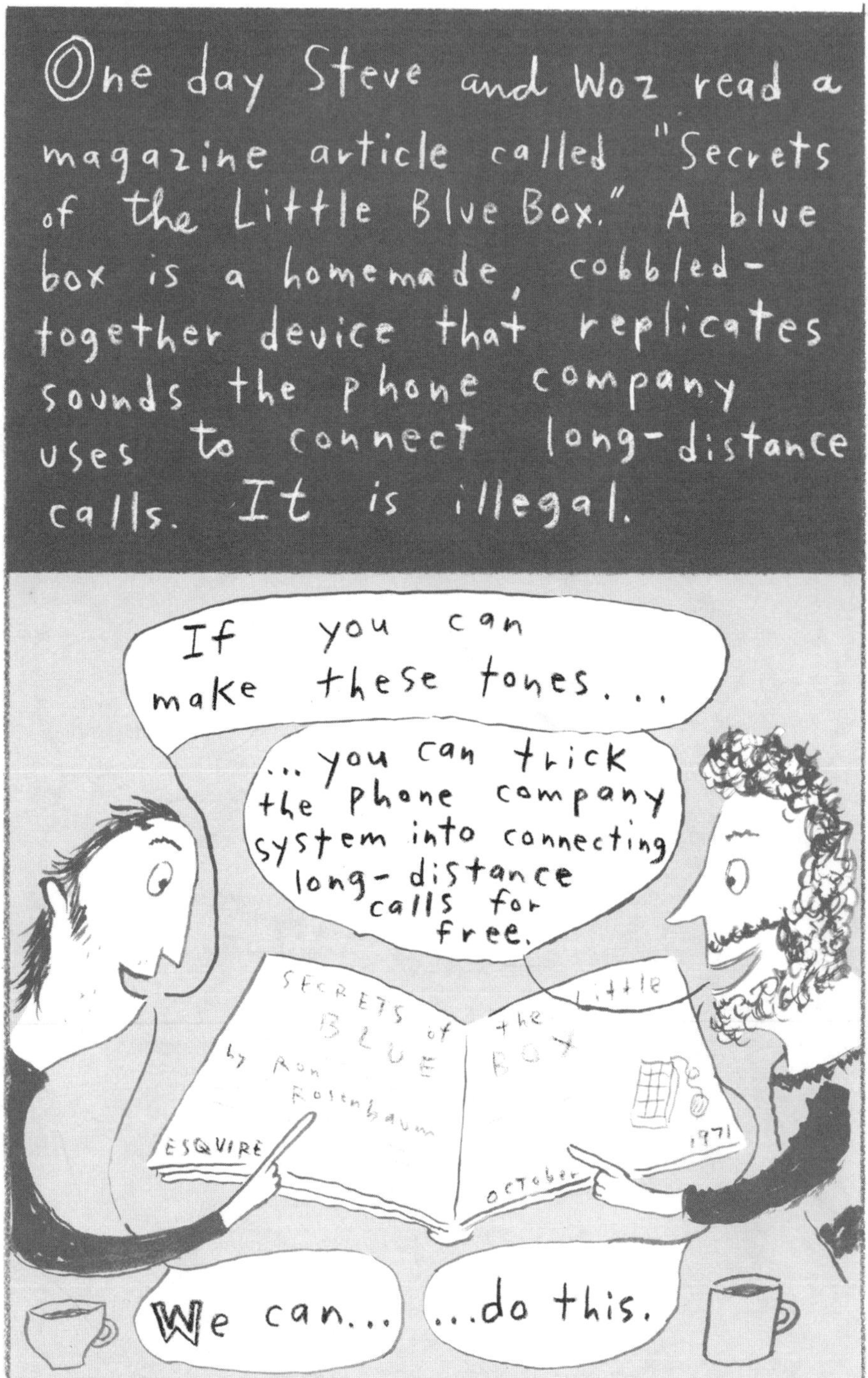
One day Steve and Woz read a magazine article called "Secrets of the Little Blue Box." A blue box is a homemade, cobbled-together device that replicates sounds the phone company uses to connect long-distance calls. It is illegal.
If you can make these tones...
...you can trick the phone company system into connecting long-distance calls for free.
SECRETS of
BLUE
by Ron Rosenbaum
Little
the
BOX
ESQUIRE
October
1971
We can...
...do this.

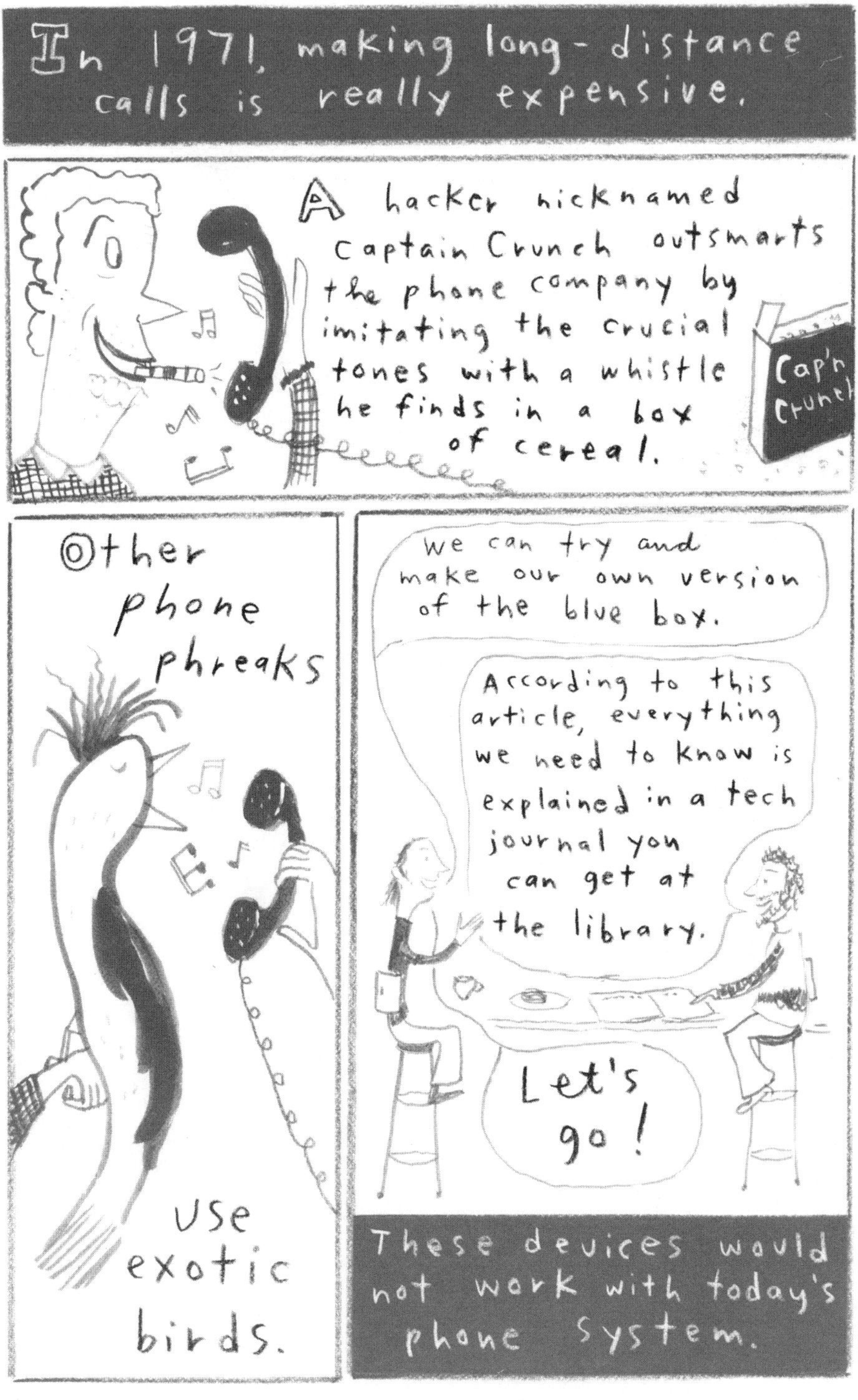
In 1971, making long-distance calls is really expensive.
A hacker nicknamed Captain Crunch outsmarts the phone company by imitating the crucial tones with a whistle he finds in a box of cereal.
Cap'n Crunch
Other phone phreaks
use exotic birds.
We can try and make our own version of the blue box.
According to this article, everything we need to know is explained in a tech journal you can get at the library.
Let's go!
These devices would not work with today's phone system.

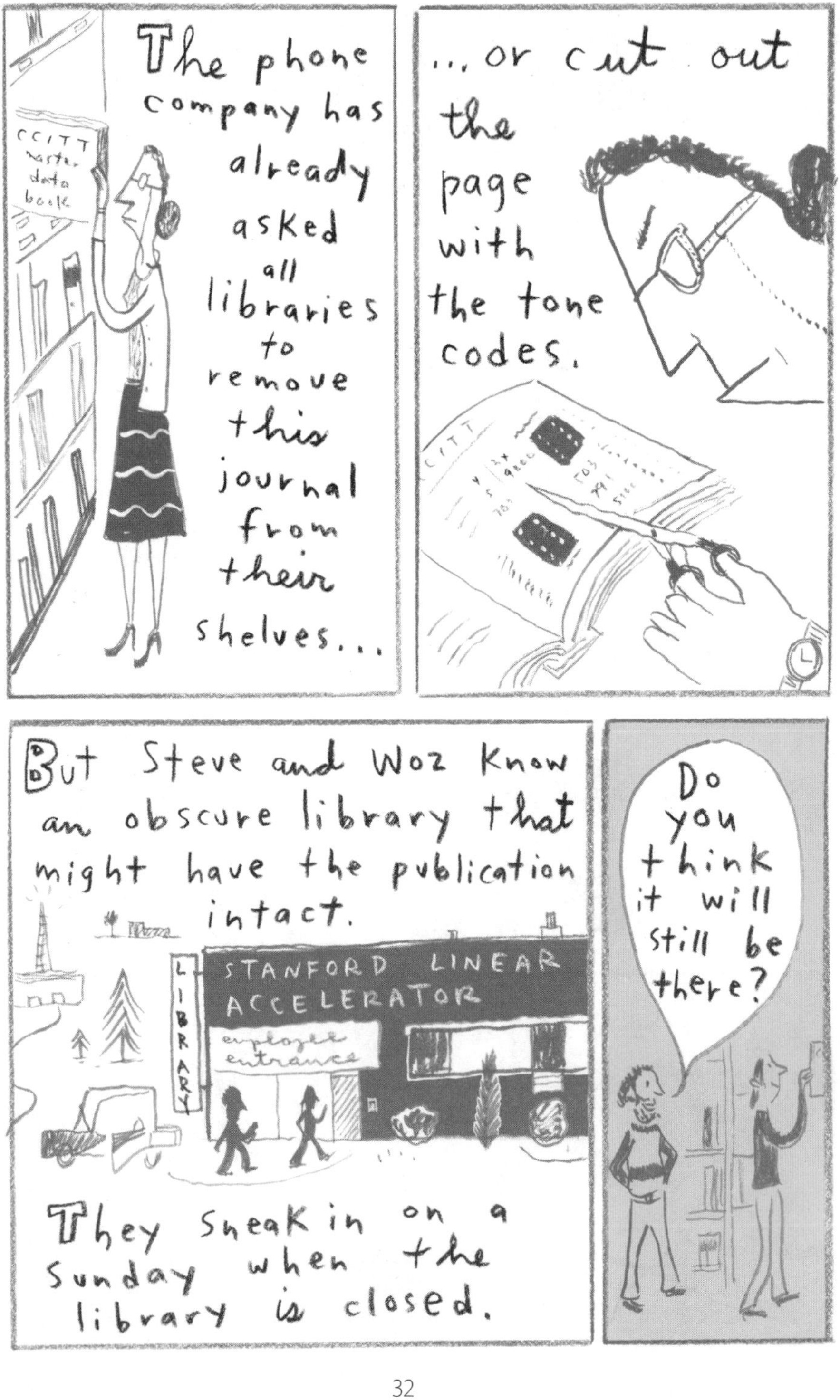
The phone company has already asked all libraries to remove this journal from their shelves...
CCITT master data book
...or cut out the page with the tone codes.
CCITT
But Steve and Woz know an obscure library that might have the publication intact.
STANFORD LINEAR ACCELERATOR
LIBRARY
employee entrance
They sneak in on a Sunday when the library is closed.
Do you think it will still be there?

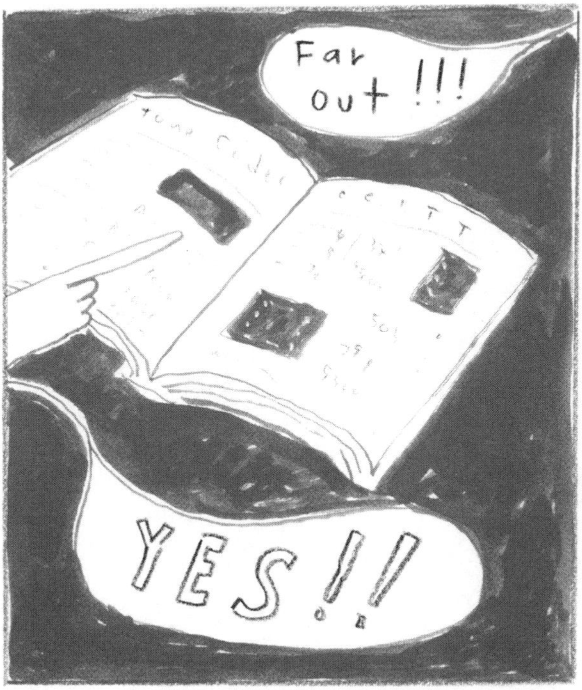
Far out !!!
YES!!

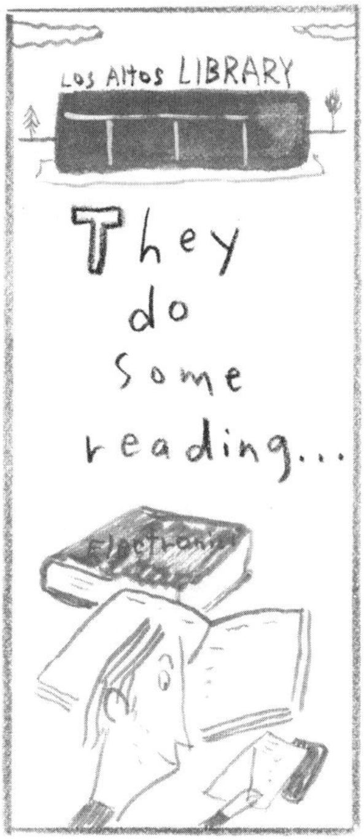
Los Altos LIBRARY
They do some reading...

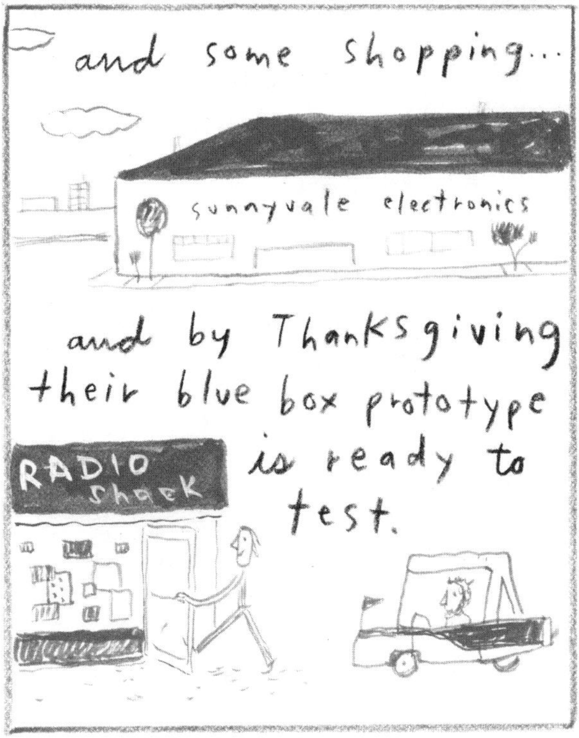
and some shopping...
sunnyvale electronics
and by Thanksgiving their blue box prototype is ready to test.
RADIO Shack

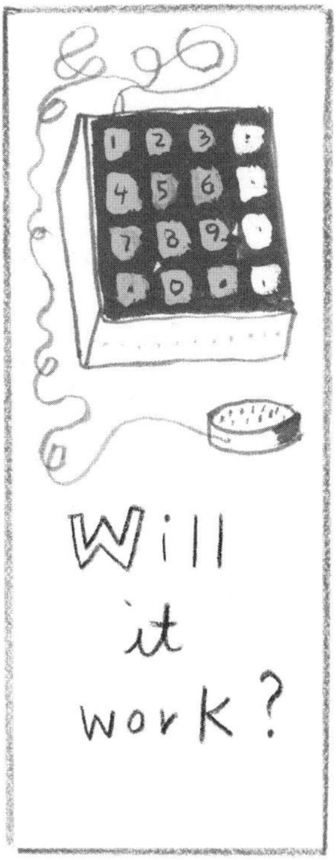
1 2 3
4 5 6
7 8 9
0
Will it work?

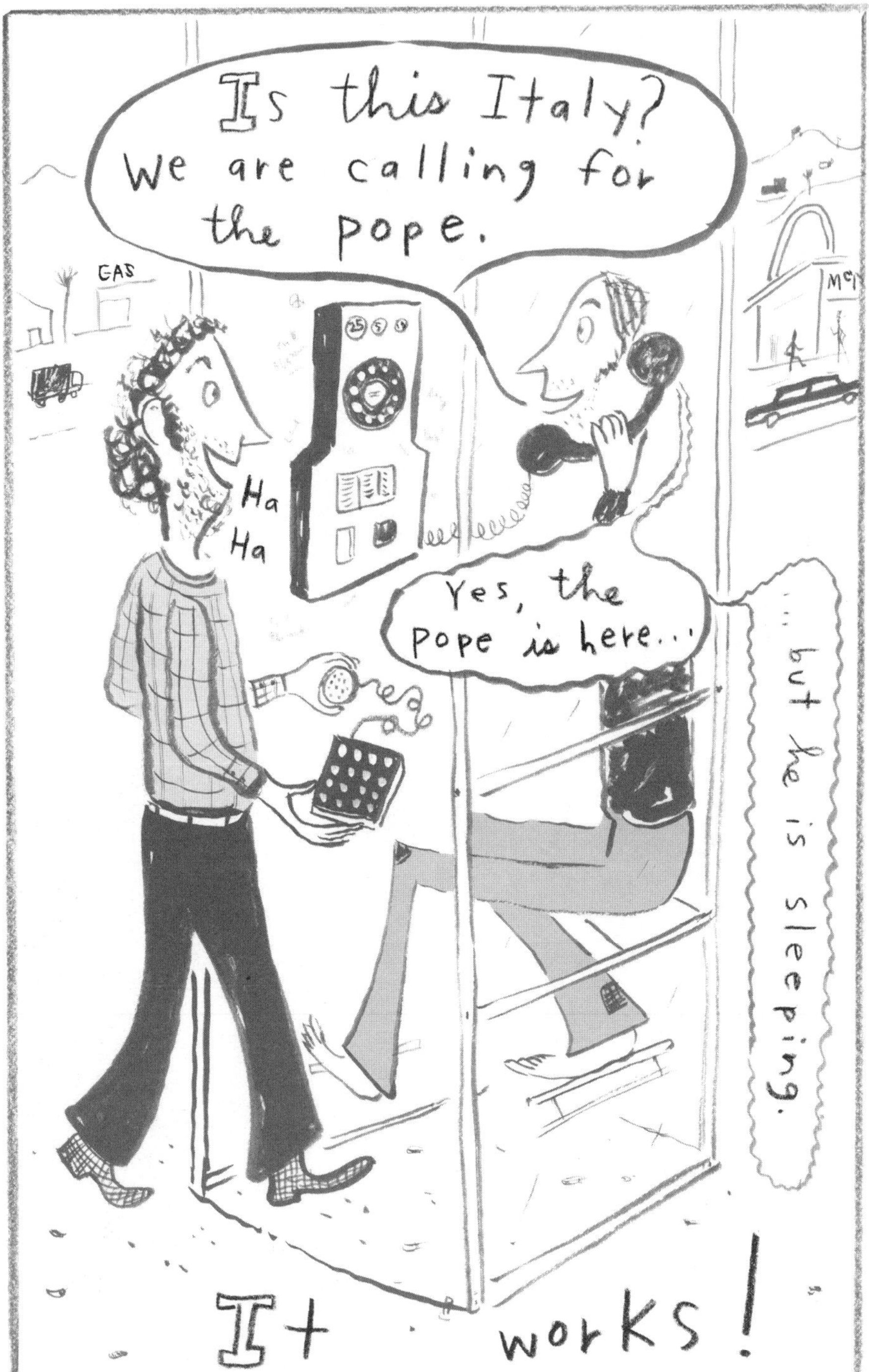
Is this Italy? We are calling for the pope.
GAS
Ha
Ha
Yes, the pope is here...
... but he is sleeping.
It works!

What do you say we make more of these and try to sell them?
Should we?
SOY
DEW
Why not? The parts cost $40 and we can maybe sell them for $150.
MOUNTAIN DEW
Steve makes sure the blue boxes are "user-friendly" so that anyone can use them, not just techy types. They happily sell them here and there until something really bad happens...

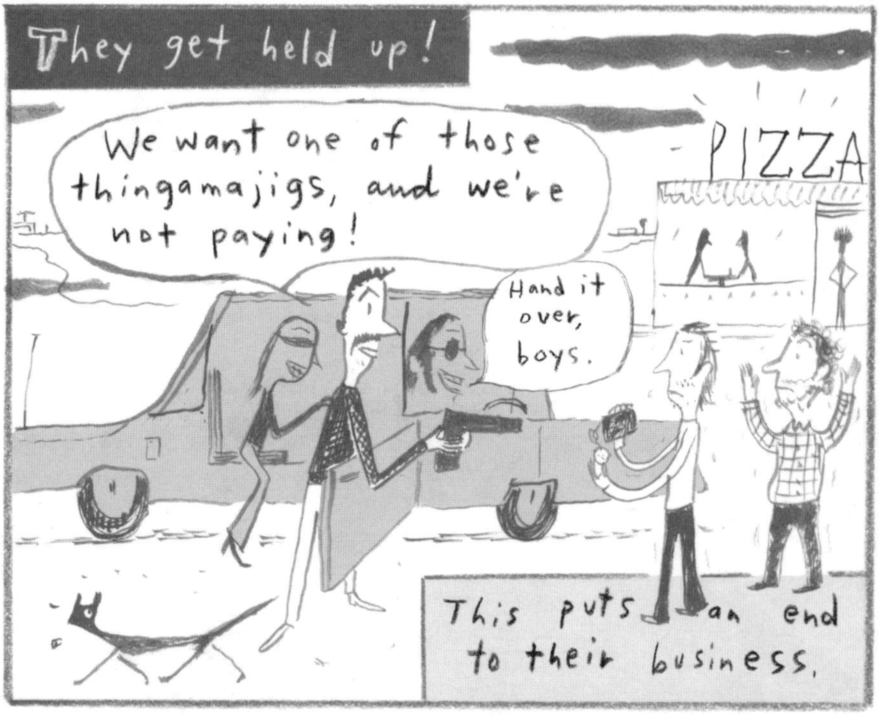
They get held up!
PIZZA
We want one of those thingamajigs, and we're not paying!
Hand it over, boys.
This puts an end to their business.

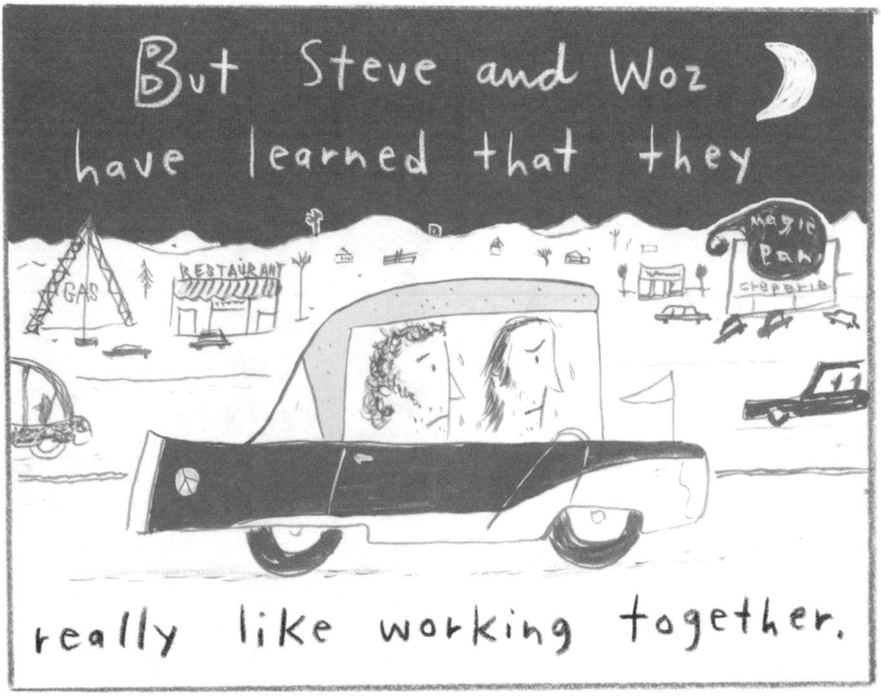
But Steve and Woz have learned that they
GAS
RESTAURANT
really like working together.

Chapter 4

College and Enlightenment (1972 – 1974)

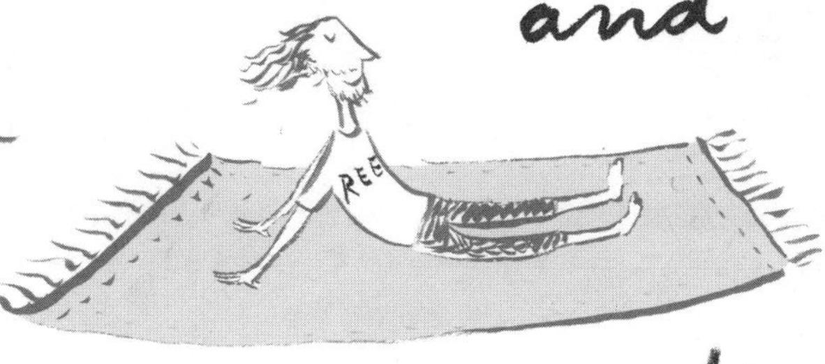
REE

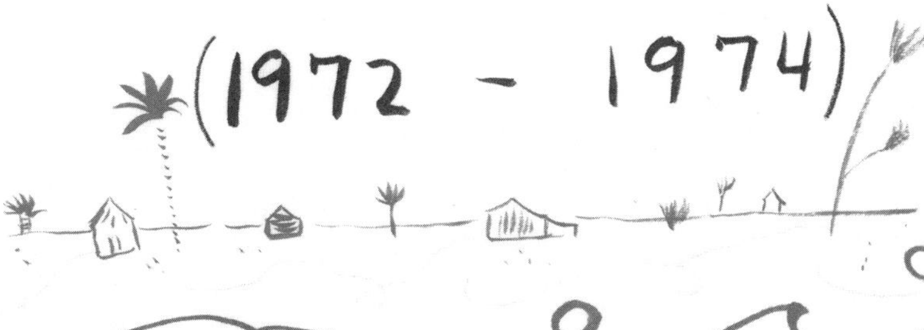

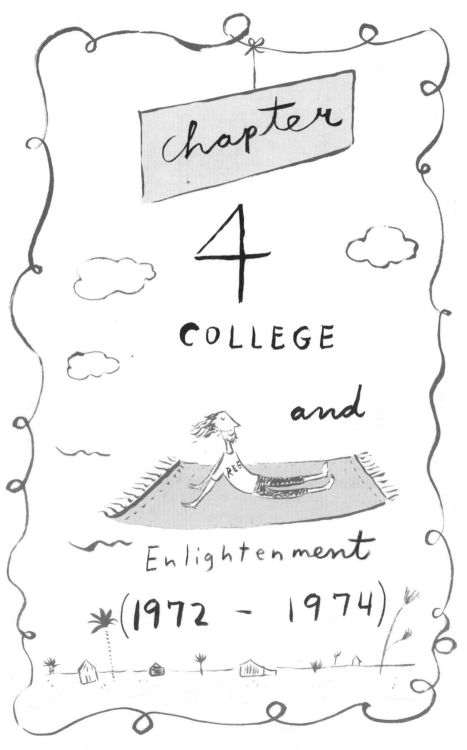

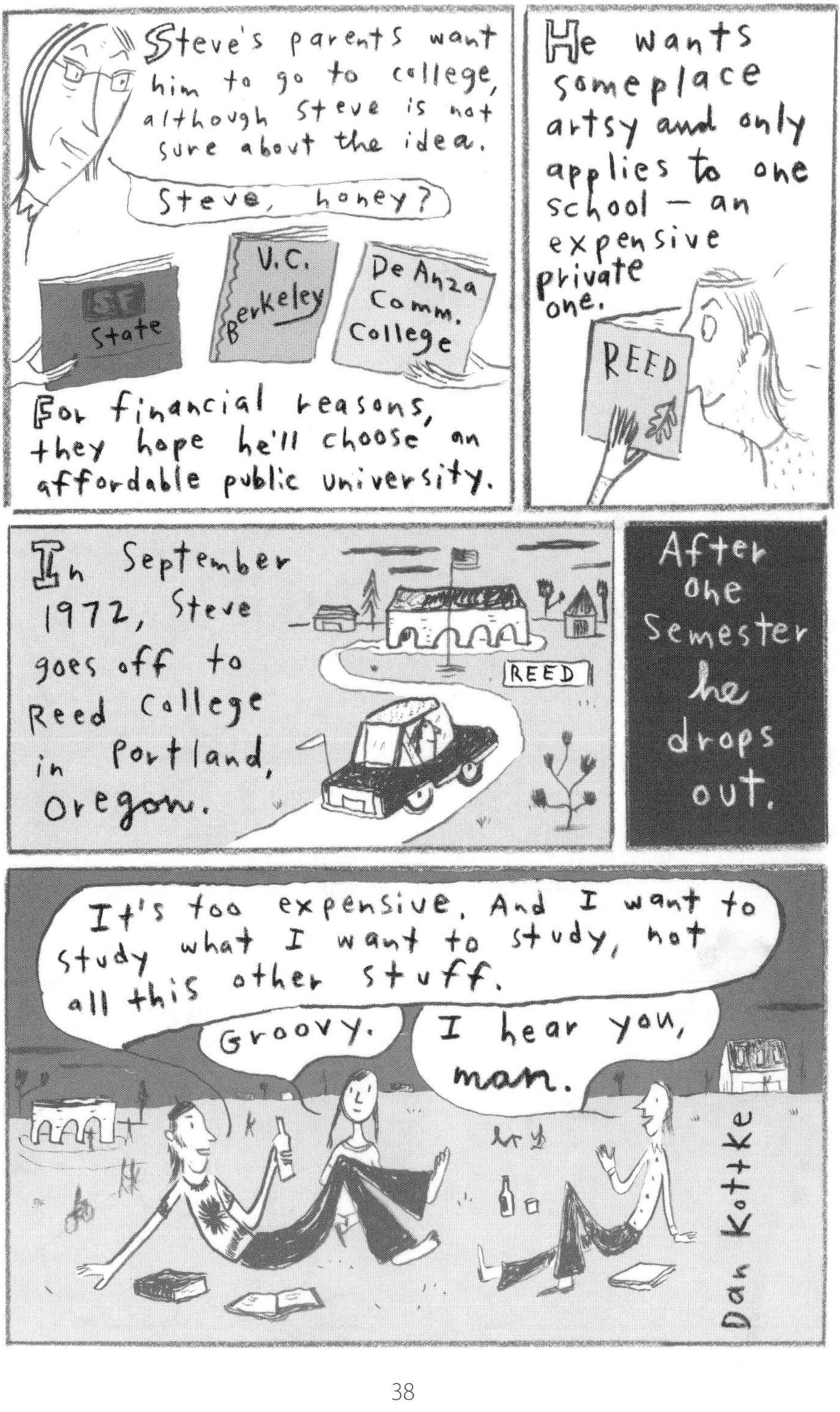
Steve's parents want him to go to college, although Steve is not sure about the idea.
Steve, honey?
SF State
U.C. Berkeley
De Anza Comm. College
For financial reasons, they hope he'll choose an affordable public university.
He wants someplace artsy and only applies to one school — an expensive private one.
REED
In September 1972, Steve goes off to Reed College in Portland, Oregon.
REED
After one semester he drops out.
It's too expensive. And I want to study what I want to study, not all this other stuff.
Groovy.
I hear you, man.
Dan Kottke

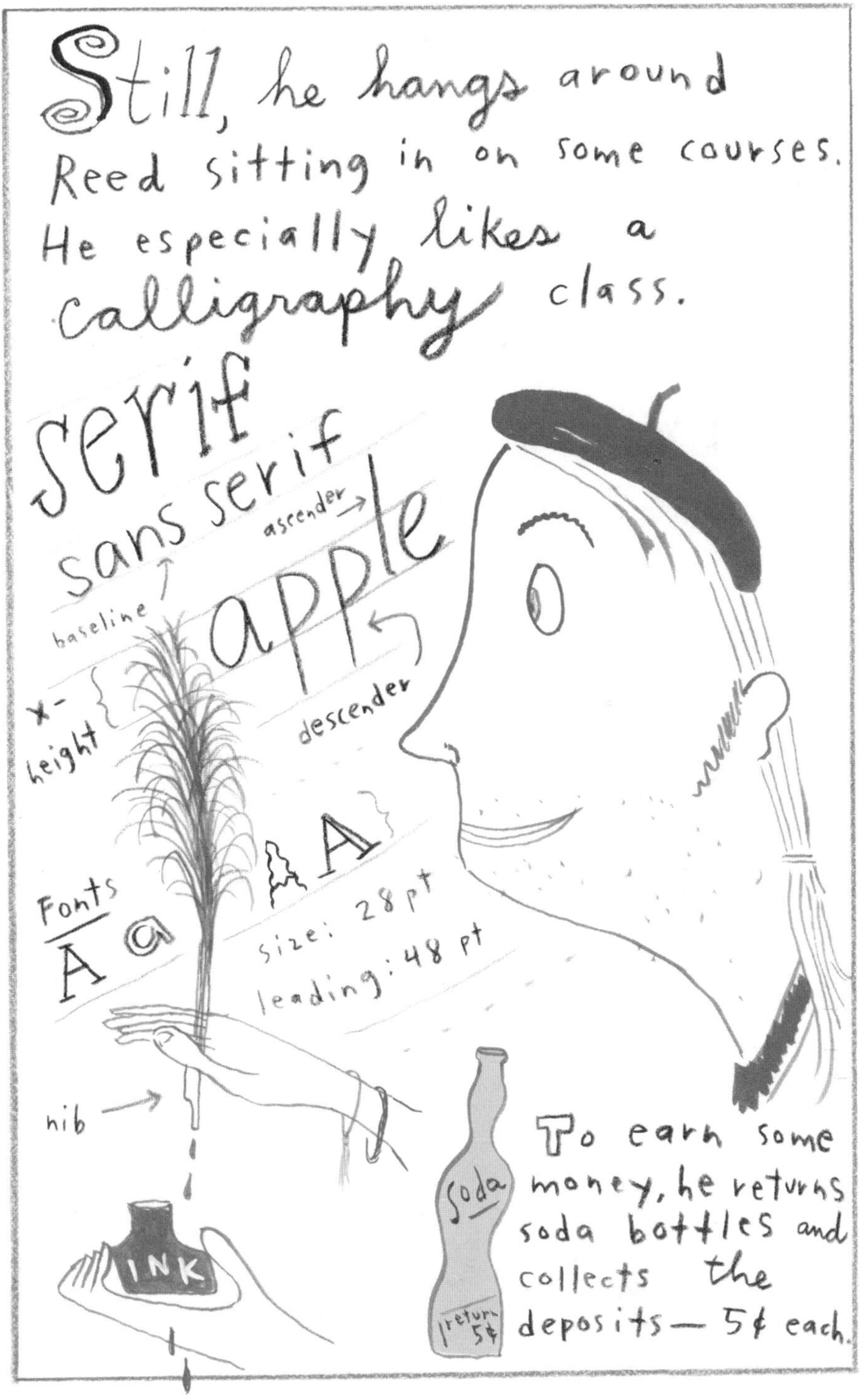
Still, he hangs around Reed sitting in on some courses. He especially likes a calligraphy class.
serif
sans serif
ascender
apple
baseline
x-height
descender
Fonts
A a A A
size: 28 pt
leading: 48 pt
nib
INK
soda
return 5¢
To earn some money, he returns soda bottles and collects the deposits — 5¢ each.

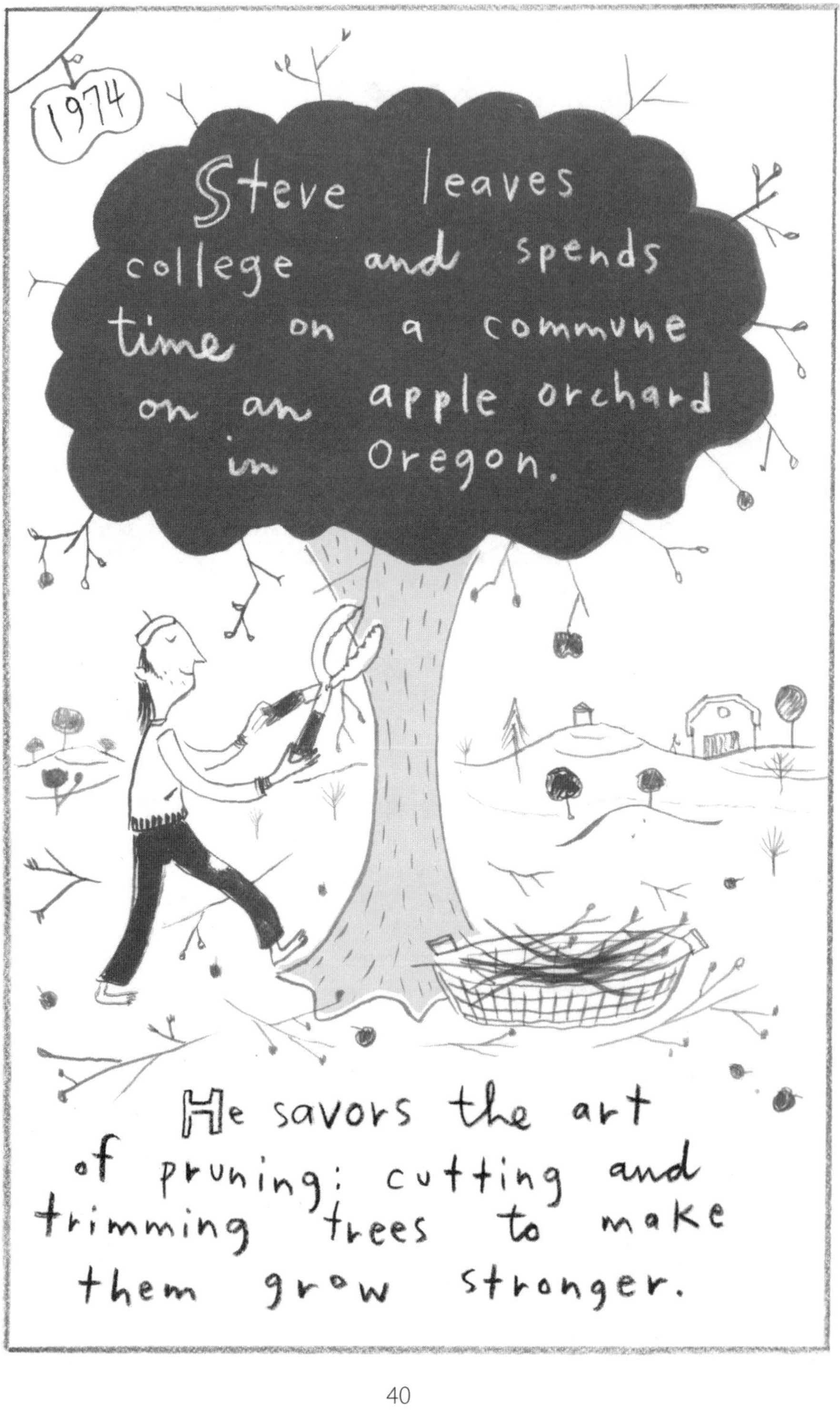
1974
Steve leaves college and spends time on a commune on an apple orchard in Oregon.
He savors the art of pruning: cutting and trimming trees to make them grow stronger.

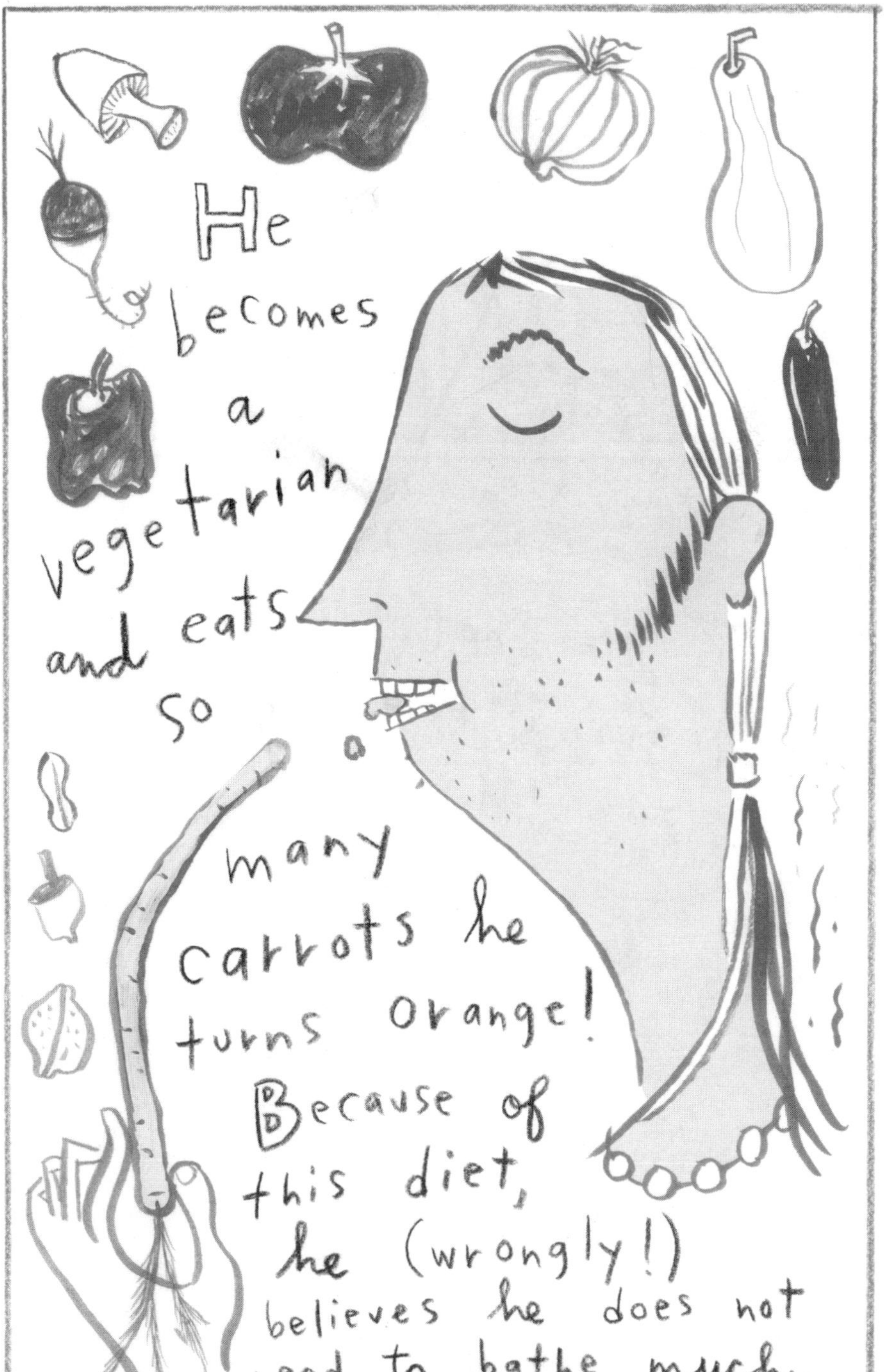
He
becomes
a
vegetarian
and eats
so
many
carrots he
turns orange!
Because of
this diet,
he (wrongly!)
believes he does not
need to bathe much.

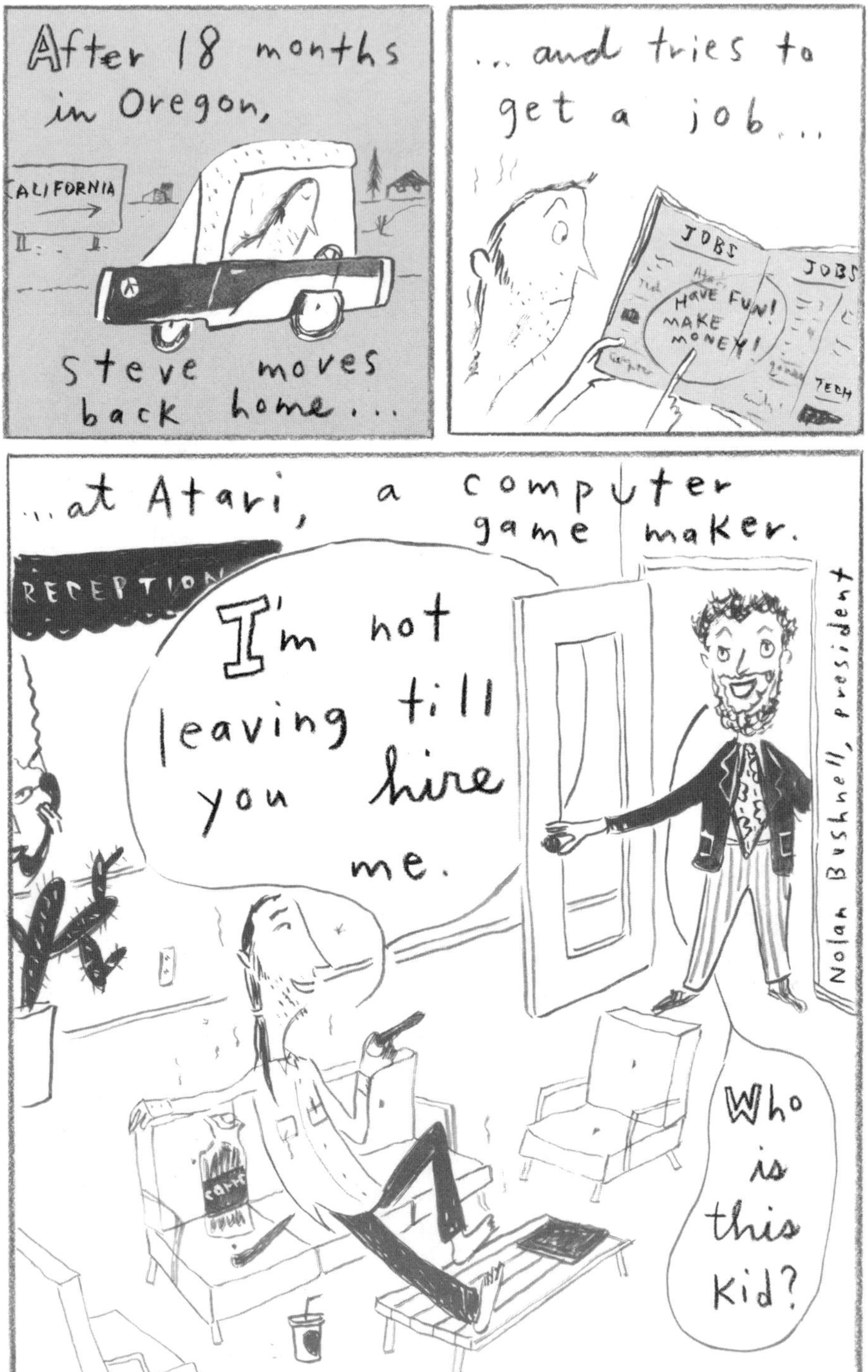
After 18 months in Oregon,
CALIFORNIA
Steve moves back home...
... and tries to get a job...
JOBS
JOBS
HAVE FUN! MAKE MONEY!
TECH
...at Atari, a computer game maker.
RECEPTION
I'm not leaving till you hire me.
Nolan Bushnell, president
Who is this Kid?

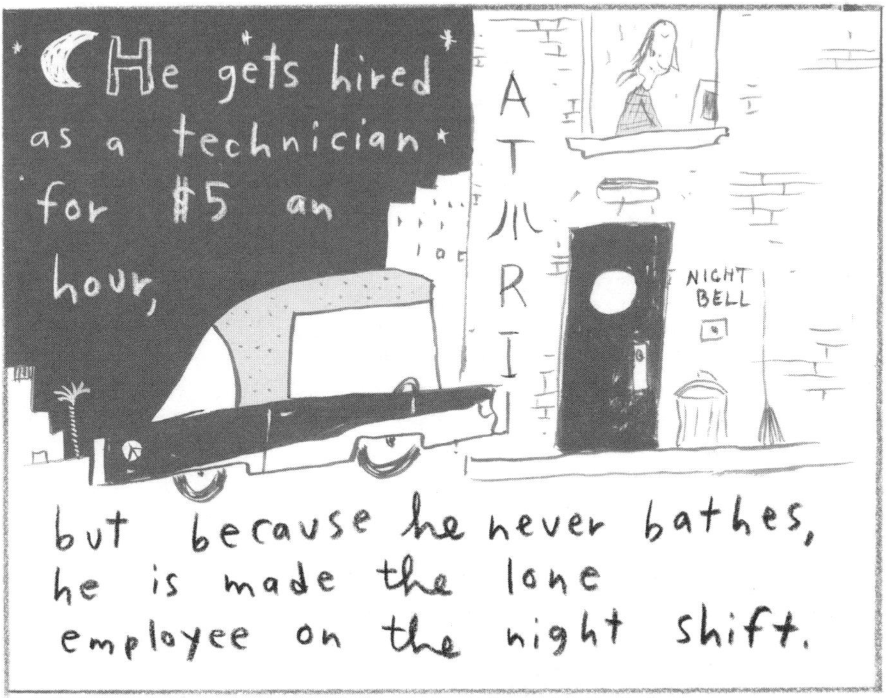
He gets hired as a technician for $5 an hour,
ATARI
NIGHT BELL
but because he never bathes, he is made the lone employee on the night shift.

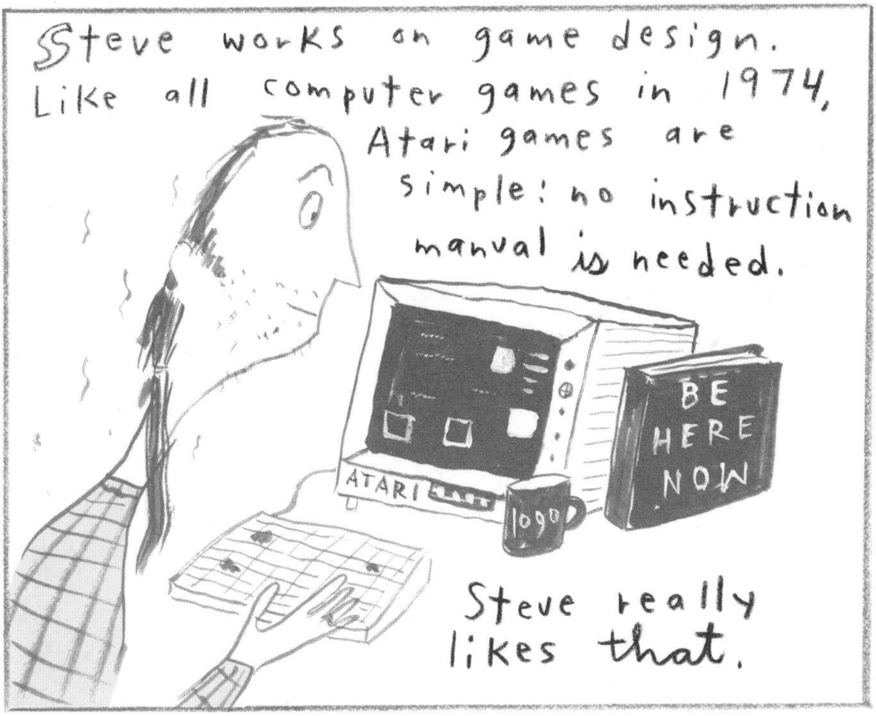
Steve works on game design. Like all computer games in 1974, Atari games are simple: no instruction manual is needed.
ATARI
BE HERE NOW
logo
Steve really likes that.

circa 1970 coin-operated computer games

all in B&W only

PONG

First commercially successful video game. Like table tennis on a screen.

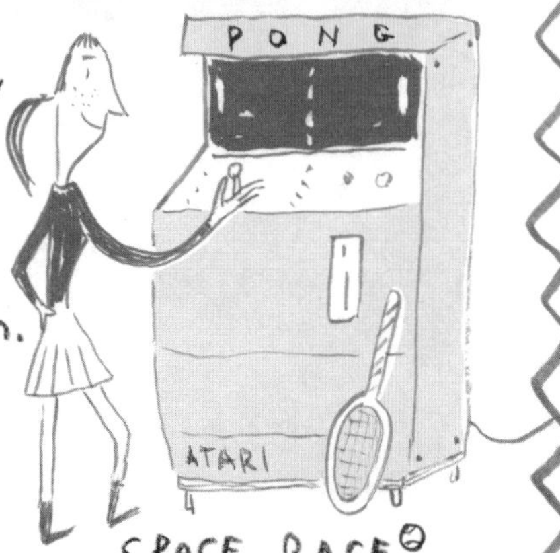
PONG
ATARI

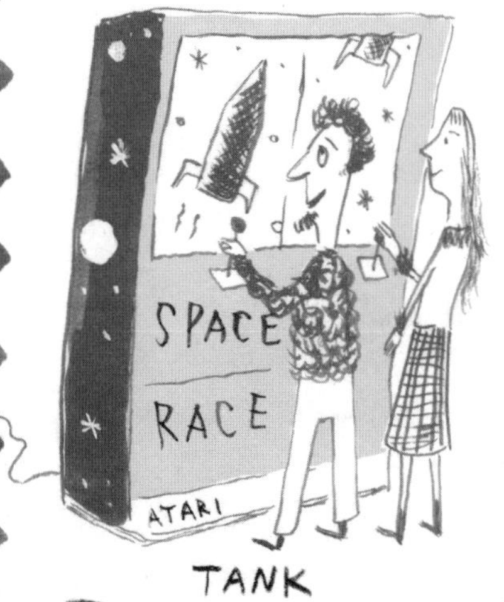
SPACE
RACE
ATARI

SPACE RACE

Two players each control a rocket ship, avoiding obstacles.

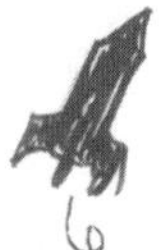

TANK

Players guide their tanks around a maze, firing at obstacles.

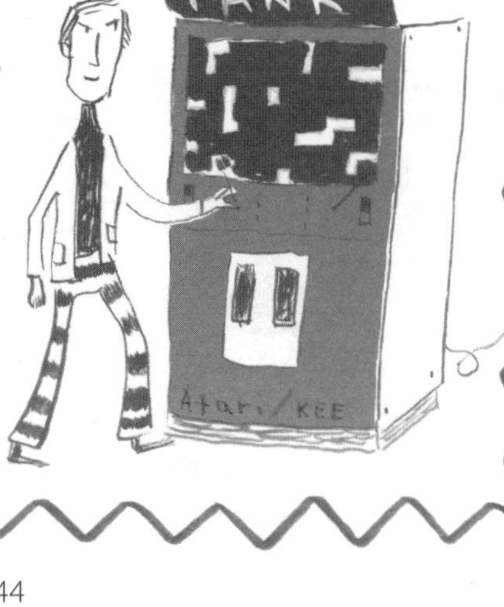
TANK
Atari/KEE

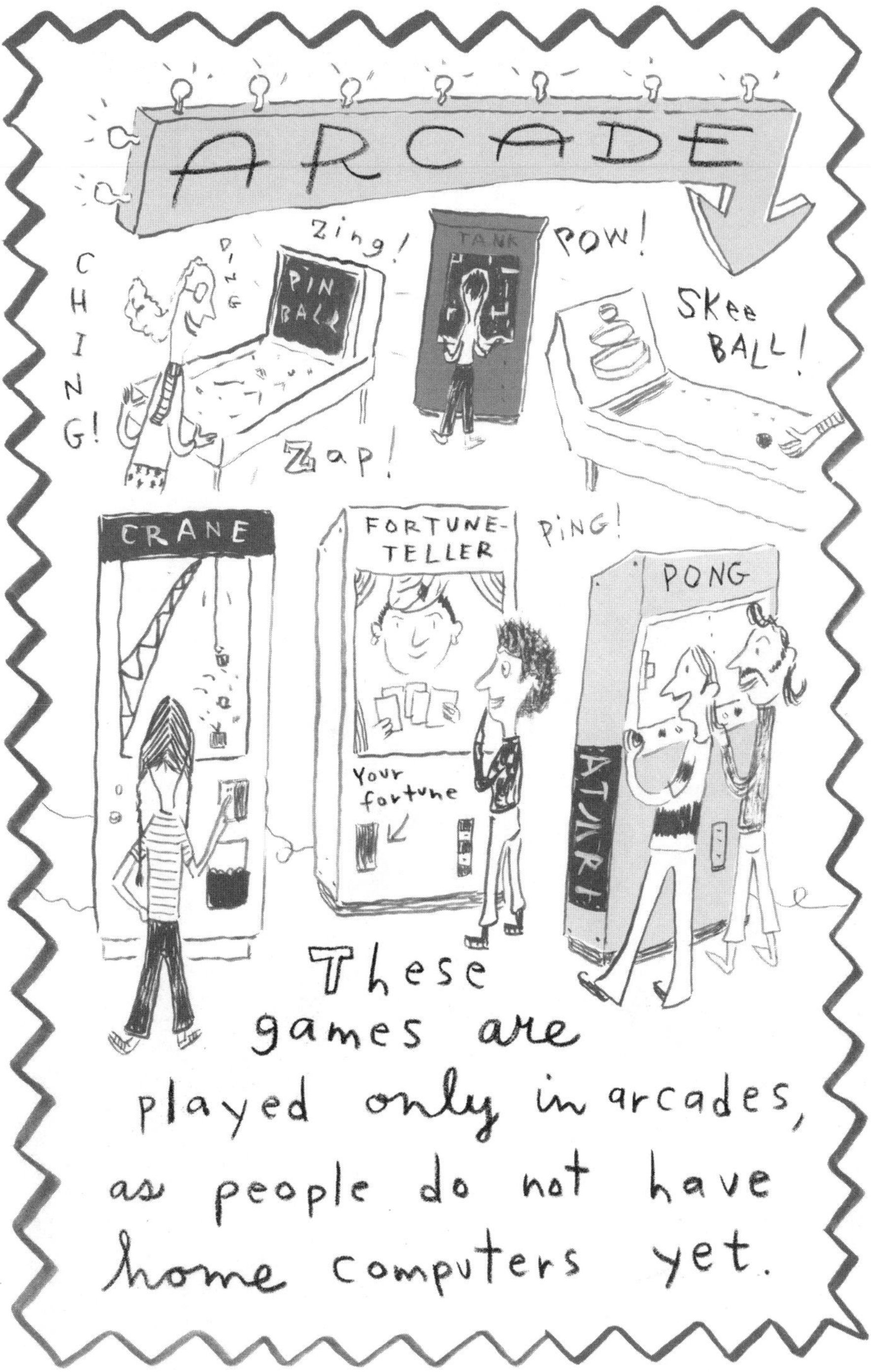
ARCADE
CHING!
DING
Zing!
PIN BALL
TANK
POW!
SKee BALL!
Zap!
CRANE
FORTUNE-TELLER
PiNG!
PONG
ATARI
Your fortune
These games are played only in arcades, as people do not have home computers yet.

Ever since he was a teenager, Steve has looked at himself in the mirror every morning and asked,
If today were the last day of my life, would I want to do what I am about to do today?
And when the answer has been "no" for too many days in a row, he knows he has to change some-thing.
CRUST

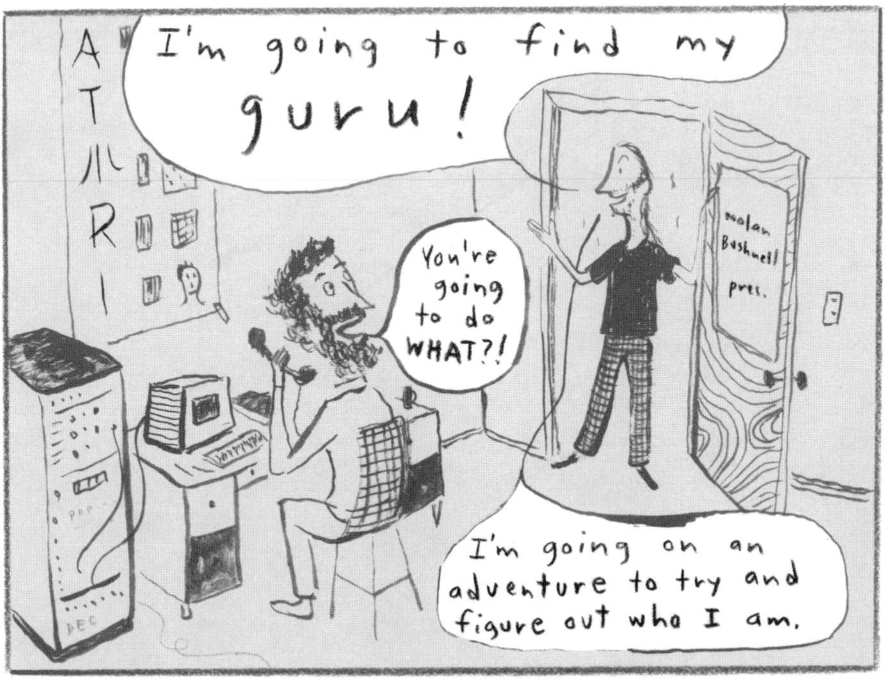
I'm going to find my guru!
You're going to do WHAT?!
I'm going on an adventure to try and figure out who I am.
ATARI
Nolan Bushnell pres.
DEC

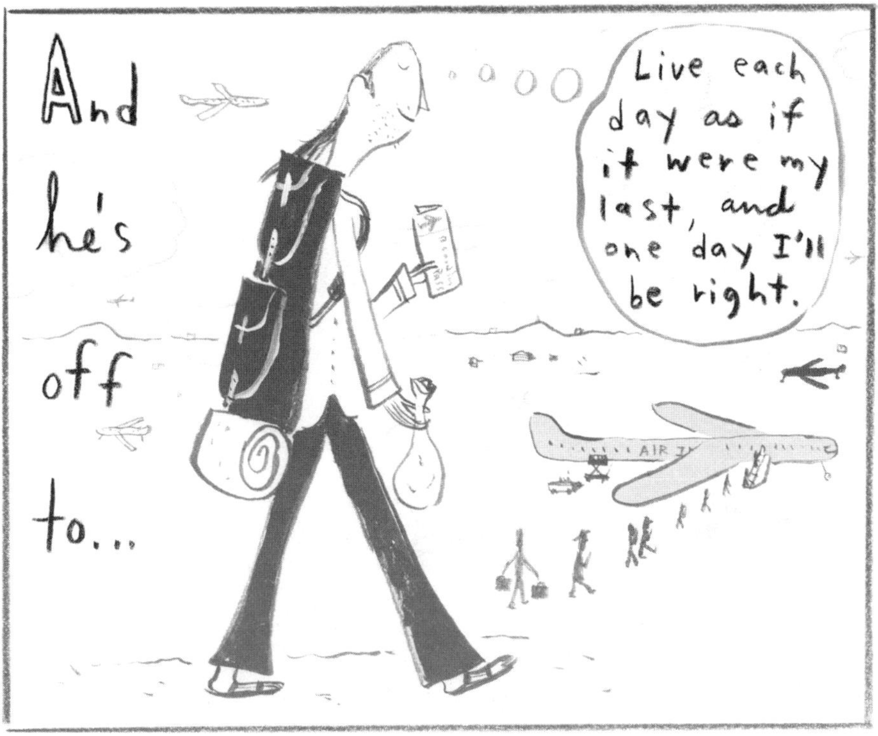
And he's off to...
Live each day as if it were my last, and one day I'll be right.

INDIA!
He travels the country with ~~his~~ friend Dan, living simply.
Expand the moment.
Delhi
seek enlightenment.
Follow your instinct.
Bombay
Search for simplicity.
IND
Buddhism

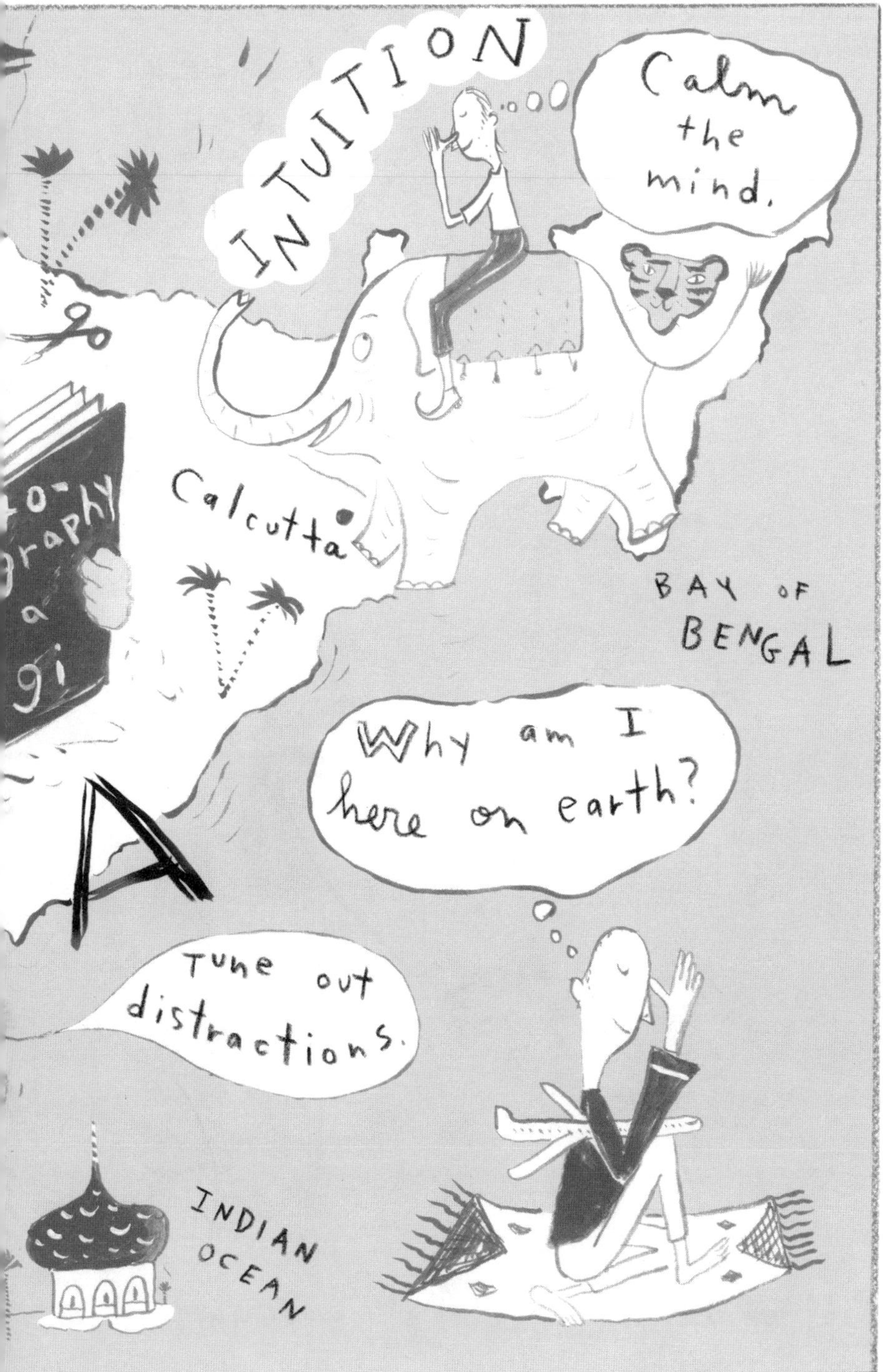
INTUITION
Calm the mind.
Calcutta
BAY OF BENGAL
Why am I here on earth?
Tune out distractions.
INDIAN OCEAN

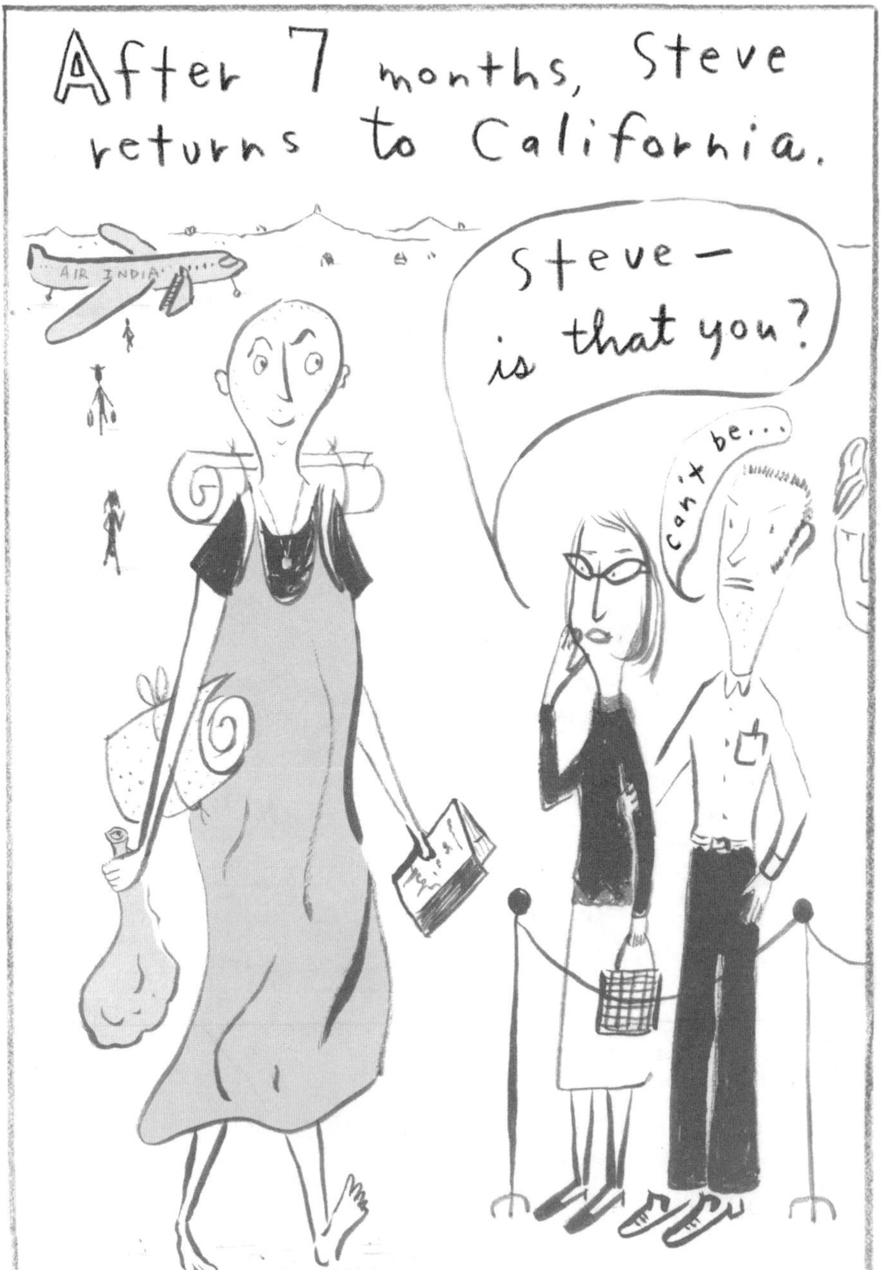
After 7 months, Steve returns to California.
AIR INDIA
Steve — is that you?
can't be...
His parents do not recognize him.

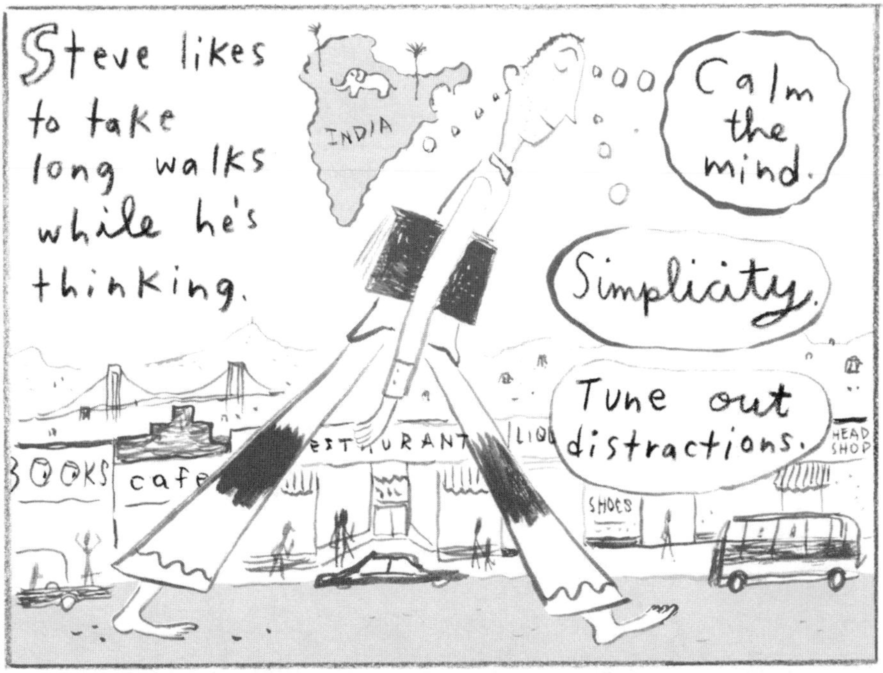
Steve likes to take long walks while he's thinking.
INDIA
Calm the mind.
Simplicity.
Tune out distractions.
BOOKS
cafe
RESTAURANT
HEAD SHOP
SHOES

He still feels restless.

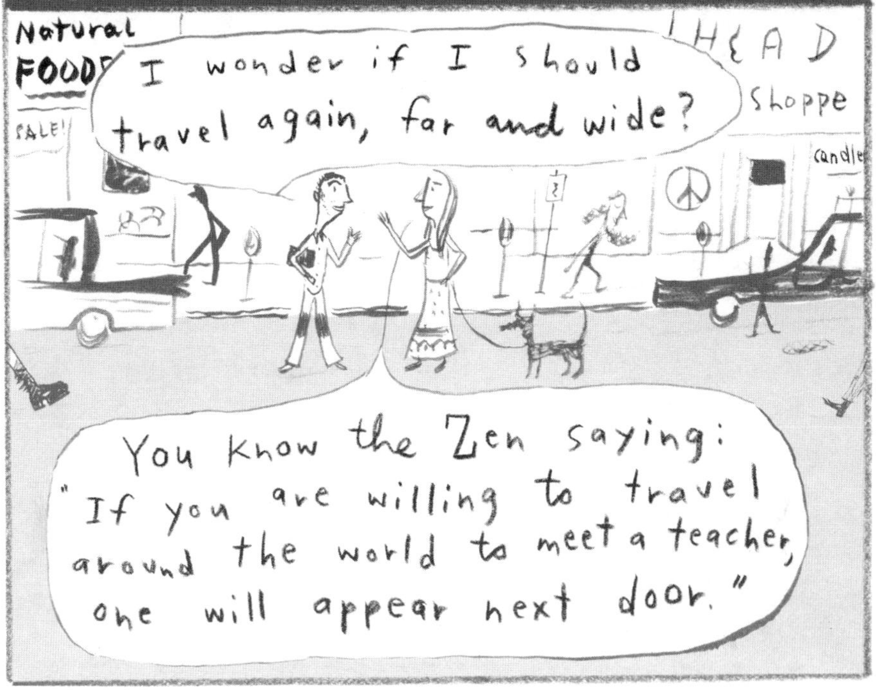
Natural FOODS
SALE!
HEAD Shoppe
candles
I wonder if I should travel again, far and wide?
You know the Zen saying: "If you are willing to travel around the world to meet a teacher, one will appear next door."

Indeed, Steve meets a local Zen master.
Shall I travel again, far and wide, or keep working in the tech industry?
EST
water BEDS
primal scream therapy
GOOD EARTH restaurant
LOS Altos ZEN CENTER
ALL SIZES
Santa Clara FOOD CO-OP
NO nukes

The Zen master thinks.
Kobun Chino Otogawa
Stick with technology, young man.

chapter

5

Apple Is Born

(1975 – 1976)

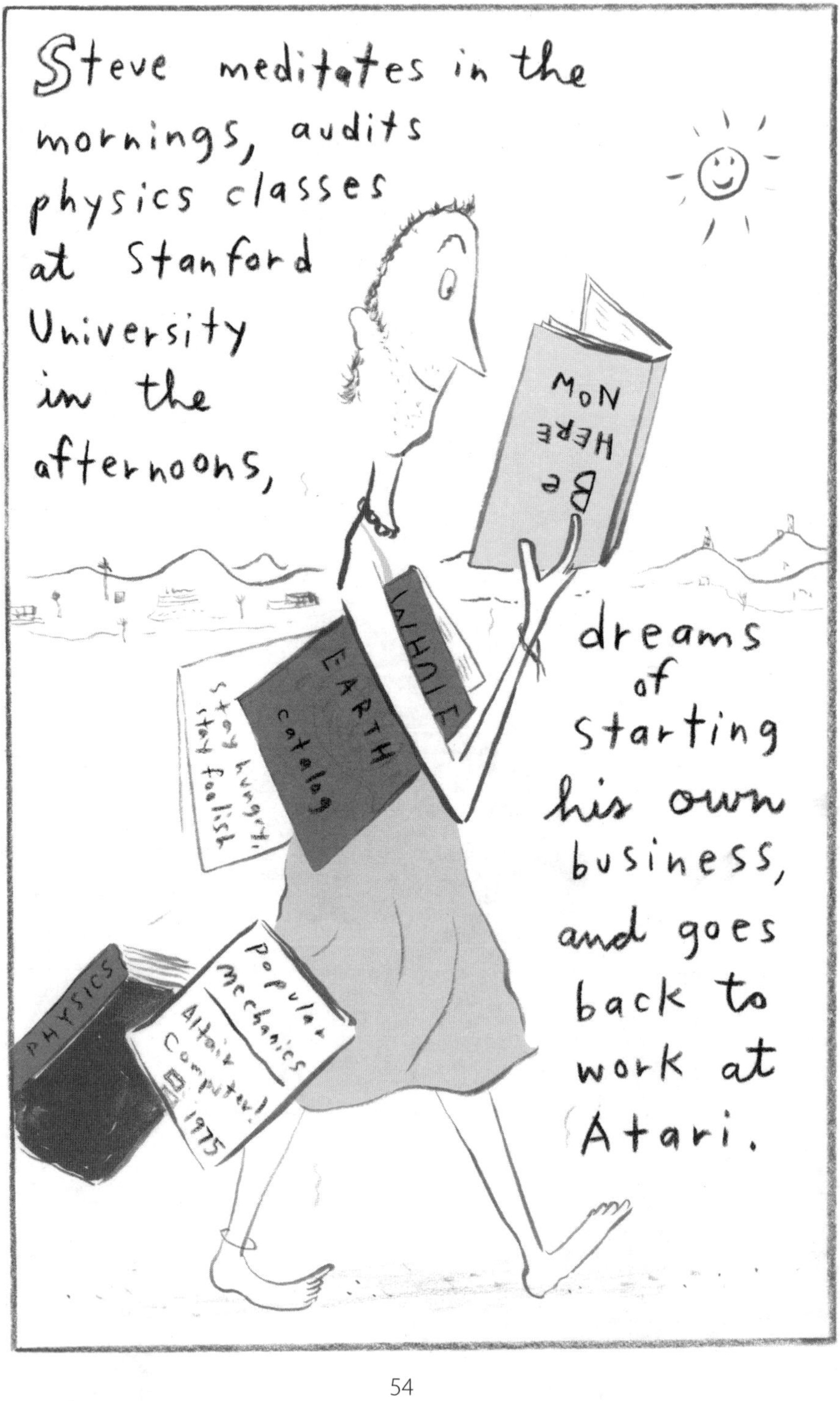
Steve meditates in the mornings, audits physics classes at Stanford University in the afternoons,
dreams of starting his own business, and goes back to work at Atari.
Be HERE NOW
WHOLE EARTH catalog
stay hungry, stay foolish
PHYSICS
Popular Mechanics
Altair Computer!
1975

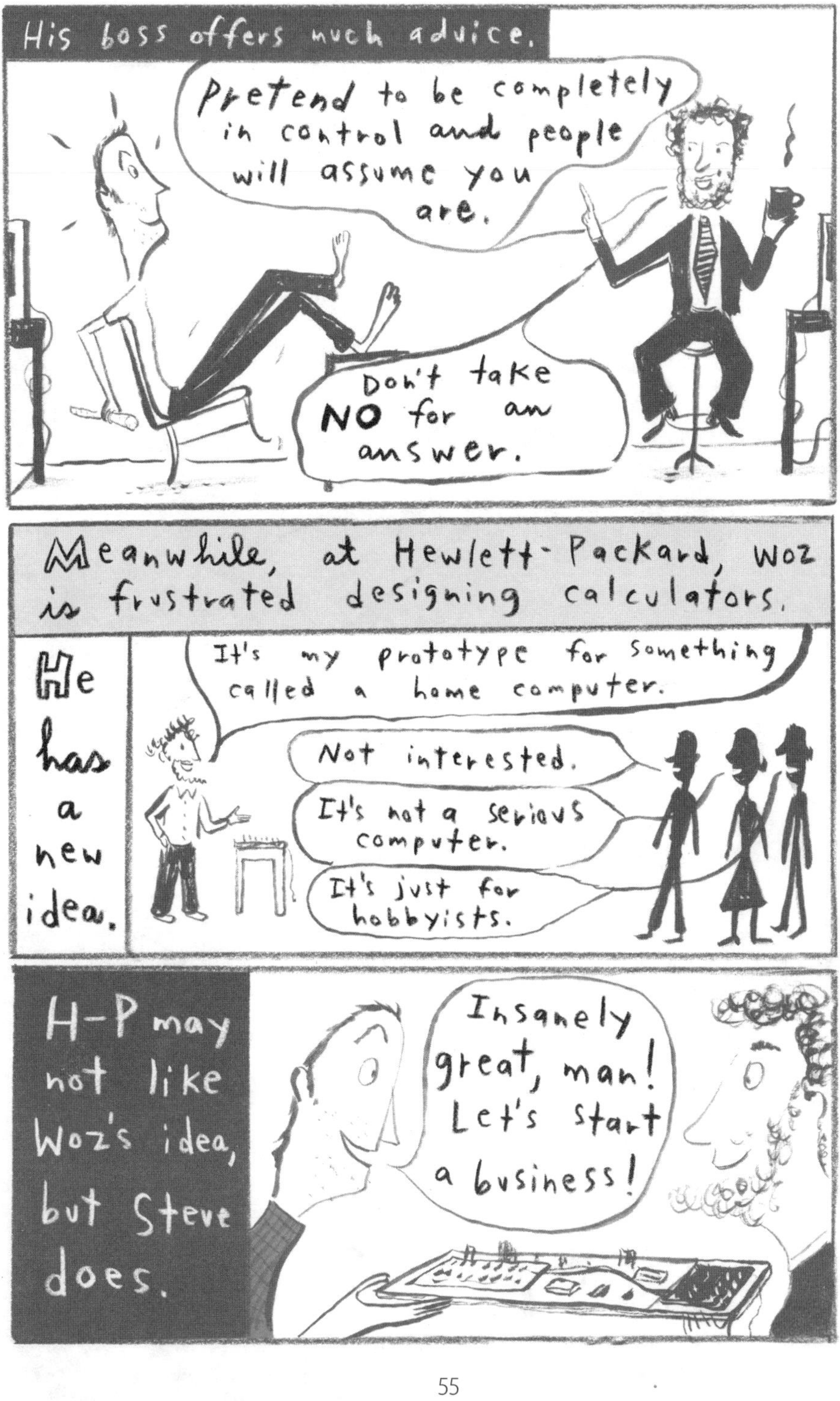

His boss offers much advice.
Pretend to be completely in control and people will assume you are.
Don't take NO for an answer.
Meanwhile, at Hewlett-Packard, Woz is frustrated designing calculators.
He has a new idea.
It's my prototype for something called a home computer.
Not interested.
It's not a serious computer.
It's just for hobbyists.
H-P may not like Woz's idea, but Steve does.
Insanely great, man! Let's start a business!

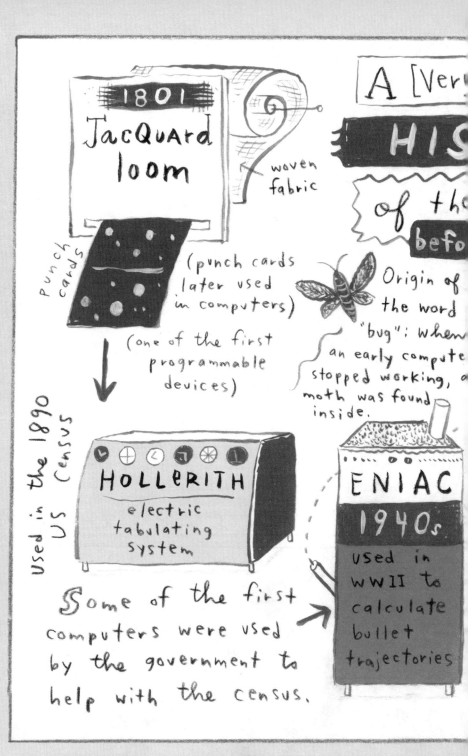

1801
JacQuard loom

woven fabric

A [Very]

HIS

of the

befo

punch cards

(punch cards later used in computers)

Origin of the word "bug"; when an early computer stopped working, a moth was found inside.

(one of the first programmable devices)

Used in the 1890 US Census

HOLLERITH
electric tabulating system

ENIAC
1940s
used in WWII to calculate bullet trajectories

Some of the first computers were used by the government to help with the census.

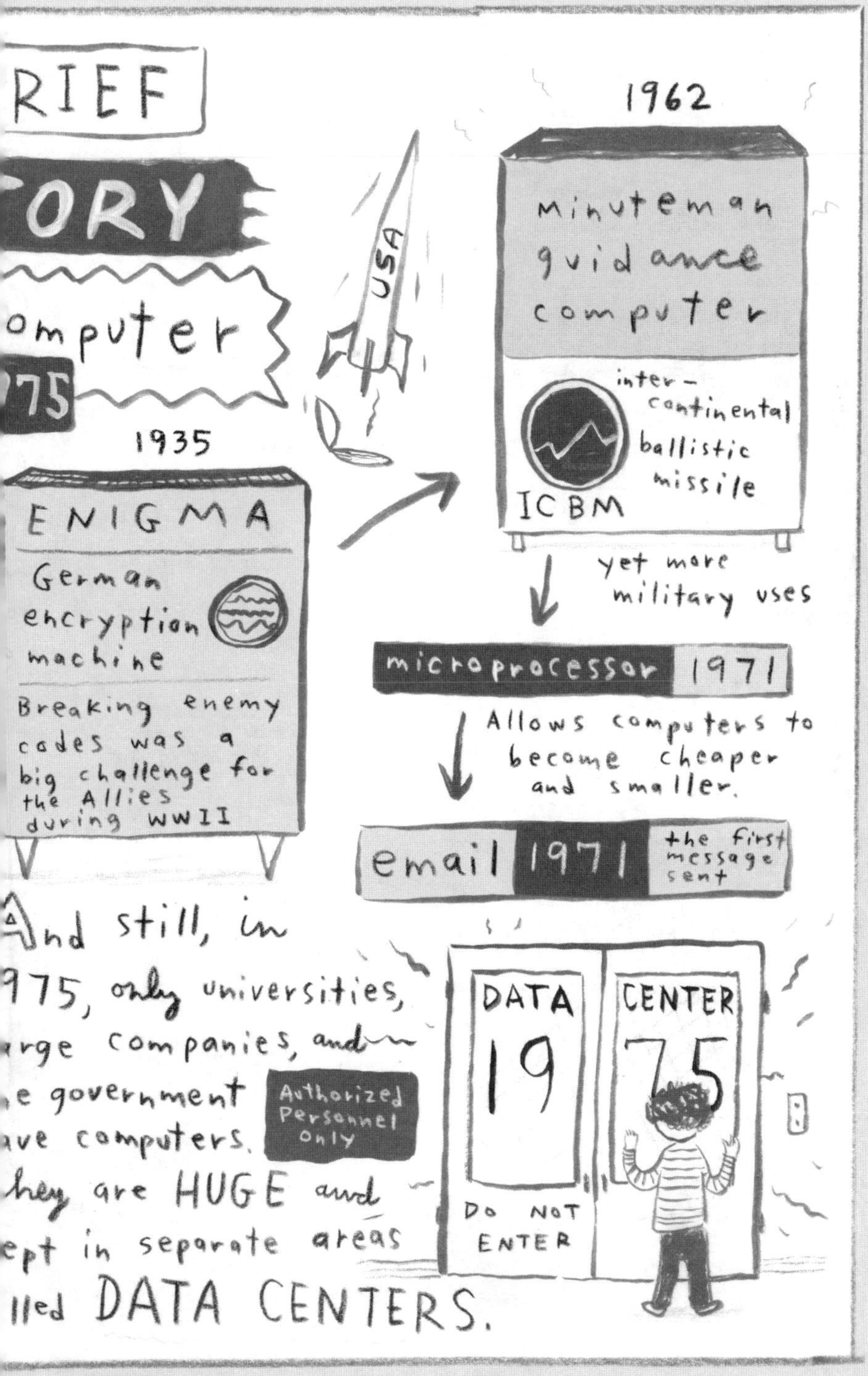

RIEF
ORY
omputer
75
1935
ENIGMA
German encryption machine
Breaking enemy codes was a big challenge for the Allies during WWII
USA
1962
minuteman guidance computer
inter-continental ballistic missile
ICBM
yet more military uses
microprocessor 1971
Allows computers to become cheaper and smaller.
email 1971
the first message sent
And still, in
975, only universities,
rge companies, and
e government
ave computers.
hey are HUGE and
ept in separate areas
lled DATA CENTERS.
Authorized Personnel Only
DATA
CENTER
1975
DO NOT ENTER

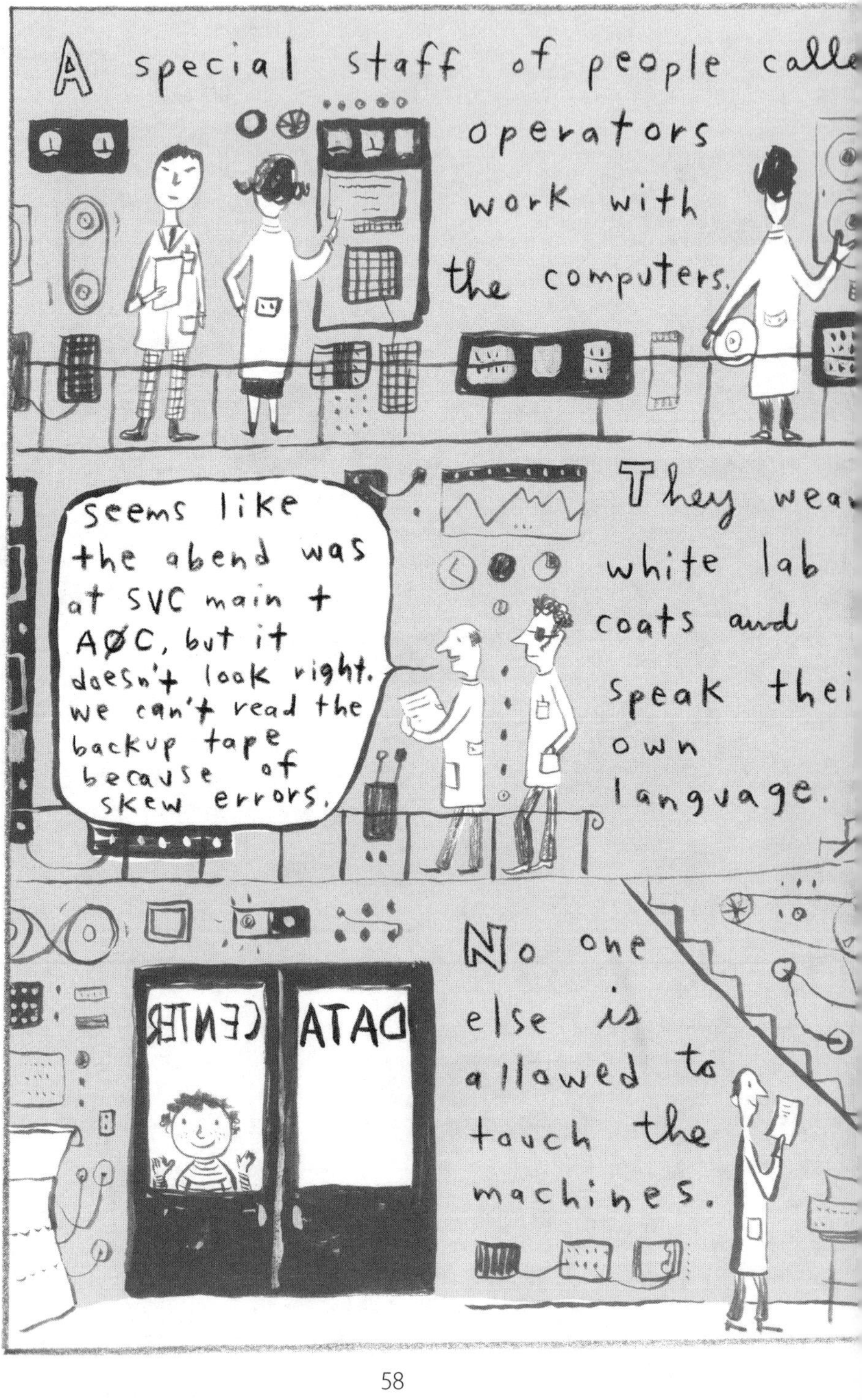
A special staff of people calle
operators work with the computers.
seems like the abend was at SVC main + AØC, but it doesn't look right. we can't read the backup tape because of skew errors.
They wea
white lab coats and
speak thei
own language.
No one else is allowed to touch the machines.

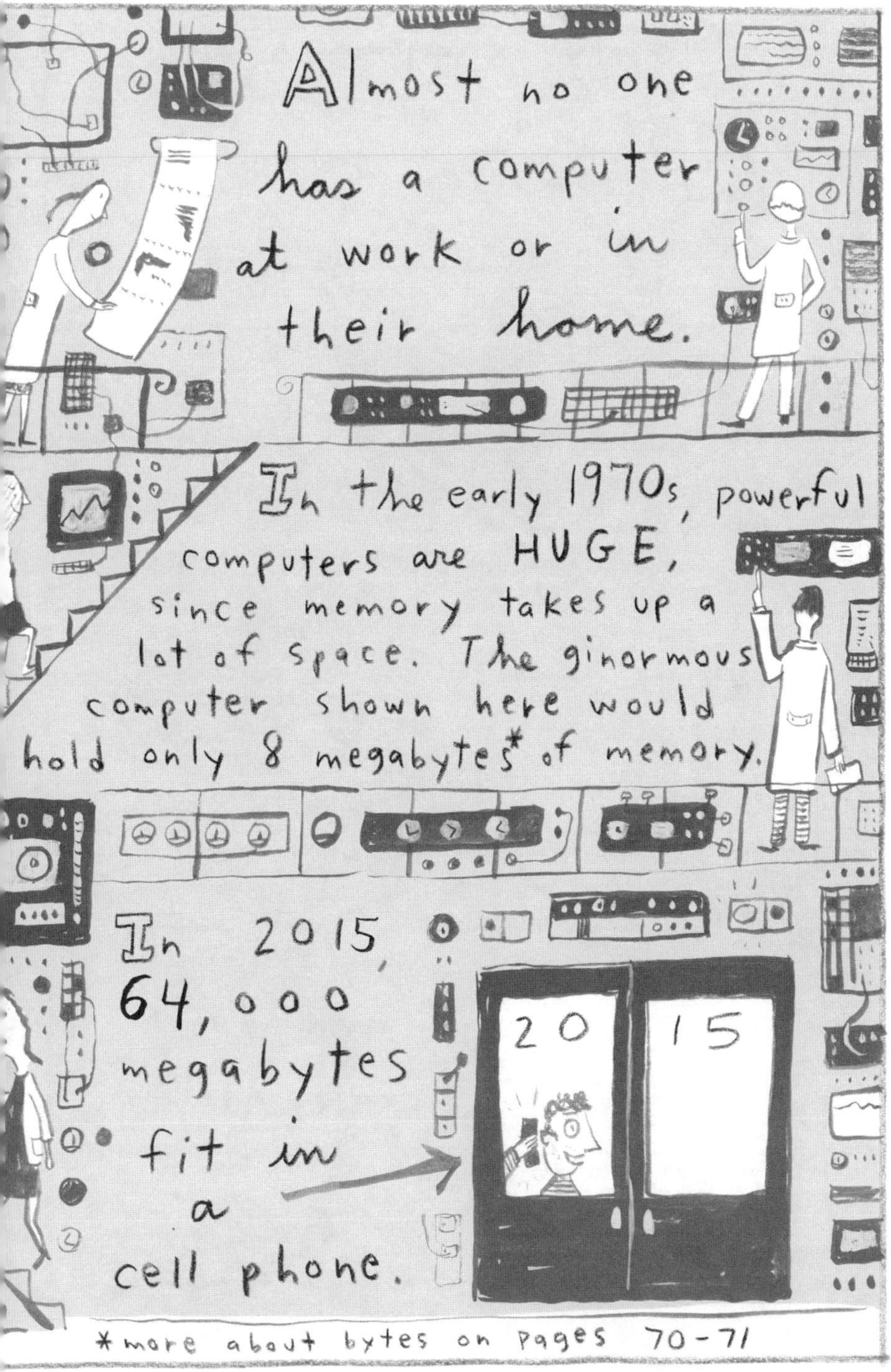
Almost no one has a computer at work or in their home.
In the early 1970s, powerful computers are HUGE, since memory takes up a lot of space. The ginormous computer shown here would hold only 8 megabytes* of memory.
In 2015, 64,000 megabytes fit in a cell phone.
2015
*more about bytes on pages 70-71

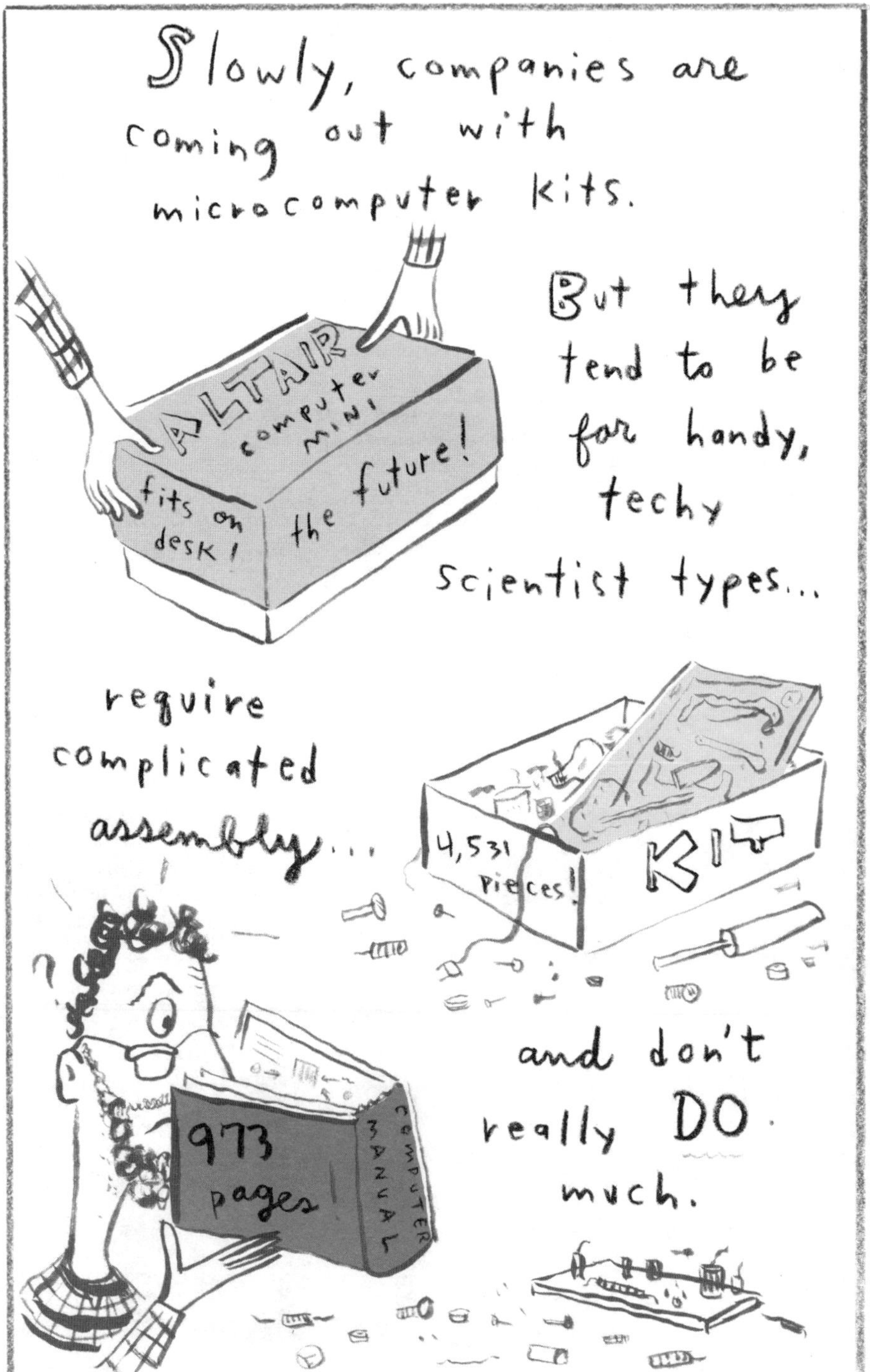
Slowly, companies are coming out with microcomputer kits.
ALTAIR computer mini
fits on desk!
the future!
But they tend to be for handy, techy scientist types...
require complicated assembly...
4,531 pieces!
KIT
973 pages
COMPUTER MANUAL
and don't really DO much.

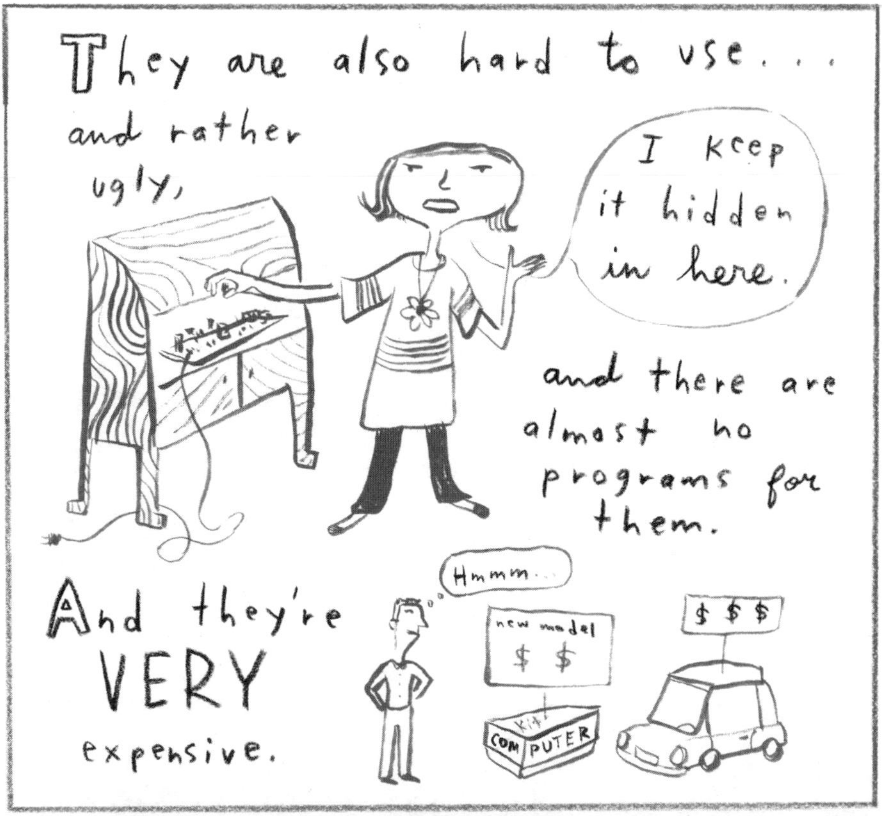
They are also hard to use...
...and rather ugly,
I keep it hidden in here.
and there are almost no programs for them.
And they're VERY expensive.
Hmmm...
new model $ $
KIT COMPUTER
$ $ $

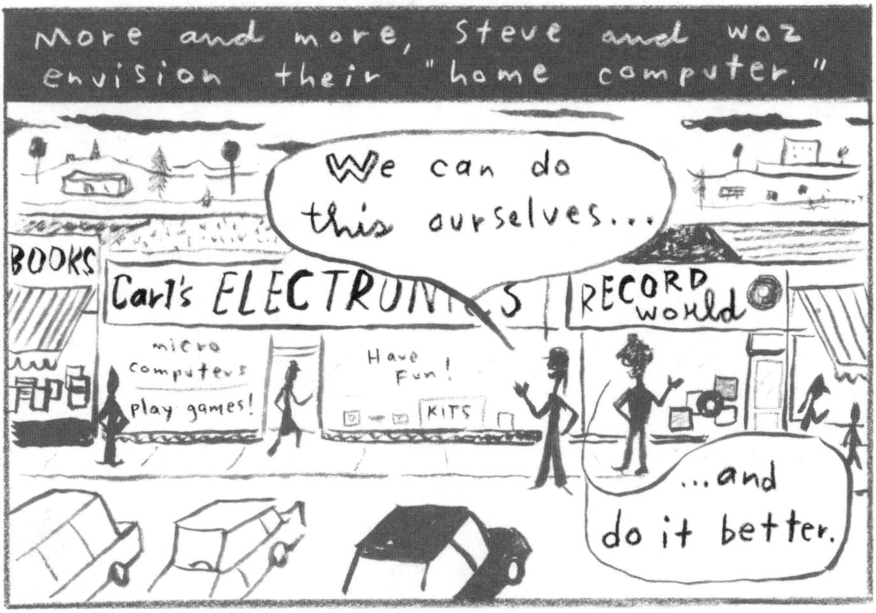
More and more, Steve and Woz envision their "home computer."
We can do this ourselves...
BOOKS
Carl's ELECTRONICS
RECORD world
micro computers play games!
Have Fun!
KITS
...and do it better.

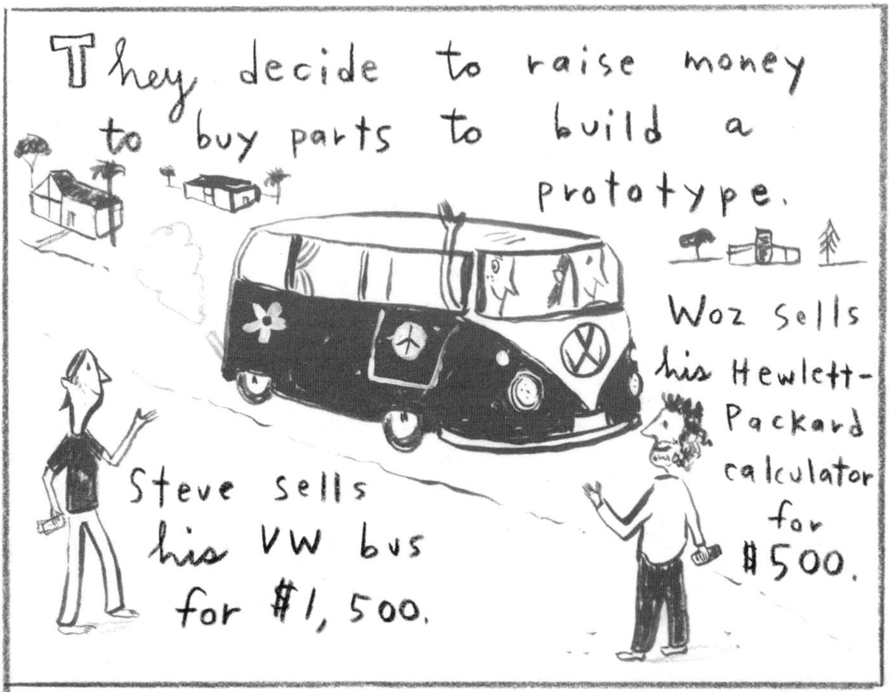
They decide to raise money to buy parts to build a prototype.
Steve sells his VW bus for $1,500.
Woz sells his Hewlett-Packard calculator for $500.

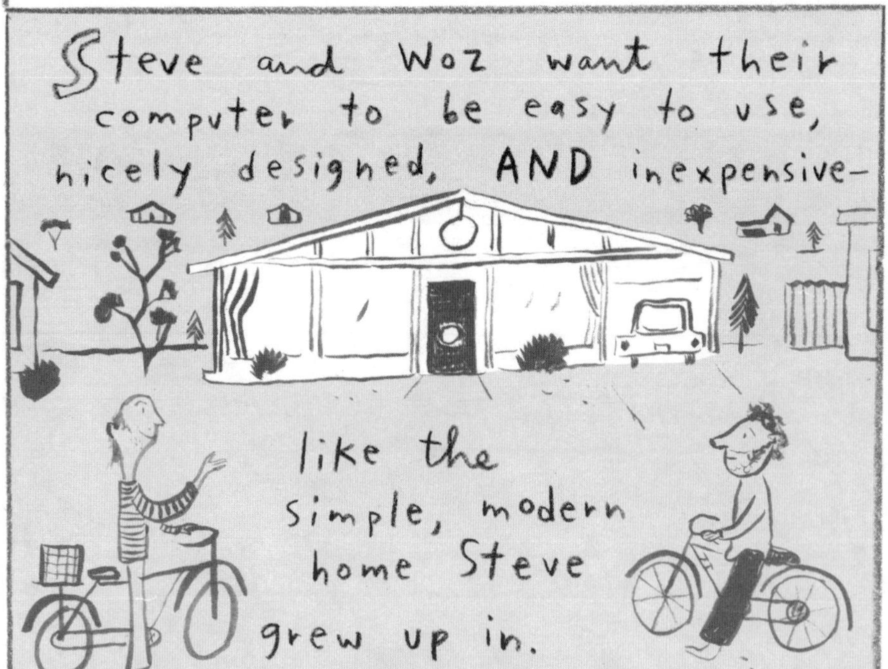
Steve and Woz want their computer to be easy to use, nicely designed, AND inexpensive-
like the simple, modern home Steve grew up in.

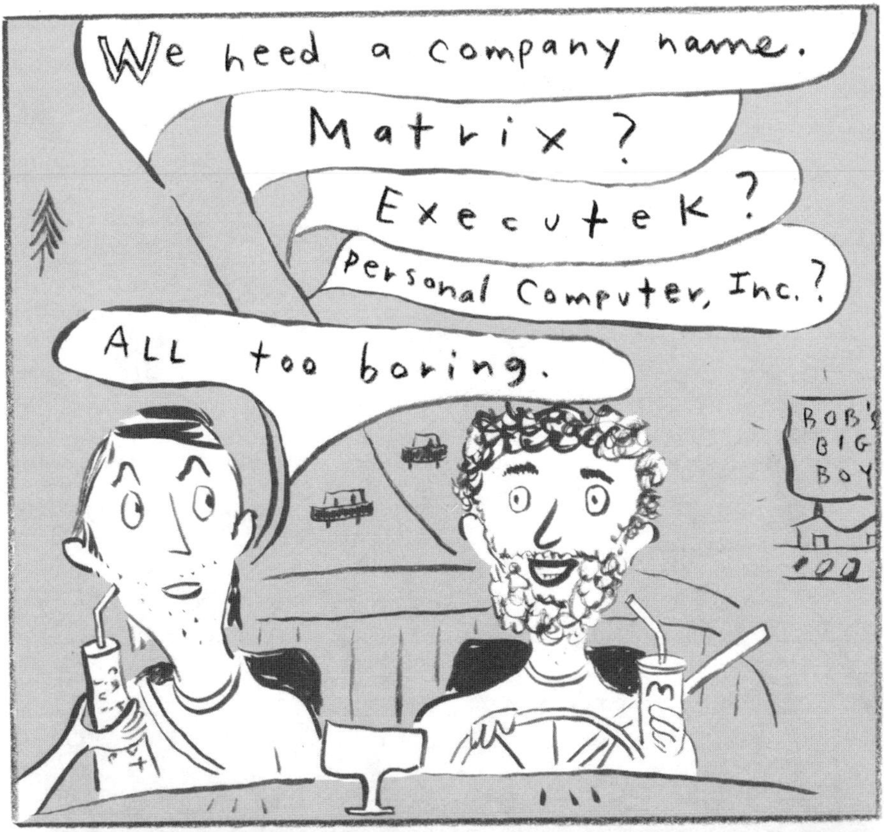
We need a company name.
Matrix?
Executek?
Personal Computer, Inc.?
ALL too boring.
BOB'S BIG BOY

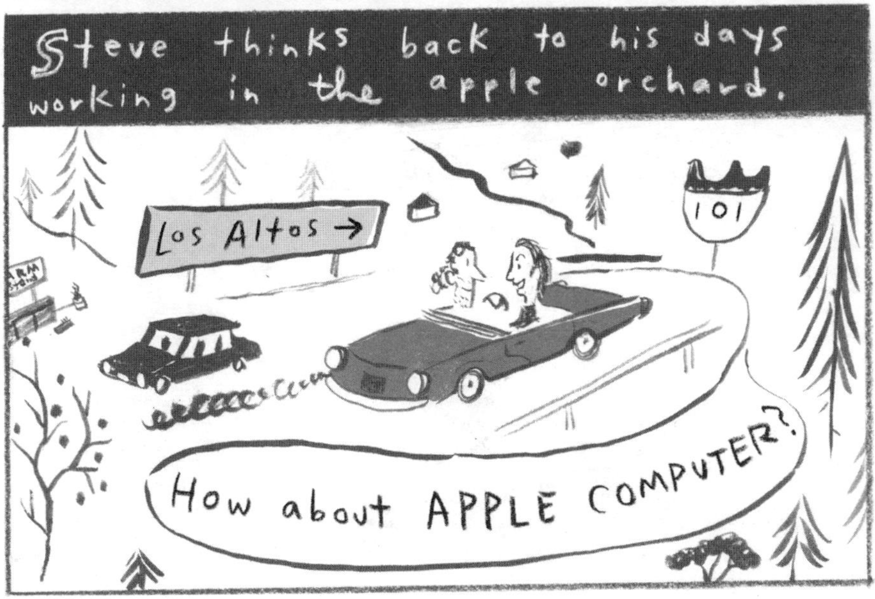
Steve thinks back to his days working in the apple orchard.
Los Altos →
101
How about APPLE COMPUTER?

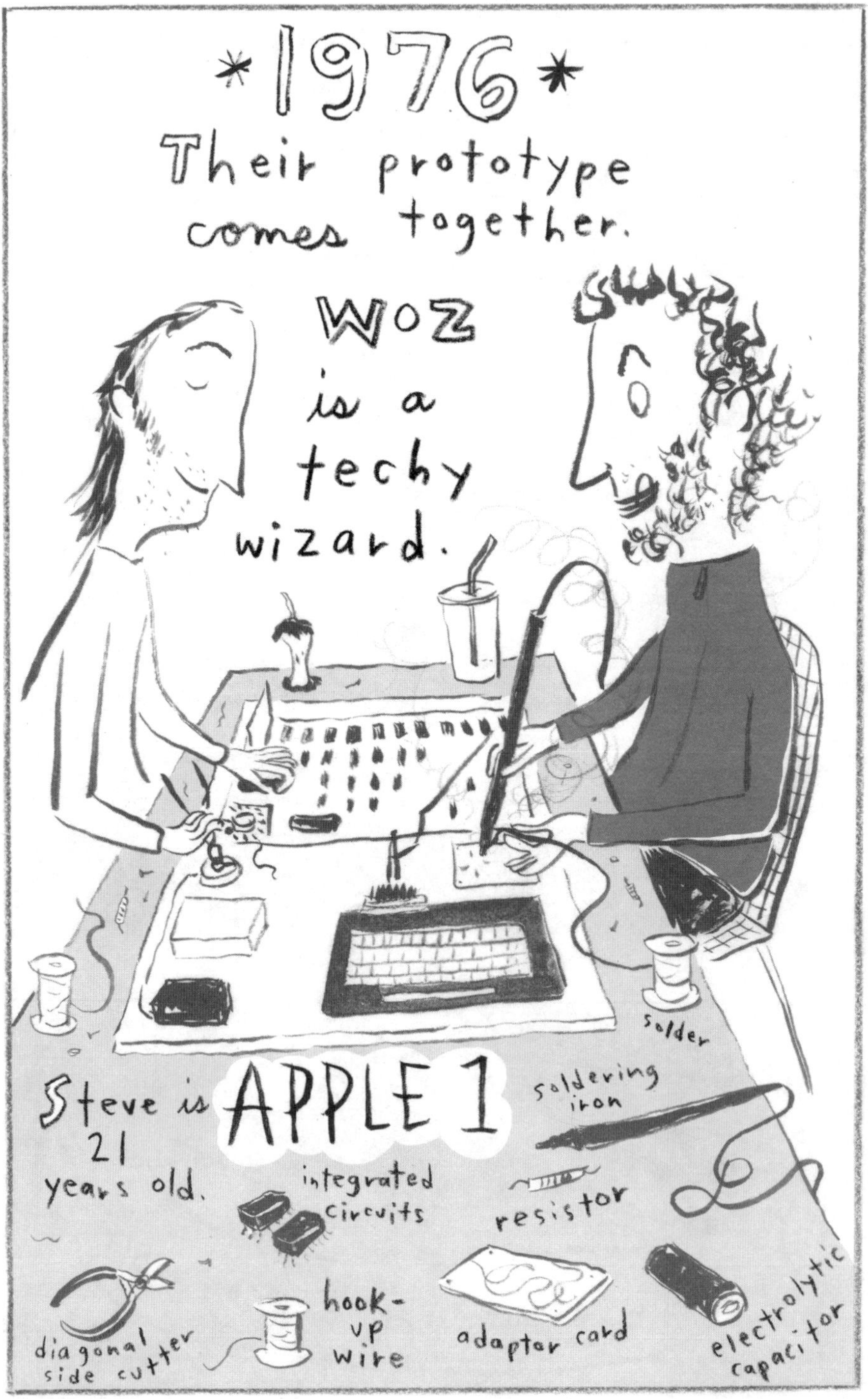
1976
Their prototype comes together.
WOZ is a techy wizard.
Steve is 21 years old.
APPLE 1
solder
soldering iron
integrated circuits
resistor
diagonal side cutter
hook-up wire
adaptor card
electrolytic capacitor

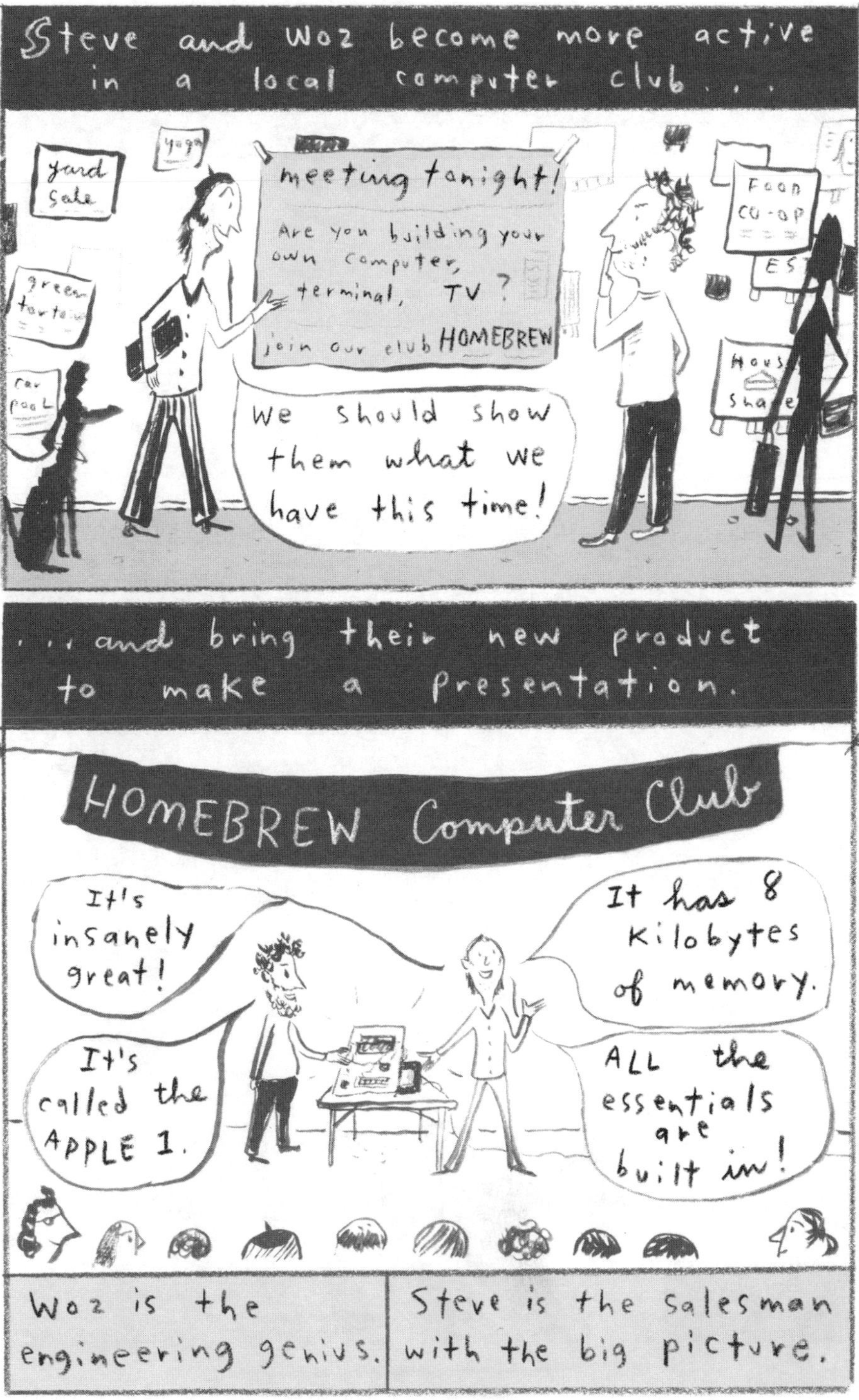
Steve and Woz become more active in a local computer club...
yard sale
yoga
meeting tonight!
Are you building your own computer, terminal, TV?
join our club HOMEBREW
Food co-op
green tortoise
car pool
House share
We should show them what we have this time!
...and bring their new product to make a presentation.
HOMEBREW Computer Club
It's insanely great!
It has 8 kilobytes of memory.
It's called the APPLE 1.
ALL the essentials are built in!
Woz is the engineering genius.
Steve is the salesman with the big picture.

Except for one man who owns a small chain of stores, the audience is not impressed.

Interesting. Keep in touch, boys!

You bet.

HOMEBREW Co

SLAC

The very next day Steve stops by...

BYTE shop

Hi— I'm keeping in touch!

...and makes a sale.

OK— I'll take 50 Apples, but I don't want build-it-yourself computer kits. I need them assembled.

PAUL TEARELL

Parts

Sure, OK. Whatever you'd like.

FOR SALE

Homebrew CLUB meetings at SLAC

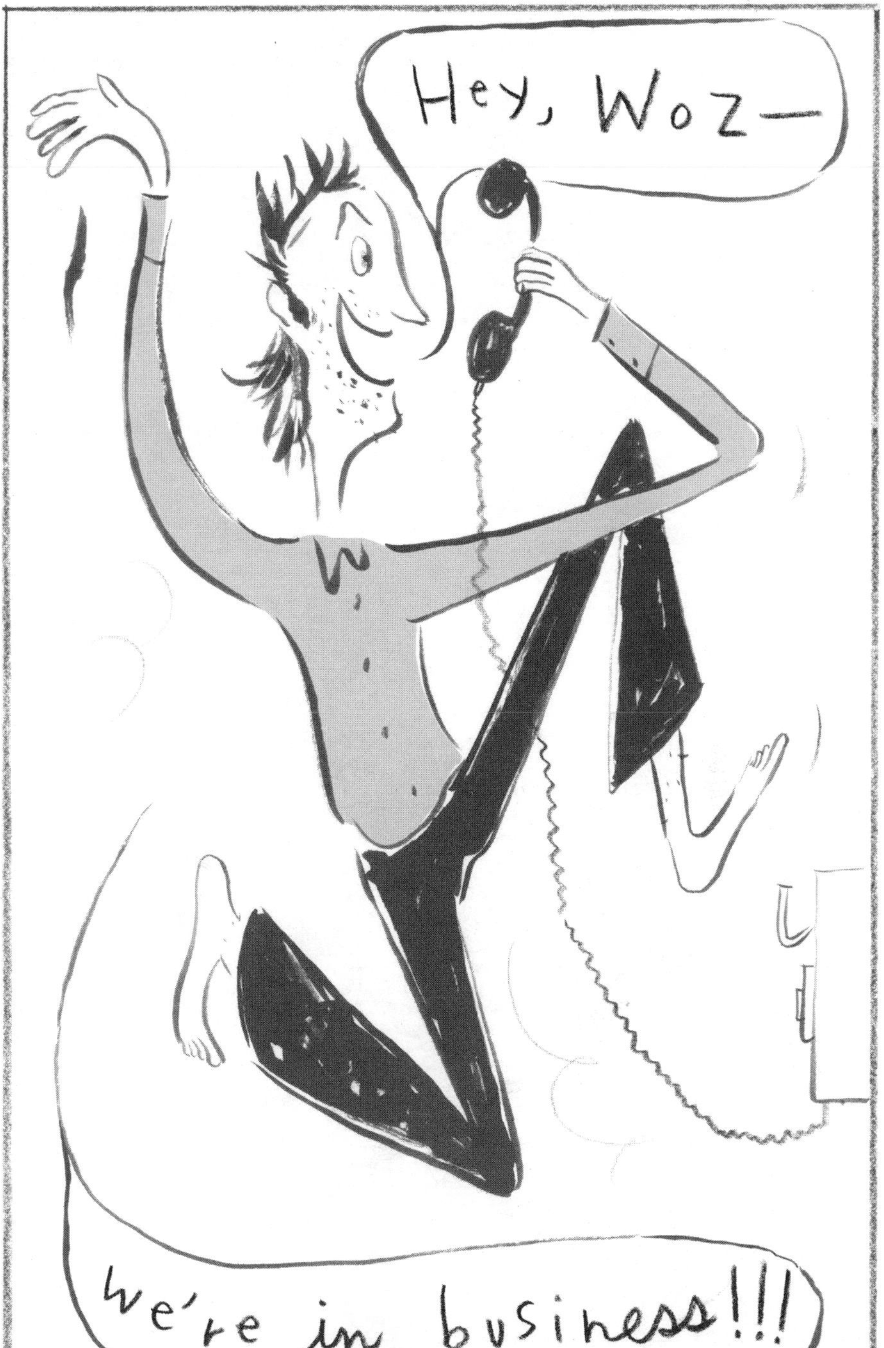
Hey, WoZ—
we're in business!!!

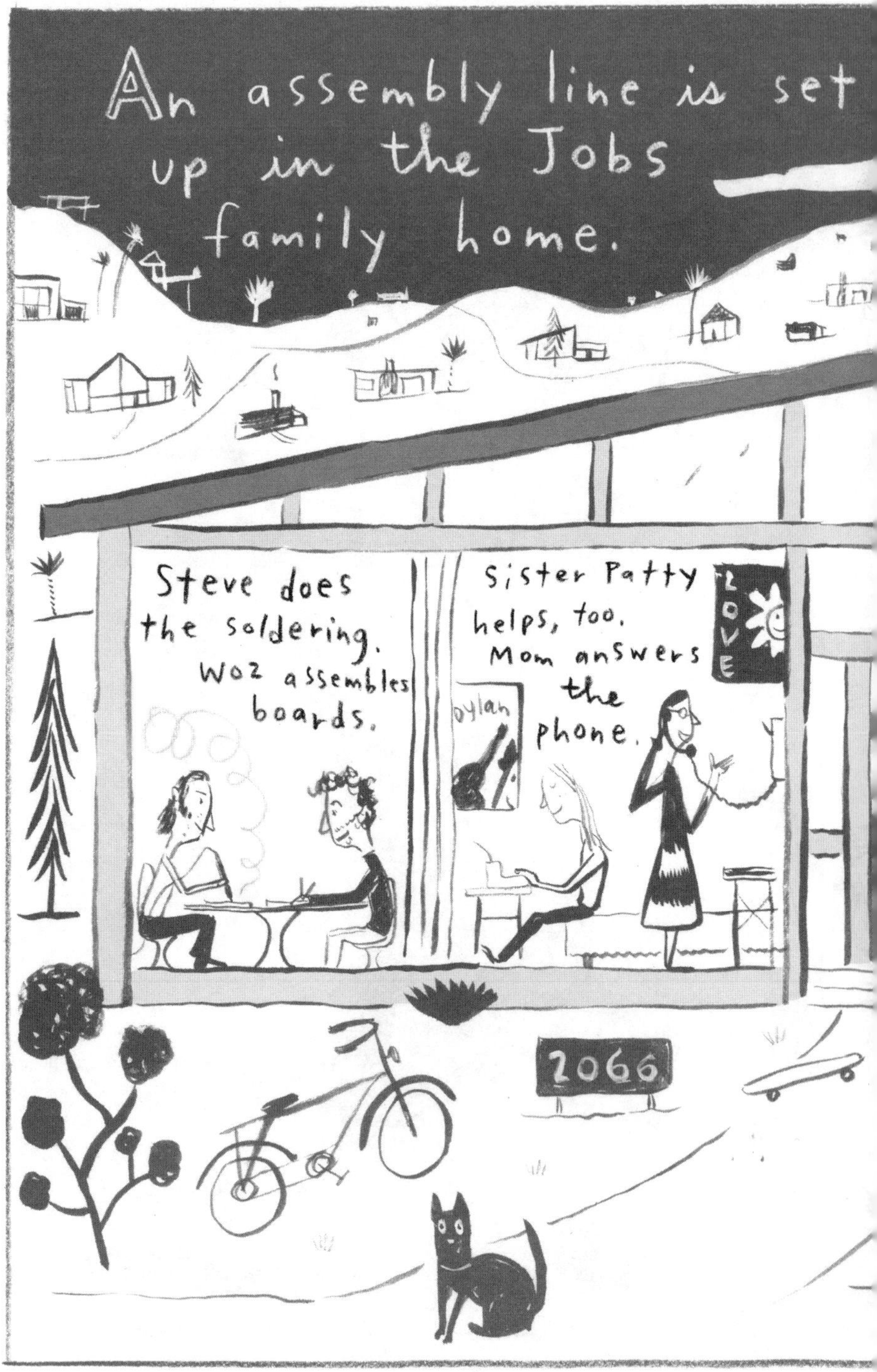
An assembly line is set up in the Jobs family home.
Steve does the soldering. Woz assembles boards.
Sister Patty helps, too. Mom answers the phone.
LOVE
Dylan
2066

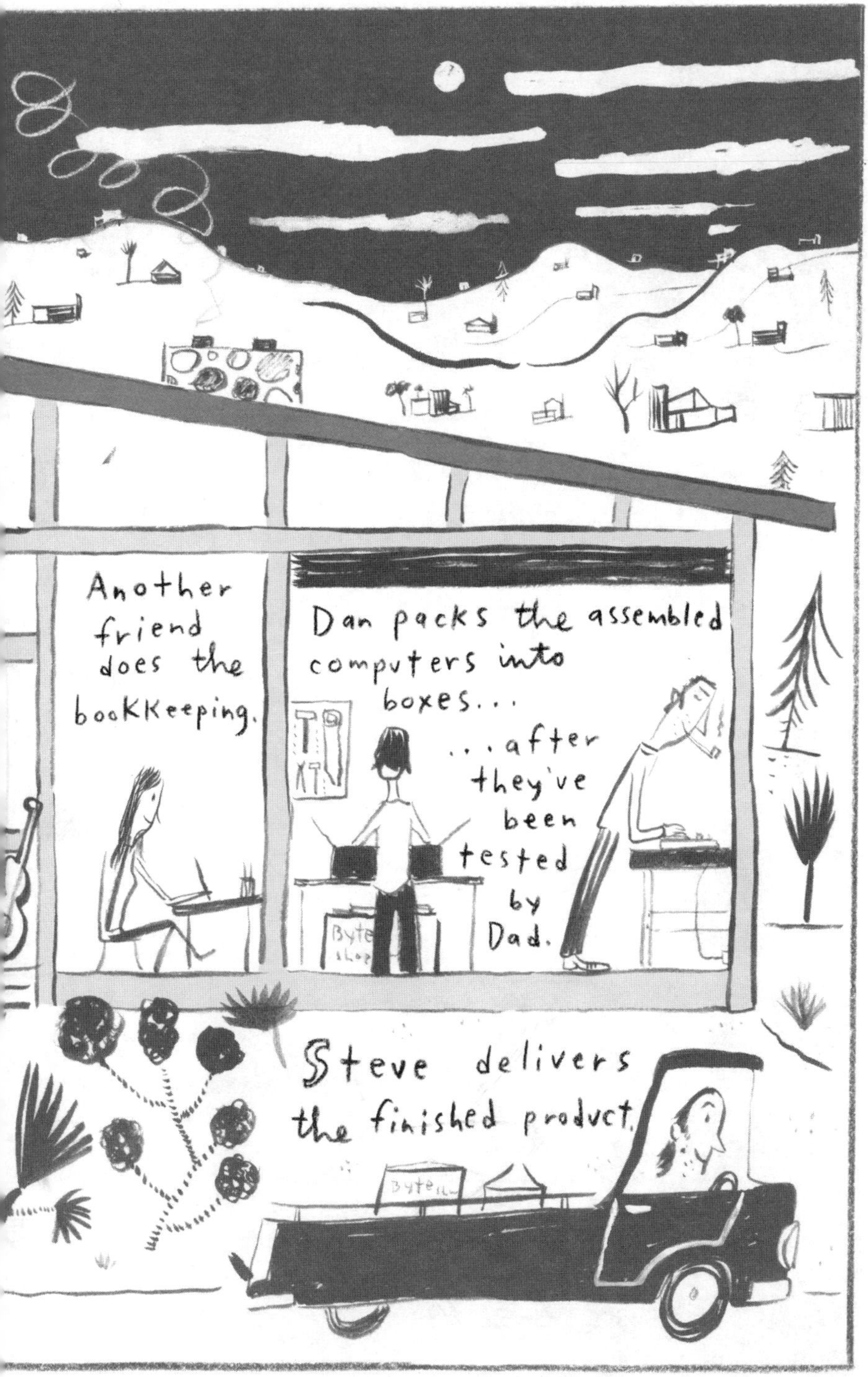
Another friend does the bookkeeping.
Dan packs the assembled computers into boxes...
...after they've been tested by Dad.
Byte Shop
Steve delivers the finished product.
Byte

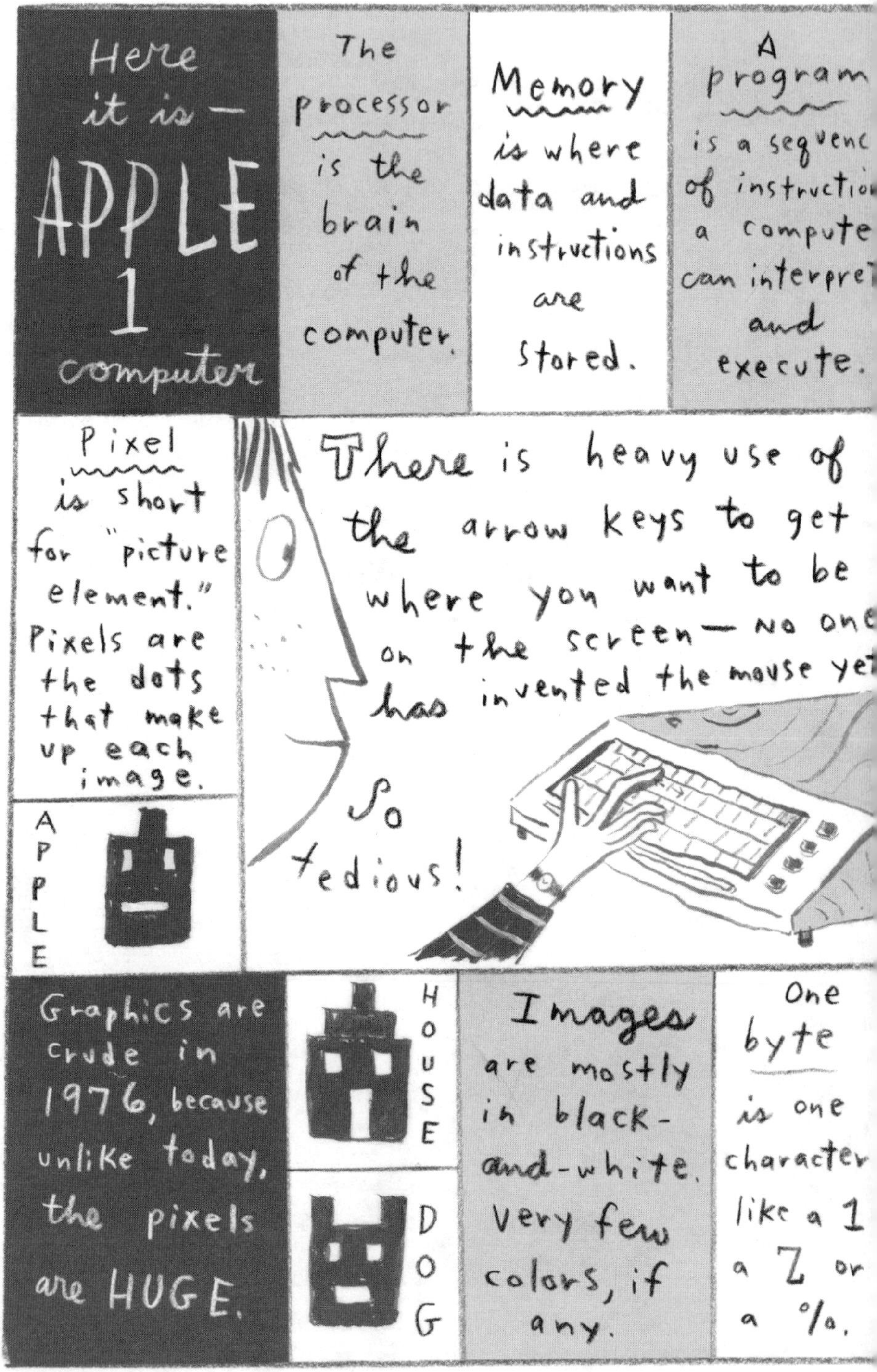
Here it is — APPLE 1 computer
The processor is the brain of the computer.
Memory is where data and instructions are stored.
A program is a sequenc of instructio a compute can interpre and execute.
Pixel is short for "picture element." Pixels are the dots that make up each image.
There is heavy use of the arrow keys to get where you want to be on the screen — no one has invented the mouse yet
So tedious!
APPLE
Graphics are crude in 1976, because unlike today, the pixels are HUGE.
HOUSE
DOG
Images are mostly in black-and-white. Very few colors, if any.
One byte is one character like a 1 a Z or a %.

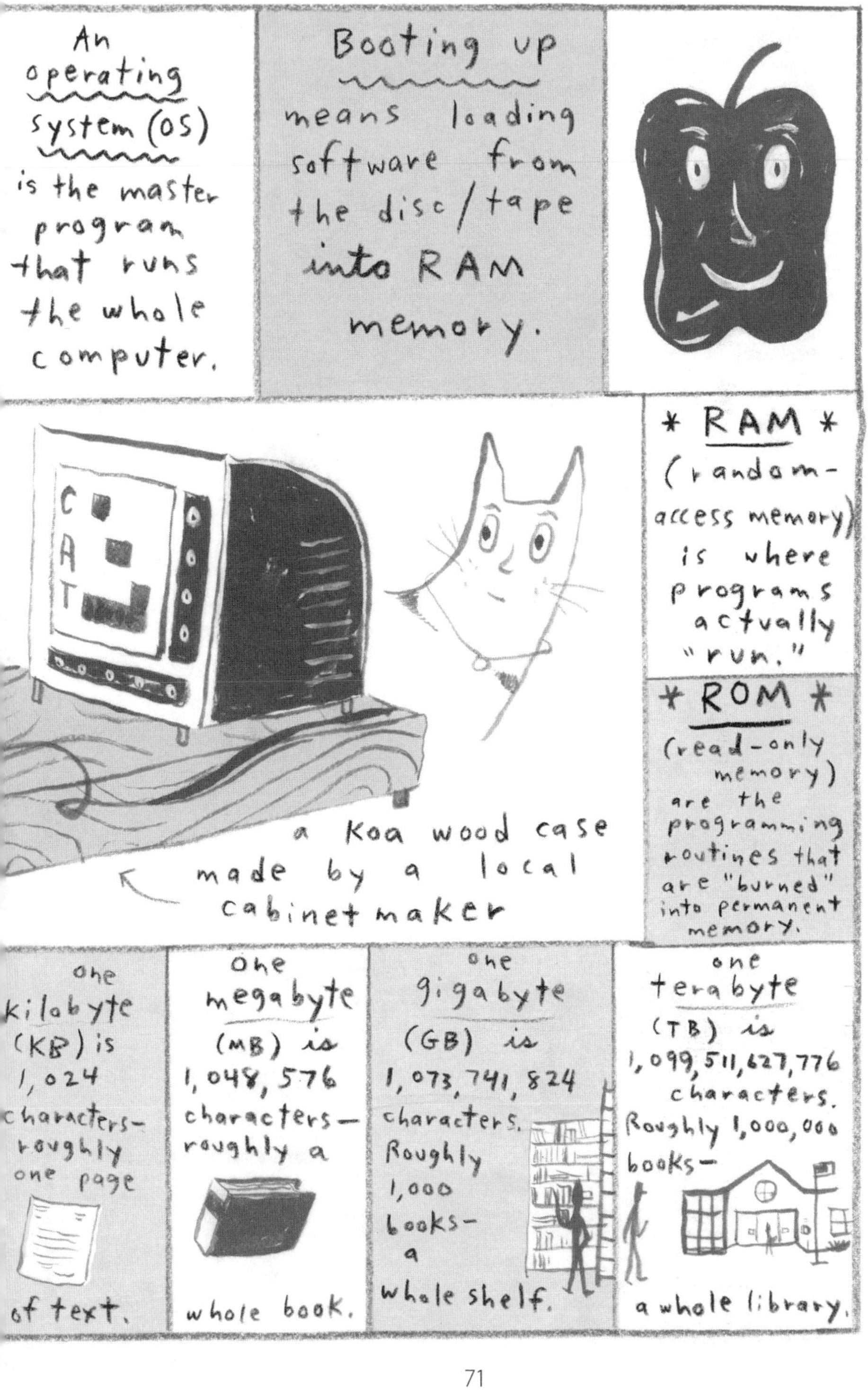
An operating system (OS) is the master program that runs the whole computer.
Booting up means loading software from the disc/tape into RAM memory.
C A T
a Koa wood case made by a local cabinetmaker
* RAM * (random-access memory) is where programs actually "run."
* ROM * (read-only memory) are the programming routines that are "burned" into permanent memory.
one kilabyte (KB) is 1,024 characters- roughly one page of text.
one megabyte (MB) is 1,048,576 characters- roughly a whole book.
one gigabyte (GB) is 1,073,741,824 characters. Roughly 1,000 books- a whole shelf.
one terabyte (TB) is 1,099,511,627,776 characters. Roughly 1,000,000 books- a whole library.

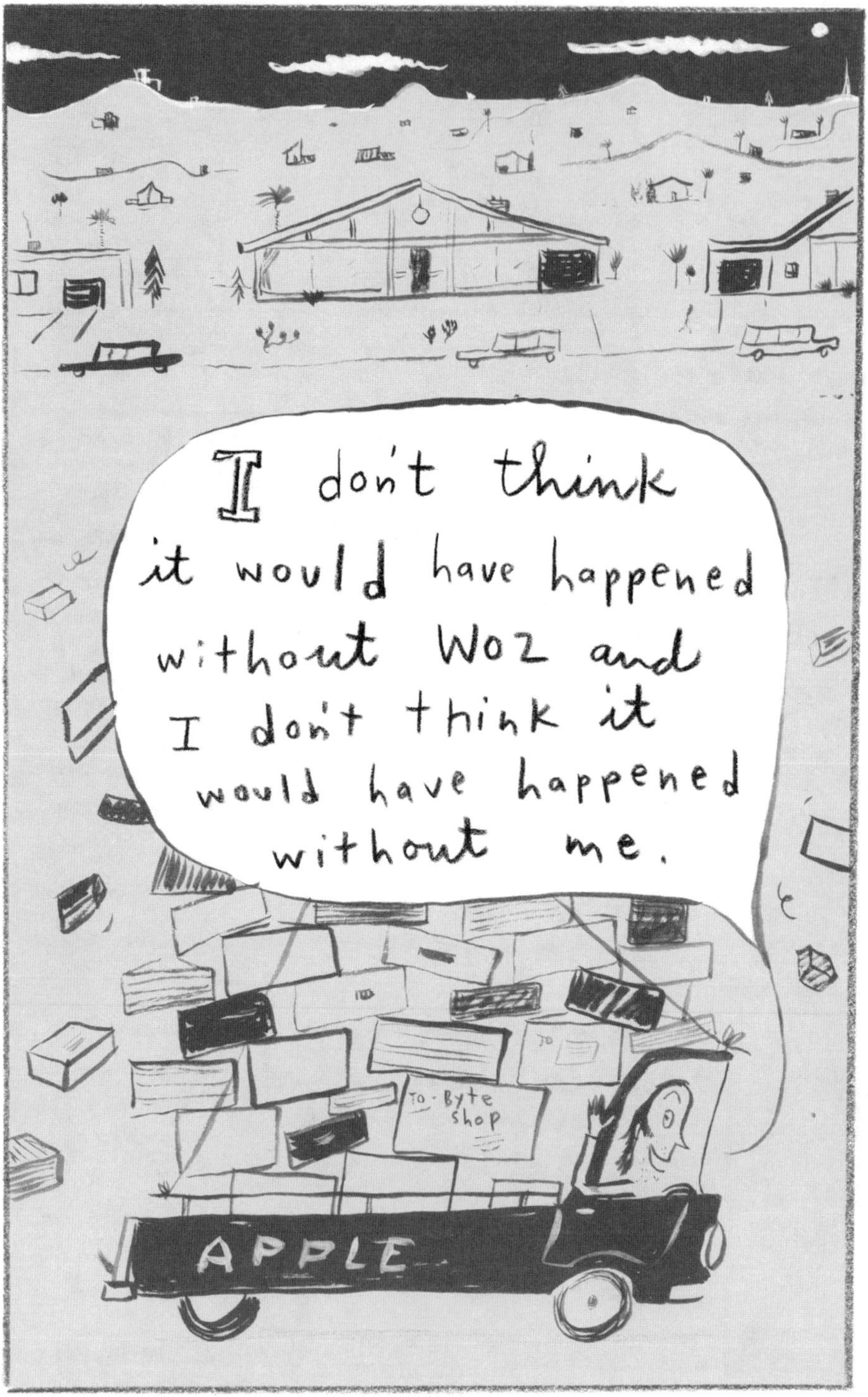
I don't think it would have happened without WOZ and I don't think it would have happened without me.
TO - Byte shop
APPLE

Chapter

6

Moving Up
(1977)

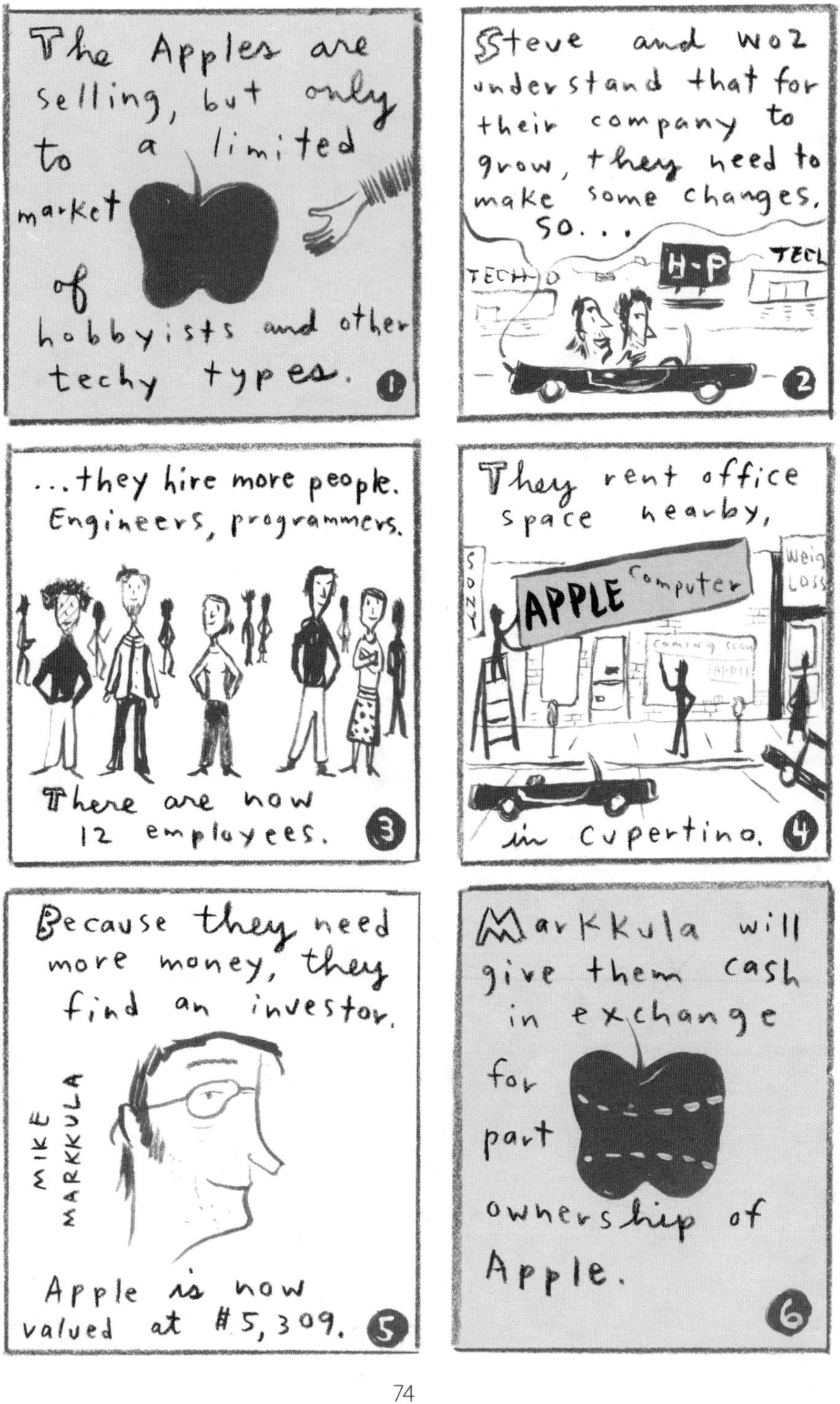
The Apples are selling, but only to a limited market of hobbyists and other techy types.
1
Steve and Woz understand that for their company to grow, they need to make some changes. So...
H-P
2
...they hire more people. Engineers, programmers.
There are now 12 employees.
3
They rent office space nearby,
SONY
APPLE Computer
in Cupertino.
4
Because they need more money, they find an investor.
MIKE MARKKULA
Apple is now valued at $5,309.
5
Markkula will give them cash in exchange for part ownership of Apple.
6

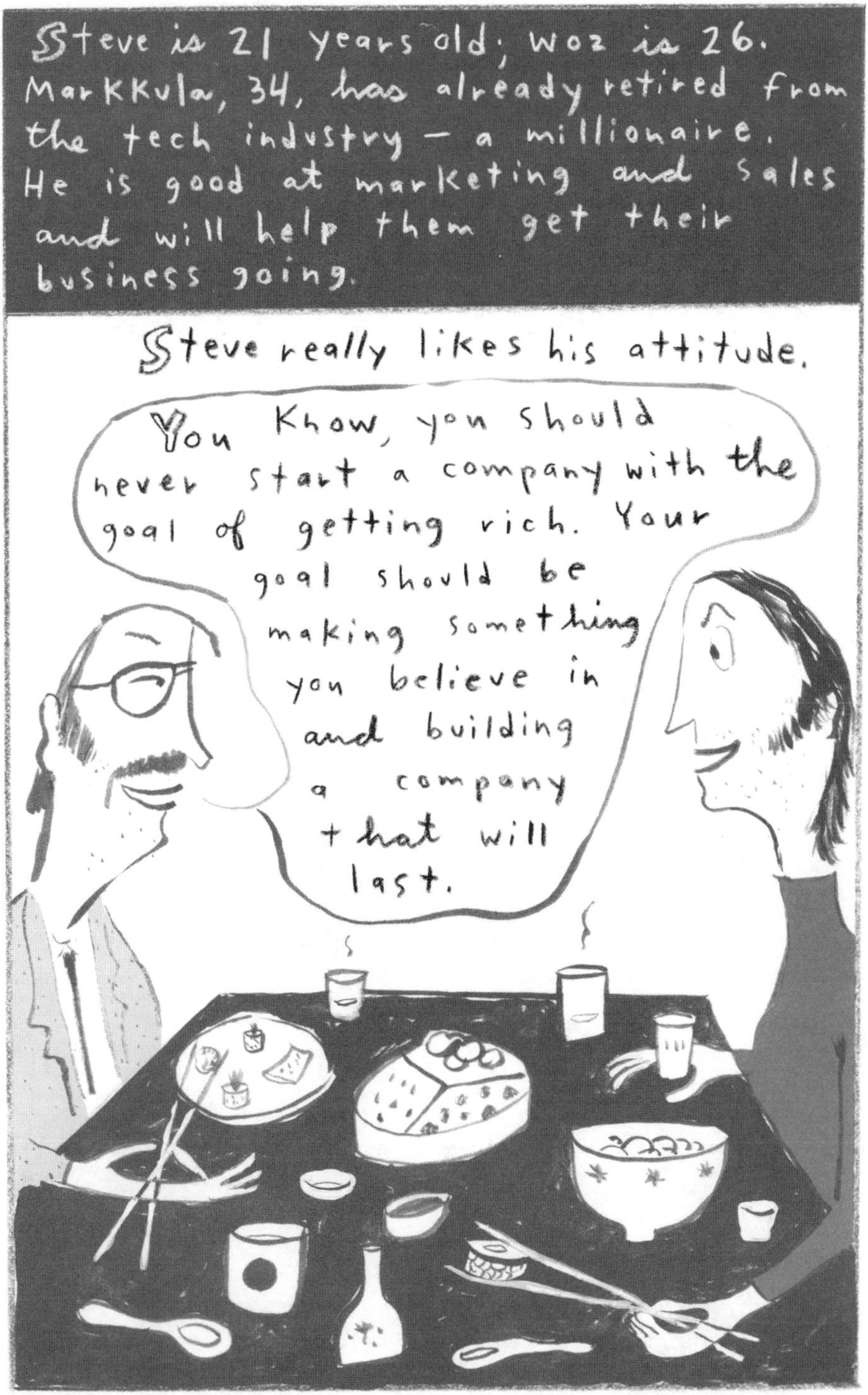
Steve is 21 years old; Woz is 26. MarKKula, 34, has already retired from the tech industry — a millionaire. He is good at marketing and sales and will help them get their business going.
Steve really likes his attitude.
You Know, you should never start a company with the goal of getting rich. Your goal should be making something you believe in and building a company that will last.

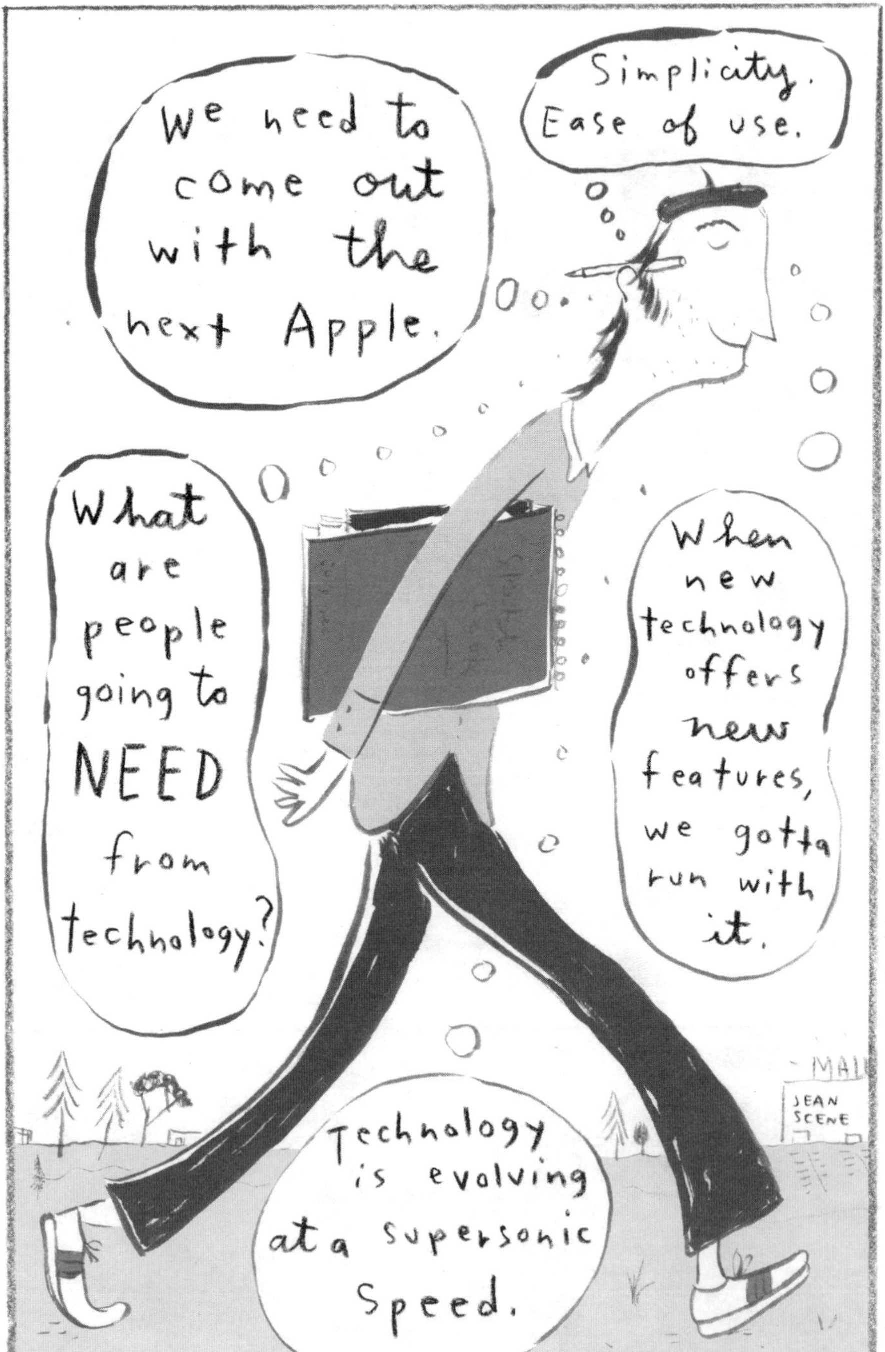
We need to come out with the next Apple.
Simplicity. Ease of use.
What are people going to NEED from technology?
When new technology offers new features, we gotta run with it.
Technology is evolving at a supersonic speed.
MALL
JEAN SCENE

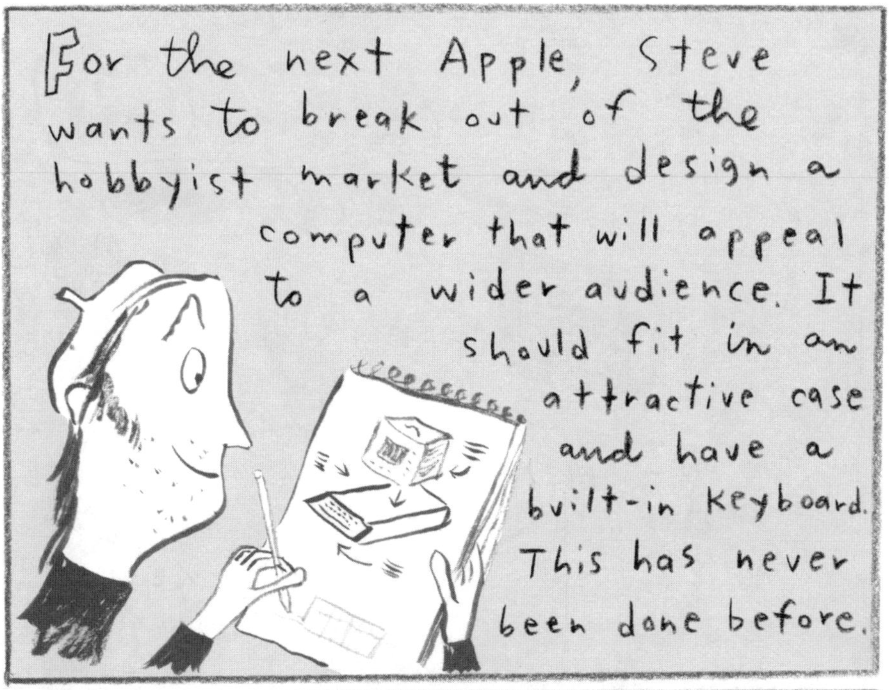
For the next Apple, Steve wants to break out of the hobbyist market and design a computer that will appeal to a wider audience. It should fit in an attractive case and have a built-in keyboard. This has never been done before.

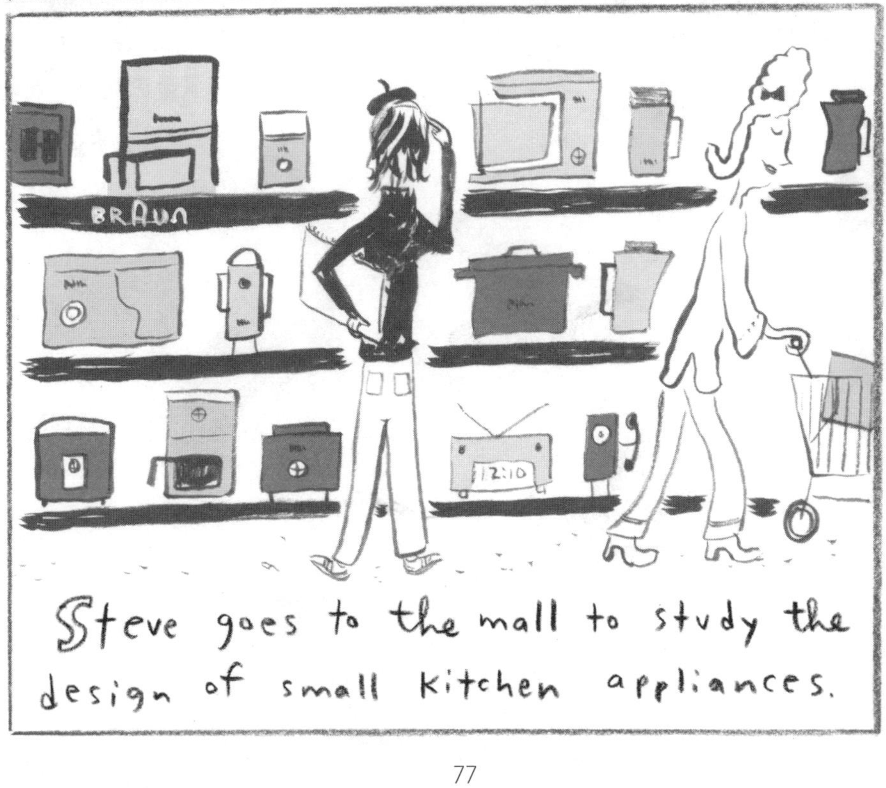
BRAUN
12:10
Steve goes to the mall to study the design of small kitchen appliances.

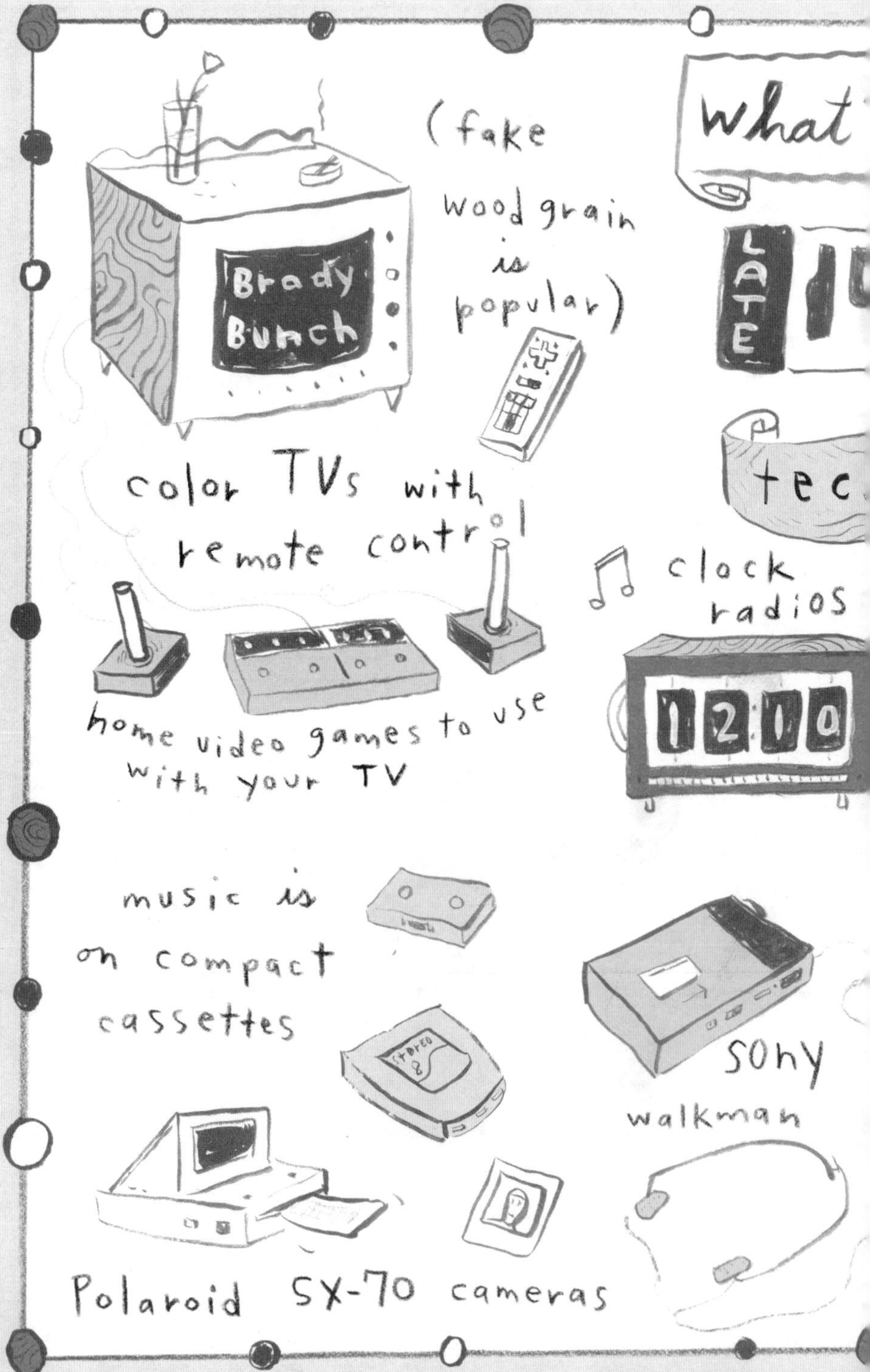
What
LATE
(fake
wood grain
is
popular)
Brady
Bunch
color TVs with
remote control
clock
radios
1210
home video games to use
with your TV
music is
on compact
cassettes
STEREO
8
SONY
walkman
Polaroid SX-70 cameras

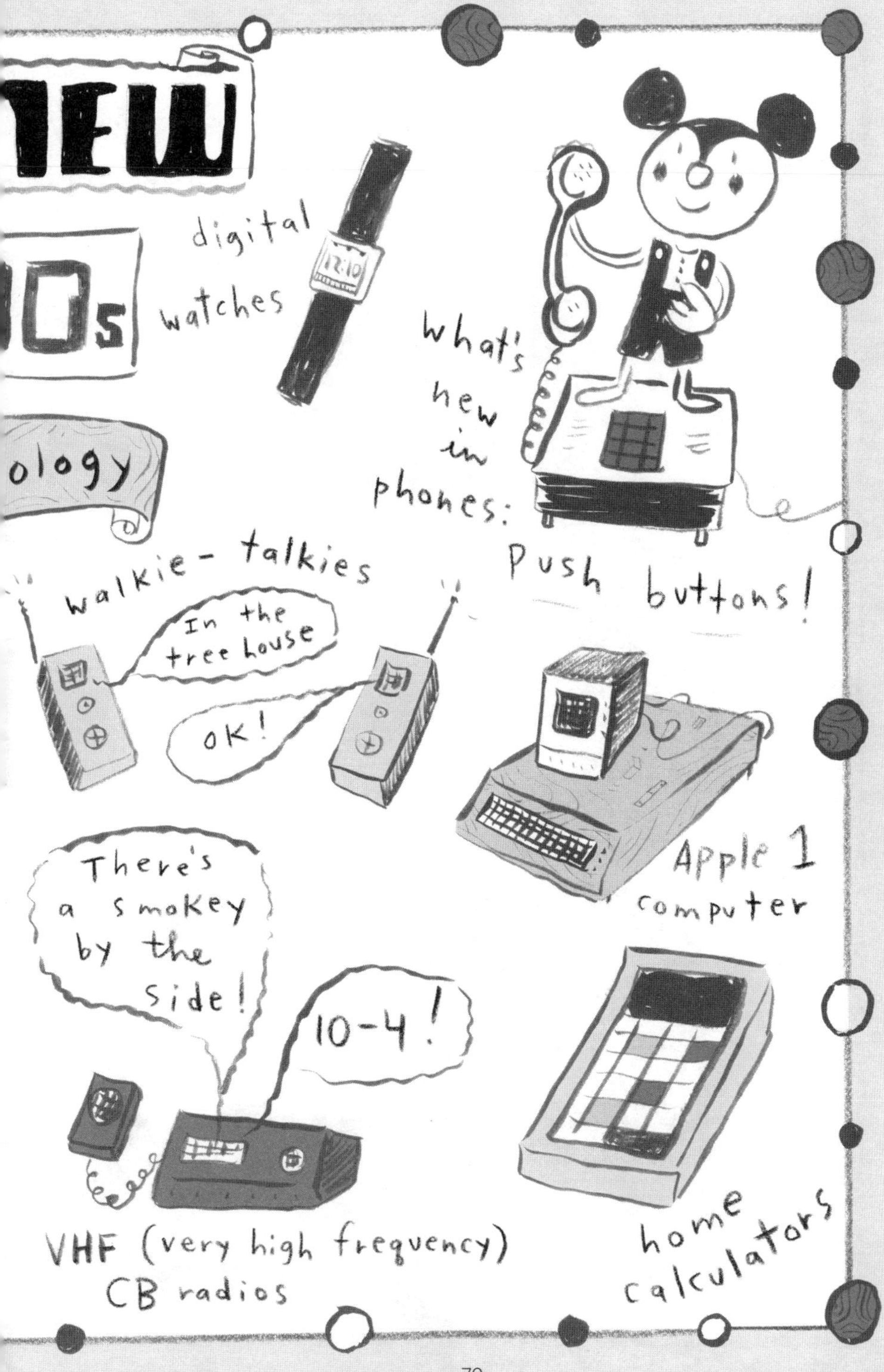
digital watches
what's new in phones: push buttons!
walkie-talkies
In the tree house
OK!
Apple 1 computer
There's a smokey by the side!
10-4!
VHF (very high frequency) CB radios
home calculators

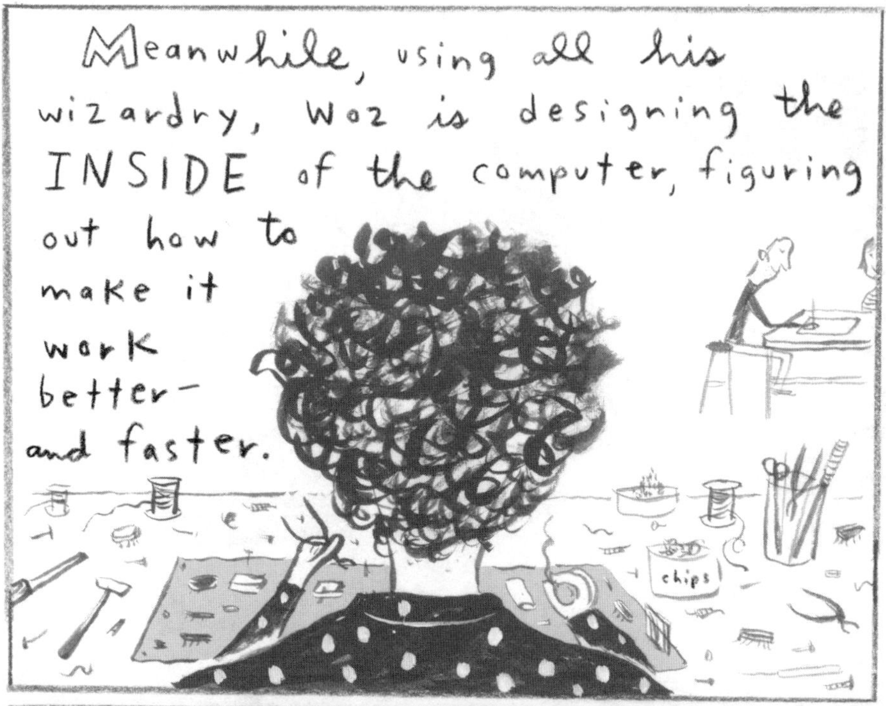
Meanwhile, using all his wizardry, Woz is designing the INSIDE of the computer, figuring out how to make it work better- and faster.
chips

He has finally quit his job at Hewlett-Packard.

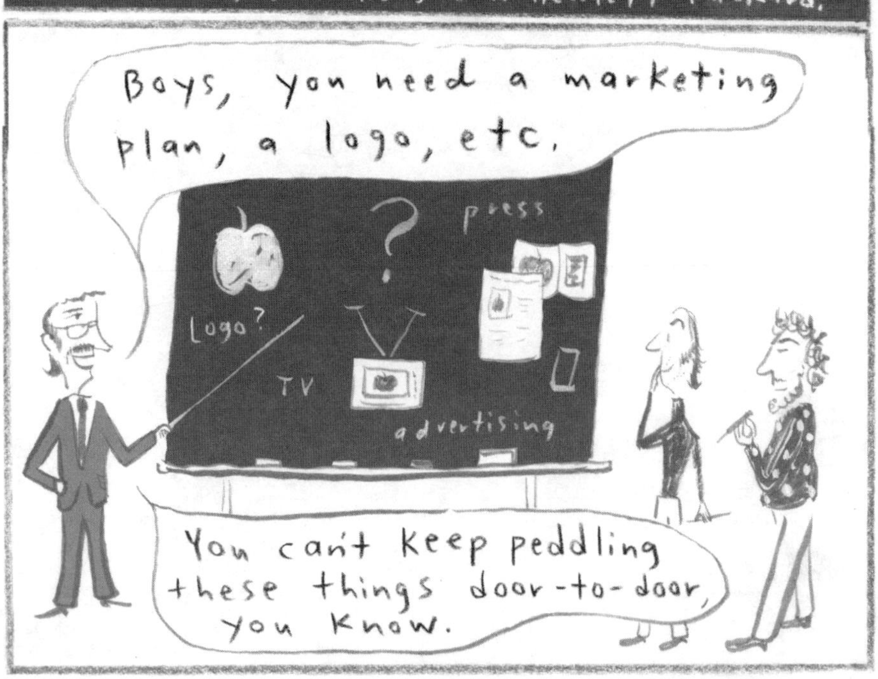
Boys, you need a marketing plan, a logo, etc.
press
Logo?
TV
advertising
You can't keep peddling these things door-to-door, you know.

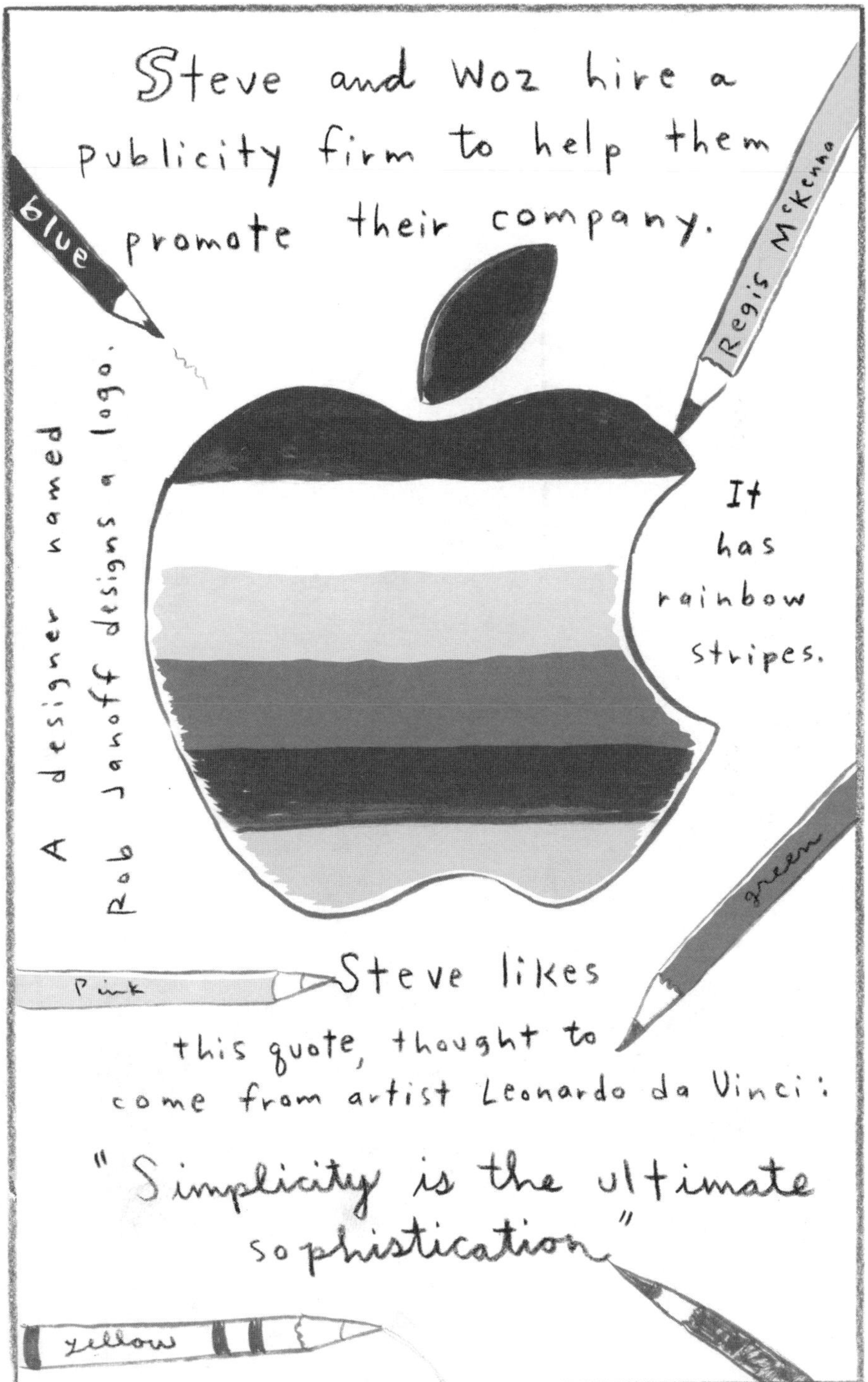
Steve and Woz hire a publicity firm to help them promote their company.
blue
Regis McKenna
A designer named Rob Janoff designs a logo.
It has rainbow stripes.
Pink
green
Steve likes this quote, thought to come from artist Leonardo da Vinci:
"Simplicity is the ultimate sophistication."
yellow

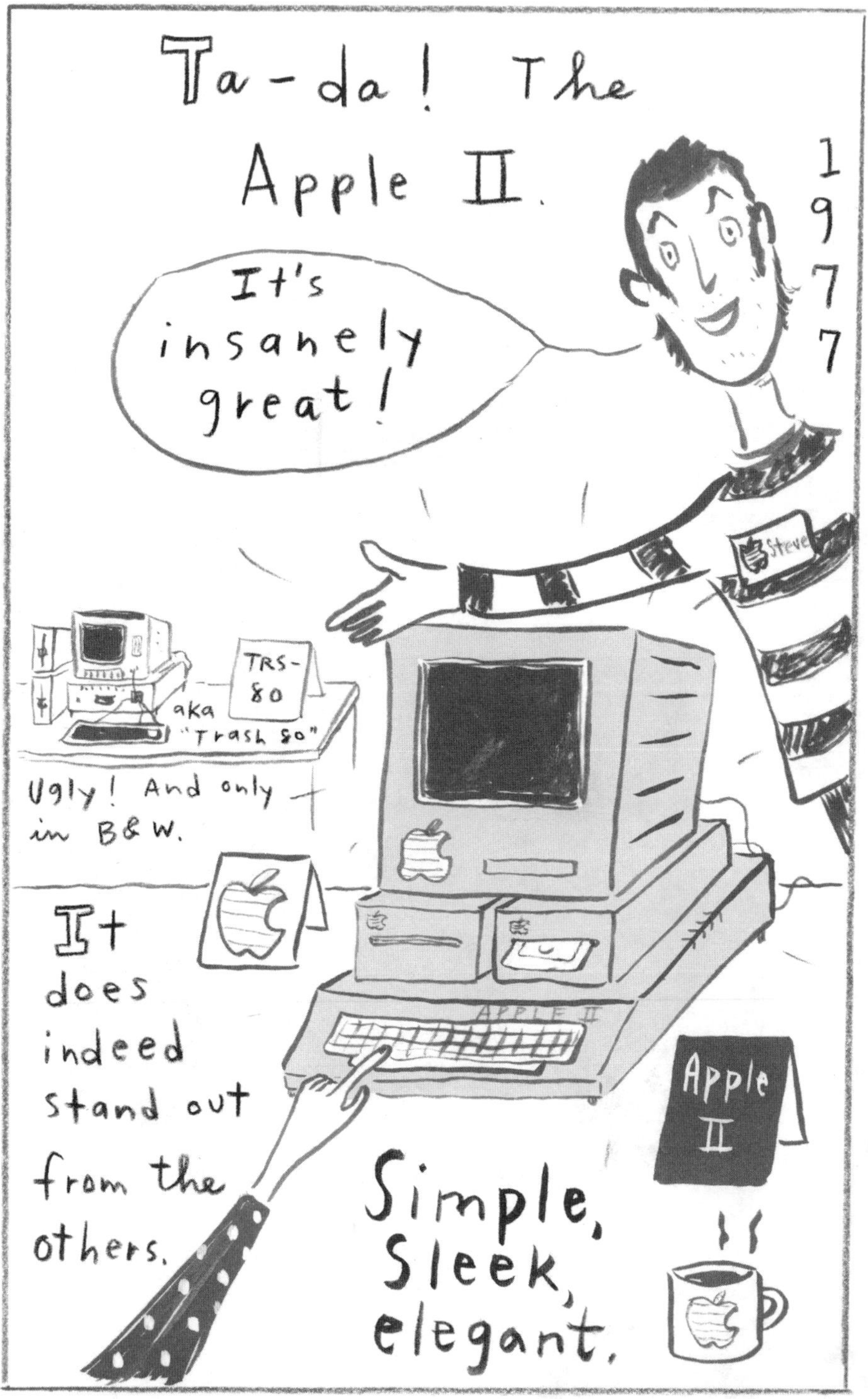
Ta-da! The Apple II.
1977
It's insanely great!
Steve
TRS-80
aka "Trash 80"
Ugly! And only in B&W.
APPLE II
Apple II
It does indeed stand out from the others.
Simple, sleek, elegant.

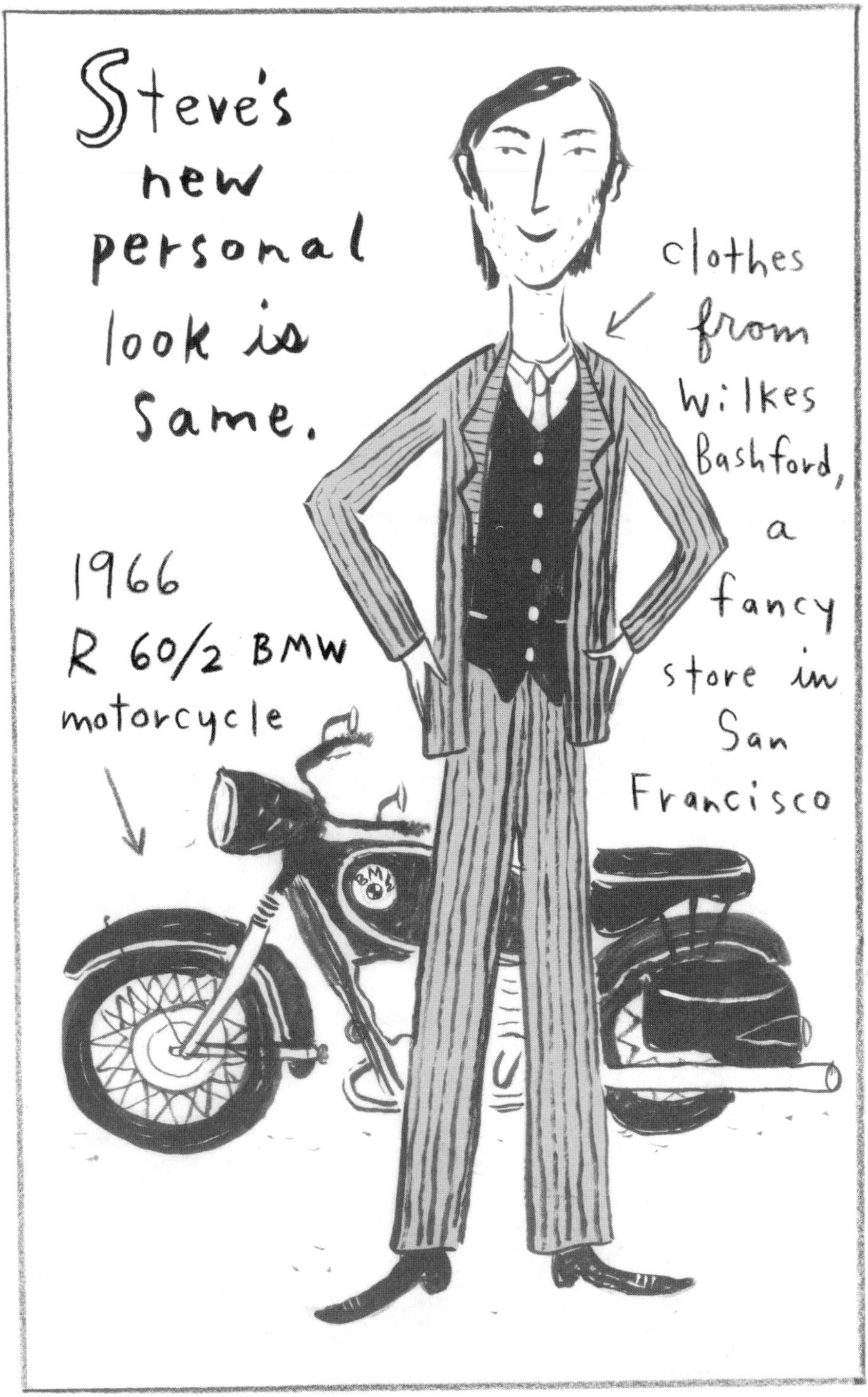
Steve's new personal look is same.
clothes from Wilkes Bashford, a fancy store in San Francisco
1966 R 60/2 BMW motorcycle
BMW

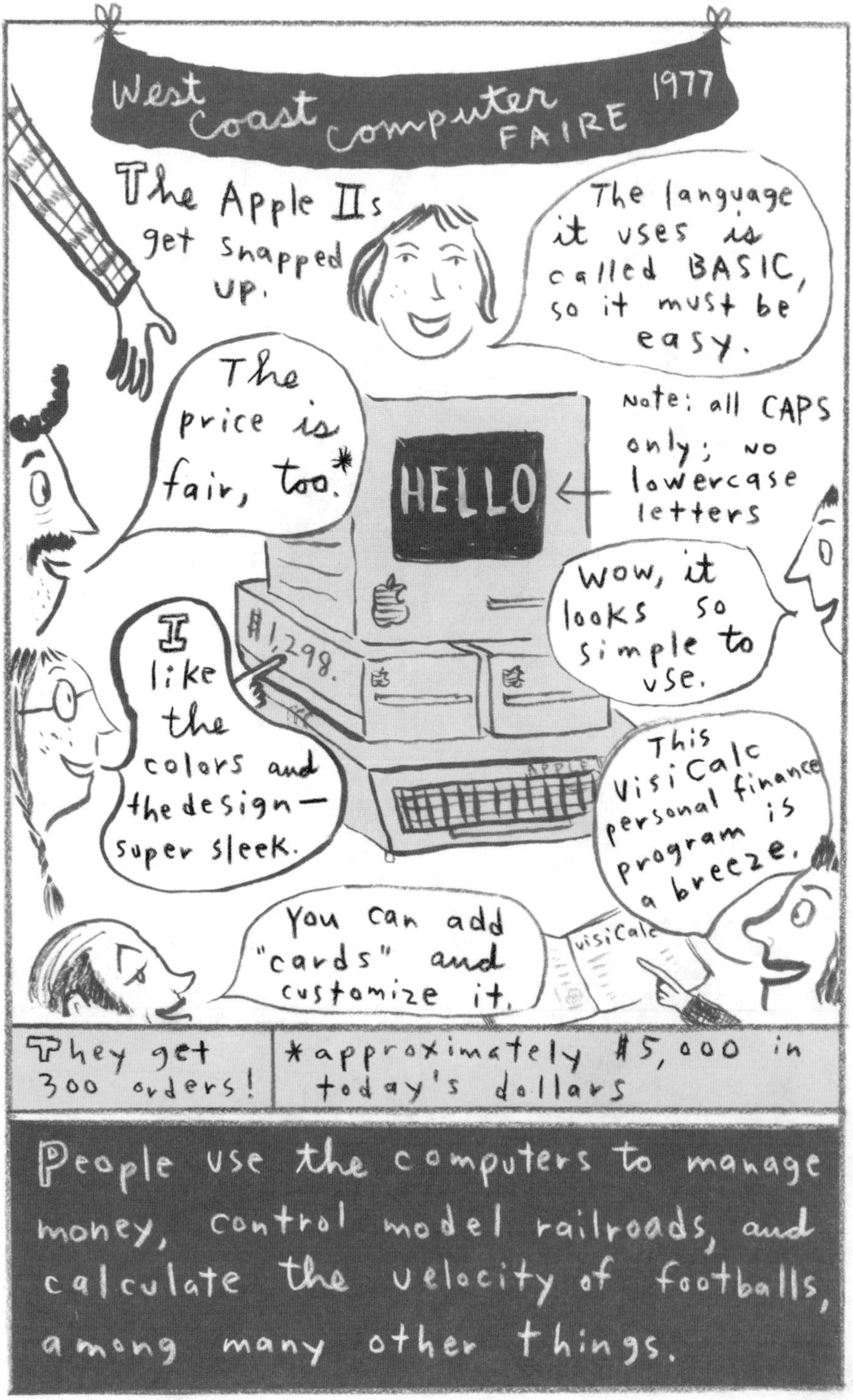
West Coast Computer FAIRE 1977
The Apple IIs get snapped up.
The language it uses is called BASIC, so it must be easy.
The price is fair, too.*
HELLO
Note: all CAPS only; no lowercase letters
Wow, it looks so simple to use.
$1,298.
I like the colors and the design—super sleek.
This VisiCalc personal finance program is a breeze.
You can add "cards" and customize it.
VisiCalc
They get 300 orders!
*approximately $5,000 in today's dollars
People use the computers to manage money, control model railroads, and calculate the velocity of footballs, among many other things.

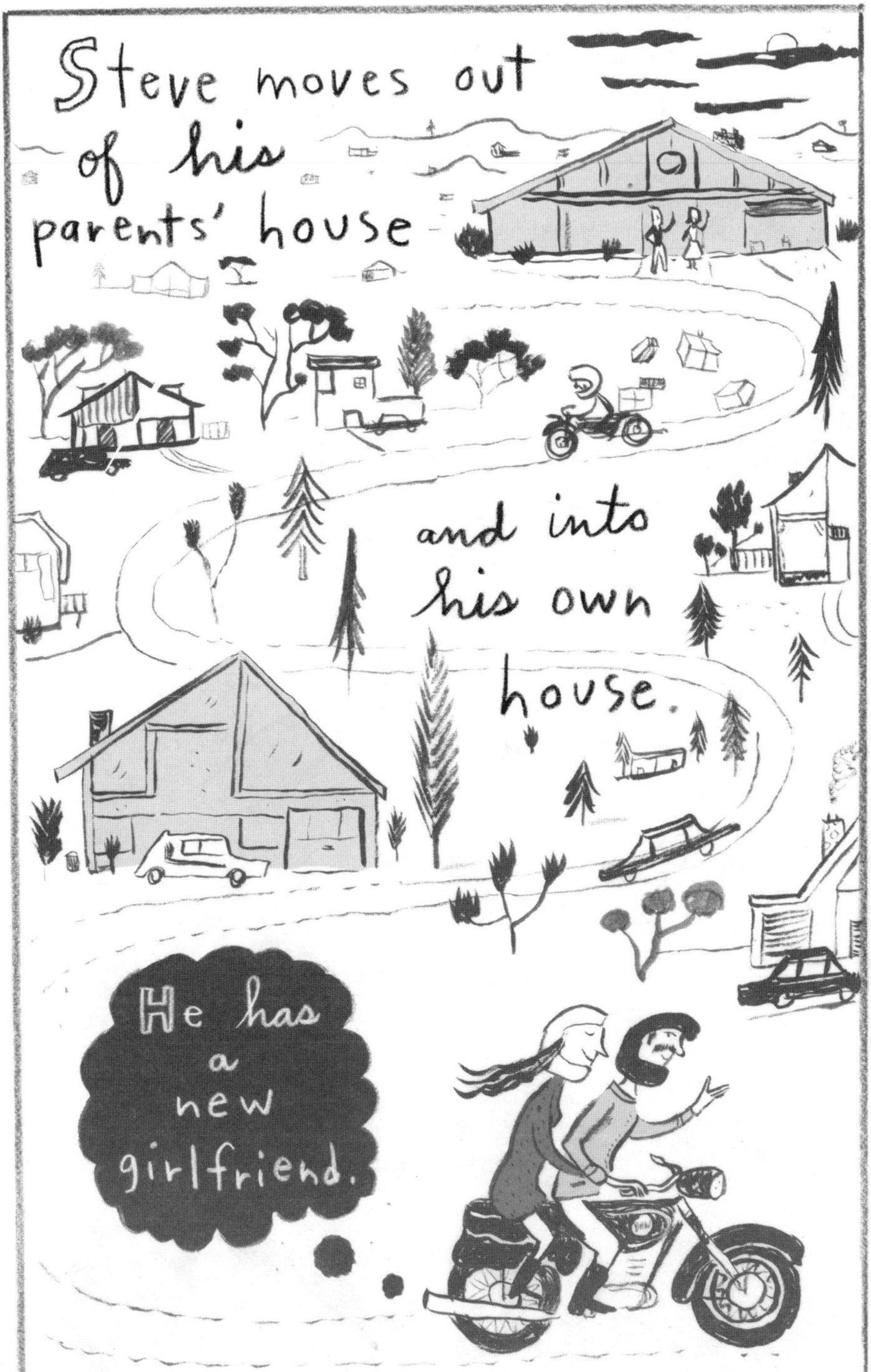
Steve moves out of his parents' house
and into his own house.
He has a new girlfriend.

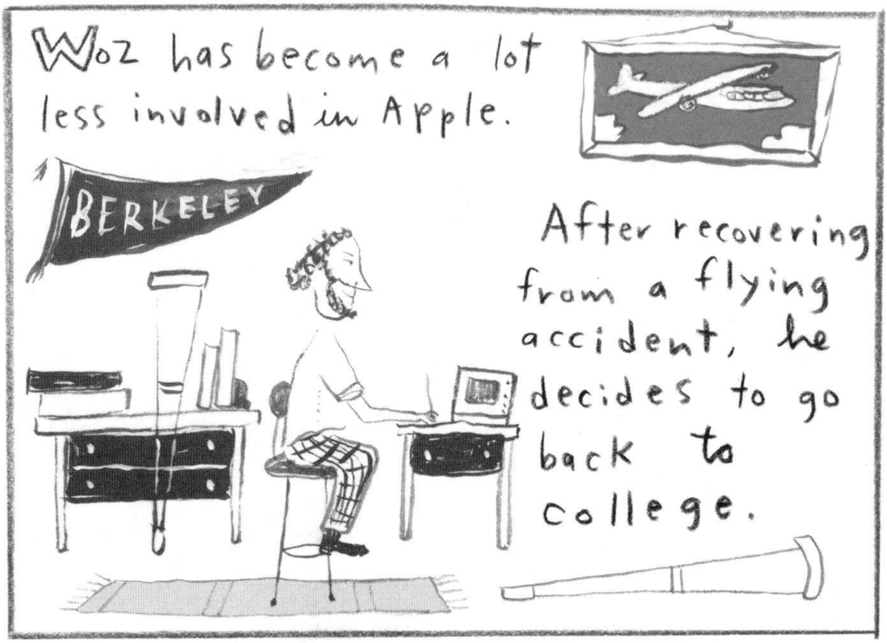
Woz has become a lot less involved in Apple.
BERKELEY
After recovering from a flying accident, he decides to go back to college.

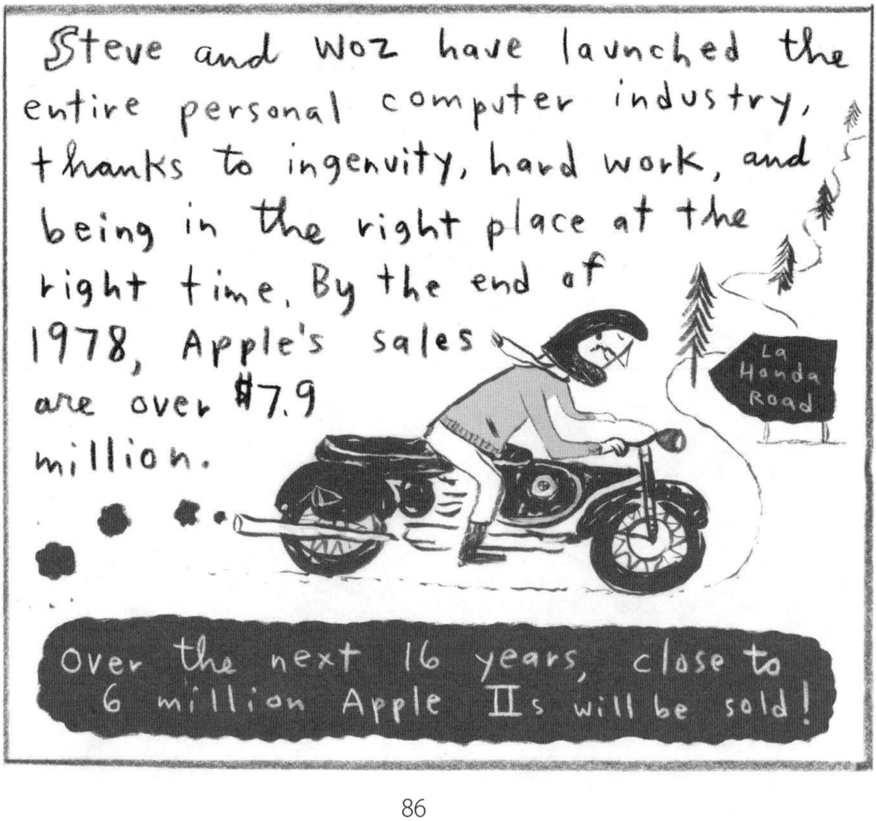
Steve and Woz have launched the entire personal computer industry, thanks to ingenuity, hard work, and being in the right place at the right time. By the end of 1978, Apple's sales are over $7.9 million.
La Honda Road
Over the next 16 years, close to 6 million Apple IIs will be sold!

Chapter 7

Moving On
(1978 – 1981)

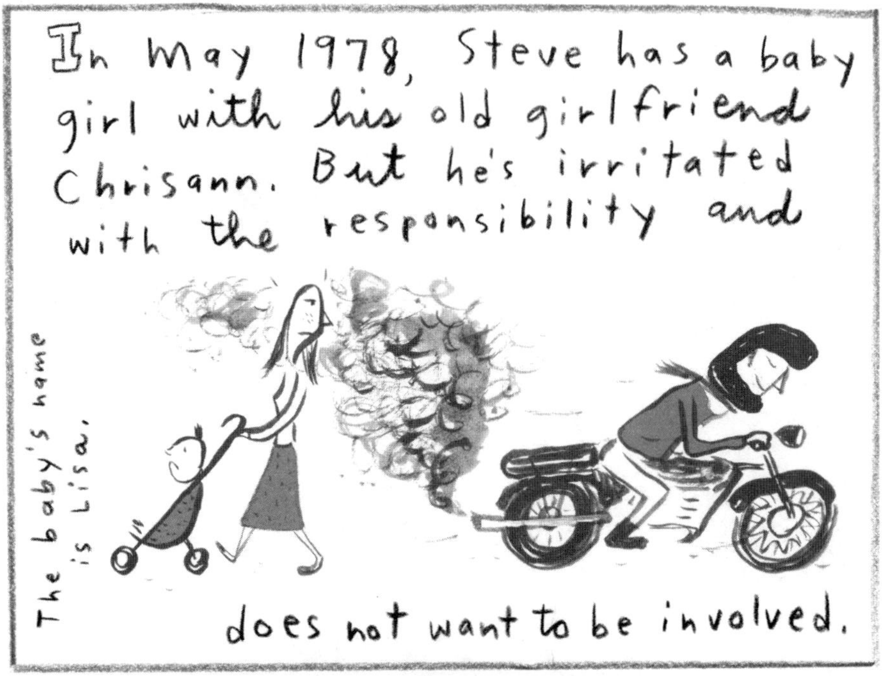
In May 1978, Steve has a baby girl with his old girlfriend Chrisann. But he's irritated with the responsibility and
The baby's name is Lisa.
does not want to be involved.

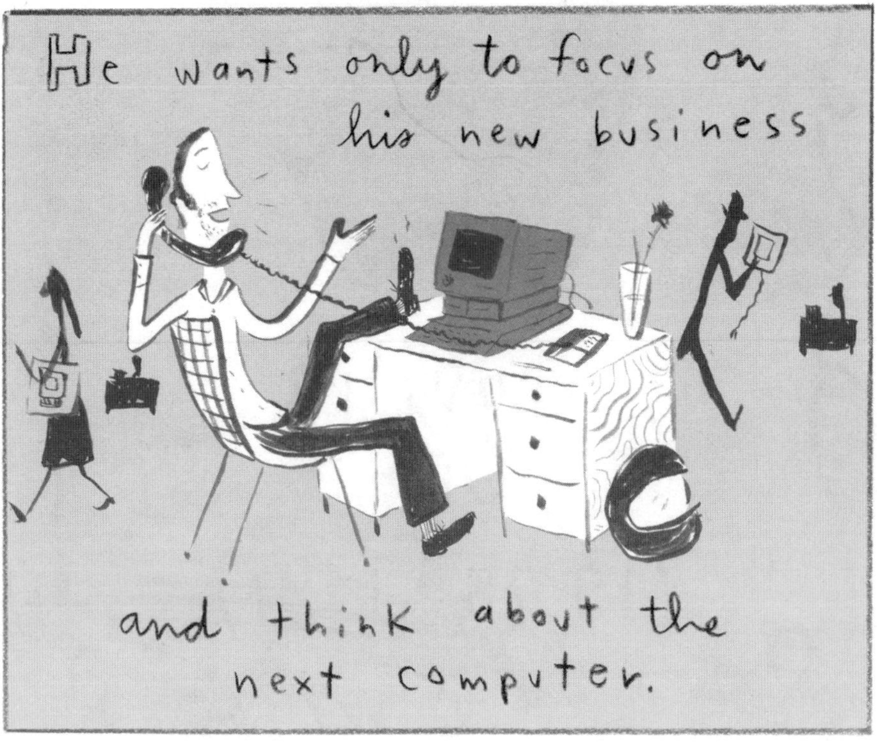
He wants only to focus on his new business
and think about the next computer.

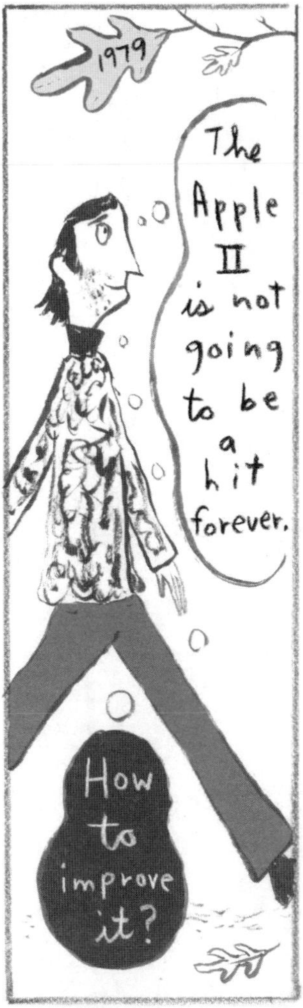
1979
The Apple II is not going to be a hit forever.
How to improve it?

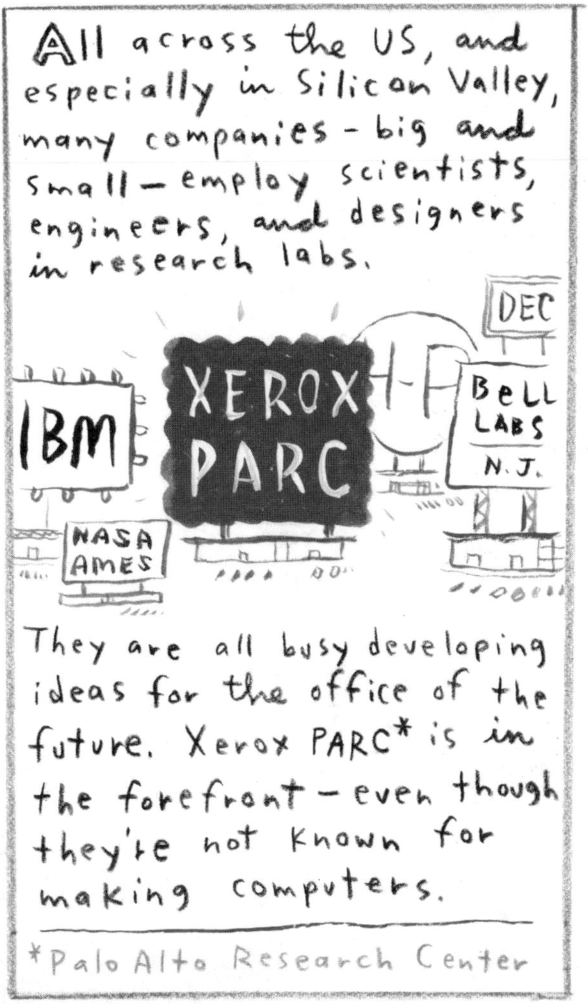
All across the US, and especially in Silicon Valley, many companies - big and small - employ scientists, engineers, and designers in research labs.
DEC
IBM
XEROX PARC
H-P
BeLL LABS N.J.
NASA AMES
They are all busy developing ideas for the office of the future. Xerox PARC* is in the forefront - even though they're not known for making computers.
*Palo Alto Research Center

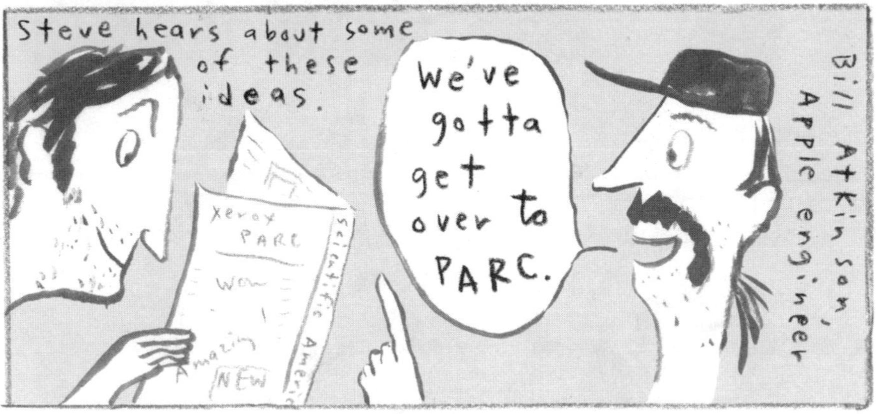
Steve hears about some of these ideas.
Xerox PARC
Wow
Amazing
NEW
Scientific Americ
We've gotta get over to PARC.
Bill Atkinson, Apple engineer

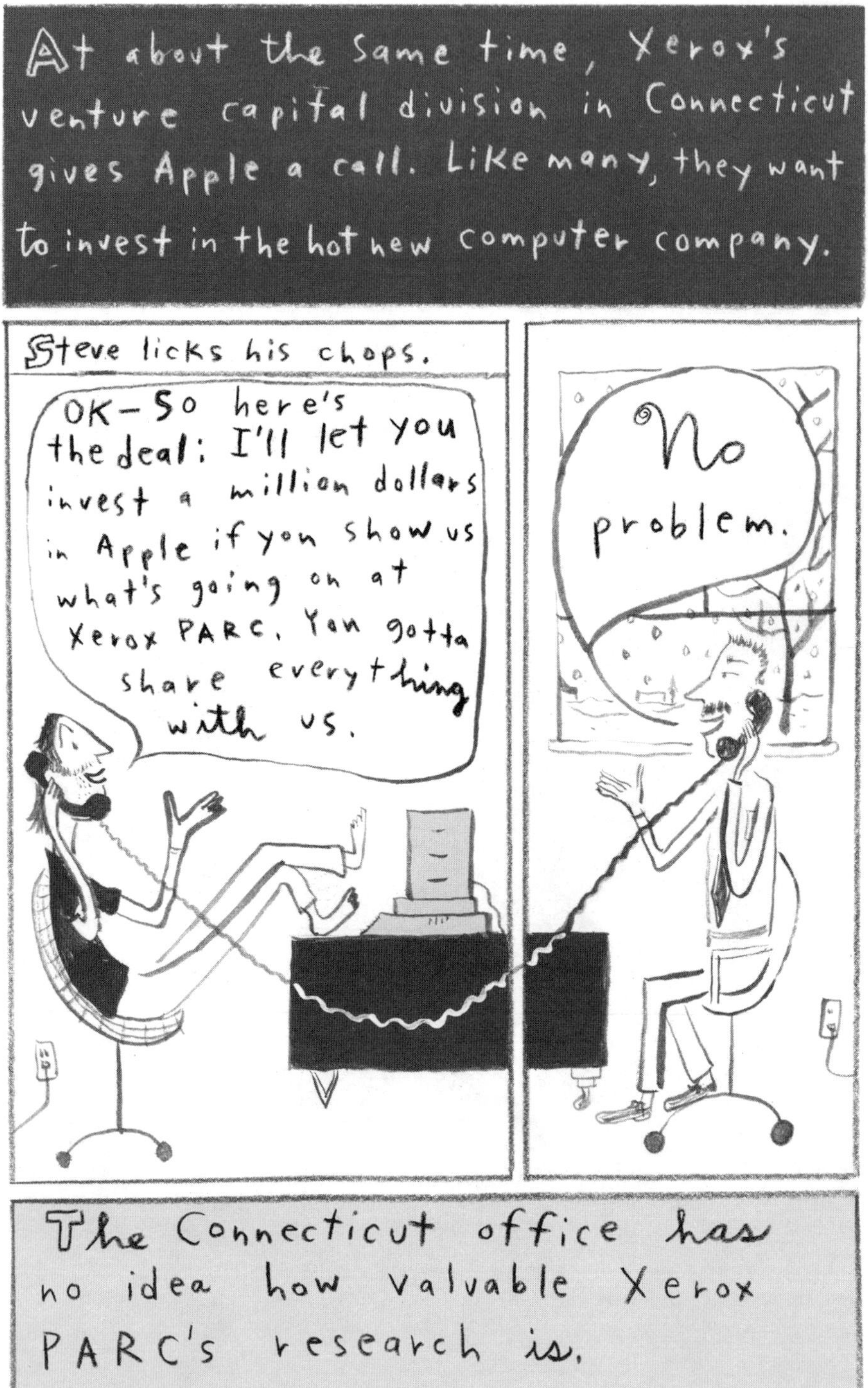
At about the same time, Xerox's venture capital division in Connecticut gives Apple a call. Like many, they want to invest in the hot new computer company.
Steve licks his chops.
OK—So here's the deal: I'll let you invest a million dollars in Apple if you show us what's going on at Xerox PARC. You gotta share everything with us.
No problem.
The Connecticut office has no idea how valuable Xerox PARC's research is.

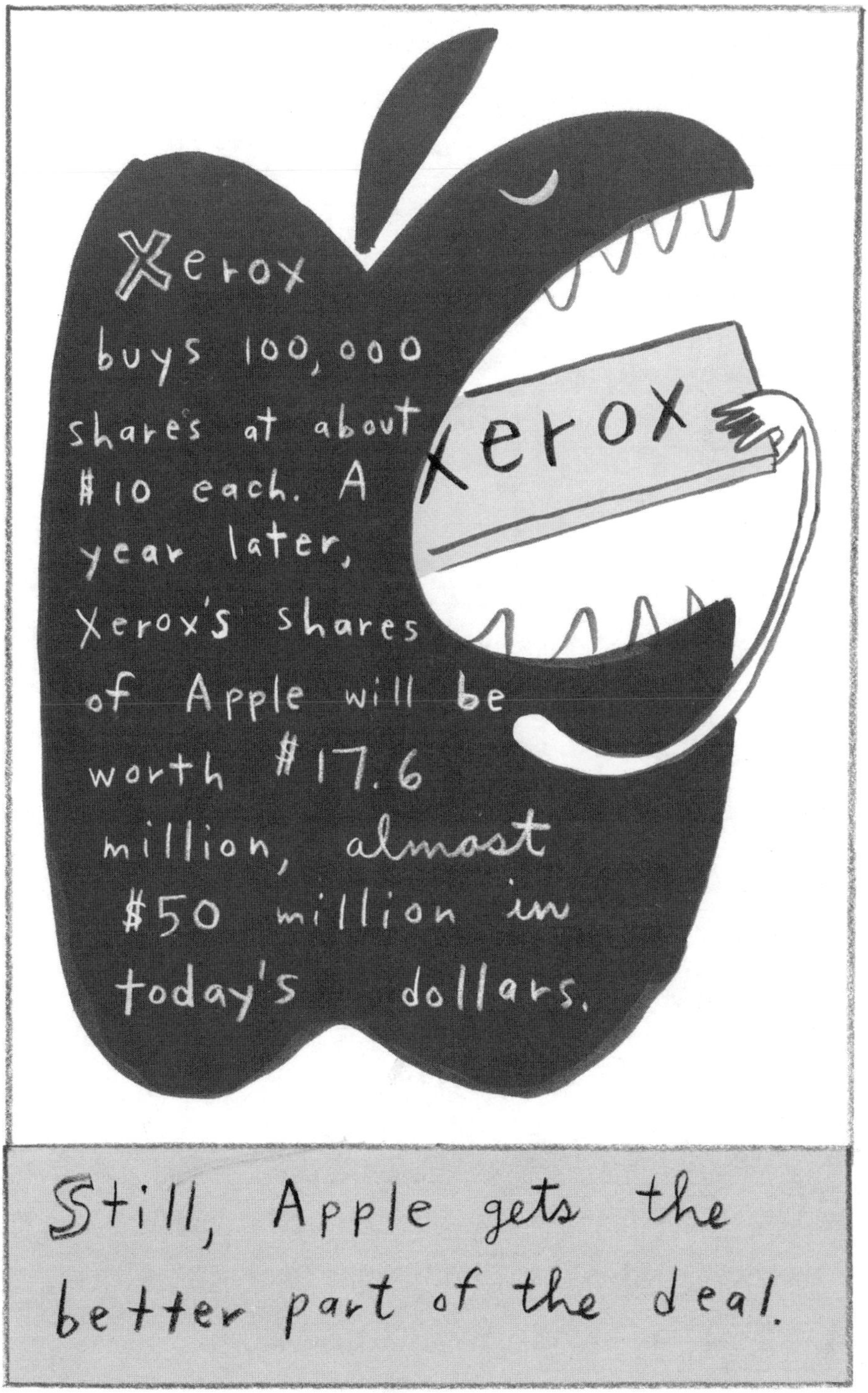
Xerox buys 100,000 shares at about $10 each. A year later, Xerox's shares of Apple will be worth $17.6 million, almost $50 million in today's dollars.
Xerox
Still, Apple gets the better part of the deal.

Steve and his crew drive 15 minutes north from Cupertino to Palo Alto.

xerox PARC

PALO Alto

We call it GUI. Say "gooey."

Advances in Computin

graphical
user
interface

networking

object-
oriented
programming

Lunch
Sandwiches
Soup
Salad

desserts
cake
pie
pudding
ice
cream

inn
pas
sala
Fis

pizz
stew
bouillab

drop-
dow
menu

As promised, the scientists show him what they've been working on.

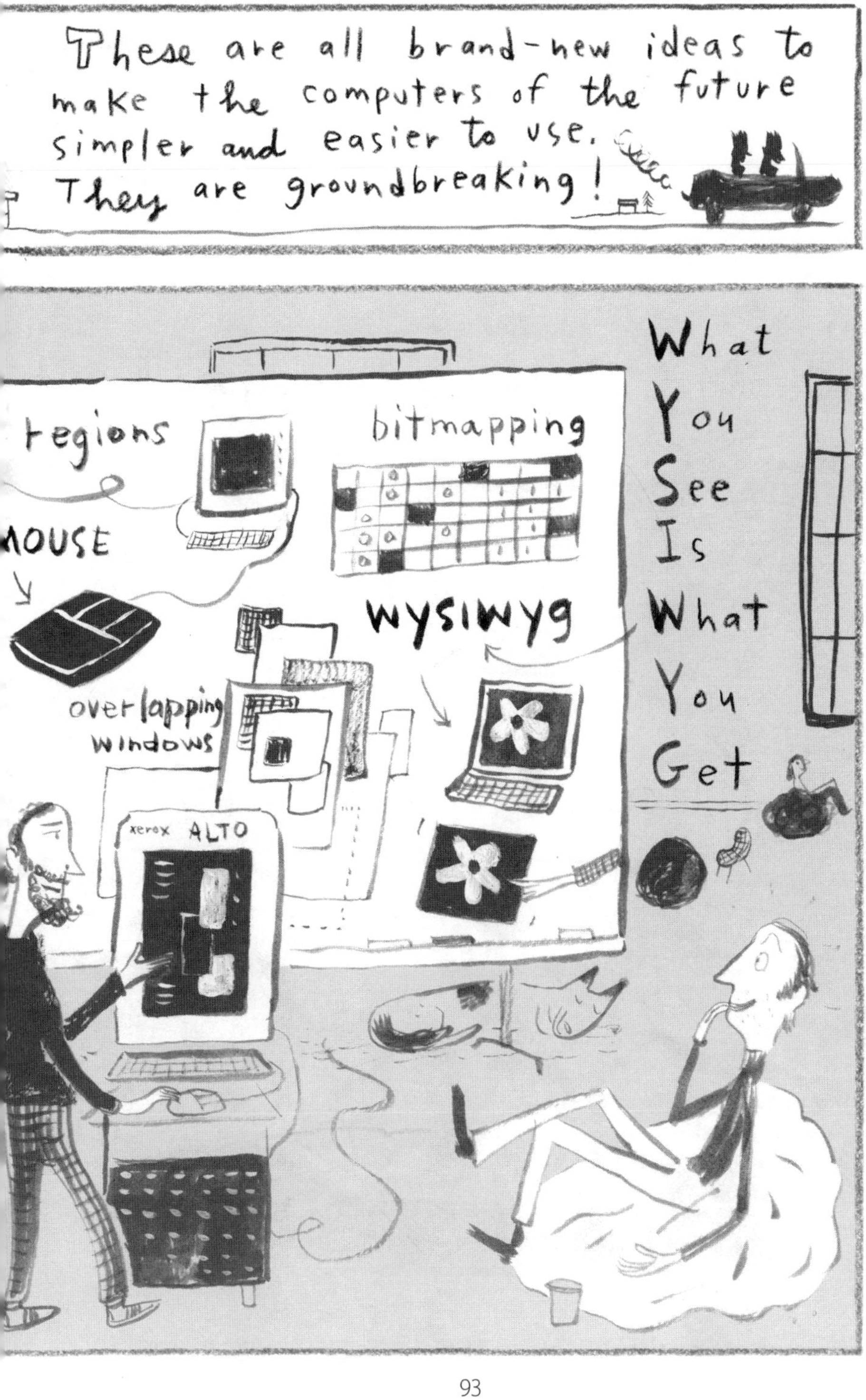
These are all brand-new ideas to make the computers of the future simpler and easier to use.
They are groundbreaking!
regions
bitmapping
MOUSE
wysiwyg
What You See Is What You Get
overlapping windows
xerox ALTO

TECH-O
LOCKHEED MISSILE
SEE'S CANDIES
It's mind-blowing!
It's APOCALYPTIC!!
Glass Slipper INN
HOT TUBS
This is the future of computing.
Insanely great!
Wagon Wheel
POLICE
101

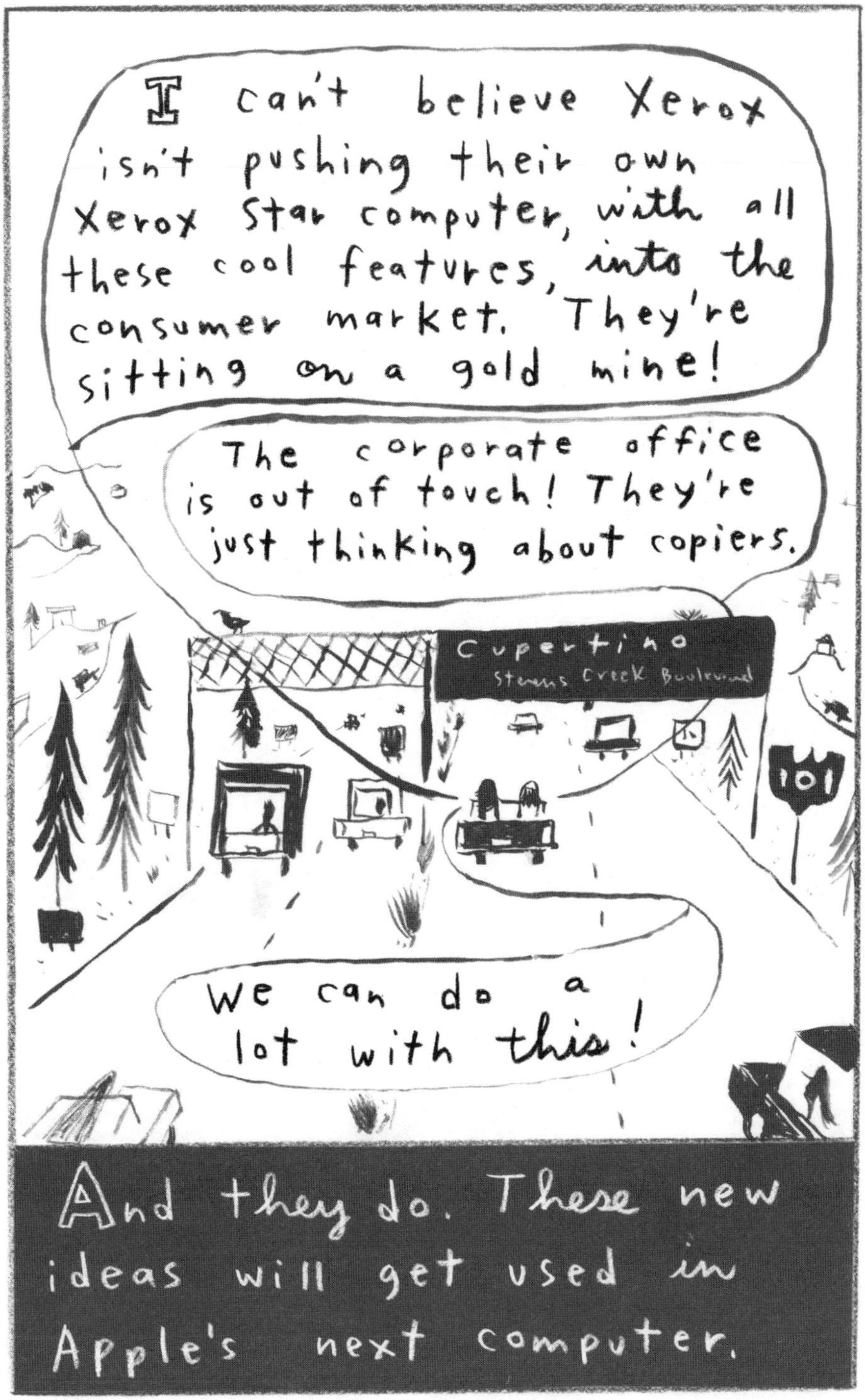
I can't believe Xerox isn't pushing their own Xerox Star computer, with all these cool features, into the consumer market. They're sitting on a gold mine!
The corporate office is out of touch! They're just thinking about copiers.
Cupertino
Stevens Creek Boulevard
101
We can do a lot with this!
And they do. These new ideas will get used in Apple's next computer.

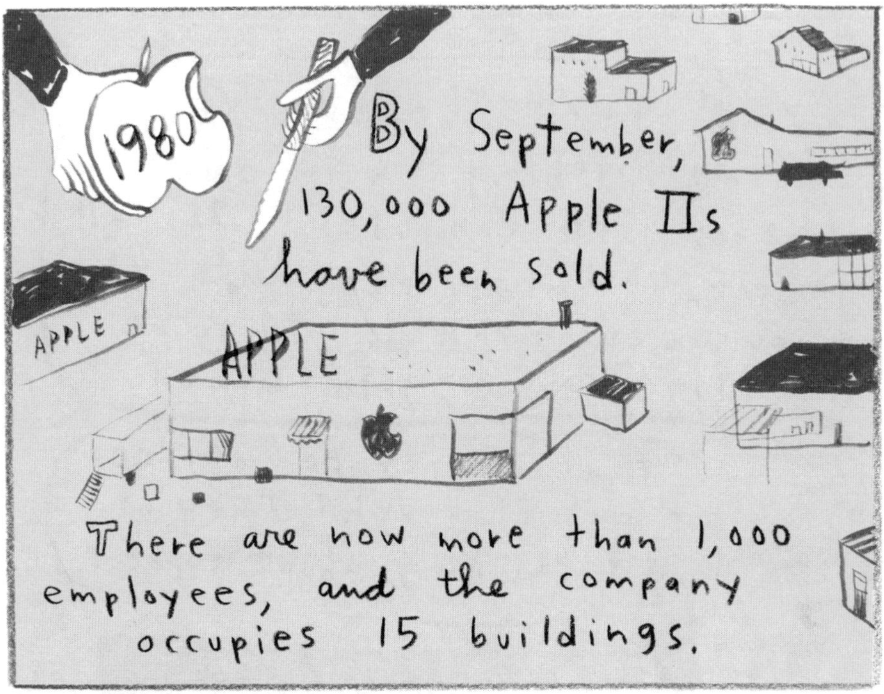
1980
By September, 130,000 Apple IIs have been sold.
APPLE
APPLE
There are now more than 1,000 employees, and the company occupies 15 buildings.

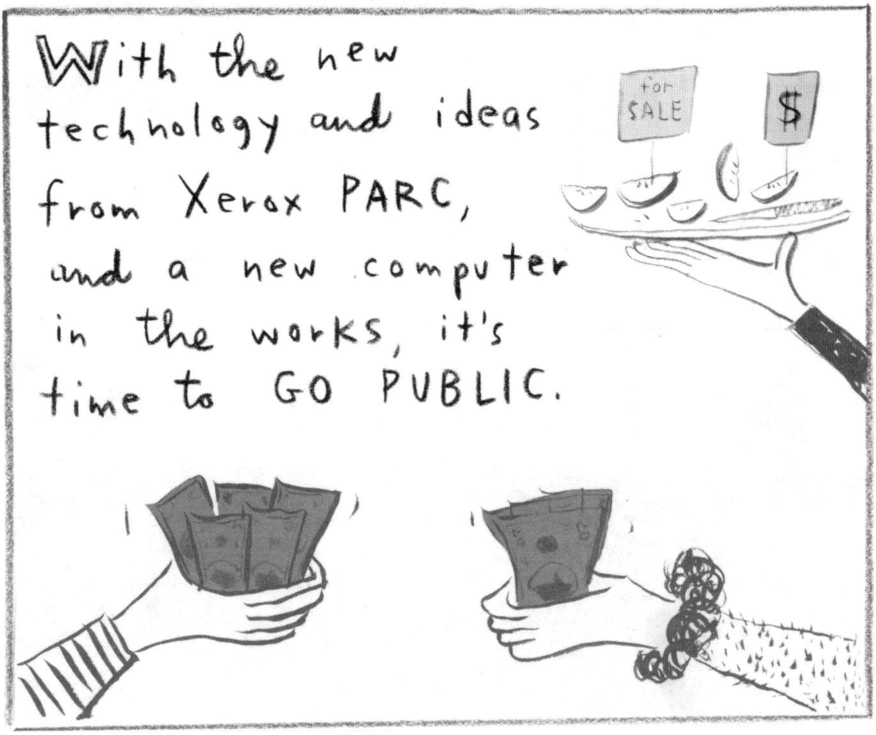
With the new technology and ideas from Xerox PARC, and a new computer in the works, it's time to GO PUBLIC.
for SALE
$

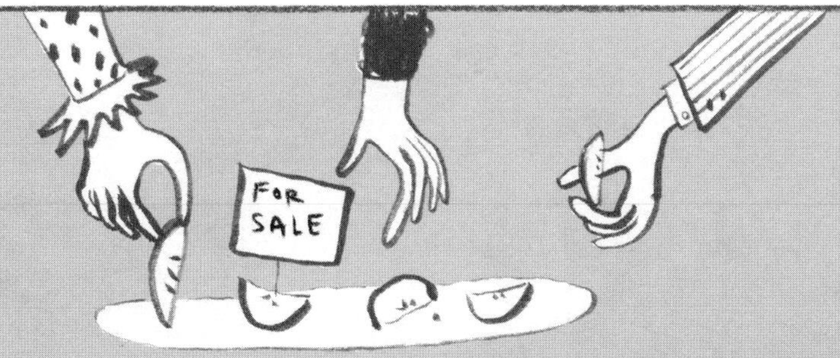
FOR SALE

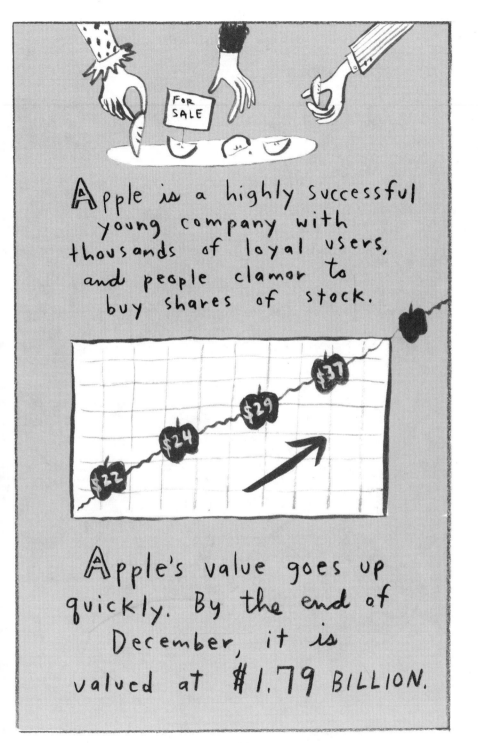

Apple is a highly successful young company with thousands of loyal users, and people clamor to buy shares of stock.

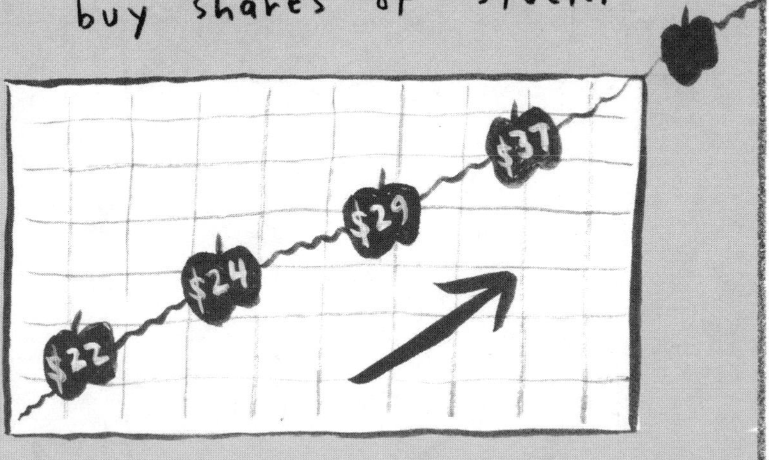
$22
$24
$29
$37

Apple's value goes up quickly. By the end of December, it is valued at $1.79 BILLION.

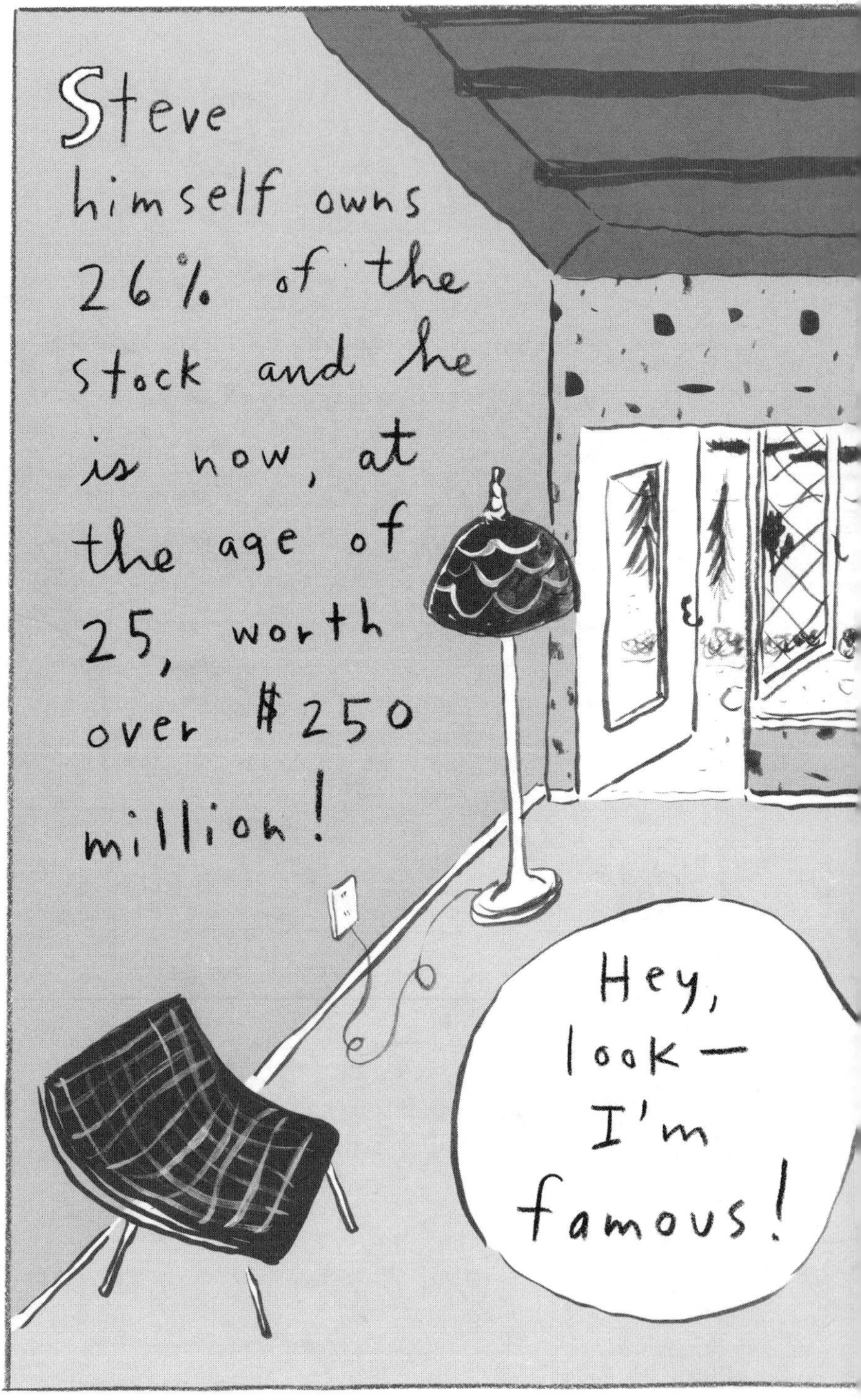
Steve himself owns 26% of the stock and he is now, at the age of 25, worth over $250 million!
Hey, look — I'm famous!

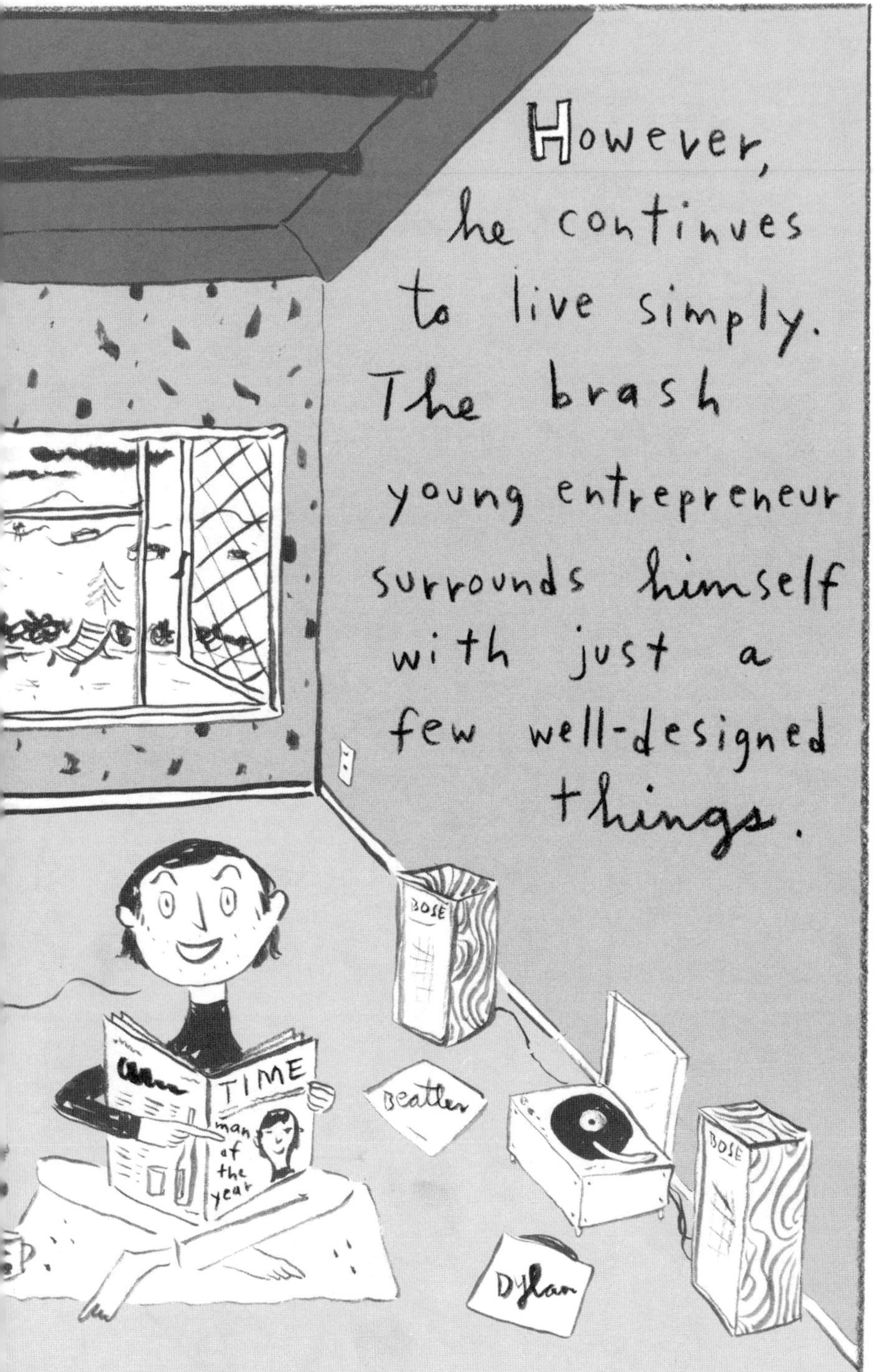
However, he continues to live simply. The brash young entrepreneur surrounds himself with just a few well-designed things.
TIME
man of the year
BOSE
Beatles
Dylan
BOSE

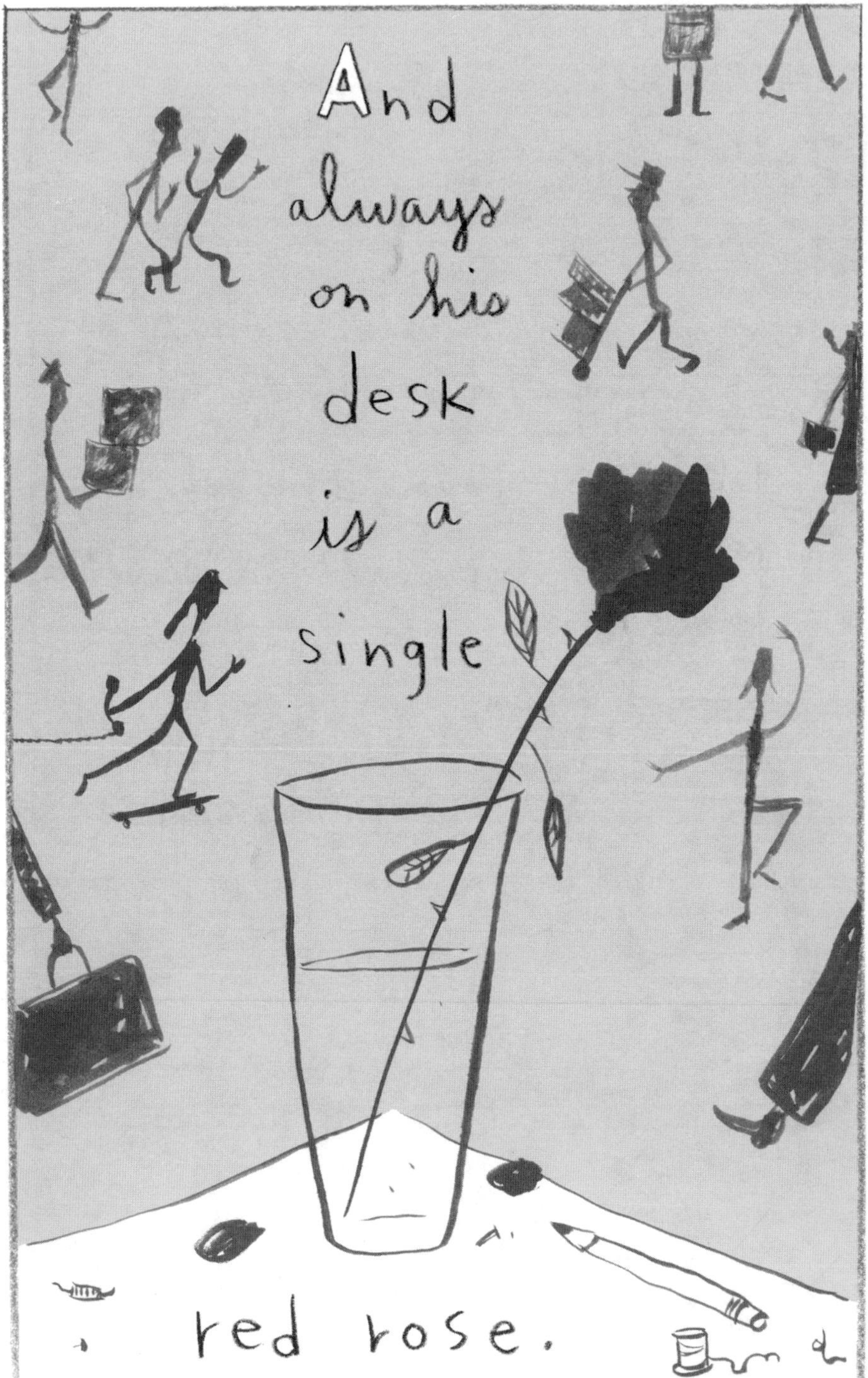
And always on his desk is a single red rose.

CHAPTER

8

RISE and FALL

(1982 — 1986)

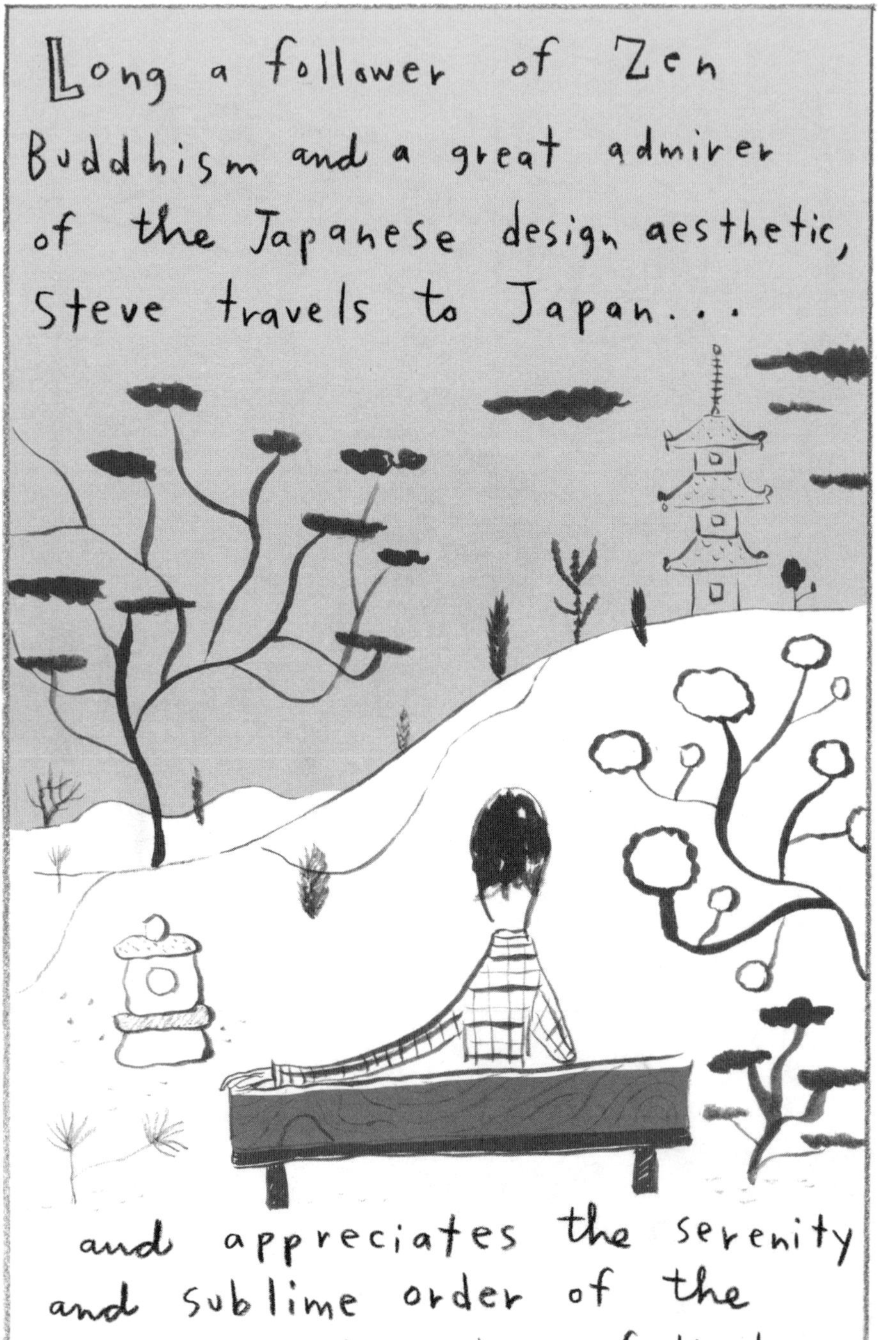
Long a follower of Zen Buddhism and a great admirer of the Japanese design aesthetic, Steve travels to Japan...
and appreciates the serenity and sublime order of the temples and gardens of Kyoto...

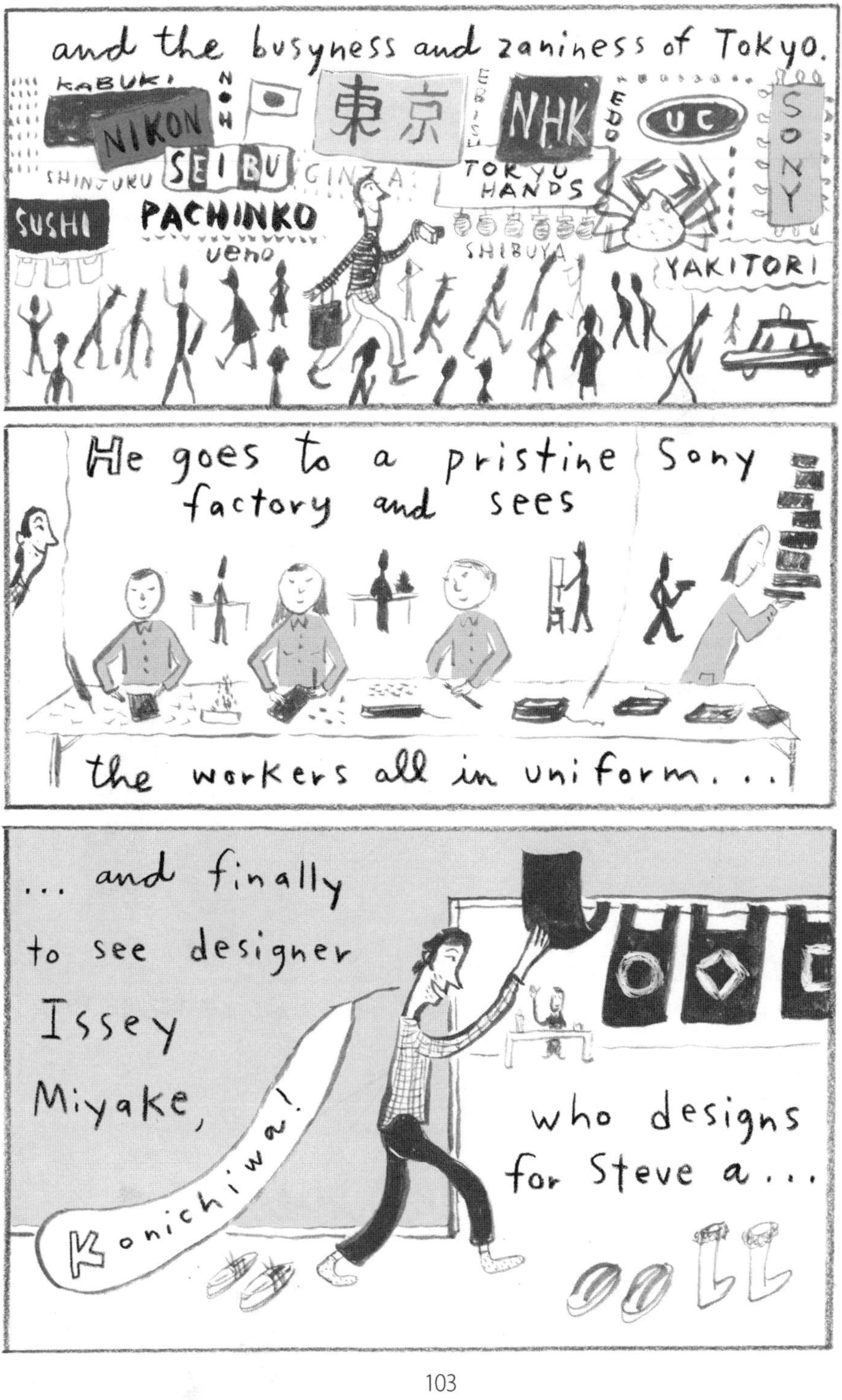

and the busyness and zaniness of Tokyo.
KABUKI
NOH
NIKON
東京
NHK
EDO
UC
SONY
SEIBU
SHINJUKU
GINZA
TOKYU HANDS
SUSHI
PACHINKO
UENO
SHIBUYA
YAKITORI
He goes to a pristine Sony factory and sees
the workers all in uniform...
... and finally to see designer Issey Miyake,
Konichiwa!
who designs for Steve a...

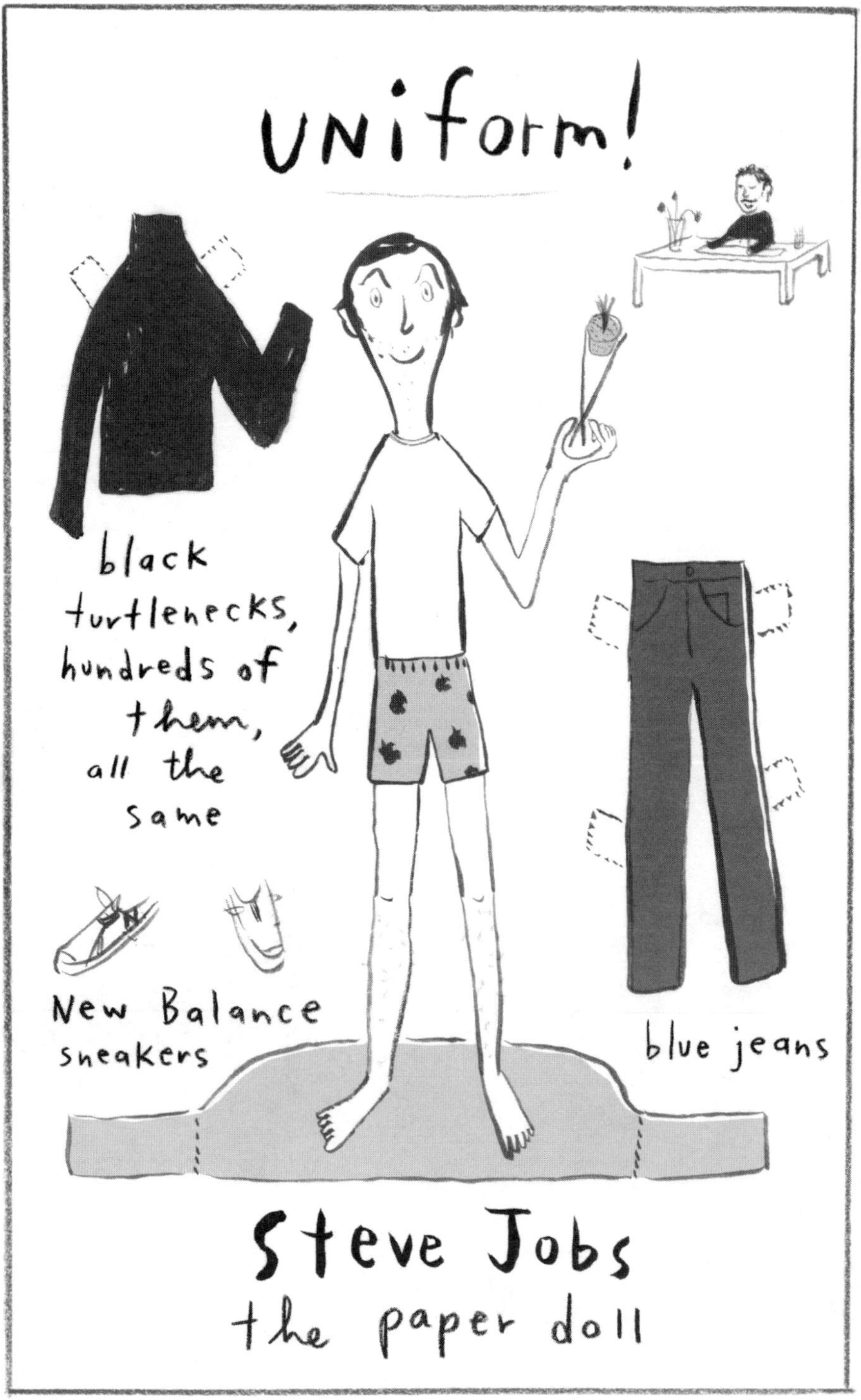
Uniform!
black turtlenecks, hundreds of them, all the same
New Balance sneakers
blue jeans
Steve Jobs
the paper doll

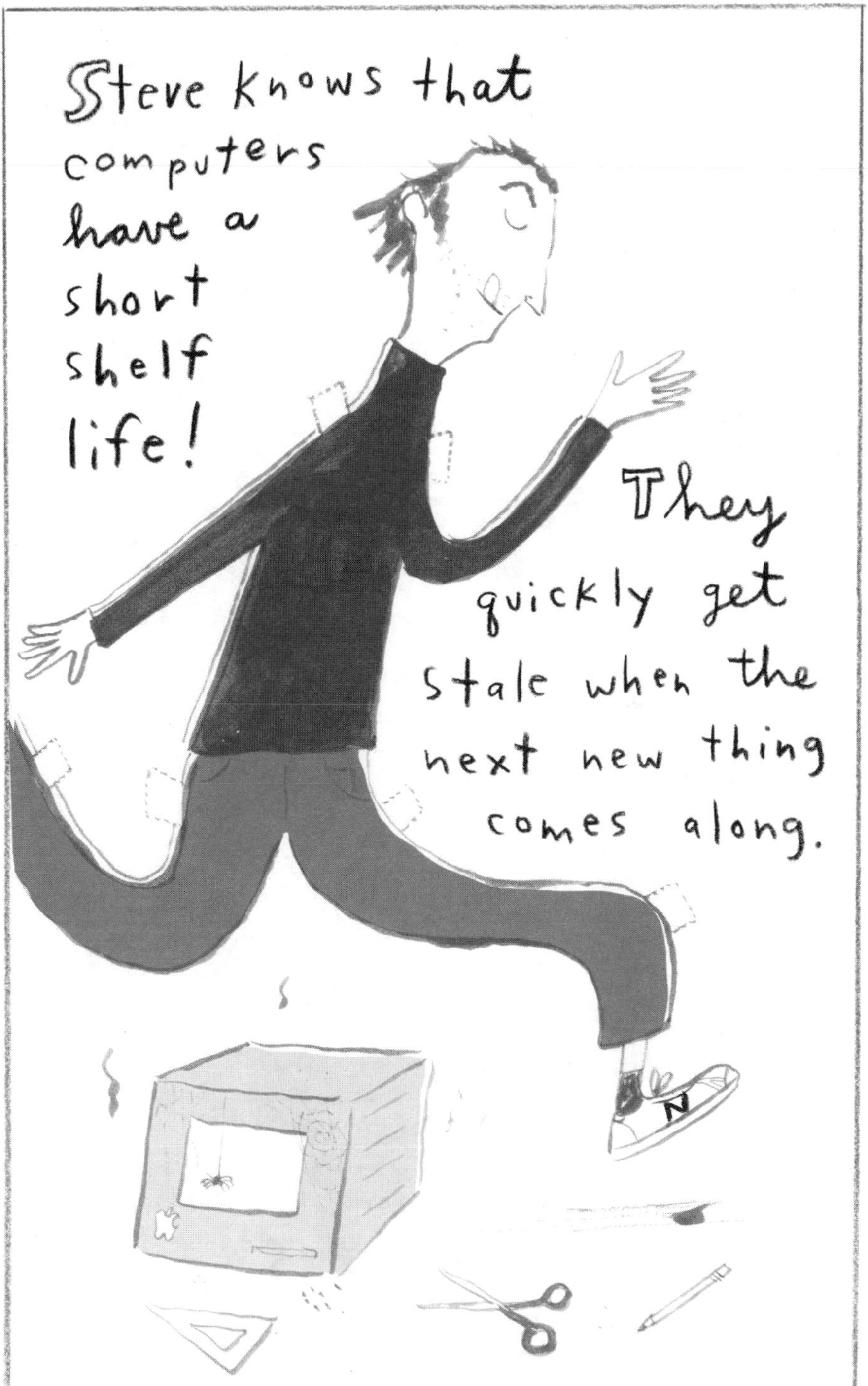
Steve knows that computers have a short shelf life!
They quickly get stale when the next new thing comes along.
N

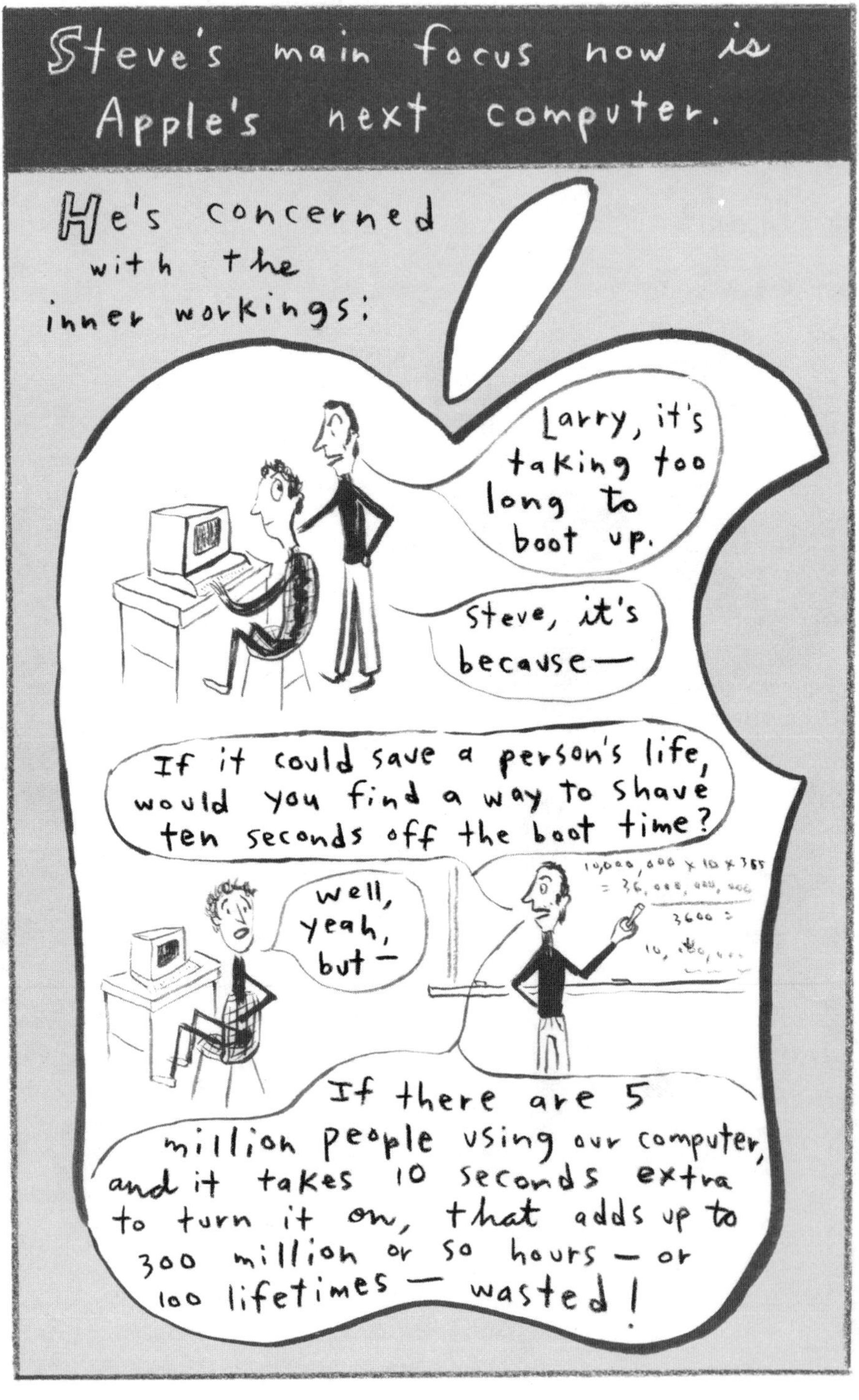
Steve's main focus now is Apple's next computer.
He's concerned with the inner workings:
Larry, it's taking too long to boot up.
Steve, it's because—
If it could save a person's life, would you find a way to shave ten seconds off the boot time?
well, yeah, but—
If there are 5 million people using our computer, and it takes 10 seconds extra to turn it on, that adds up to 300 million or so hours — or 100 lifetimes — wasted!

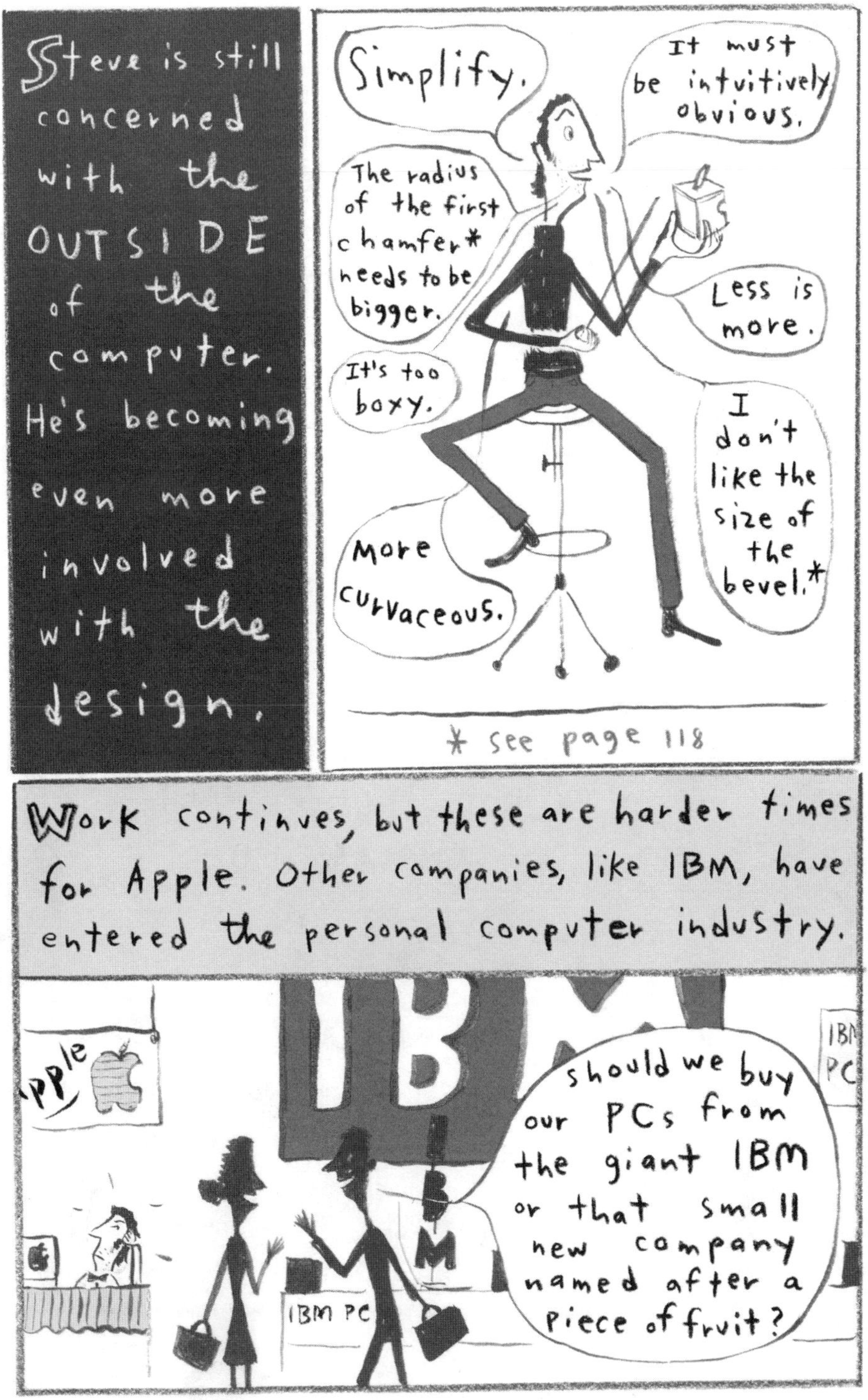
Steve is still concerned with the OUTSIDE of the computer. He's becoming even more involved with the design.
Simplify.
It must be intuitively obvious.
The radius of the first chamfer* needs to be bigger.
Less is more.
It's too boxy.
I don't like the size of the bevel.*
More curvaceous.
* see page 118
Work continues, but these are harder times for Apple. Other companies, like IBM, have entered the personal computer industry.
IBM PC
Should we buy our PCs from the giant IBM or that small new company named after a piece of fruit?

PC by IBM

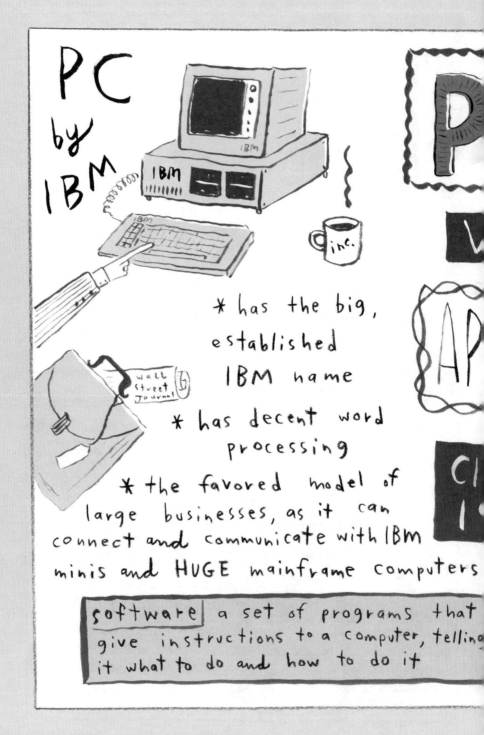

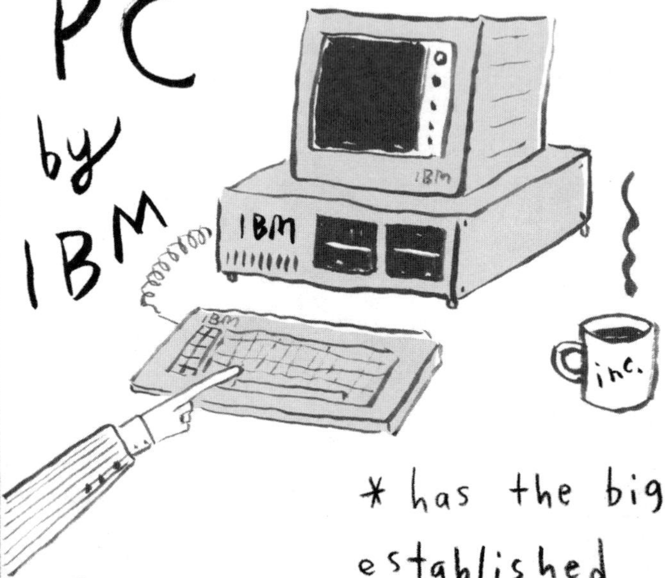
IBM
IBM
IBM
inc.

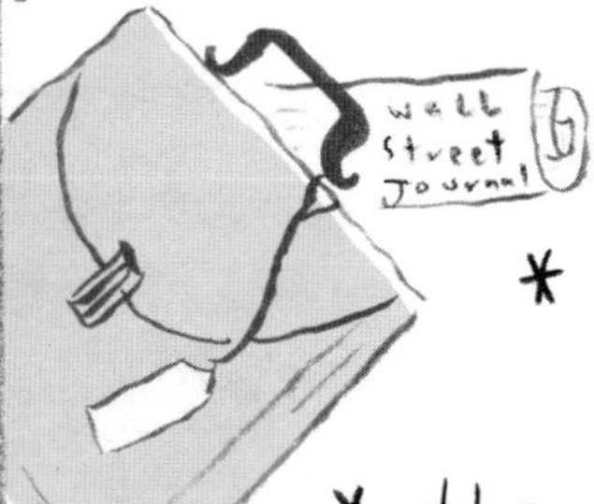
Wall Street Journal

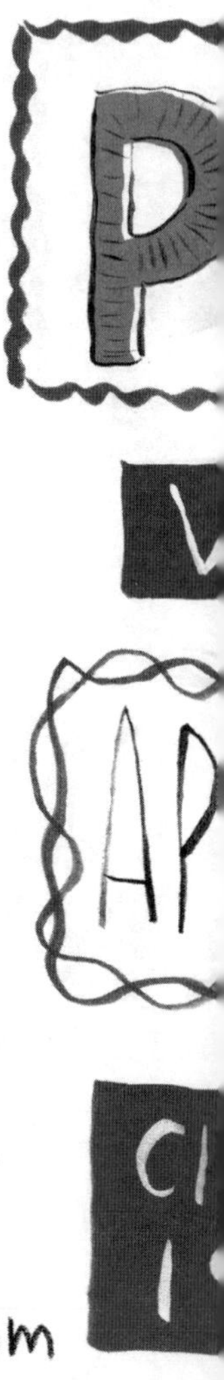

* has the big, established IBM name
* has decent word processing
* the favored model of large businesses, as it can connect and communicate with IBM minis and HUGE mainframe computers

software a set of programs that give instructions to a computer, telling it what to do and how to do it

APPLE II

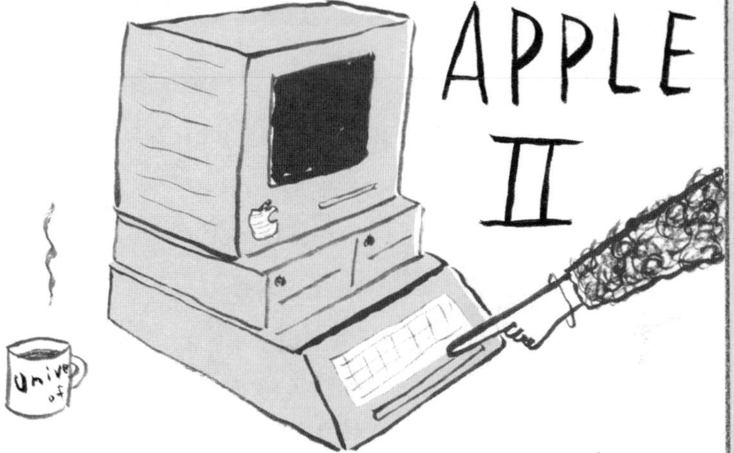

* has VisiCalc, a terrific program for visualizing spreadsheets
* offers pioneering programs for writing and making music
* has games, graphics, and educational software
* the favored model of schools and universities

hardware the physical pieces of a computer

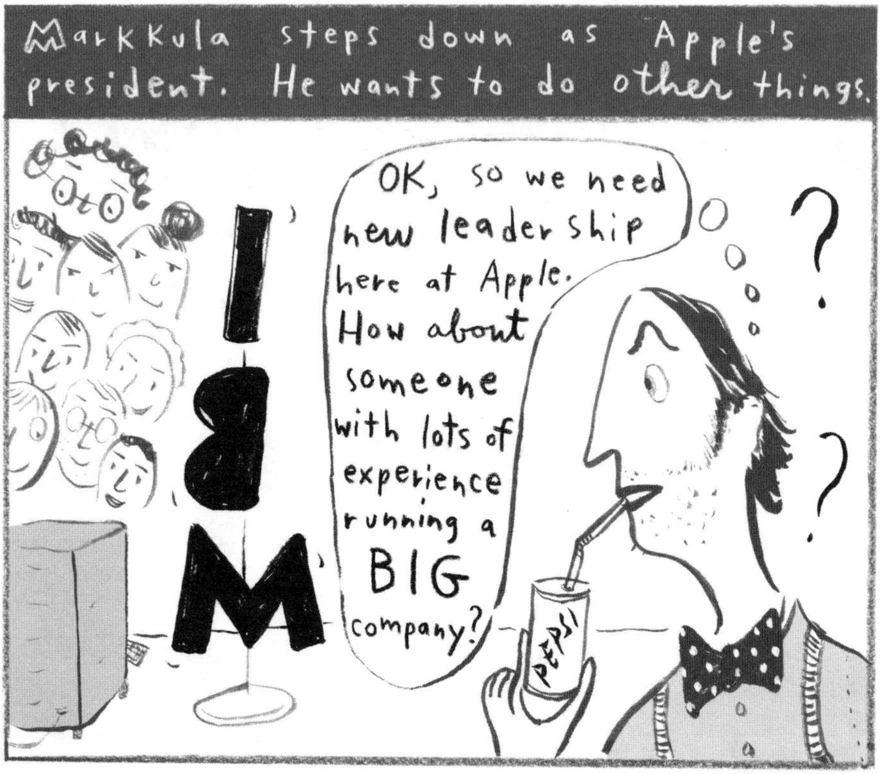
Markkula steps down as Apple's president. He wants to do other things.
IBM
OK, so we need new leadership here at Apple. How about someone with lots of experience running a BIG company?
?
?
Pepsi

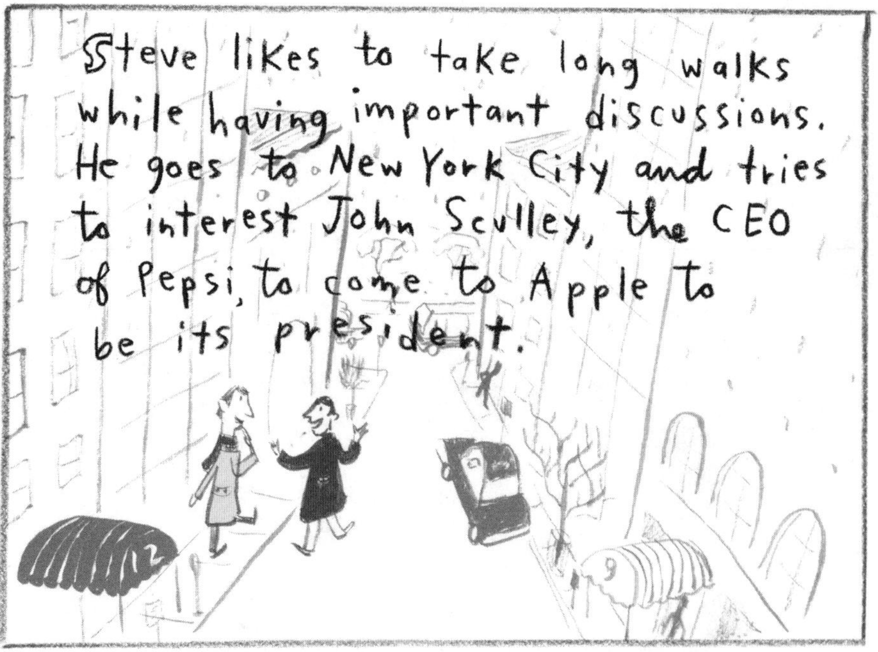
Steve likes to take long walks while having important discussions. He goes to New York City and tries to interest John Sculley, the CEO of Pepsi, to come to Apple to be its president.
12
9

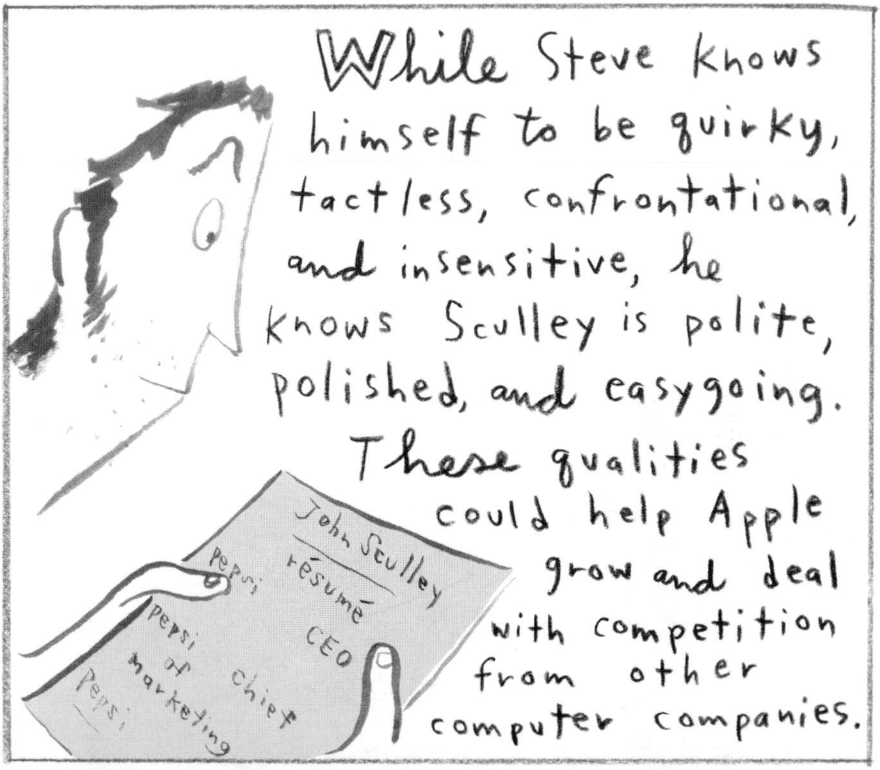
While Steve knows himself to be quirky, tactless, confrontational, and insensitive, he knows Sculley is polite, polished, and easygoing.
These qualities could help Apple grow and deal with competition from other computer companies.
John Sculley
résumé
Pepsi
CEO
Pepsi
of
chief
marketing
Pepsi

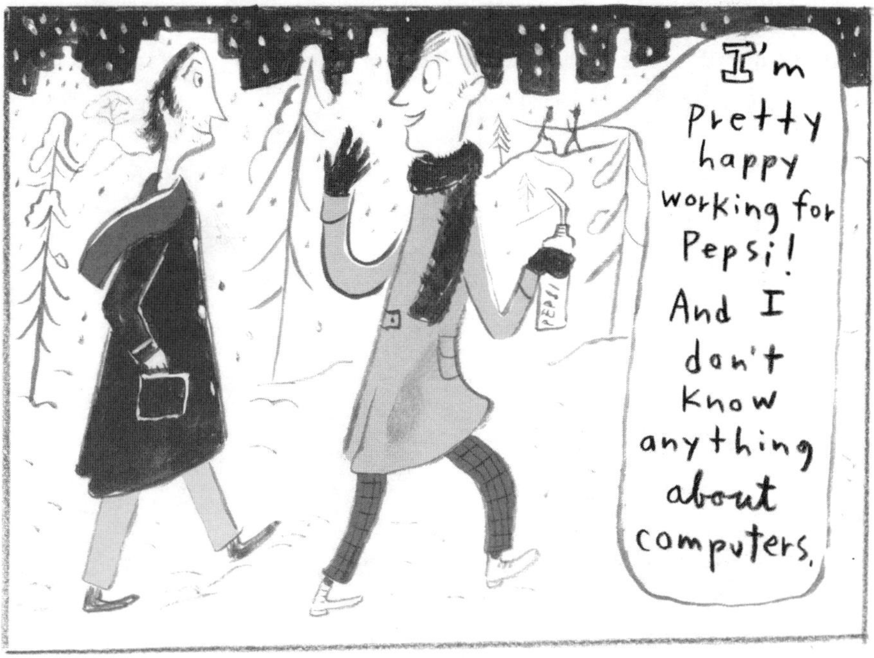
I'm pretty happy working for Pepsi! And I don't know anything about computers.
PEPSI

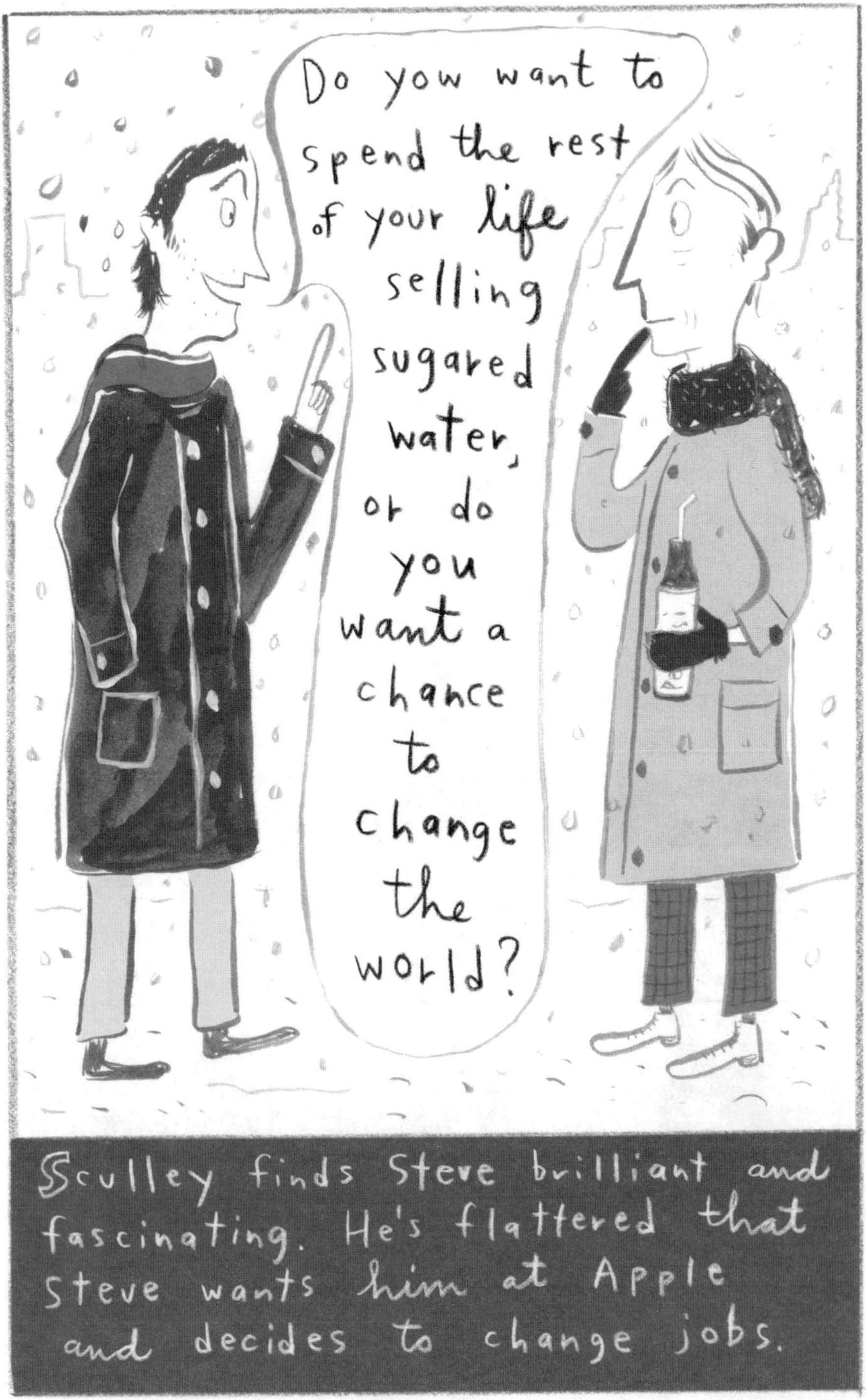
Do you want to spend the rest of your life selling sugared water, or do you want a chance to change the world?
Sculley finds Steve brilliant and fascinating. He's flattered that Steve wants him at Apple and decides to change jobs.

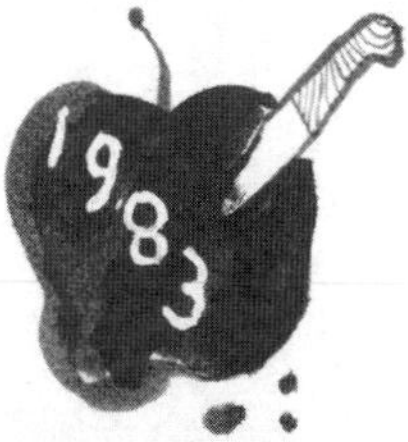
1983

Sculley comes on board, but right away there are disagreements.

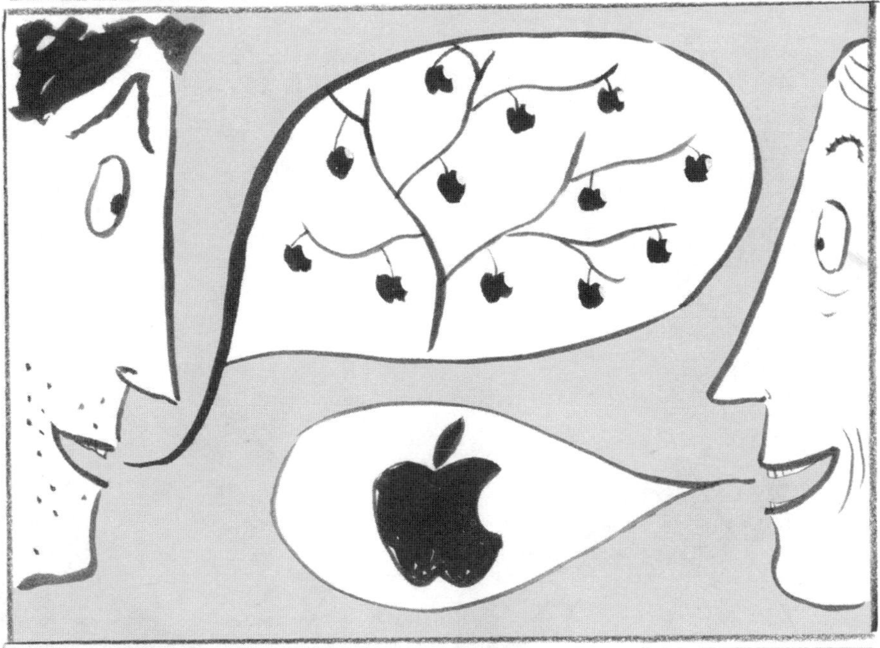

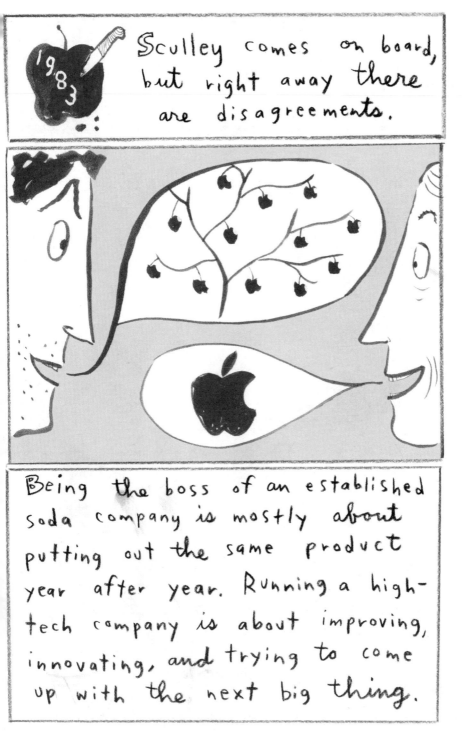

Being the boss of an established soda company is mostly about putting out the same product year after year. Running a high-tech company is about improving, innovating, and trying to come up with the next big thing.

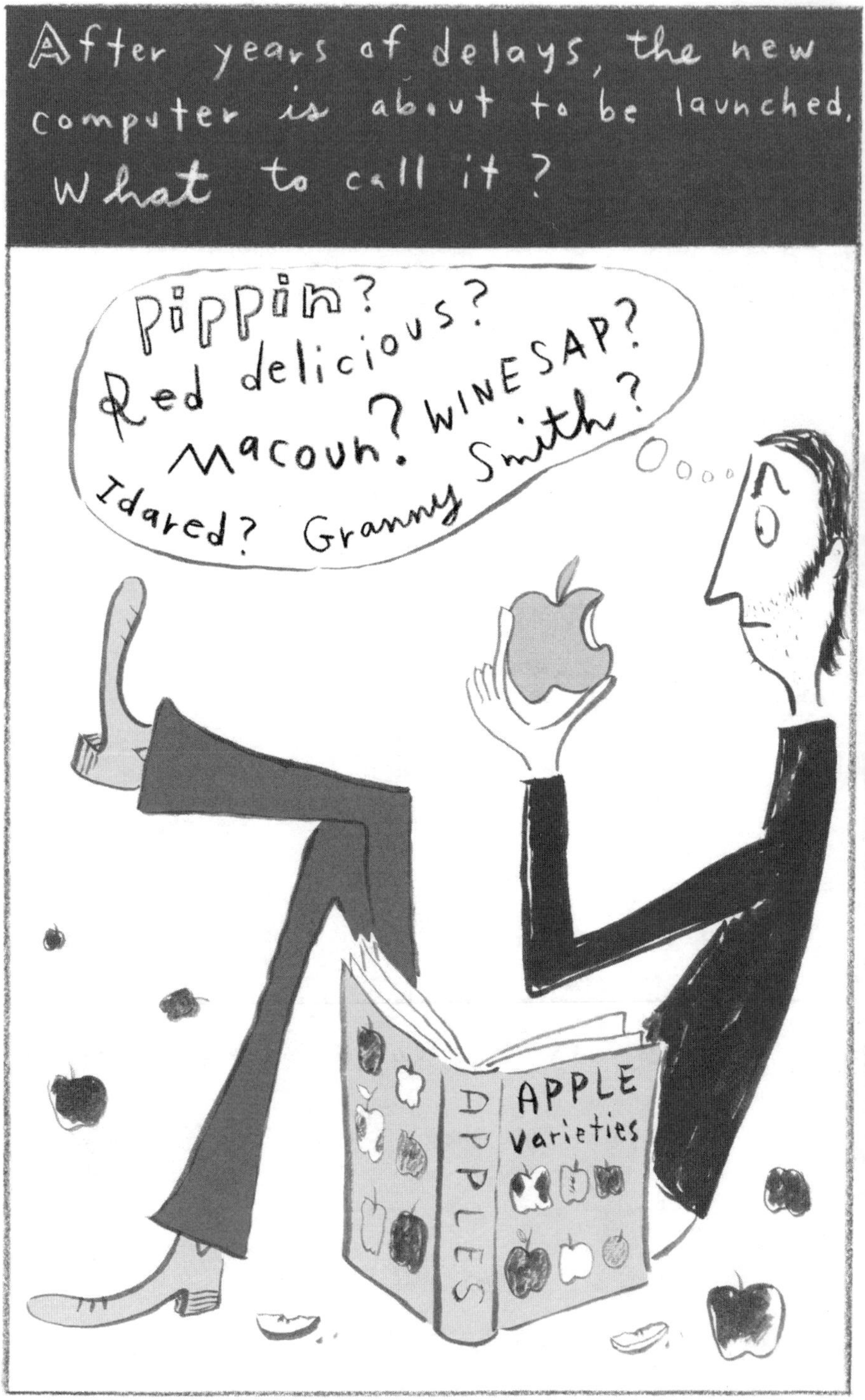
After years of delays, the new computer is about to be launched. What to call it?
Pippin? Red delicious? WINESAP? Macoun? Granny Smith? Idared?
APPLE varieties
APPLES

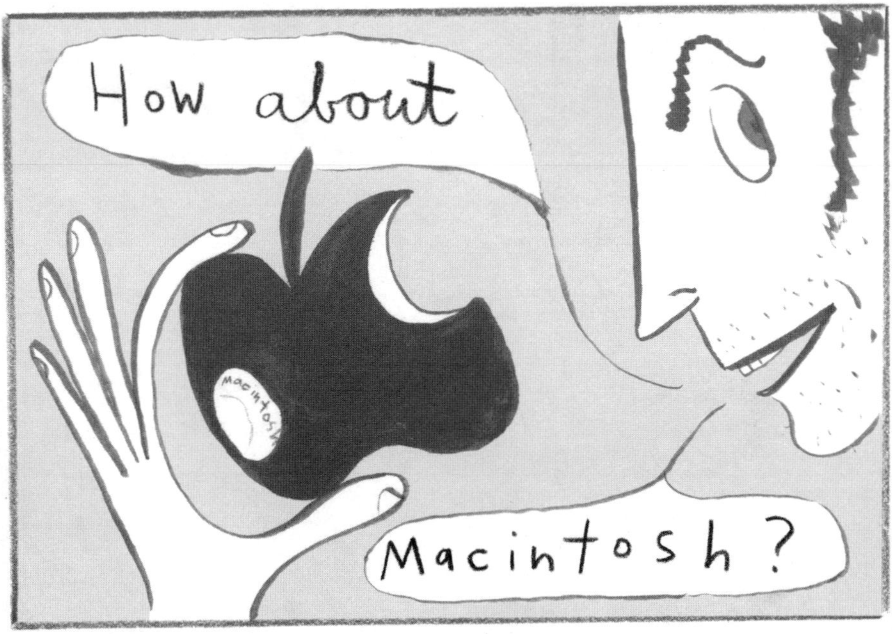
How about
Macintosh
Macintosh?

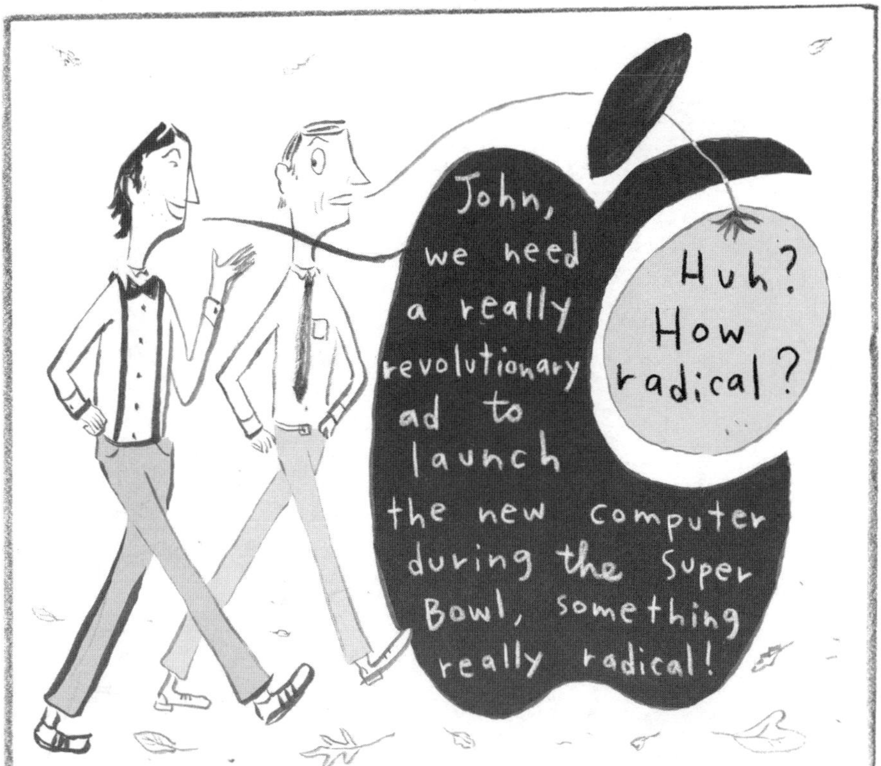
John, we need a really revolutionary ad to launch the new computer during the Super Bowl, something really radical!
Huh? How radical?

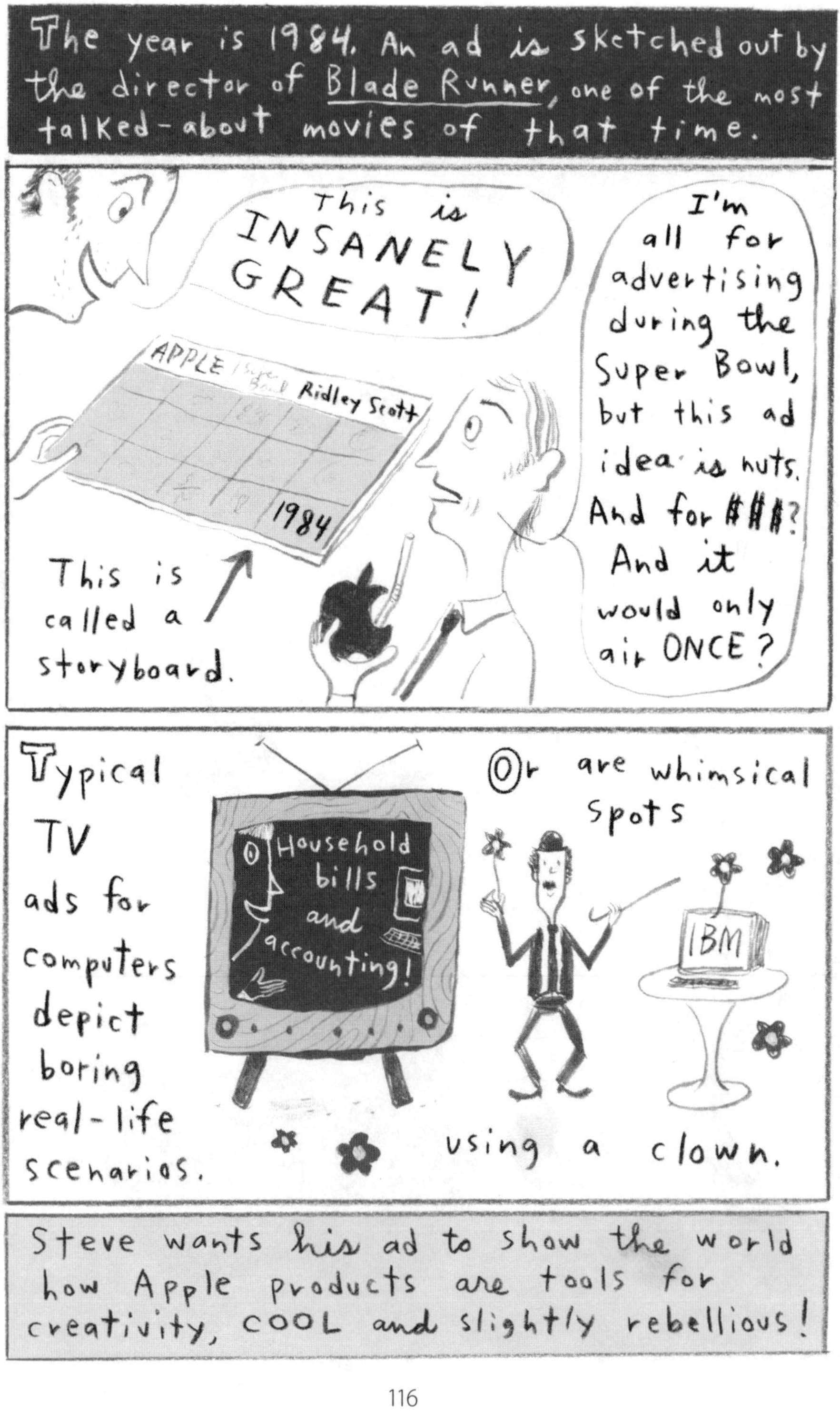
The year is 1984. An ad is sketched out by the director of Blade Runner, one of the most talked-about movies of that time.
This is INSANELY GREAT!
APPLE
Ridley Scott
1984
This is called a storyboard.
I'm all for advertising during the Super Bowl, but this ad idea is nuts. And for ###? And it would only air ONCE?
Typical TV ads for computers depict boring real-life scenarios.
Household bills and accounting!
Or are whimsical spots
IBM
using a clown.
Steve wants his ad to show the world how Apple products are tools for creativity, COOL and slightly rebellious!

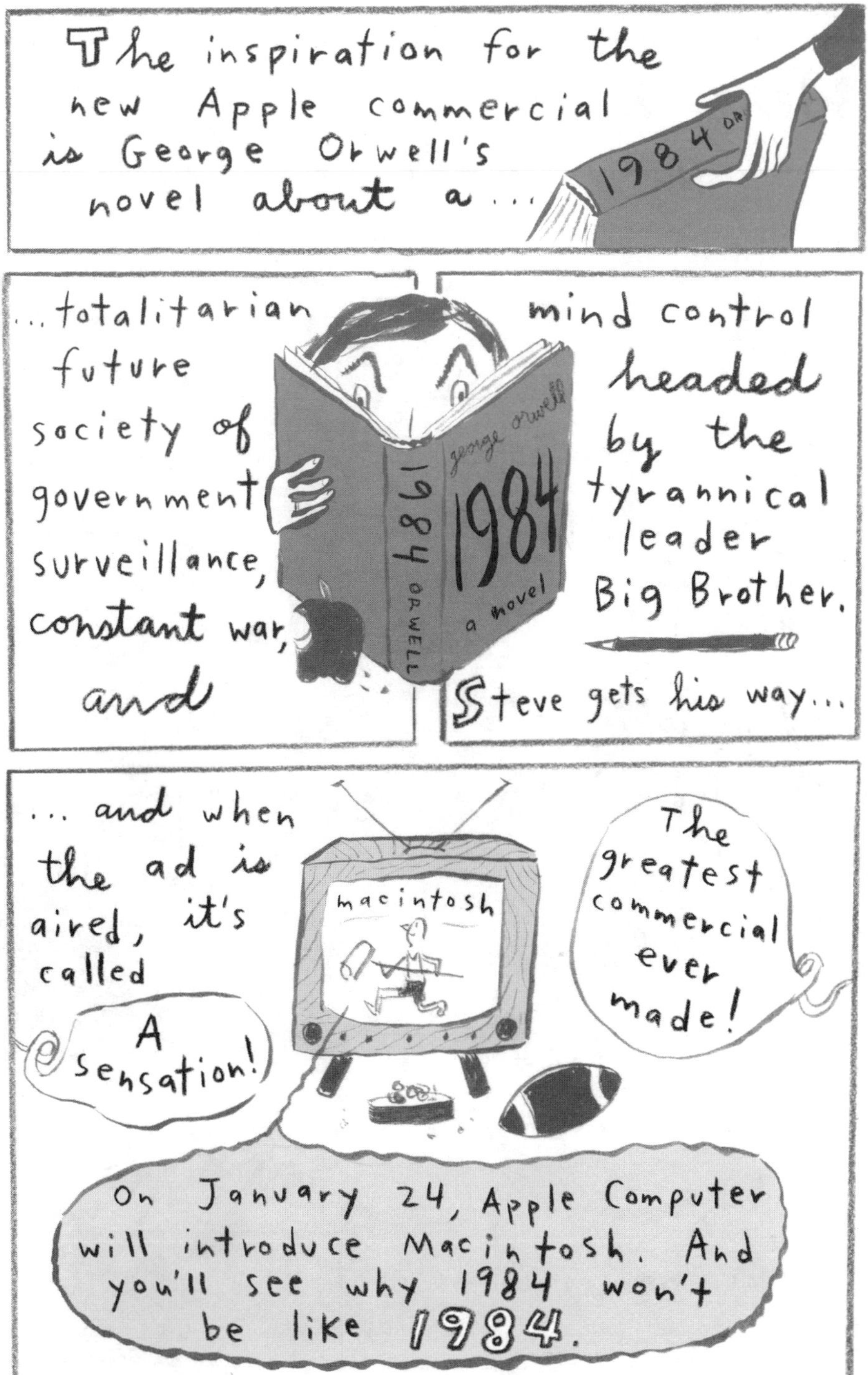
The inspiration for the new Apple commercial is George Orwell's novel about a...
1984
...totalitarian future society of government surveillance, constant war, and
mind control headed by the tyrannical leader Big Brother.
george orwell
1984
a novel
1984 ORWELL
Steve gets his way...
... and when the ad is aired, it's called
A sensation!
The greatest commercial ever made!
macintosh
On January 24, Apple Computer will introduce Macintosh. And you'll see why 1984 won't be like 1984.

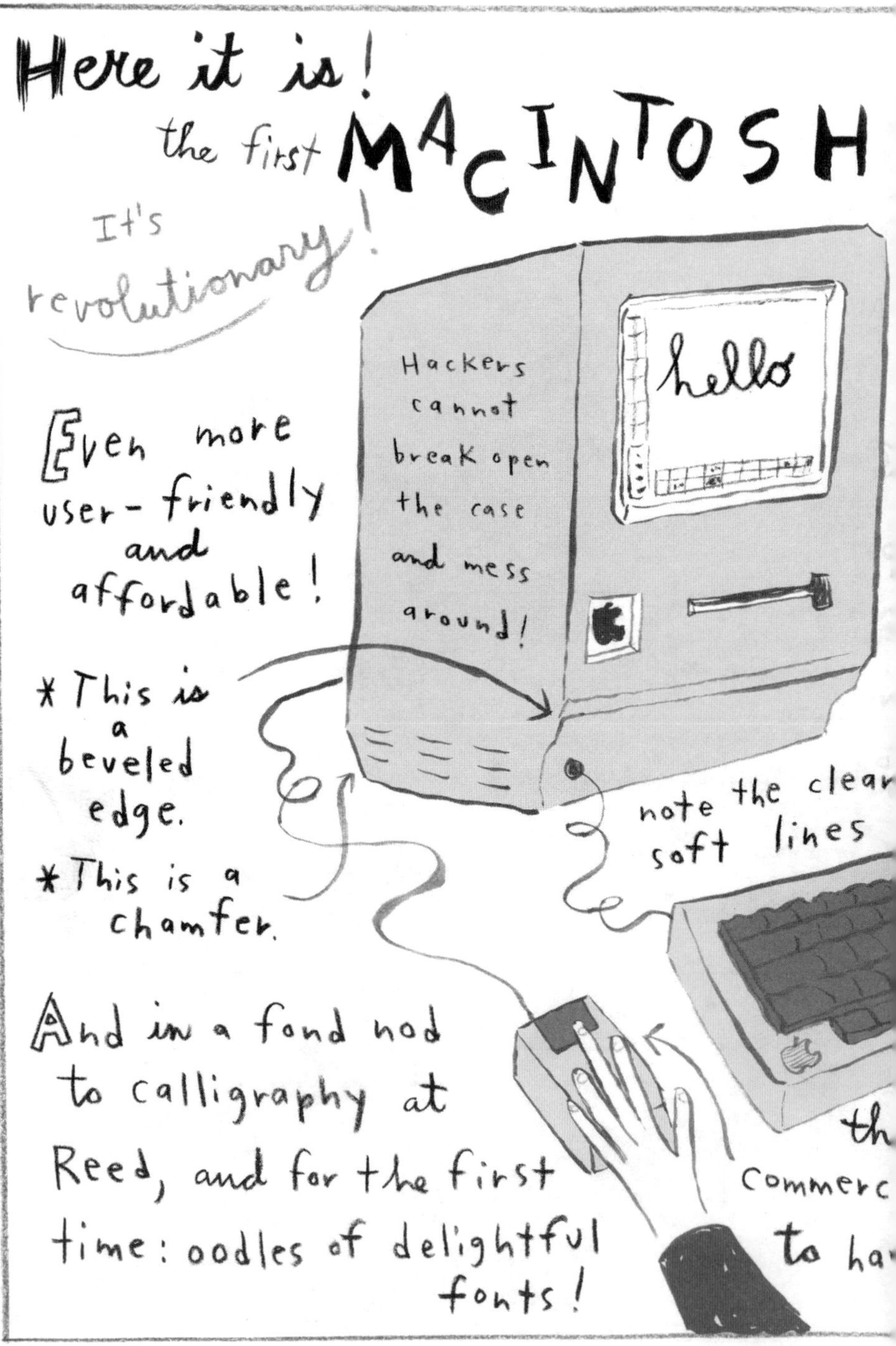
Here it is!
the first MACINTOSH
It's revolutionary!
hello
Hackers cannot break open the case and mess around!
Even more user-friendly and affordable!
* This is a beveled edge.
* This is a chamfer.
note the clear soft lines
And in a fond nod to calligraphy at Reed, and for the first time: oodles of delightful fonts!
th
commerc
to ha

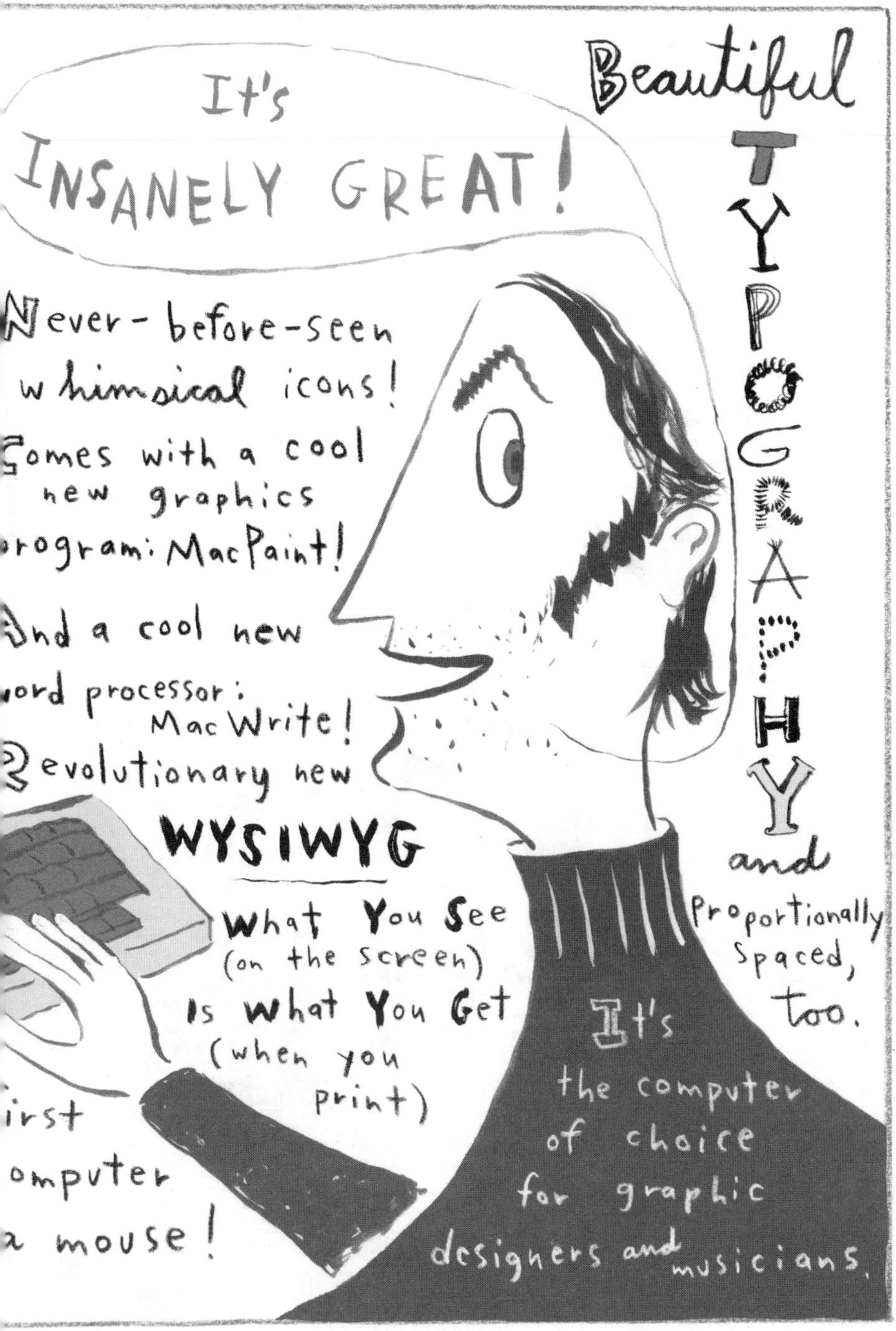
It's INSANELY GREAT!
Beautiful TYPOGRAPHY and Proportionally Spaced, too.
Never-before-seen whimsical icons!
Comes with a cool new graphics program: MacPaint!
And a cool new word processor: MacWrite!
Revolutionary new WYSIWYG
What You See (on the screen) Is What You Get (when you print)
irst omputer a mouse!
It's the computer of choice for graphic designers and musicians.

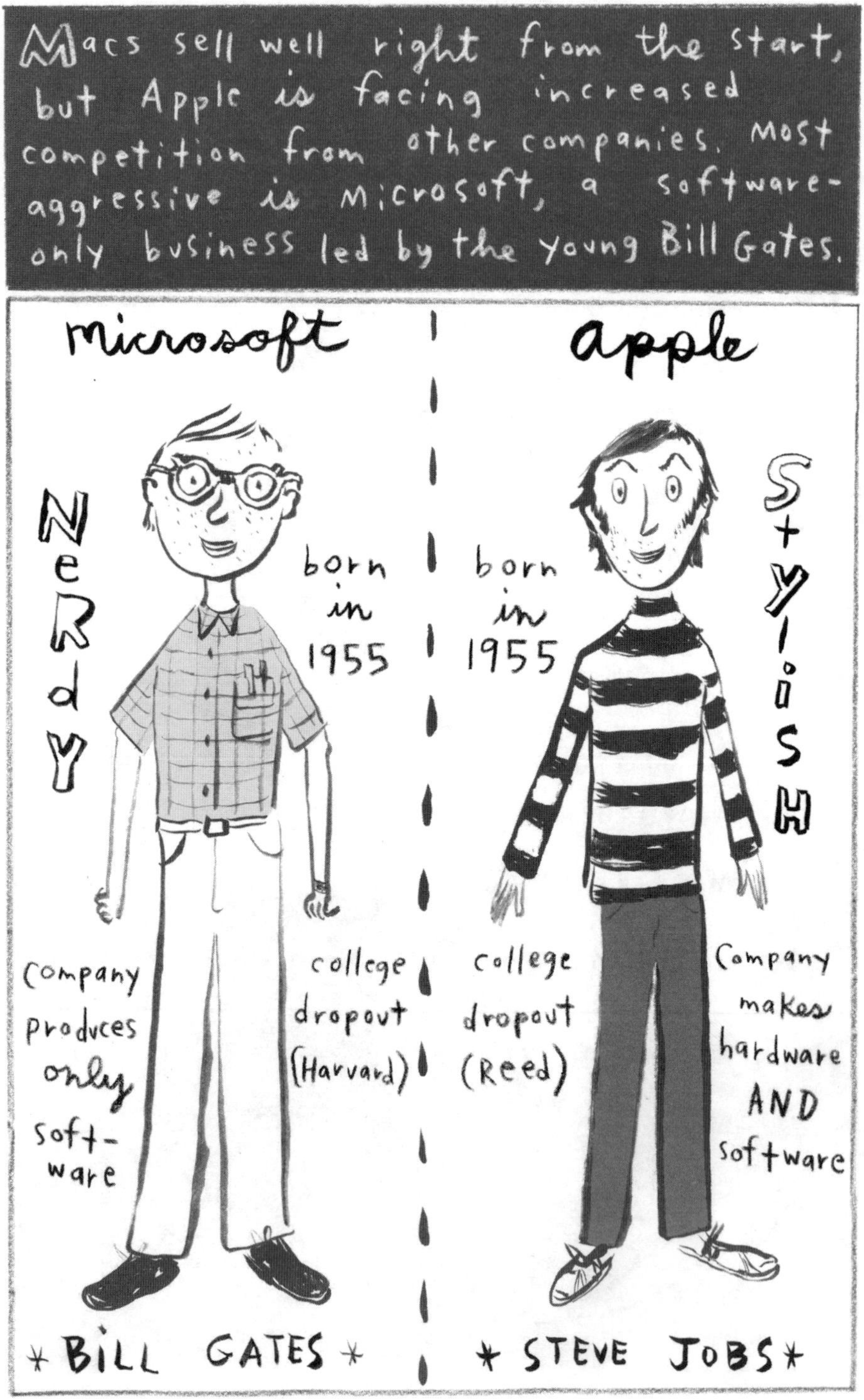
Macs sell well right from the start, but Apple is facing increased competition from other companies. Most aggressive is Microsoft, a software-only business led by the young Bill Gates.
microsoft
apple
NeRdY
born in 1955
born in 1955
StYlISH
company produces only soft-ware
college dropout (Harvard)
college dropout (Reed)
Company makes hardware AND software
* BILL GATES *
* STEVE JOBS *

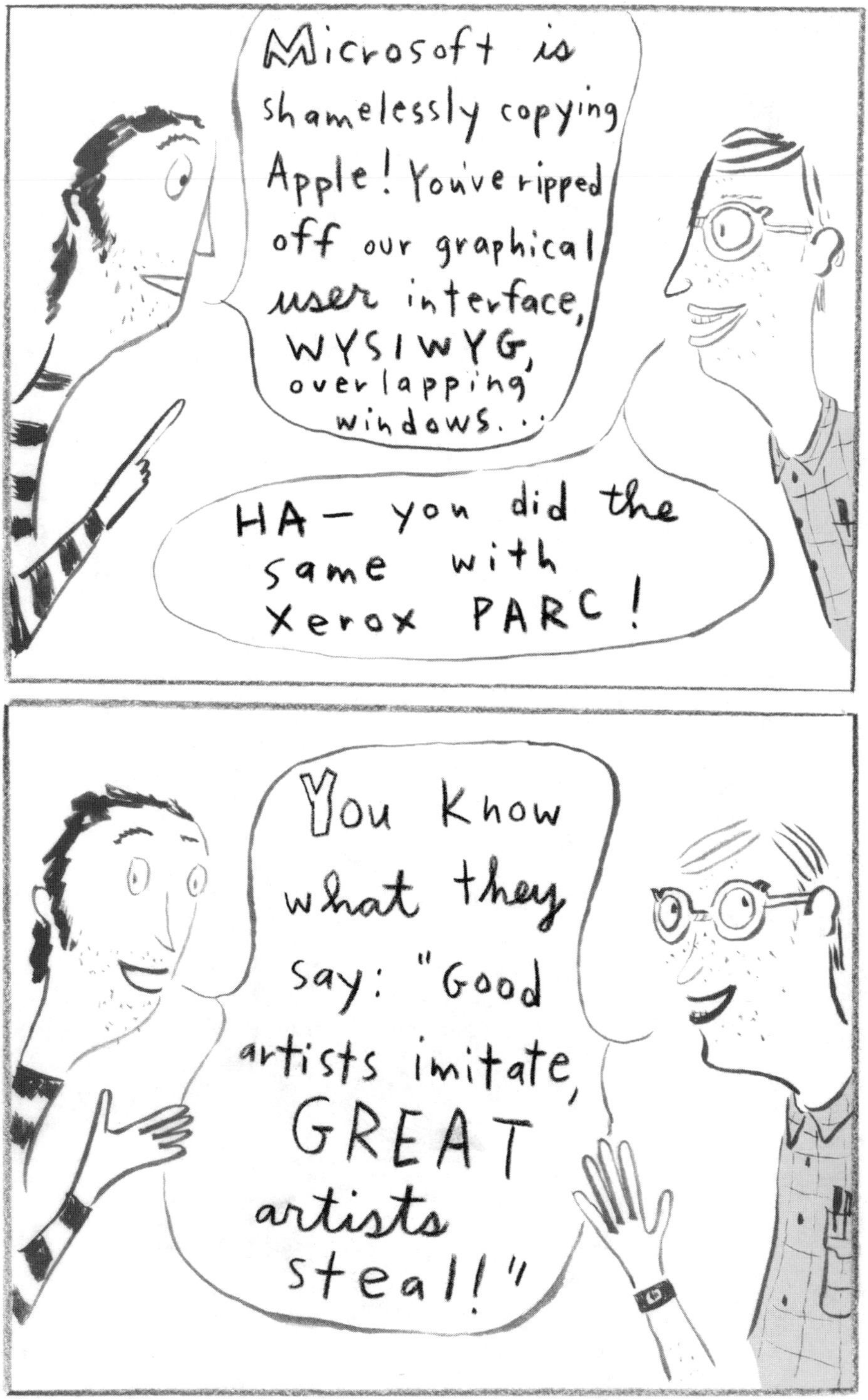
Microsoft is shamelessly copying Apple! You've ripped off our graphical user interface, WYSIWYG, overlapping windows...
HA – you did the same with Xerox PARC!
You know what they say: "Good artists imitate, GREAT artists steal!"

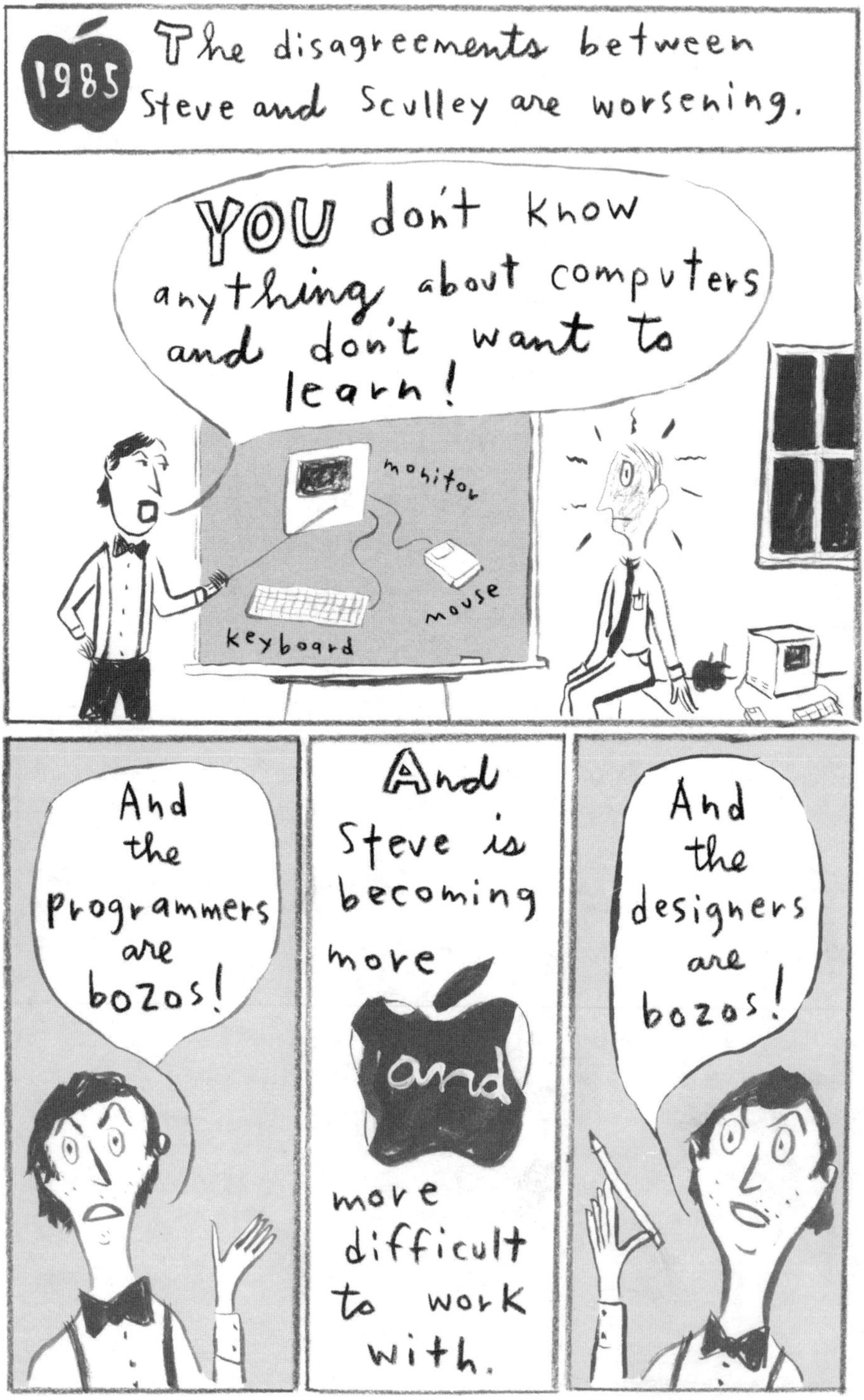
1985
The disagreements between Steve and Sculley are worsening.
YOU don't know anything about computers and don't want to learn!
monitor
mouse
keyboard
And the programmers are bozos!
And Steve is becoming more
and
more difficult to work with.
And the designers are bozos!

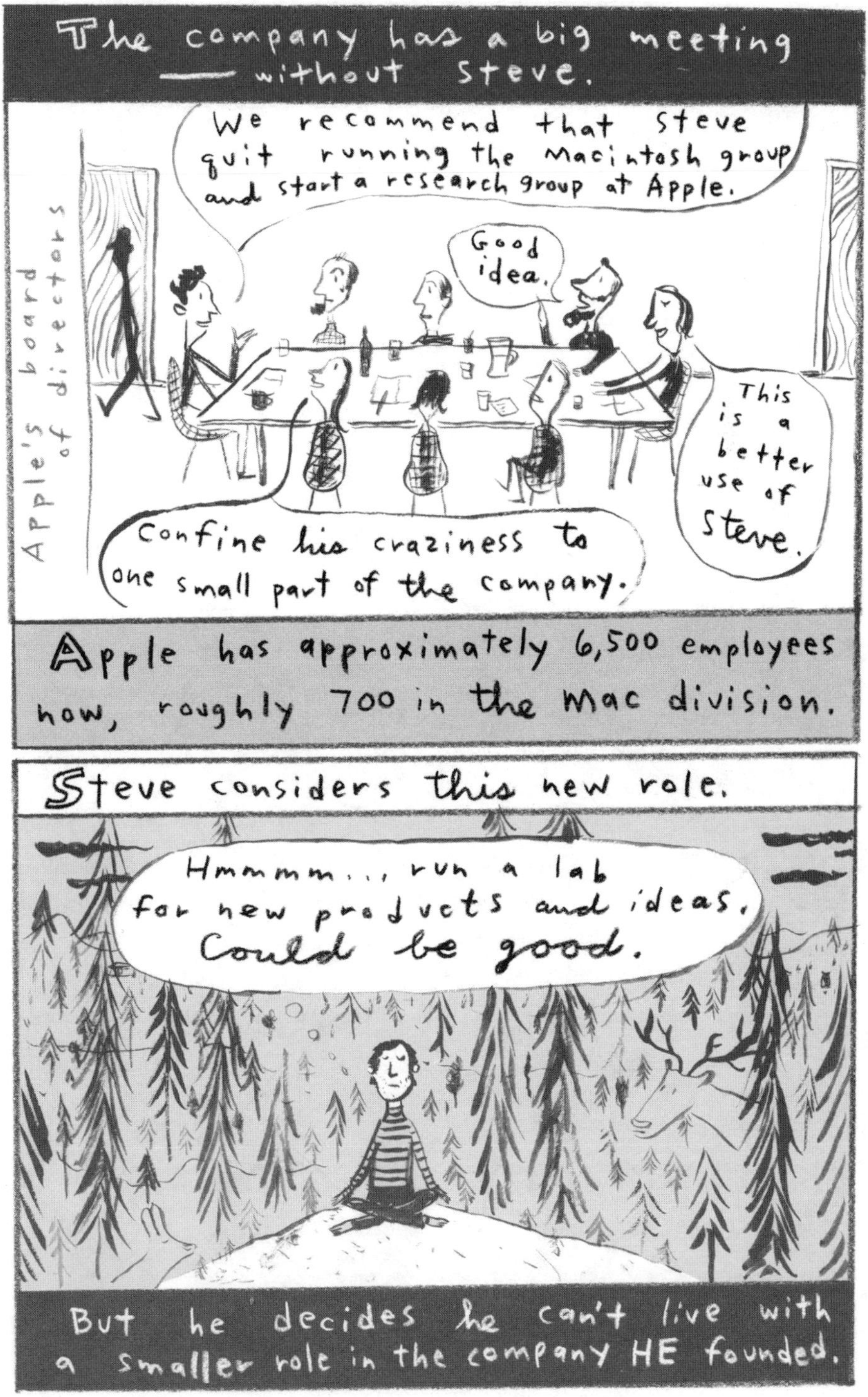
The company has a big meeting — without Steve.
Apple's board of directors
We recommend that Steve quit running the Macintosh group and start a research group at Apple.
Good idea.
This is a better use of Steve.
Confine his craziness to one small part of the company.
Apple has approximately 6,500 employees now, roughly 700 in the Mac division.
Steve considers this new role.
Hmmmm... run a lab for new products and ideas. Could be good.
But he decides he can't live with a smaller role in the company HE founded.

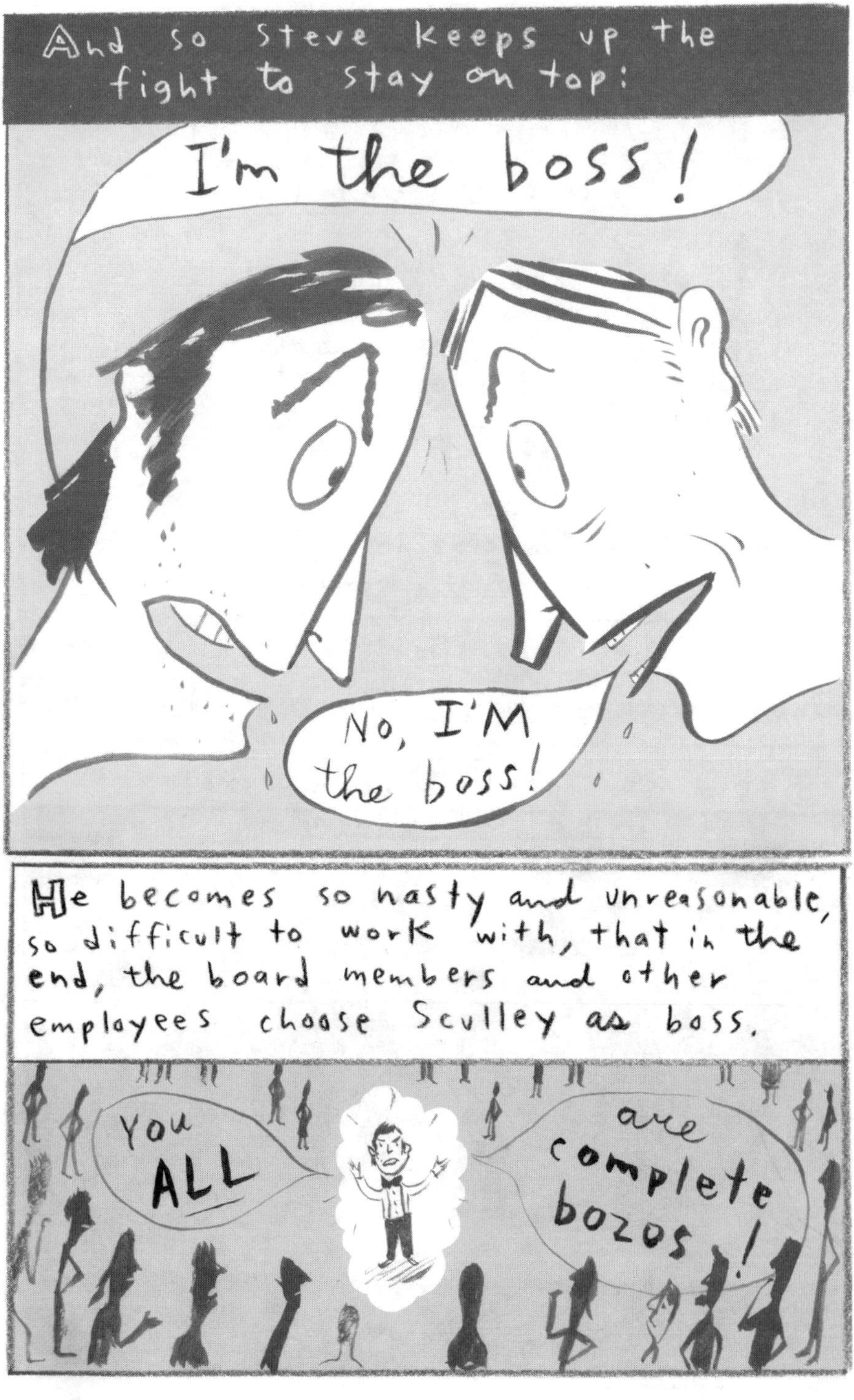
And so Steve keeps up the fight to stay on top:
I'm the boss!
No, I'M the boss!
He becomes so nasty and unreasonable, so difficult to work with, that in the end, the board members and other employees choose Sculley as boss.
You ALL
are complete bozos!

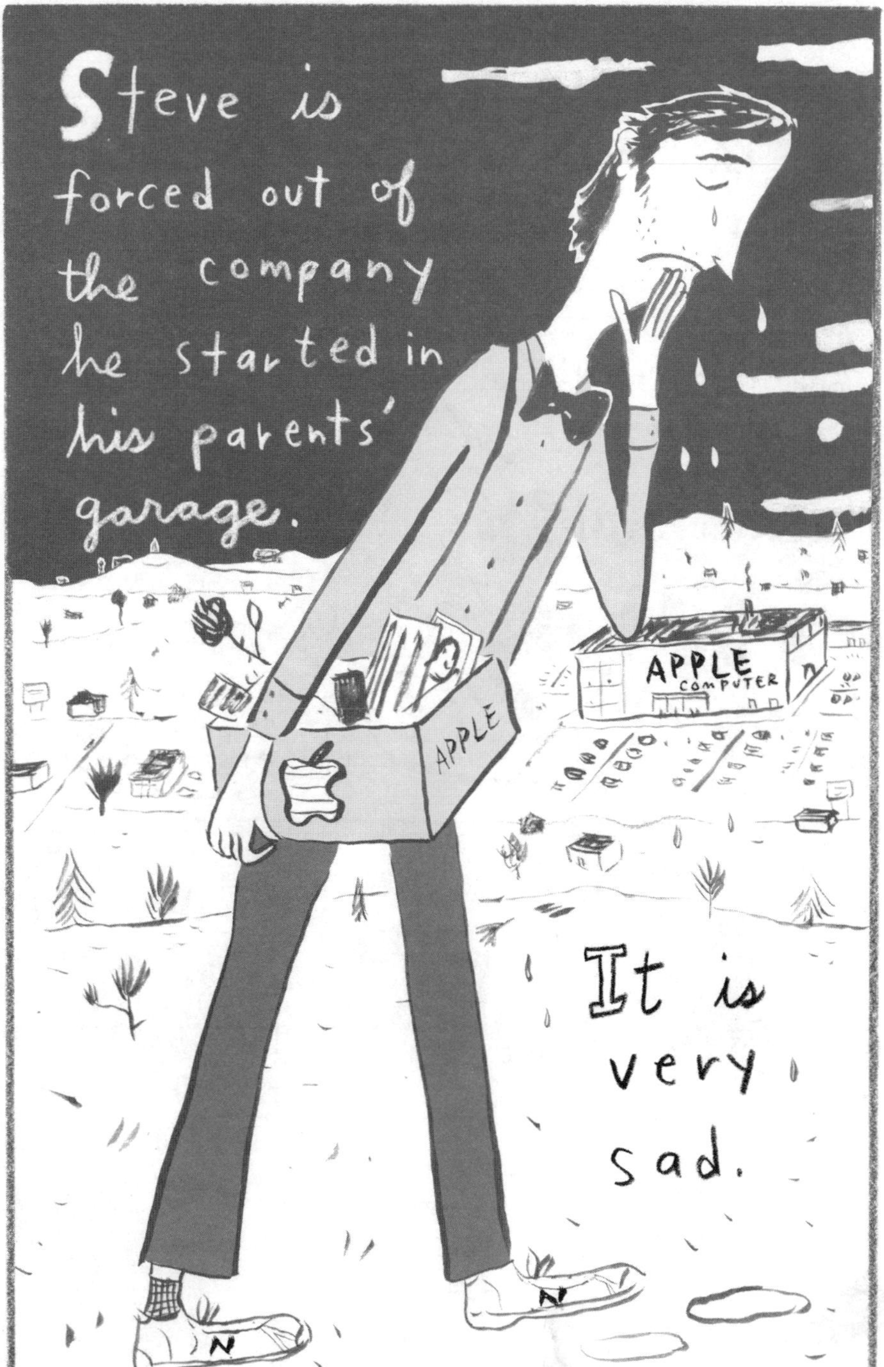
Steve is forced out of the company he started in his parents' garage.
APPLE COMPUTER
APPLE
It is very sad.

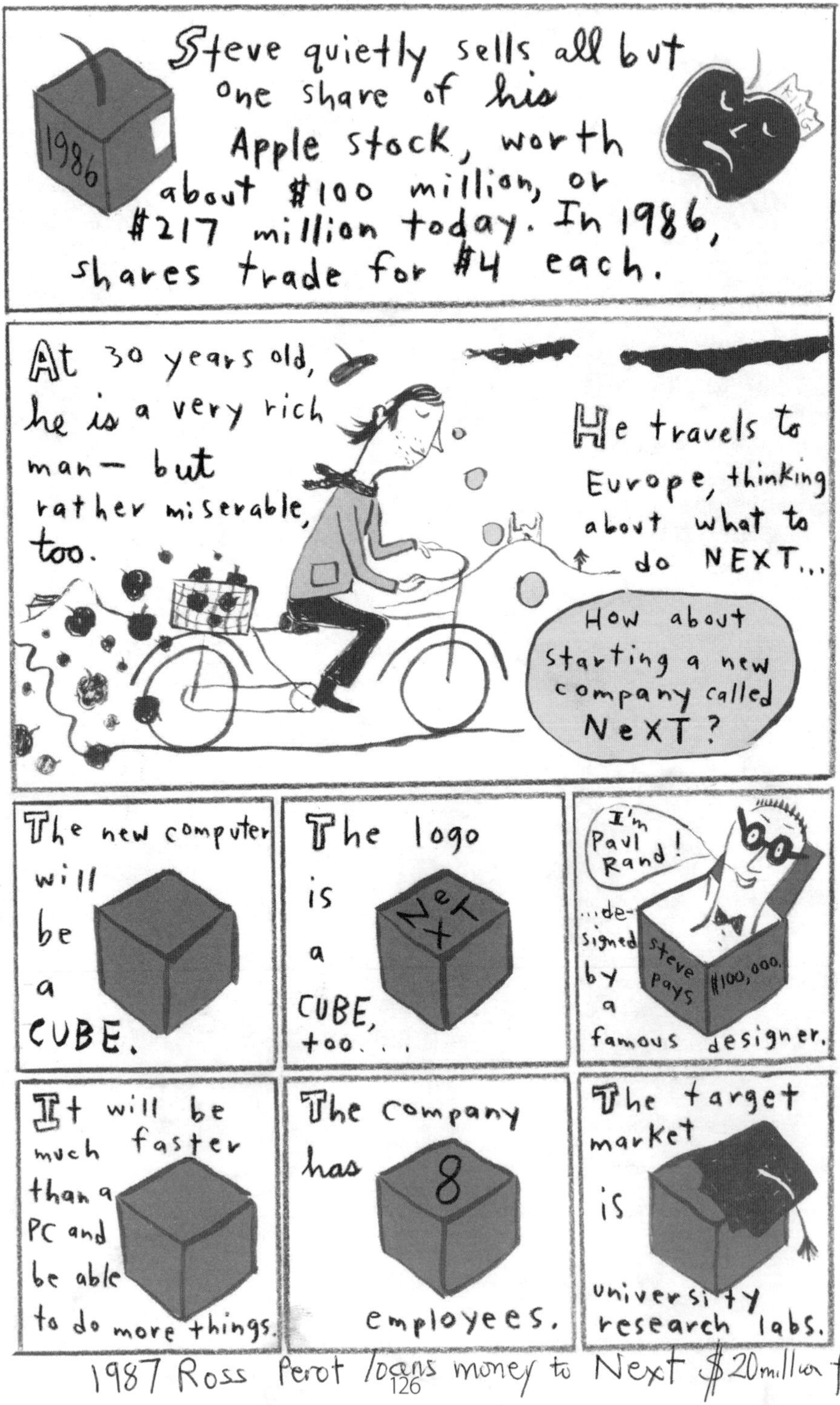
1986
Steve quietly sells all but one share of his Apple stock, worth about $100 million, or $217 million today. In 1986, shares trade for $4 each.
KING
At 30 years old, he is a very rich man— but rather miserable, too.
He travels to Europe, thinking about what to do NEXT...
How about starting a new company called NeXT?
The new computer will be a CUBE.
The logo is a CUBE, too...
NeXT
I'm Paul Rand!
...designed by a famous designer.
Steve pays $100,000.
It will be much faster than a PC and be able to do more things.
The company has 8 employees.
The target market is university research labs.

1987 Ross Perot loans money to Next $20million for/

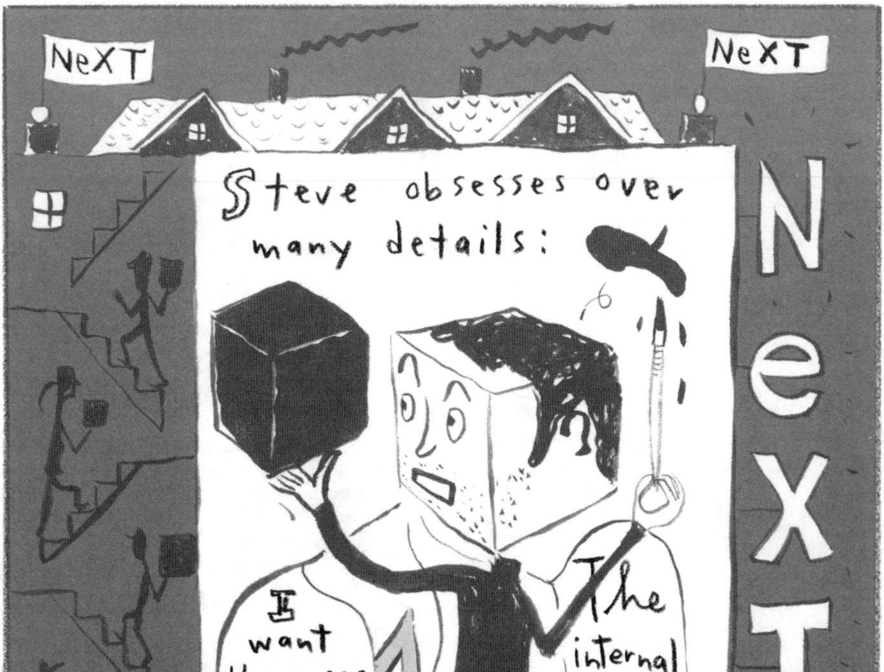

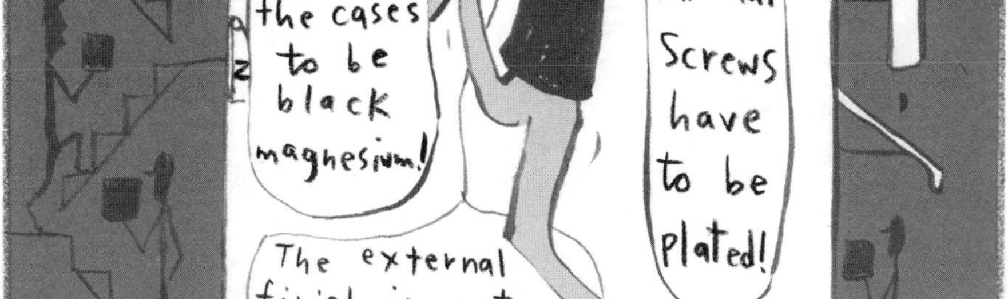

1989 Cannon invest $100 million for 16% stake

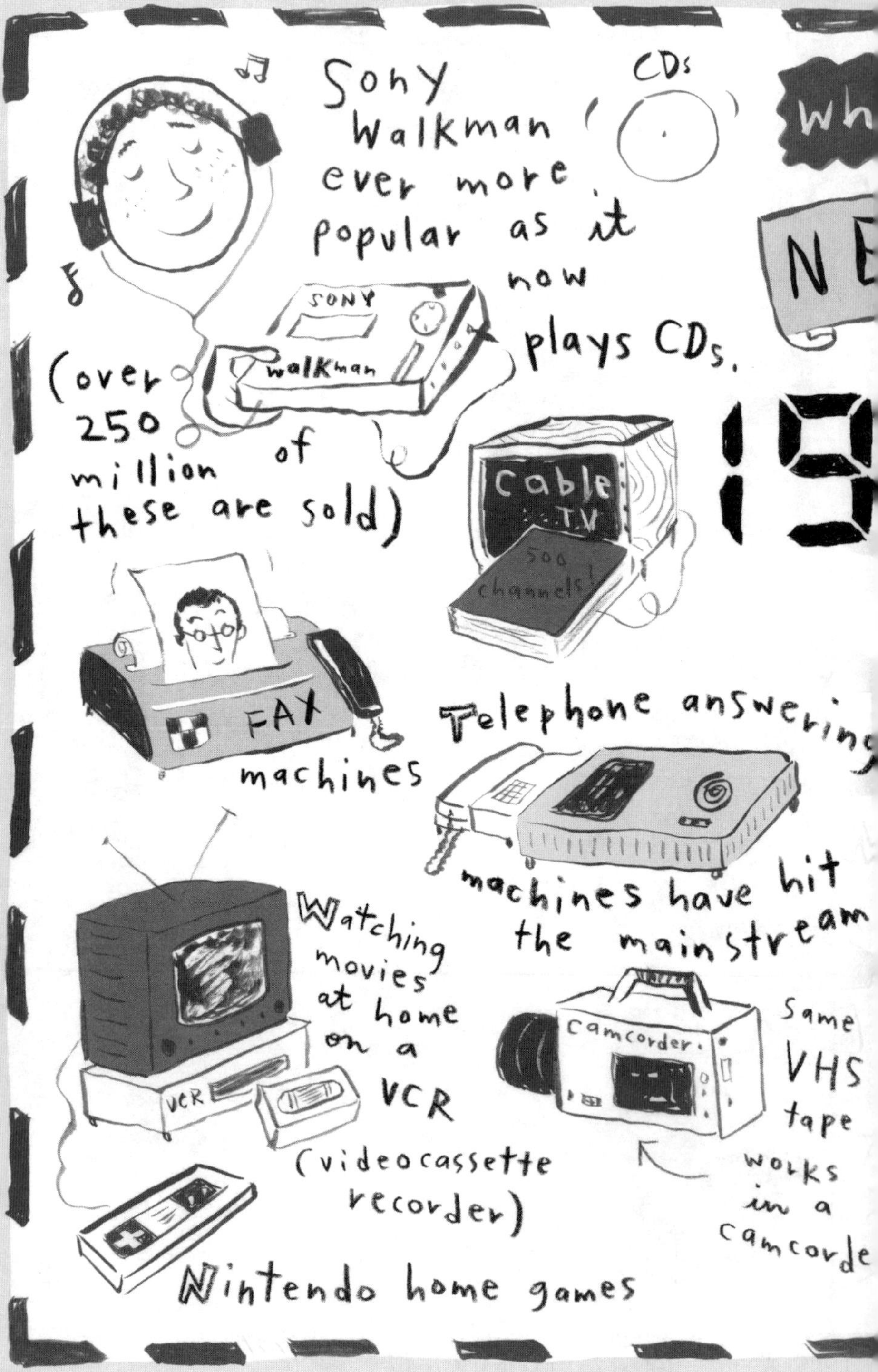
Sony Walkman ever more popular as it now plays CDs.
CDs
(over 250 million of these are sold)
SONY
walkman
Wh
NE
19
Cable TV
500 channels!
FAX machines
Telephone answering machines have hit the mainstream
Watching movies at home on a VCR
(videocassette recorder)
VCR
camcorder.
Same VHS tape works in a camcorde
Nintendo home games

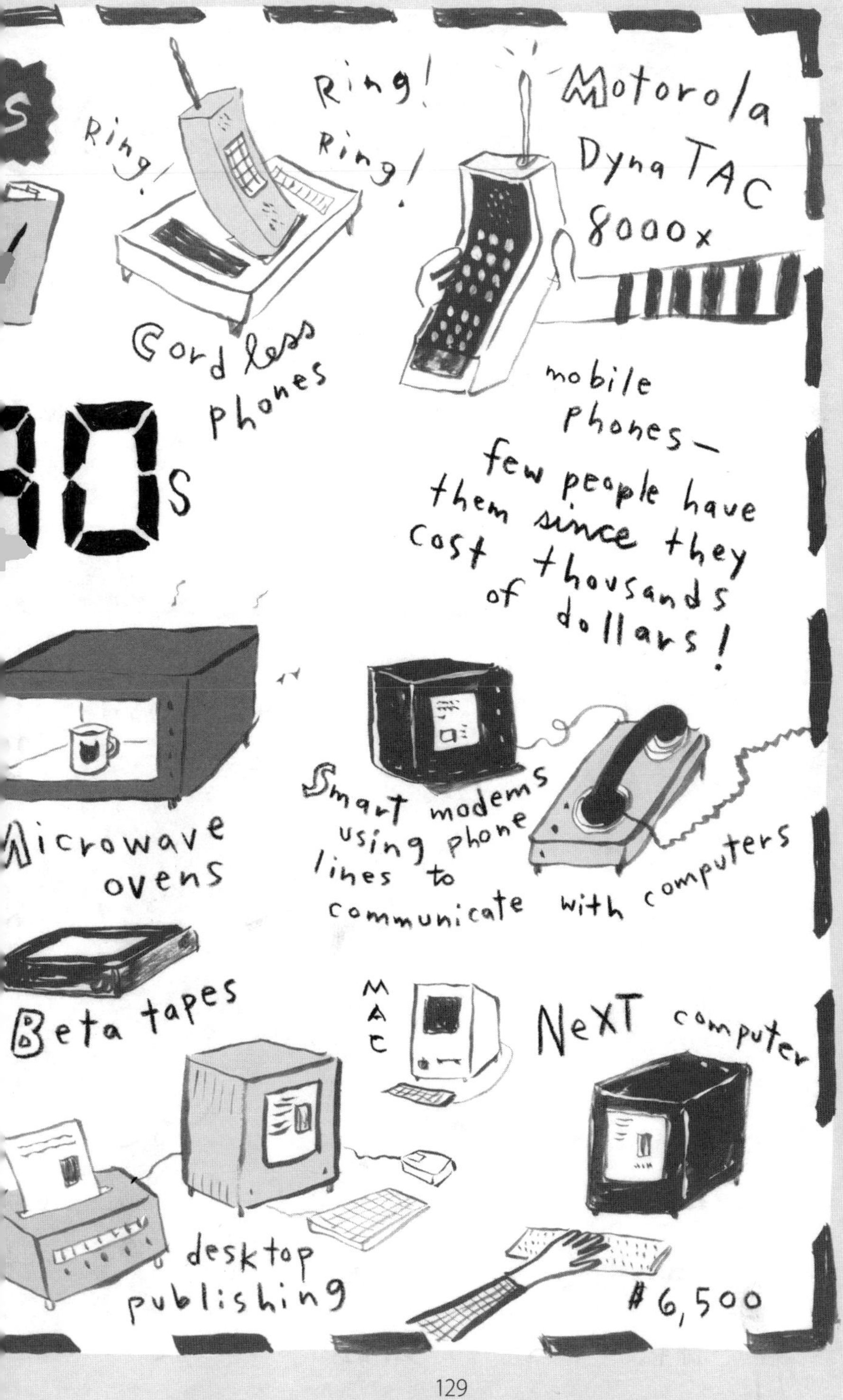
Ring!
Ring!
Ring!
Motorola DynaTAC 8000x
Cordless phones
80s
mobile phones— few people have them since they cost thousands of dollars!
Microwave ovens
Smart modems using phone lines to communicate with computers
Beta tapes
MAC
NeXT computer
desktop publishing
$6,500

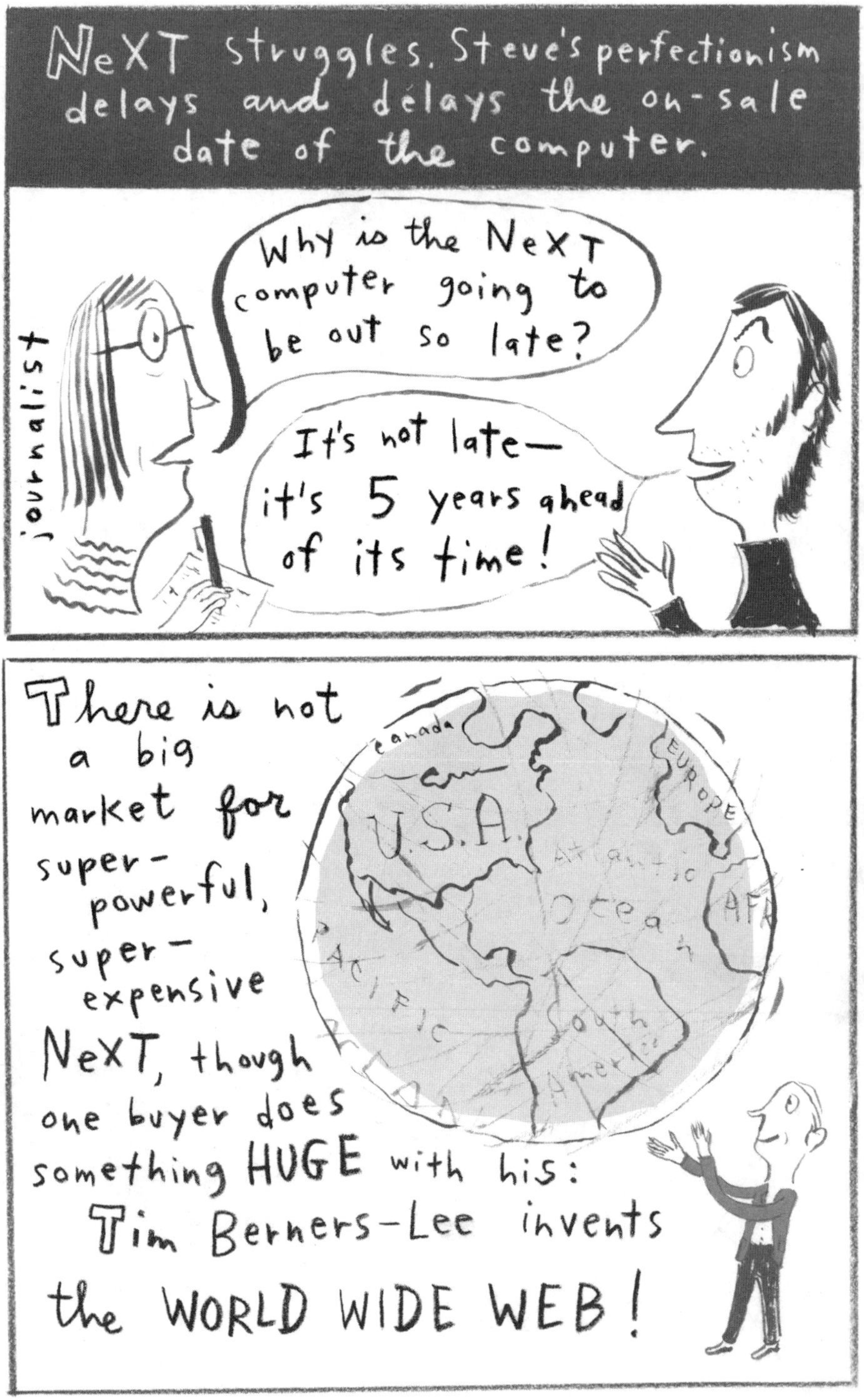
NeXT struggles. Steve's perfectionism delays and delays the on-sale date of the computer.
journalist
Why is the NeXT computer going to be out so late?
It's not late— it's 5 years ahead of its time!
There is not a big market for super-powerful, super-expensive NeXT, though one buyer does something HUGE with his: Tim Berners-Lee invents the WORLD WIDE WEB!
Canada
EUROPE
U.S.A.
Atlantic Ocean
AFR
PACIFIC
South America

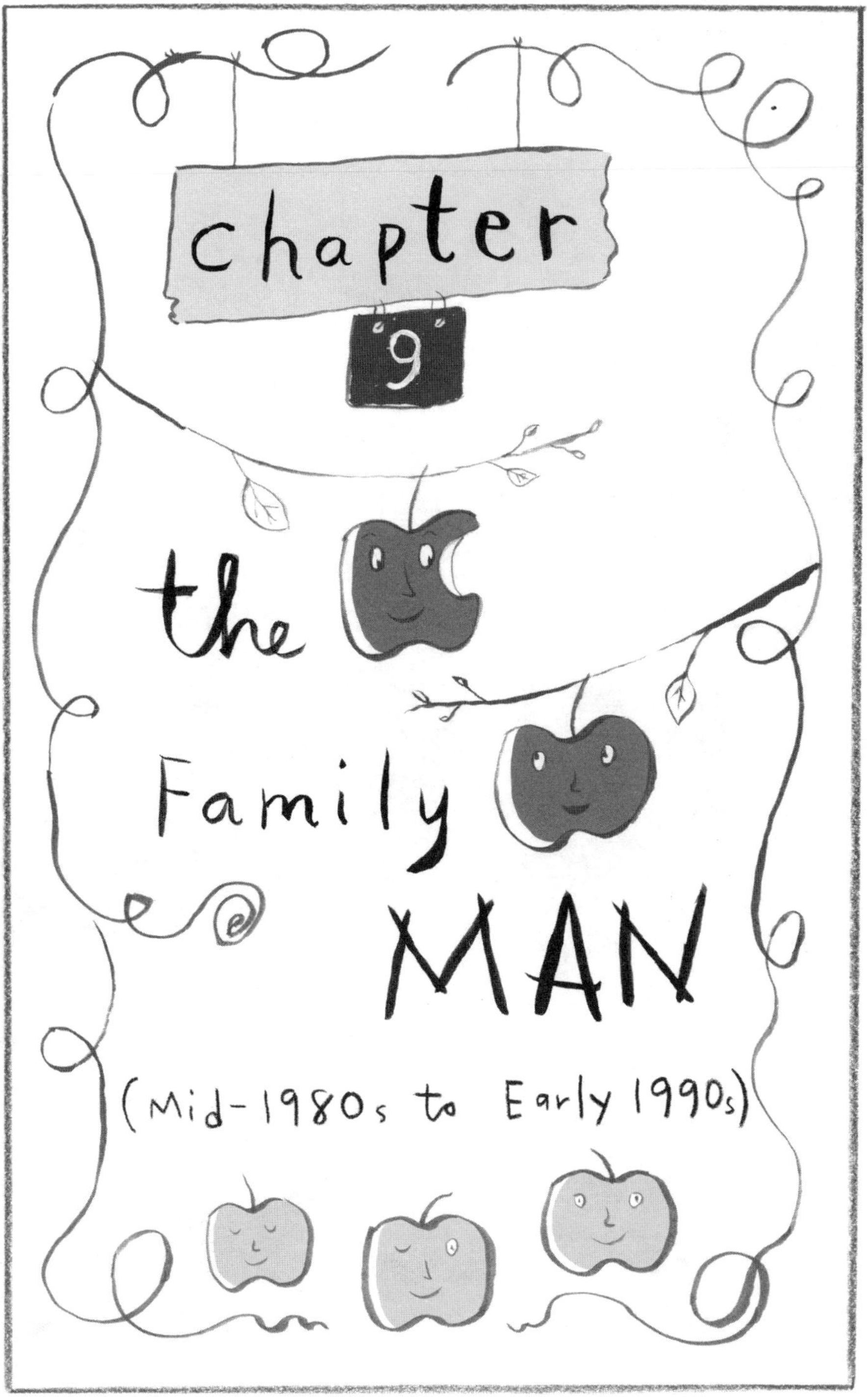
chapter
9
the Family MAN
(Mid-1980s to Early 1990s)

Like many people who have been adopted, Steve becomes curious about his BIOLOGICAL parents. He is now 31.

Yes, Detective— I know I was born in San Francisco in 1955 and...

I found your mother. Her name is Joanne Simpson and she lives in L.A.

Steve flies down to meet her.

And you have a sister.

No kidding!

She's a writer named Mona Simpson and she lives in NYC.

MUSTARD RELISH

TAIL o' the PUP

FRANKS ONIONS

I'd like to meet her, too! She's an artist!

132

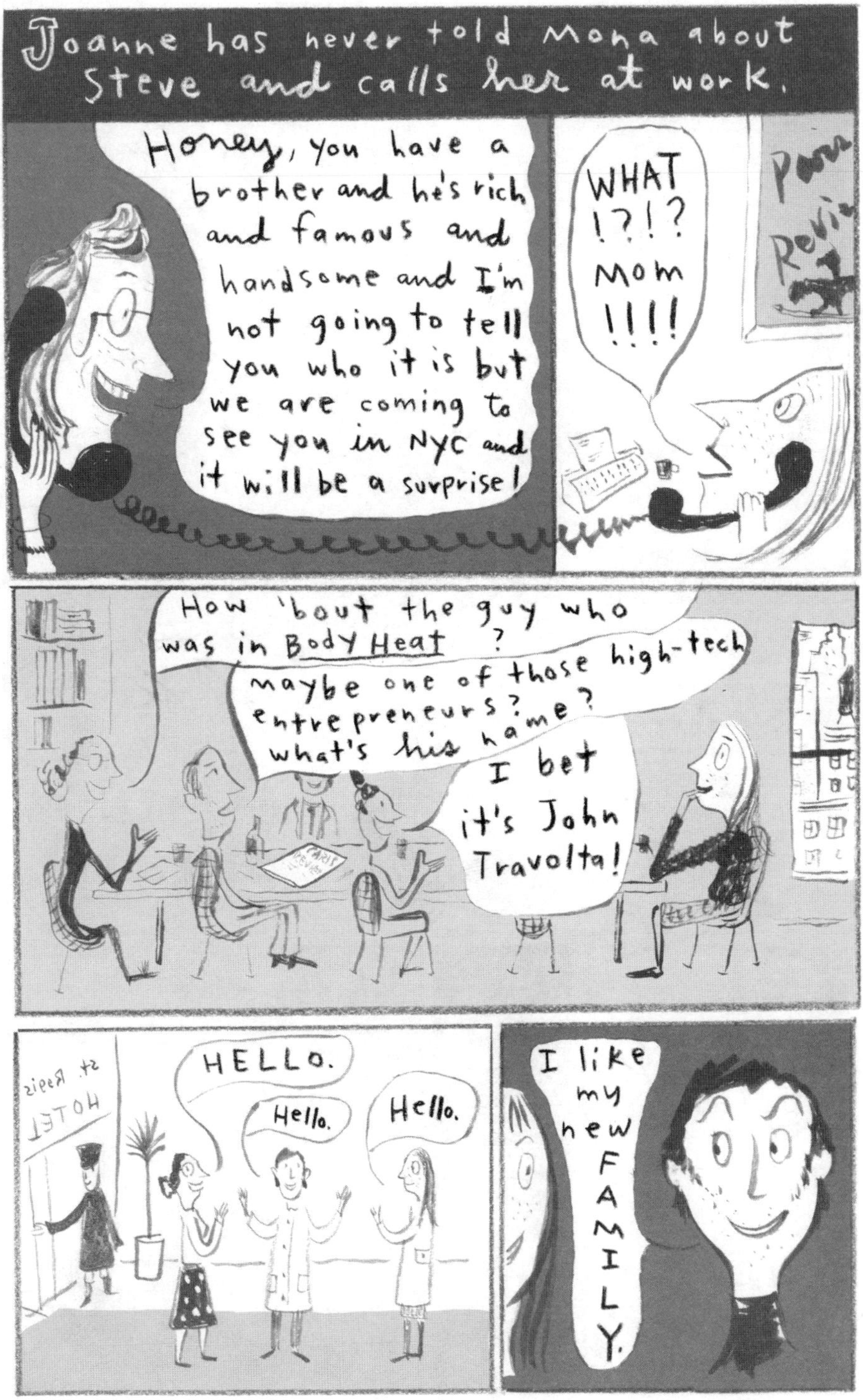

Joanne has never told Mona about Steve and calls her at work.
Honey, you have a brother and he's rich and famous and handsome and I'm not going to tell you who it is but we are coming to see you in NYC and it will be a surprise!
WHAT !?!? MOM !!!!
How 'bout the guy who was in Body Heat ?
maybe one of those high-tech entrepreneurs? what's his name?
I bet it's John Travolta!
HELLO.
Hello.
Hello.
St. Regis HOTEL
I like my new FAMILY.

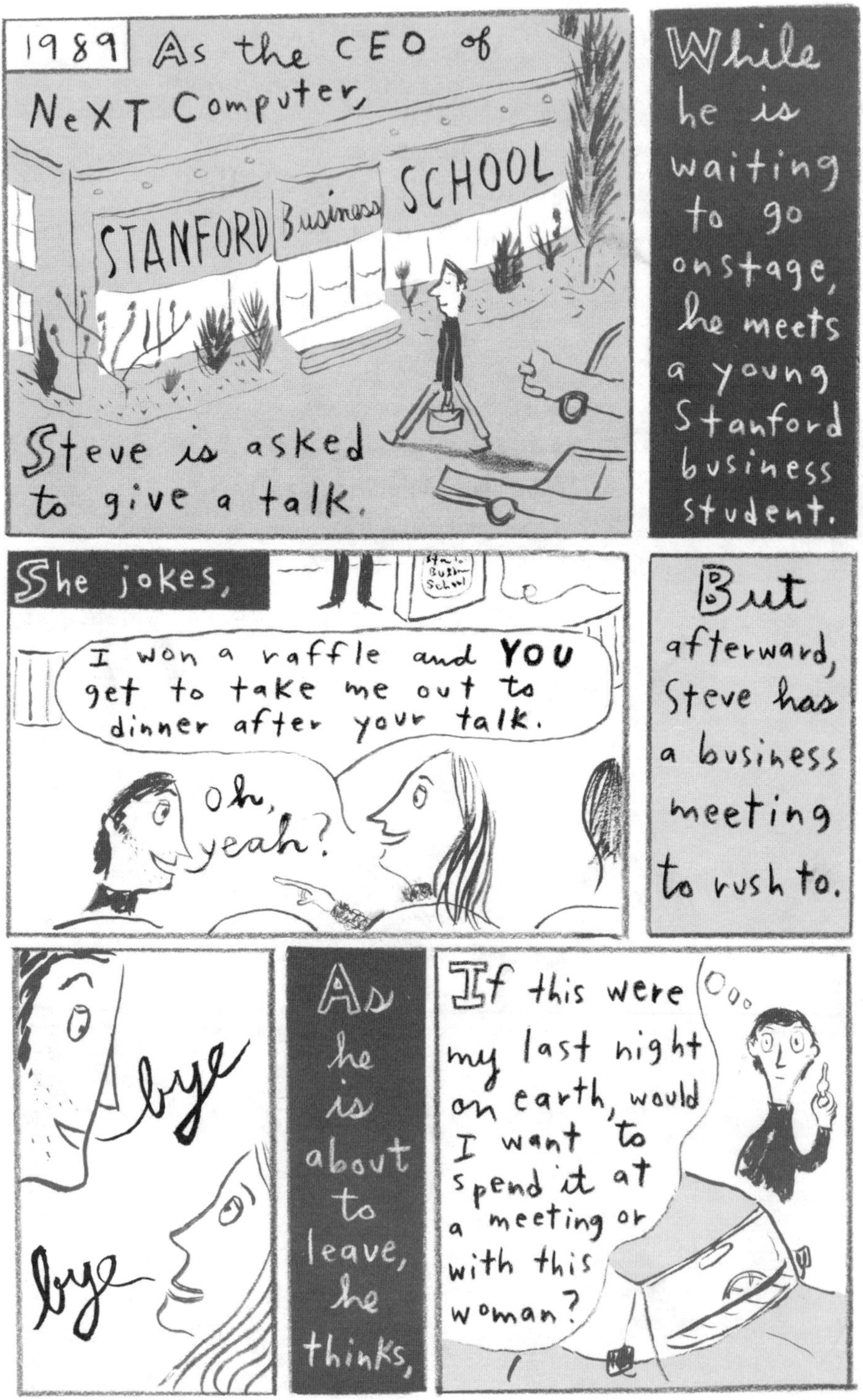
1989
As the CEO of NeXT Computer,
STANFORD Business SCHOOL
Steve is asked to give a talk.
While he is waiting to go onstage, he meets a young Stanford business student.
She jokes,
I won a raffle and YOU get to take me out to dinner after your talk.
Oh, yeah?
But afterward, Steve has a business meeting to rush to.
bye
bye
As he is about to leave, he thinks,
If this were my last night on earth, would I want to spend it at a meeting or with this woman?

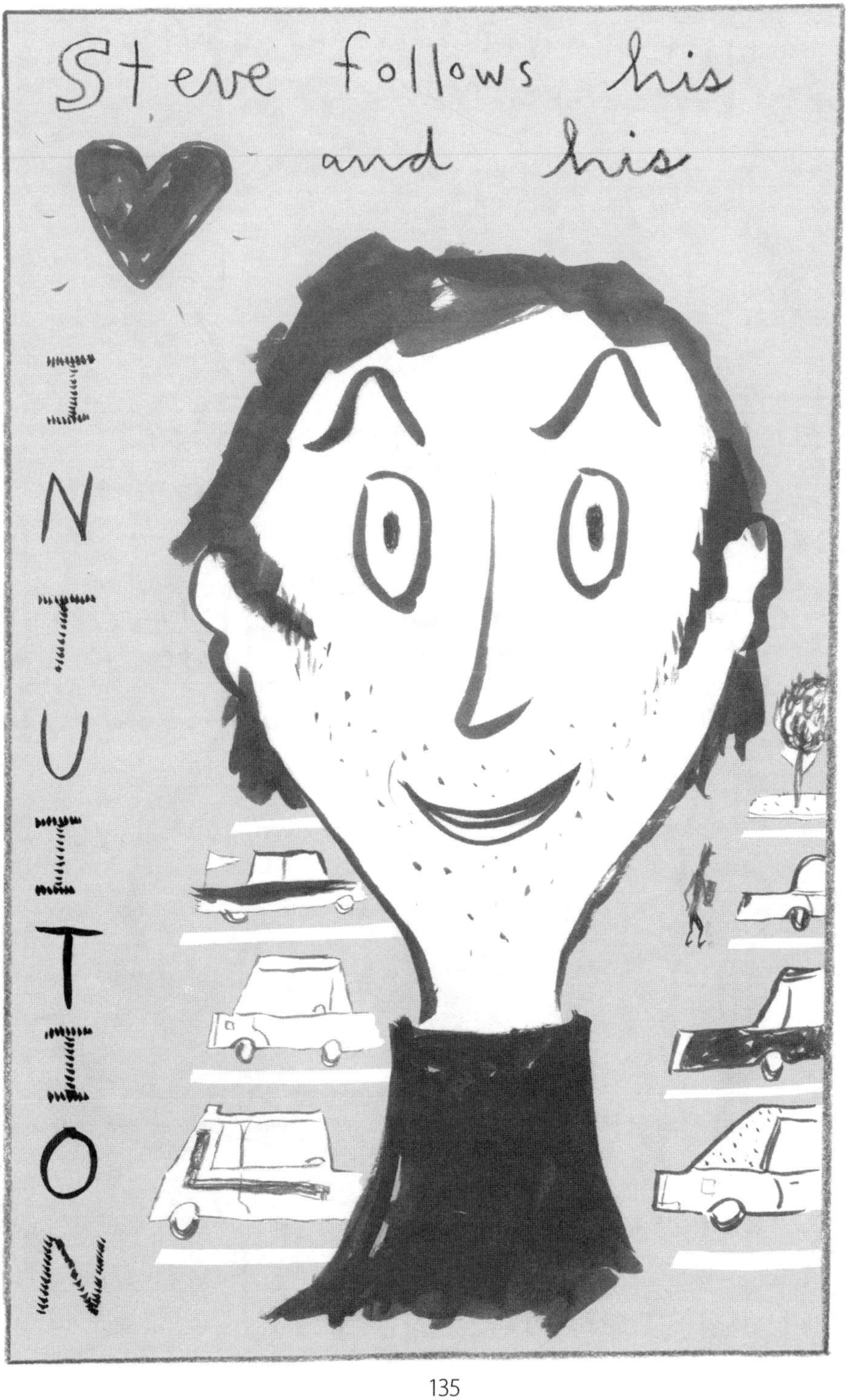
Steve follows his
and his
INTUITION

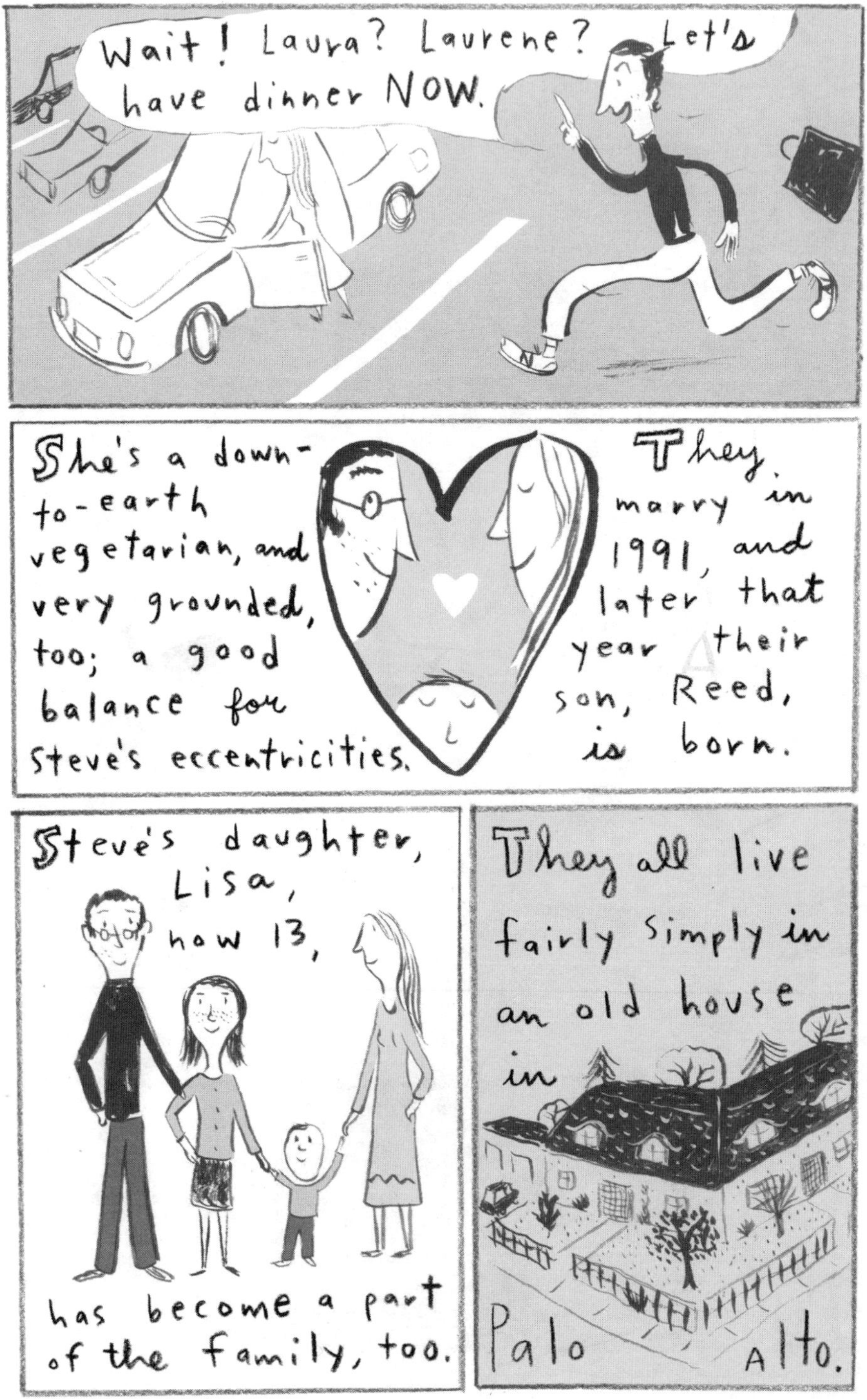
Wait! Laura? Laurene? Let's have dinner NOW.
She's a down-to-earth vegetarian, and very grounded, too; a good balance for Steve's eccentricities.
They marry in 1991, and later that year their son, Reed, is born.
Steve's daughter, Lisa, now 13,
has become a part of the family, too.
They all live fairly simply in an old house in
Palo Alto.

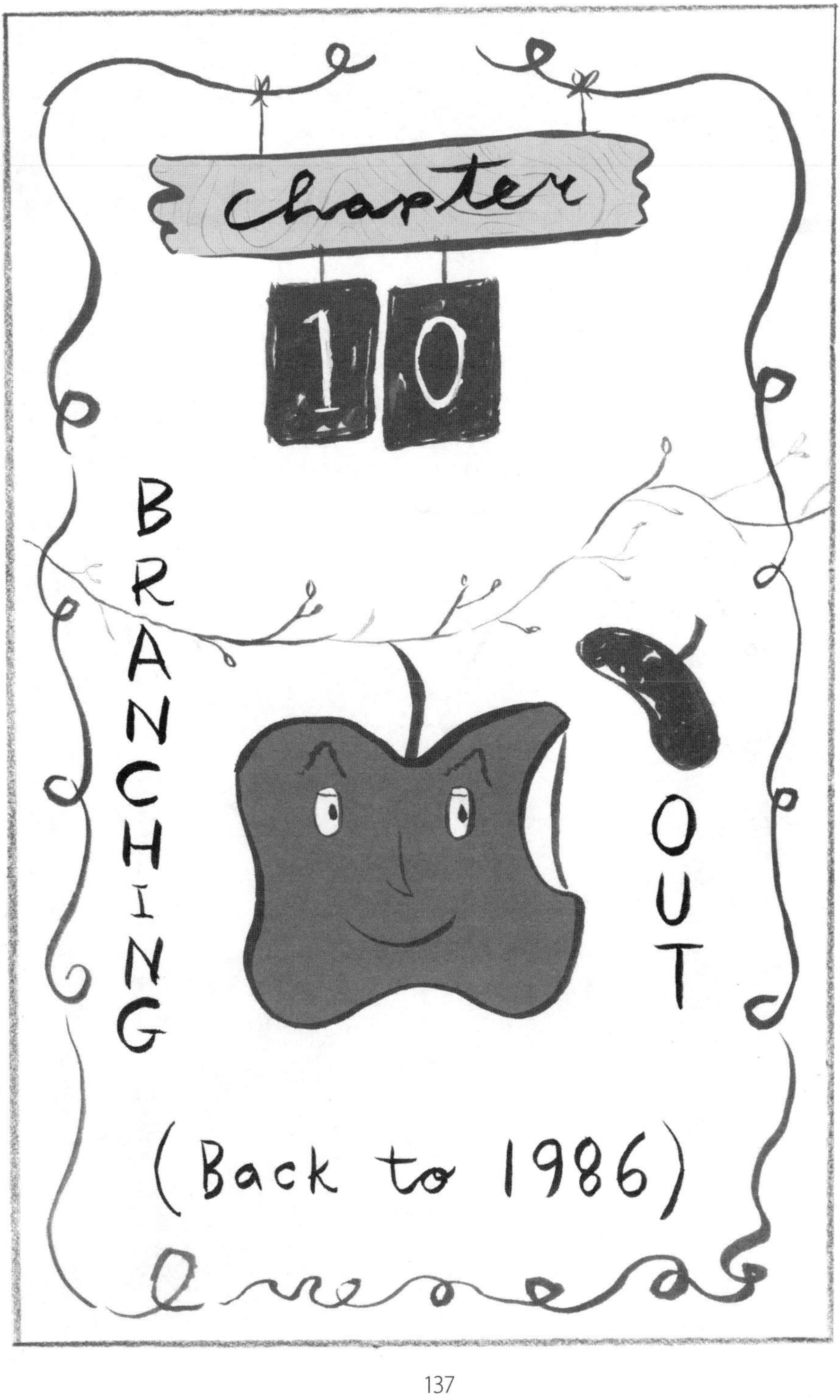
Chapter
10
BRANCHING
OUT
(Back to 1986)

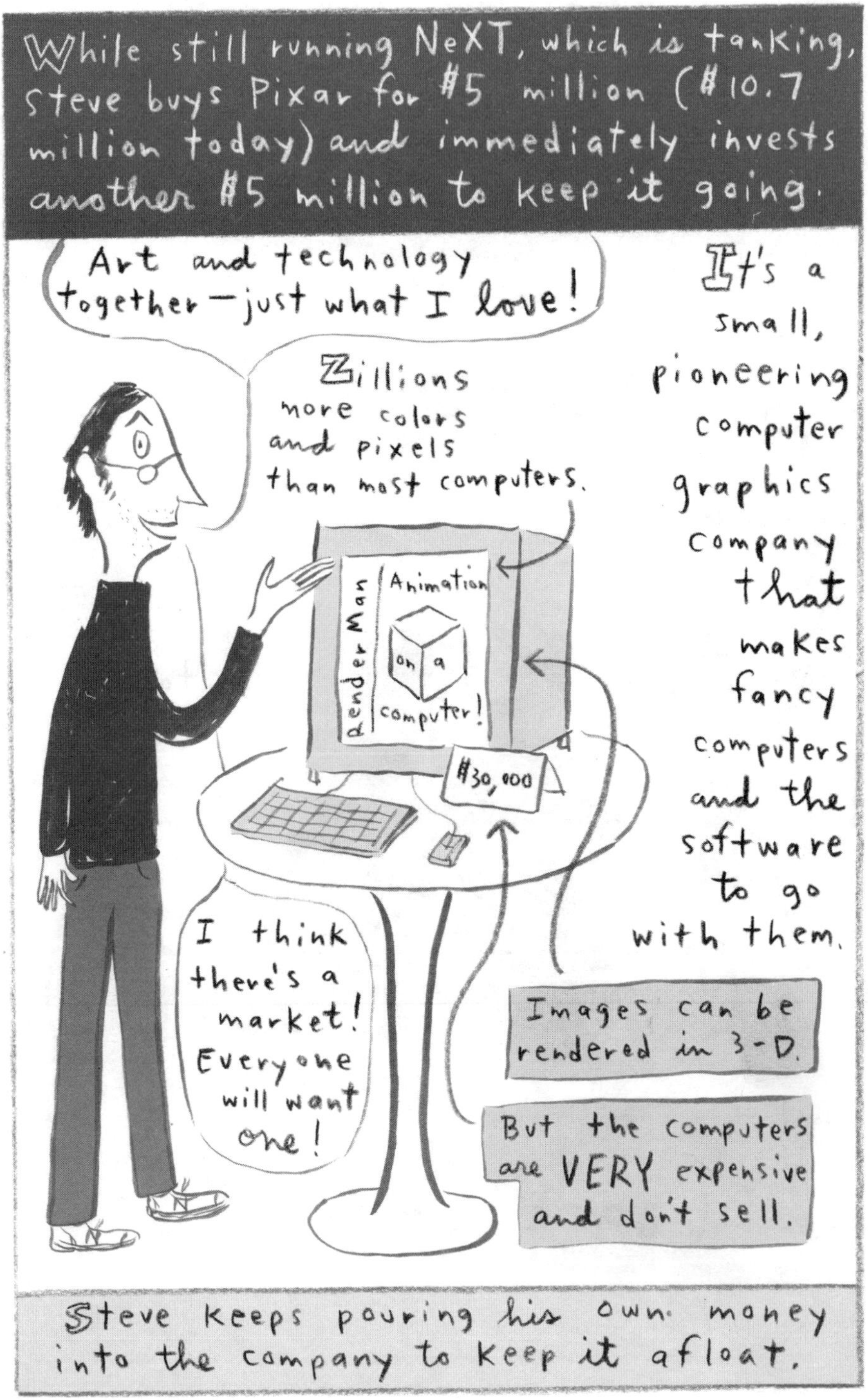
While still running NeXT, which is tanking, Steve buys Pixar for $5 million ($10.7 million today) and immediately invests another $5 million to keep it going.
Art and technology together—just what I love!
It's a small, pioneering computer graphics company that makes fancy computers and the software to go with them.
Zillions more colors and pixels than most computers.
RenderMan
Animation on a computer!
$30,000
I think there's a market! Everyone will want one!
Images can be rendered in 3-D.
But the computers are VERY expensive and don't sell.
Steve keeps pouring his own money into the company to keep it afloat.

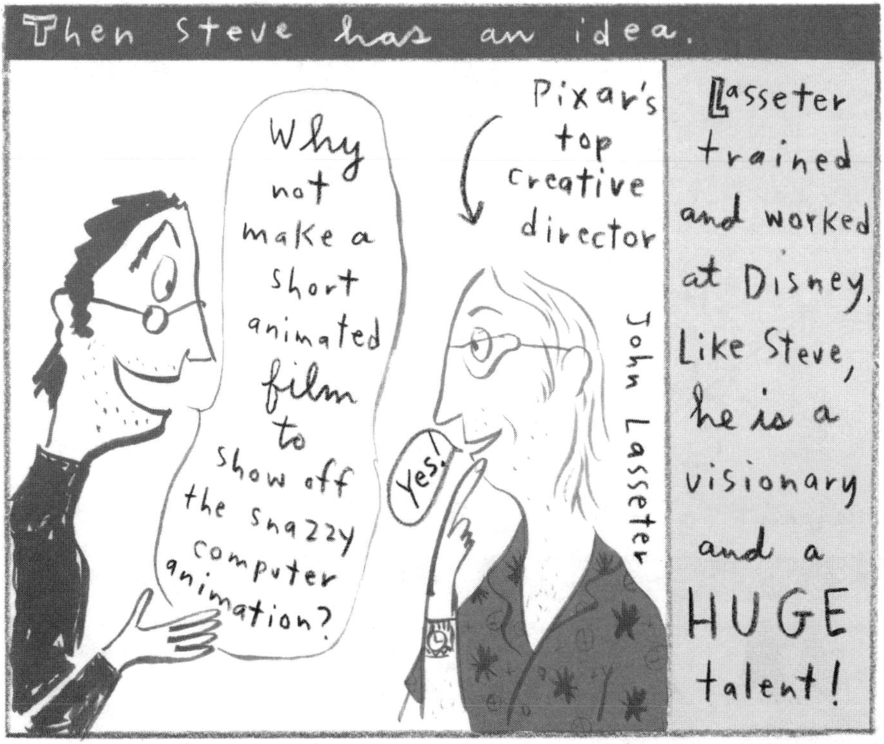
Then Steve has an idea.
Why not make a short animated film to show off the snazzy computer animation?
Yes!
Pixar's top creative director
John Lasseter
Lasseter trained and worked at Disney. Like Steve, he is a visionary and a HUGE talent!

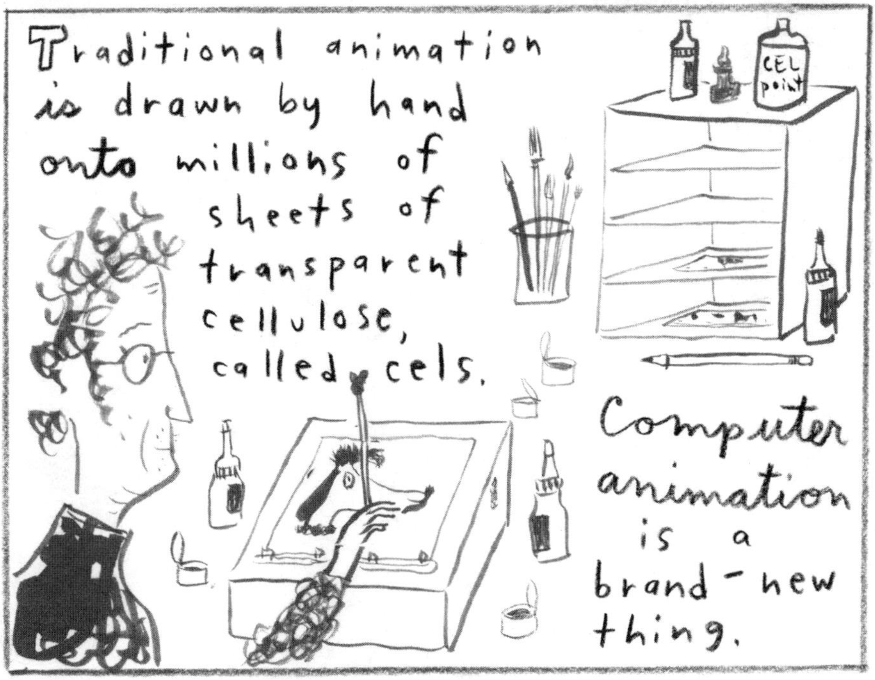
Traditional animation is drawn by hand onto millions of sheets of transparent cellulose, called cels.
CEL paint
Computer animation is a brand-new thing.

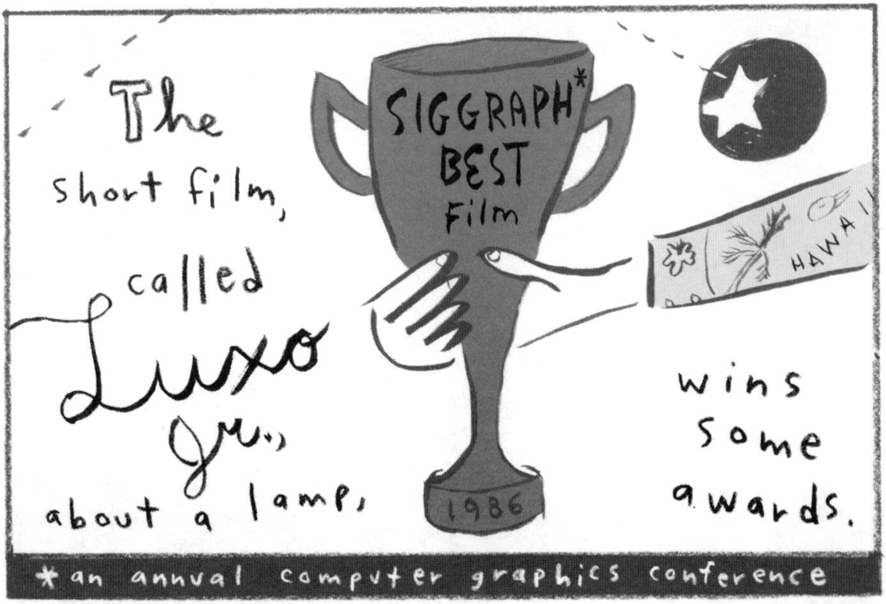
The short film, called Luxo Jr., about a lamp,
SIGGRAPH* BEST Film
1986
HAWAII
wins some awards.
*an annual computer graphics conference

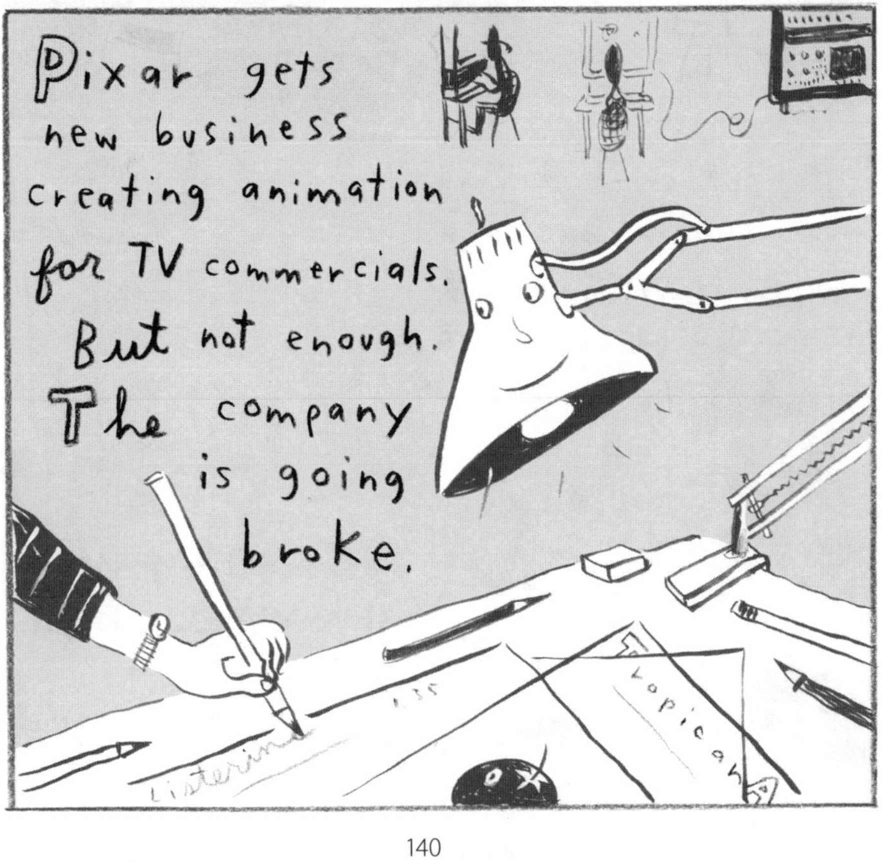
Pixar gets new business creating animation for TV commercials. But not enough. The company is going broke.

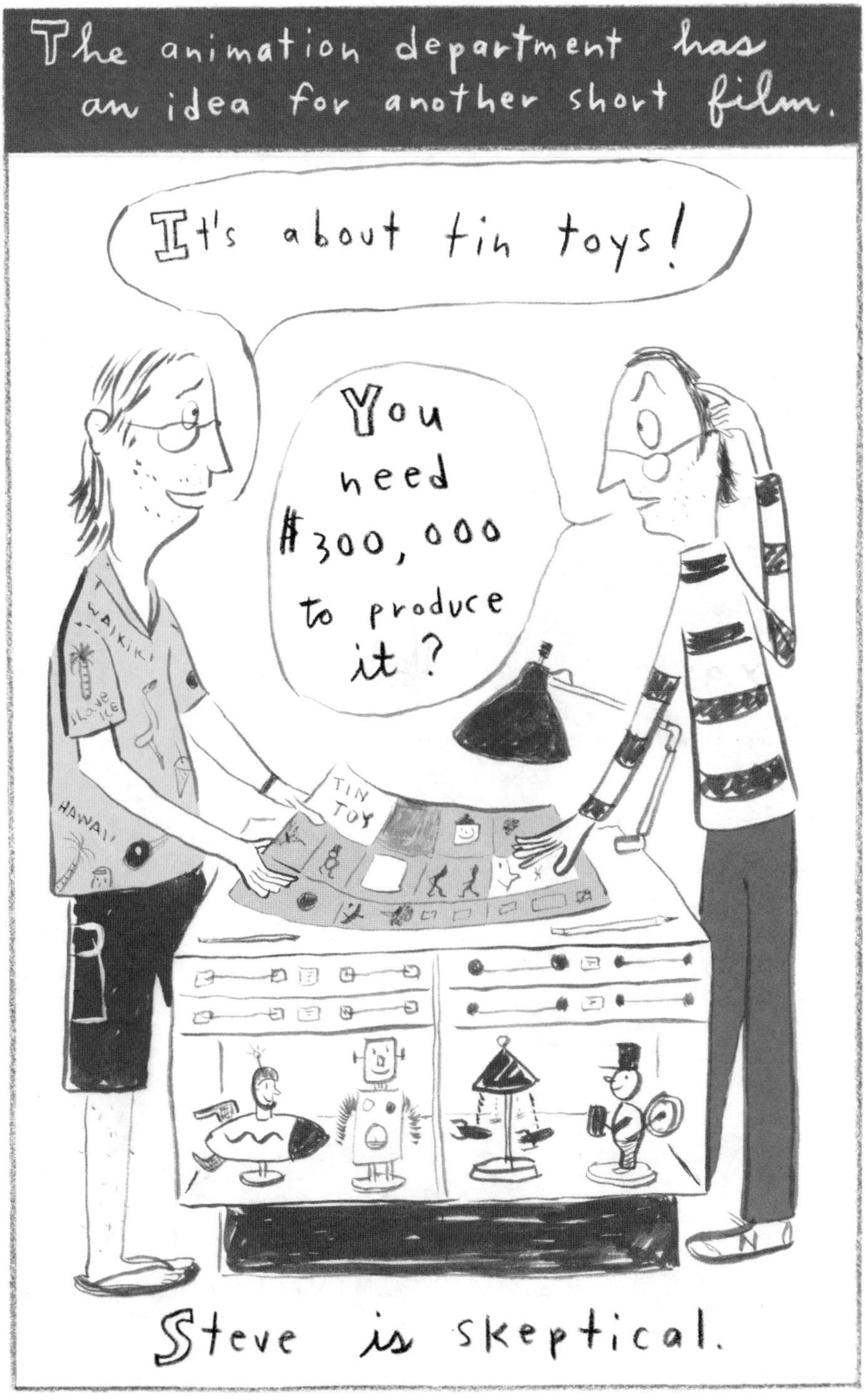
The animation department has an idea for another short film.
It's about tin toys!
You need $300,000 to produce it?
WAIKIKI
SHAVE ICE
HAWAII
TIN TOY
Steve is skeptical.

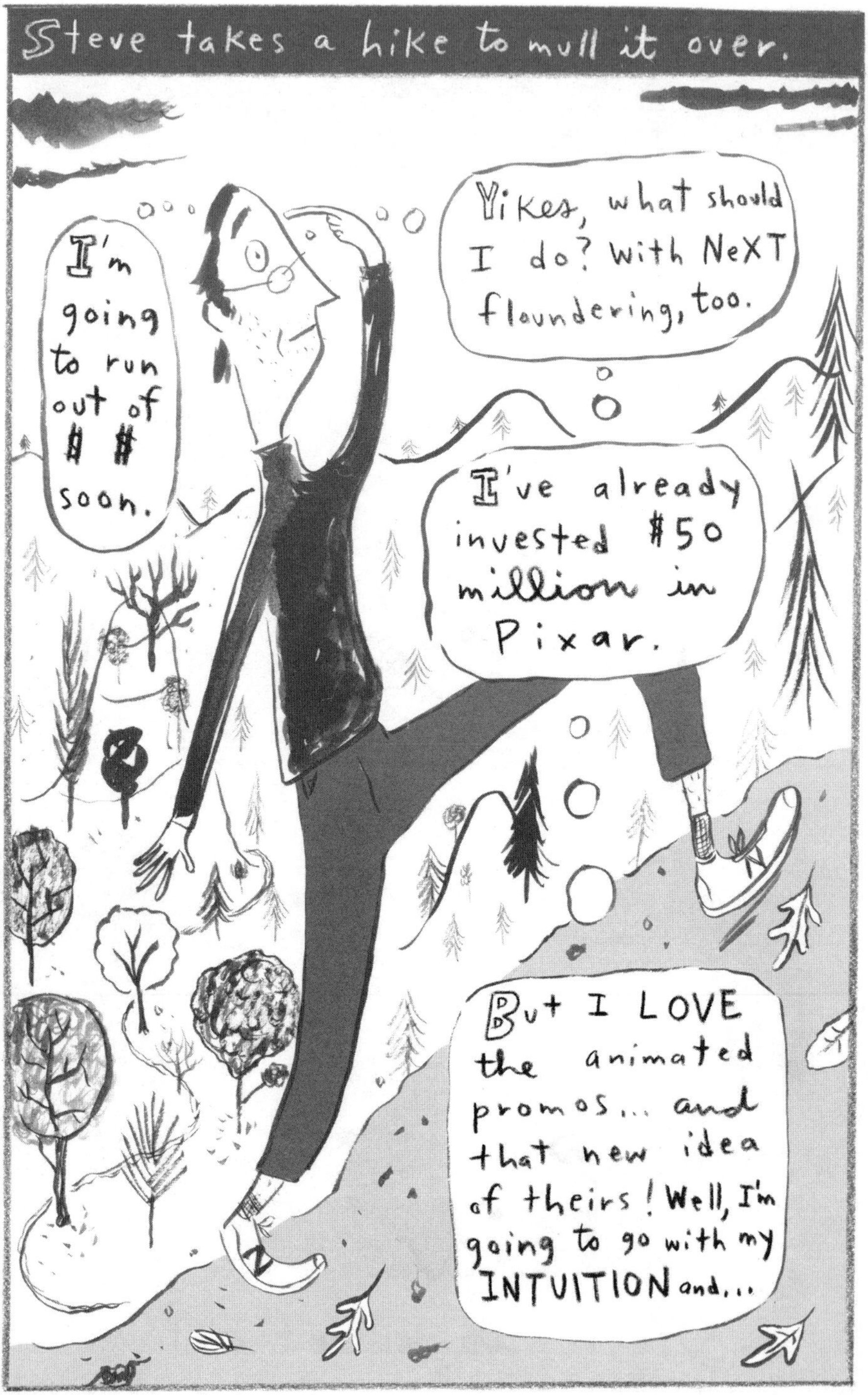

Steve takes a hike to mull it over.
I'm going to run out of $$ soon.
Yikes, what should I do? With NeXT floundering, too.
I've already invested $50 million in Pixar.
But I LOVE the animated promos... and that new idea of theirs! Well, I'm going to go with my INTUITION and...

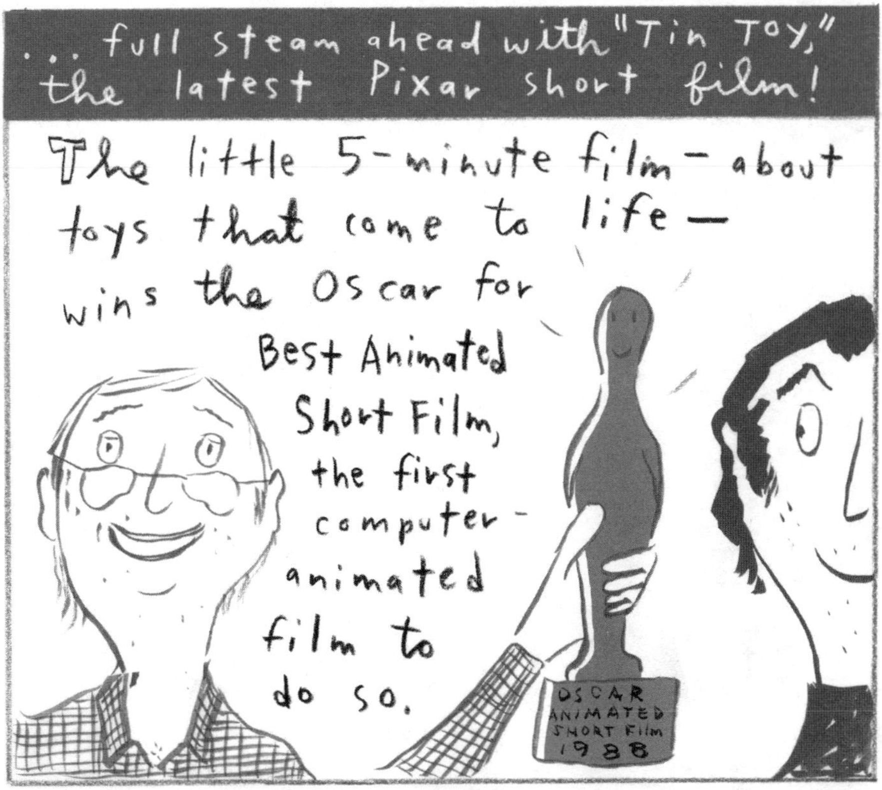
... full steam ahead with "Tin Toy," the latest Pixar short film!
The little 5-minute film – about toys that come to life – wins the Oscar for Best Animated Short Film, the first computer-animated film to do so.
OSCAR ANIMATED SHORT FILM 1988

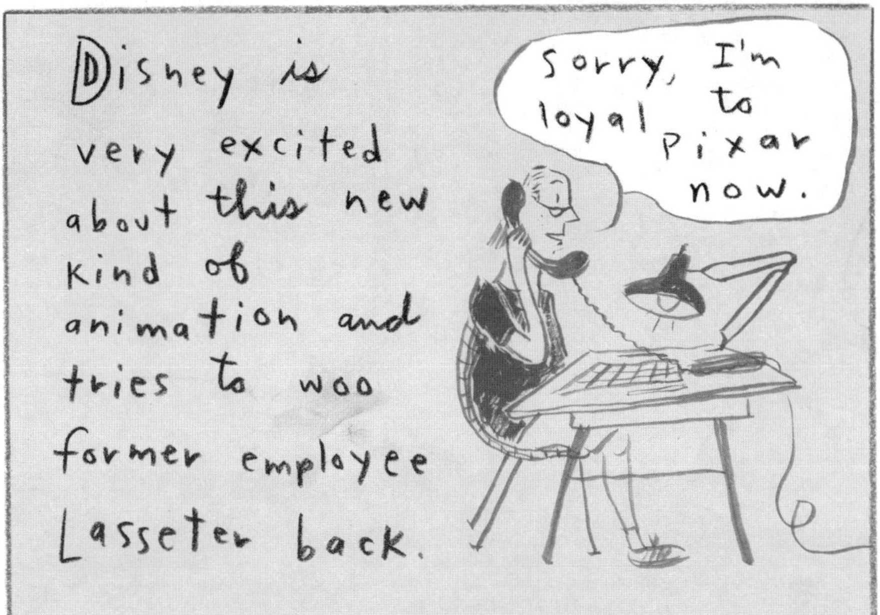
Disney is very excited about this new kind of animation and tries to woo former employee Lasseter back.
Sorry, I'm loyal to Pixar now.

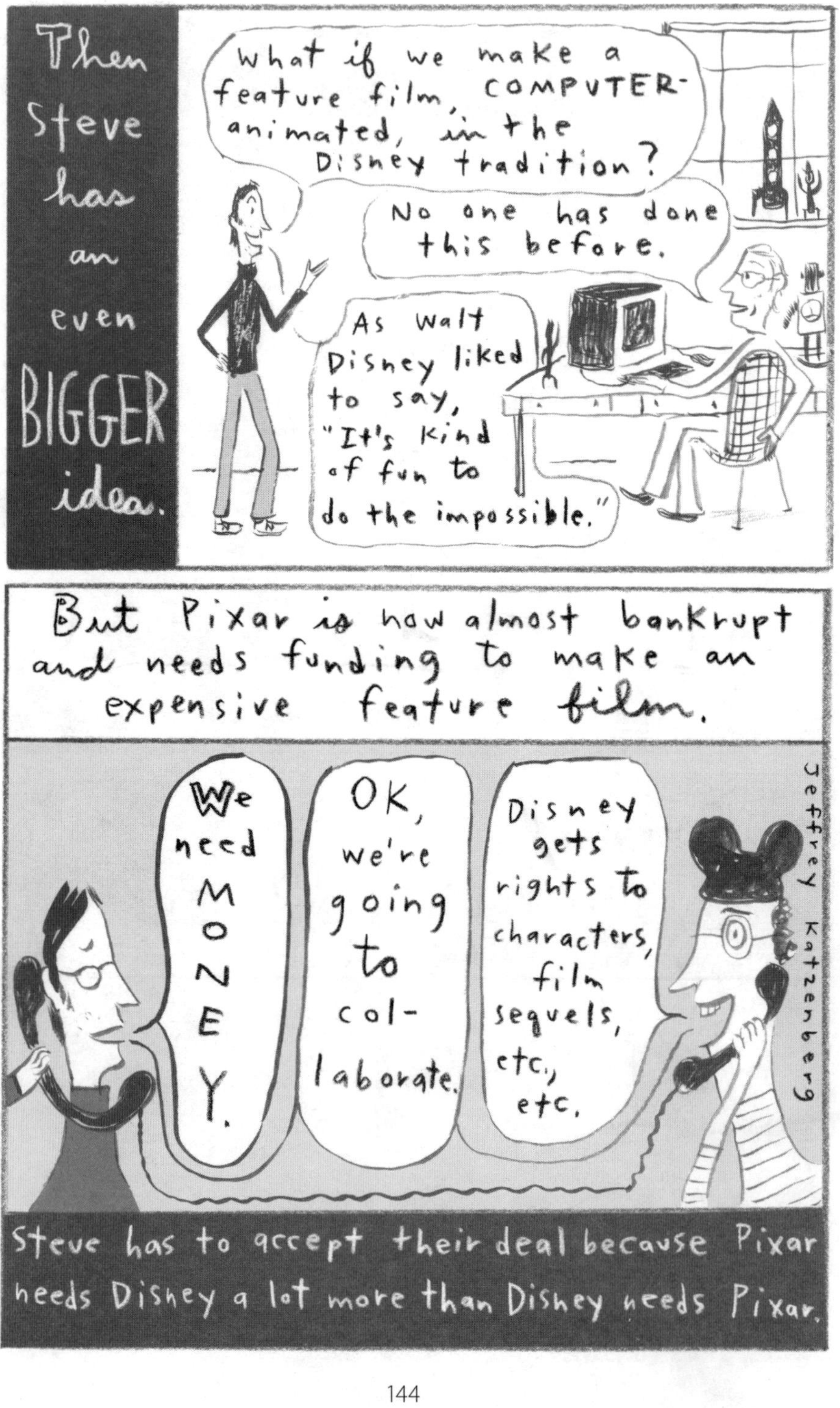
Then Steve has an even BIGGER idea.
What if we make a feature film, COMPUTER-animated, in the Disney tradition?
No one has done this before.
As Walt Disney liked to say, "It's kind of fun to do the impossible."
But Pixar is now almost bankrupt and needs funding to make an expensive feature film.
We need MONEY.
OK, we're going to col-laborate.
Disney gets rights to characters, film sequels, etc., etc.
Jeffrey Katzenberg
Steve has to accept their deal because Pixar needs Disney a lot more than Disney needs Pixar.

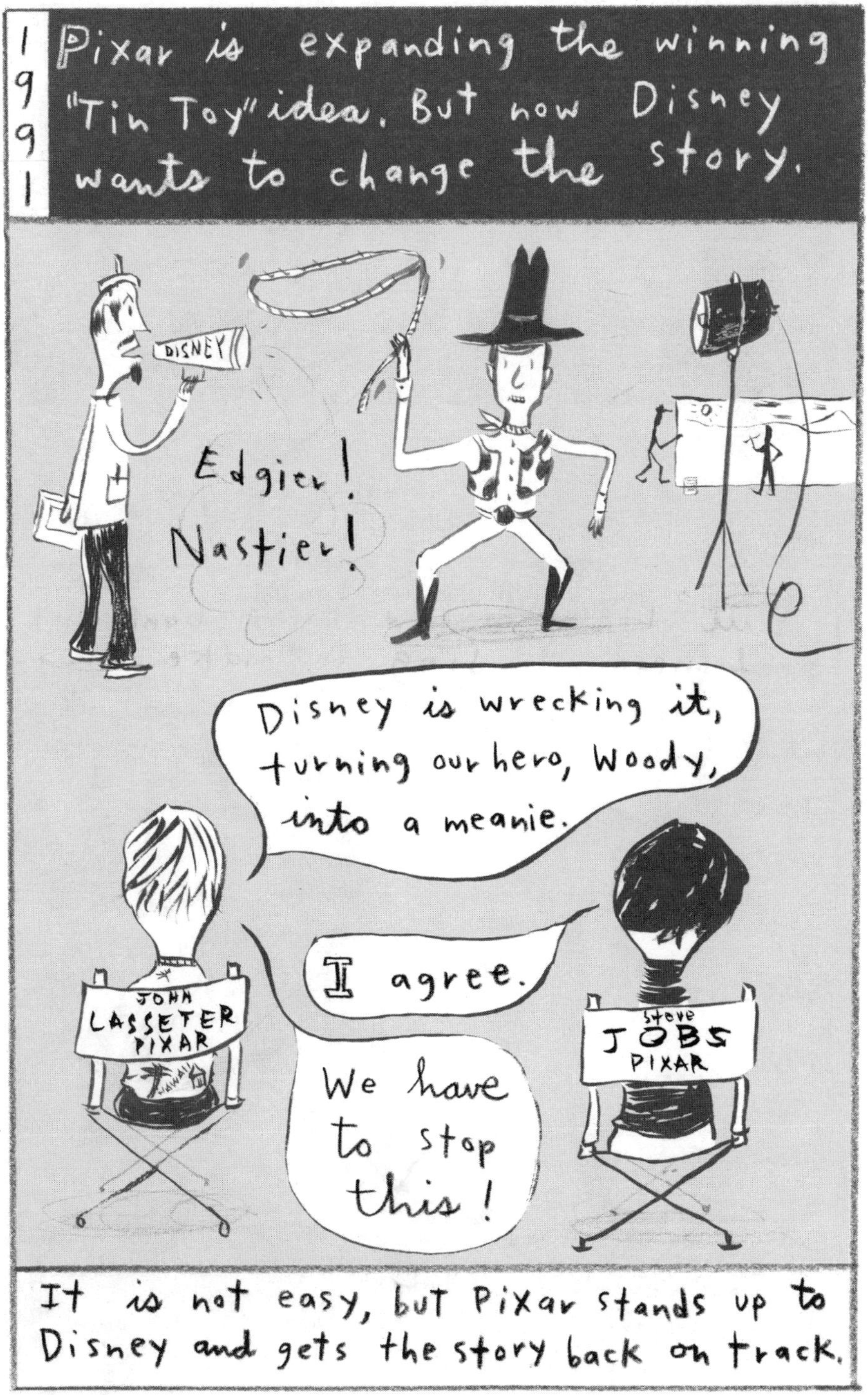
1991
Pixar is expanding the winning "Tin Toy" idea. But now Disney wants to change the story.
DISNEY
Edgier! Nastier!
Disney is wrecking it, turning our hero, Woody, into a meanie.
I agree.
We have to stop this!
JOHN LASSETER PIXAR
STEVE JOBS PIXAR
It is not easy, but Pixar stands up to Disney and gets the story back on track.

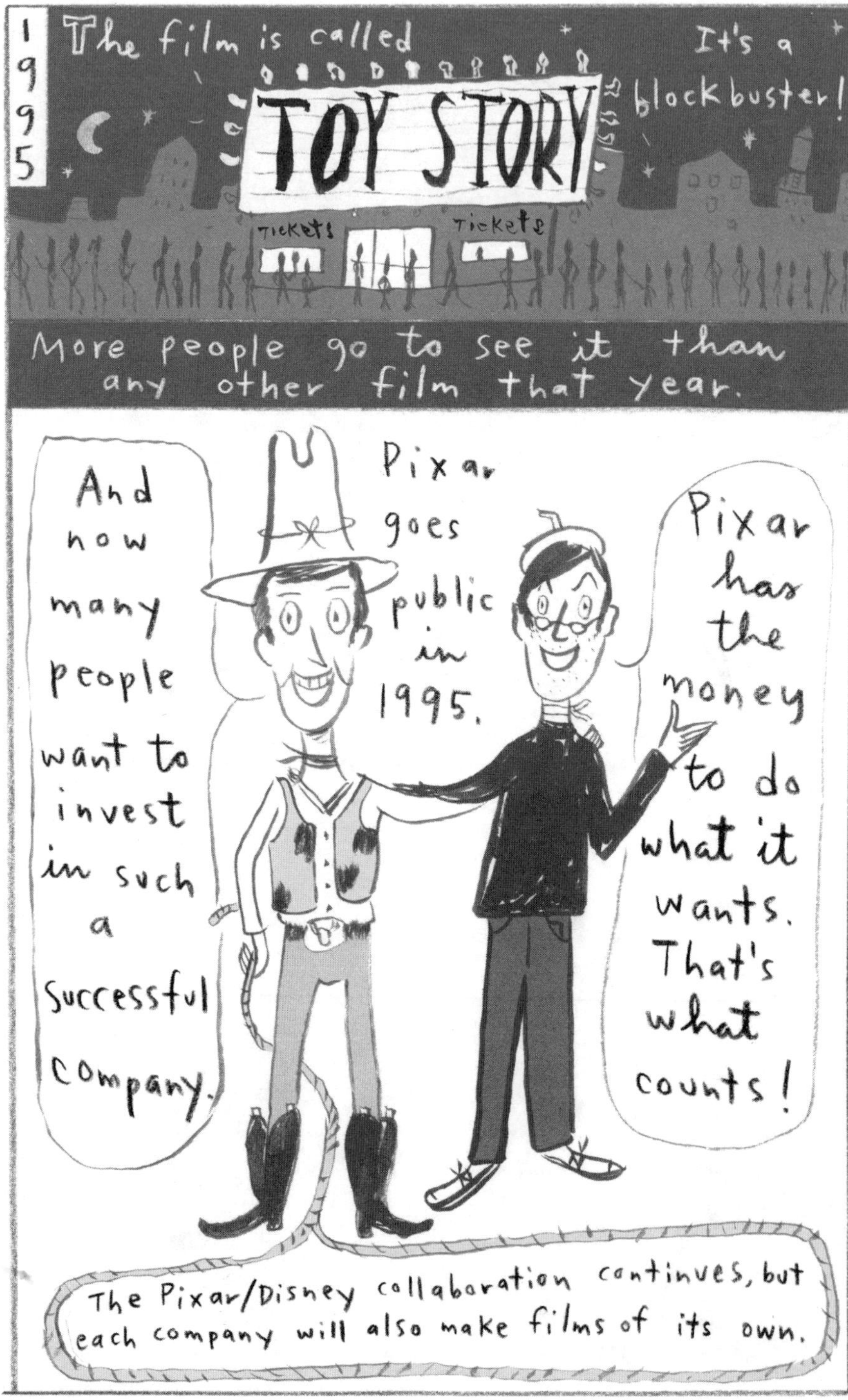
1995
The film is called
TOY STORY
It's a blockbuster!
TICKETS
TICKETS
More people go to see it than any other film that year.
And now many people want to invest in such a successful company.
Pixar goes public in 1995.
Pixar has the money to do what it wants. That's what counts!
The Pixar/Disney collaboration continues, but each company will also make films of its own.

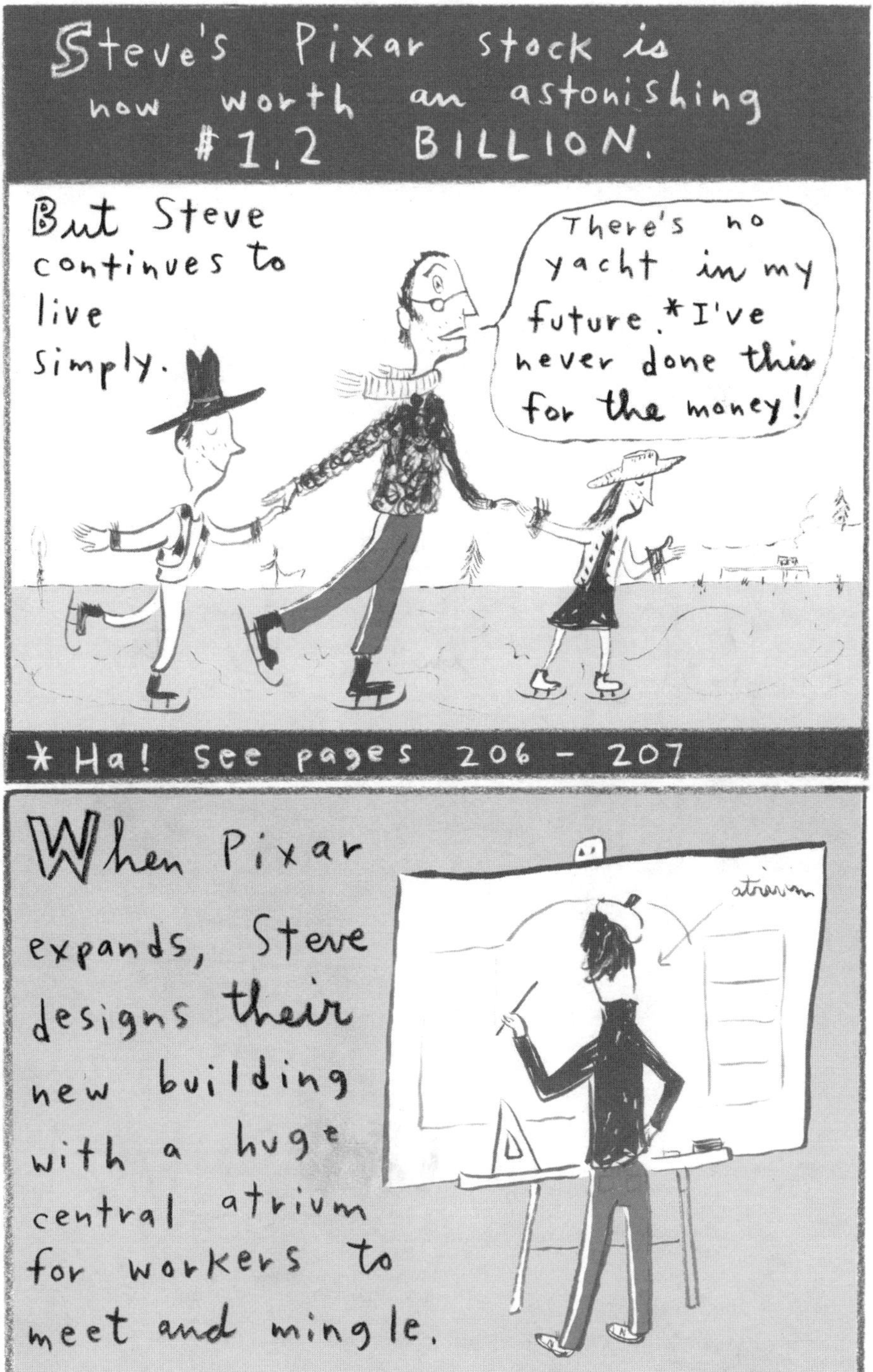
Steve's Pixar stock is now worth an astonishing $1.2 BILLION.
But Steve continues to live simply.
There's no yacht in my future.* I've never done this for the money!
* Ha! See pages 206 - 207
When Pixar expands, Steve designs their new building with a huge central atrium for workers to meet and mingle.

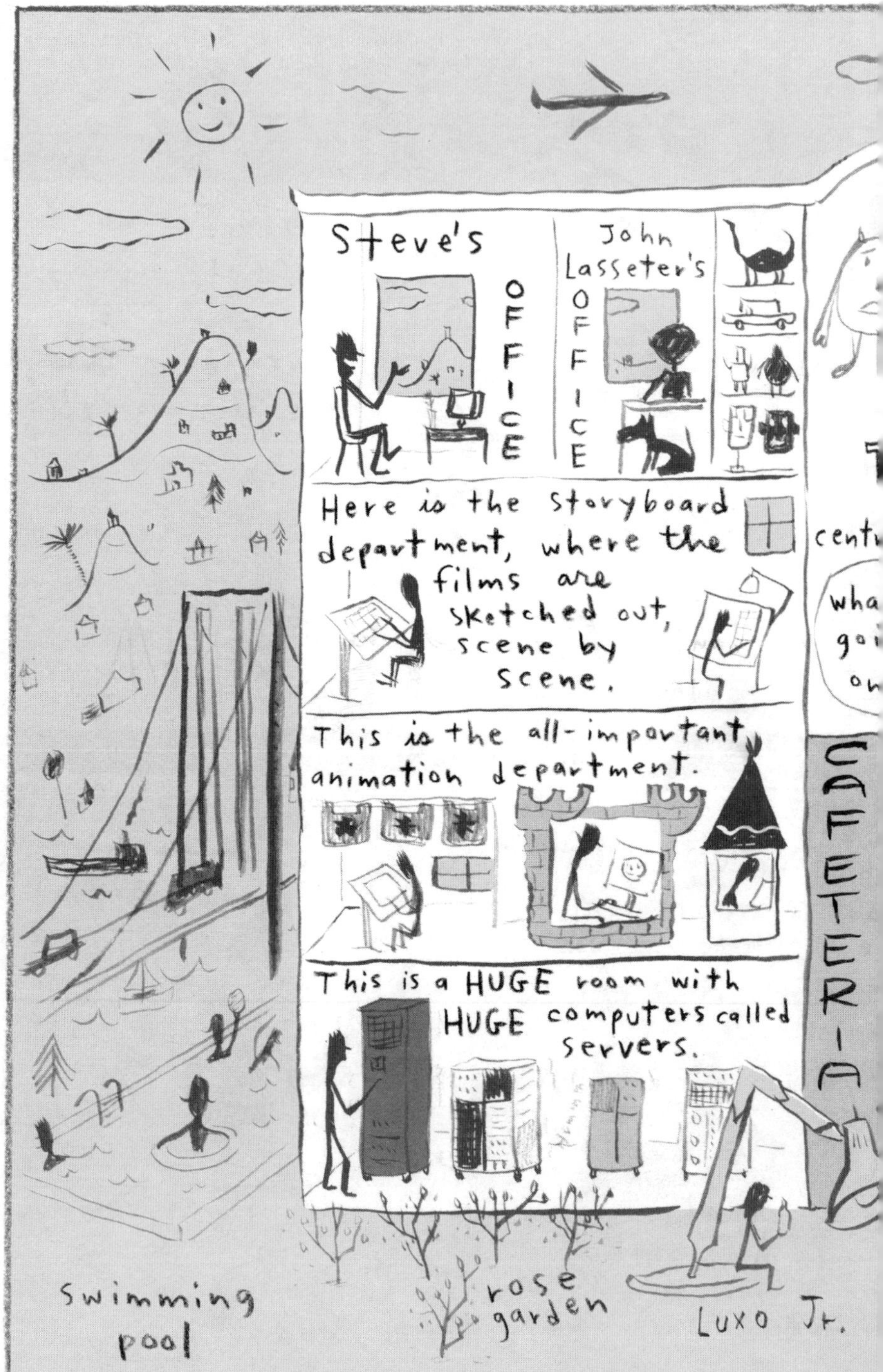
Steve's
OFFICE
John Lasseter's
OFFICE
Here is the storyboard department, where the films are sketched out, scene by scene.
This is the all-important animation department.
This is a HUGE room with HUGE computers called servers.
CAFETERIA
Swimming pool
rose garden
Luxo Jr.

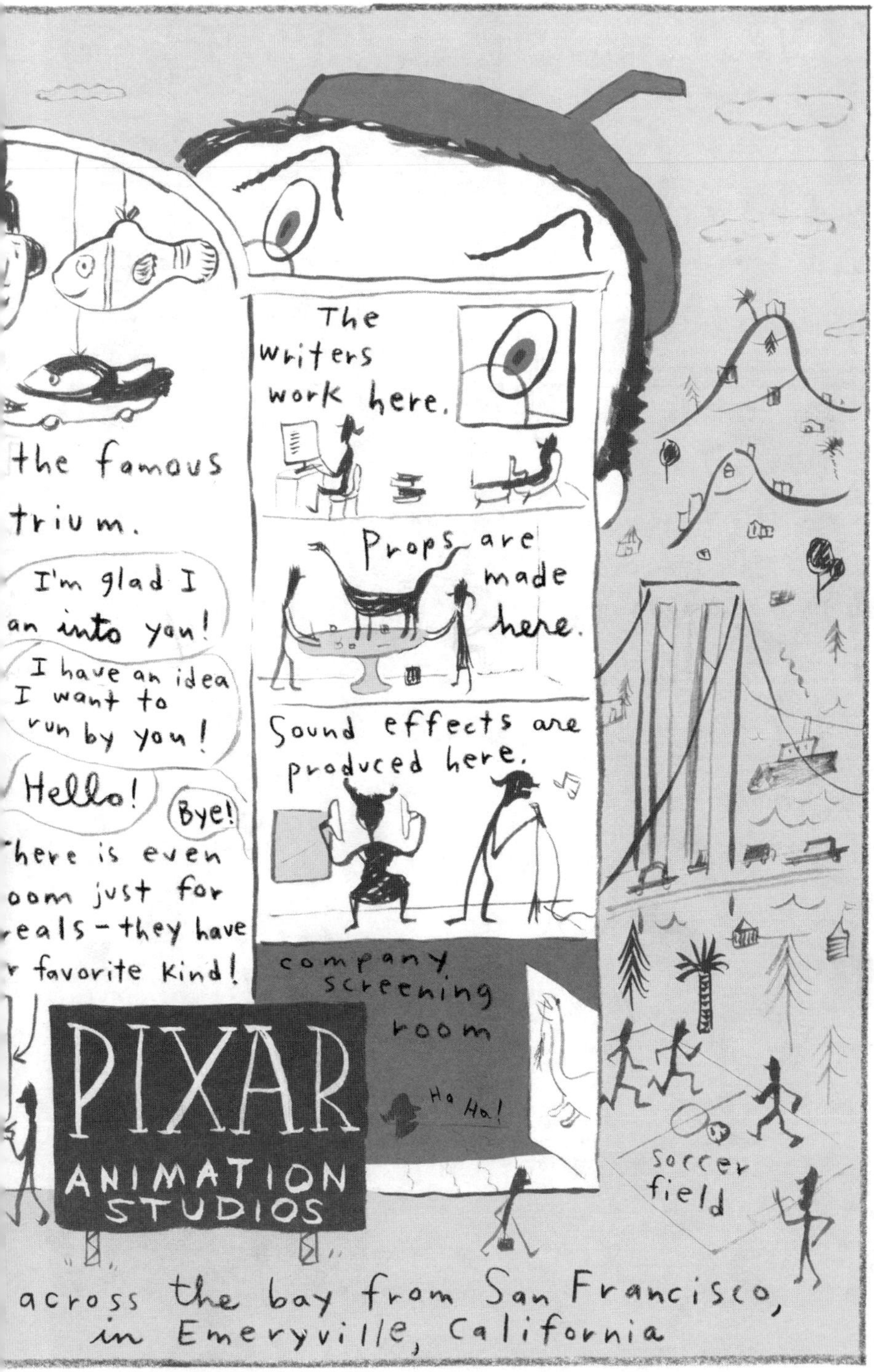
the famous
trium.
I'm glad I
an into you!
I have an idea
I want to
run by you!
Hello!
Bye!
here is even
oom just for
eals - they have
favorite kind!
The
writers
work here.
Props are
made
here.
Sound effects are
produced here.
company
screening
room
Ha Ha!
PIXAR
ANIMATION
STUDIOS
soccer
field
across the bay from San Francisco,
in Emeryville, California

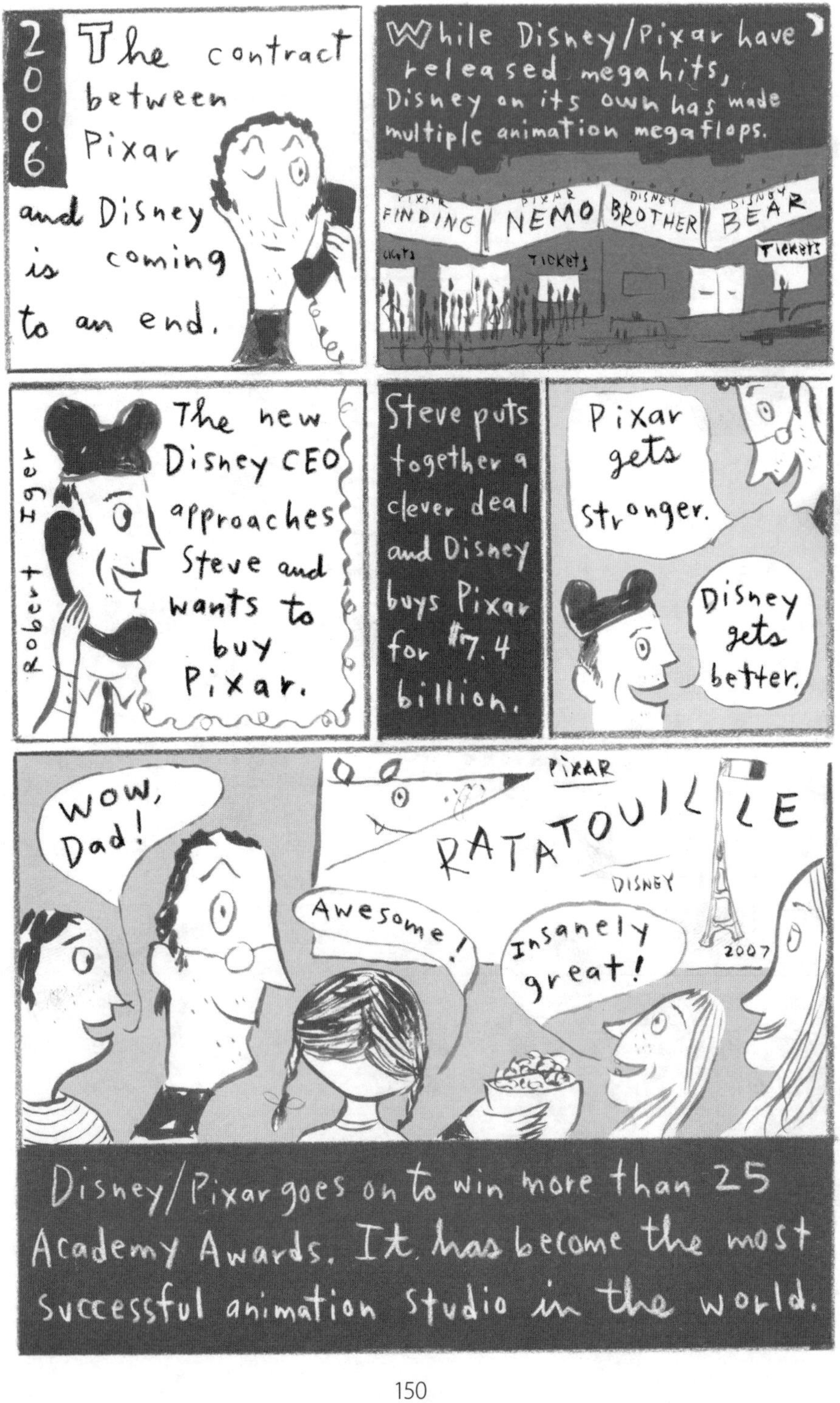
2006
The contract between Pixar and Disney is coming to an end.
While Disney/Pixar have released megahits, Disney on its own has made multiple animation megaflops.
PIXAR
FINDING
PIXAR
NEMO
DISNEY
BROTHER
DISNEY
BEAR
TICKETS
TICKETS
Robert Iger
The new Disney CEO approaches Steve and wants to buy Pixar.
Steve puts together a clever deal and Disney buys Pixar for $7.4 billion.
Pixar gets stronger.
Disney gets better.
WOW, Dad!
PIXAR
RATATOUILLE
DISNEY
2007
Awesome!
Insanely great!
Disney/Pixar goes on to win more than 25 Academy Awards. It has become the most successful animation studio in the world.

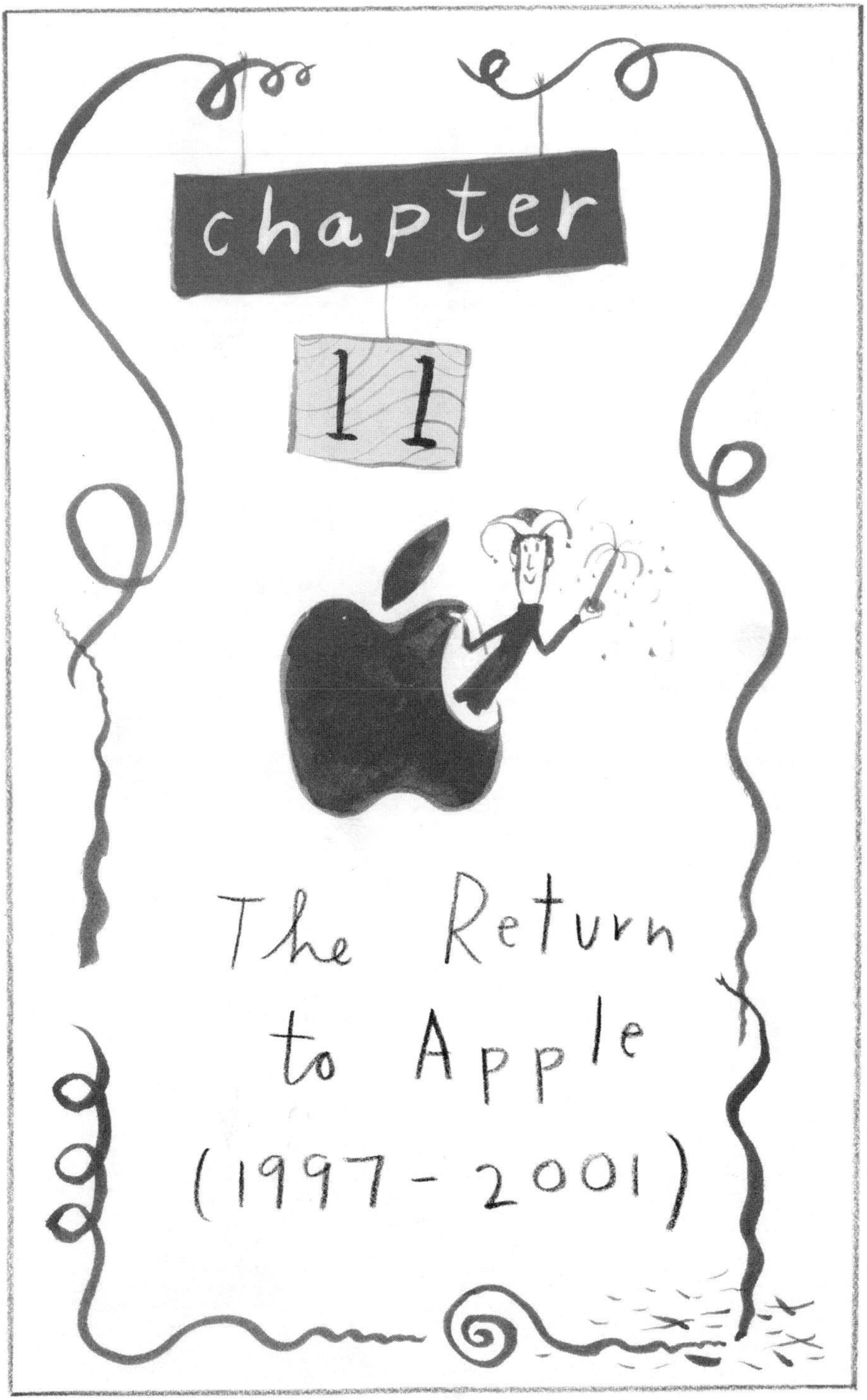
chapter
11
The Return to Apple (1997 - 2001)

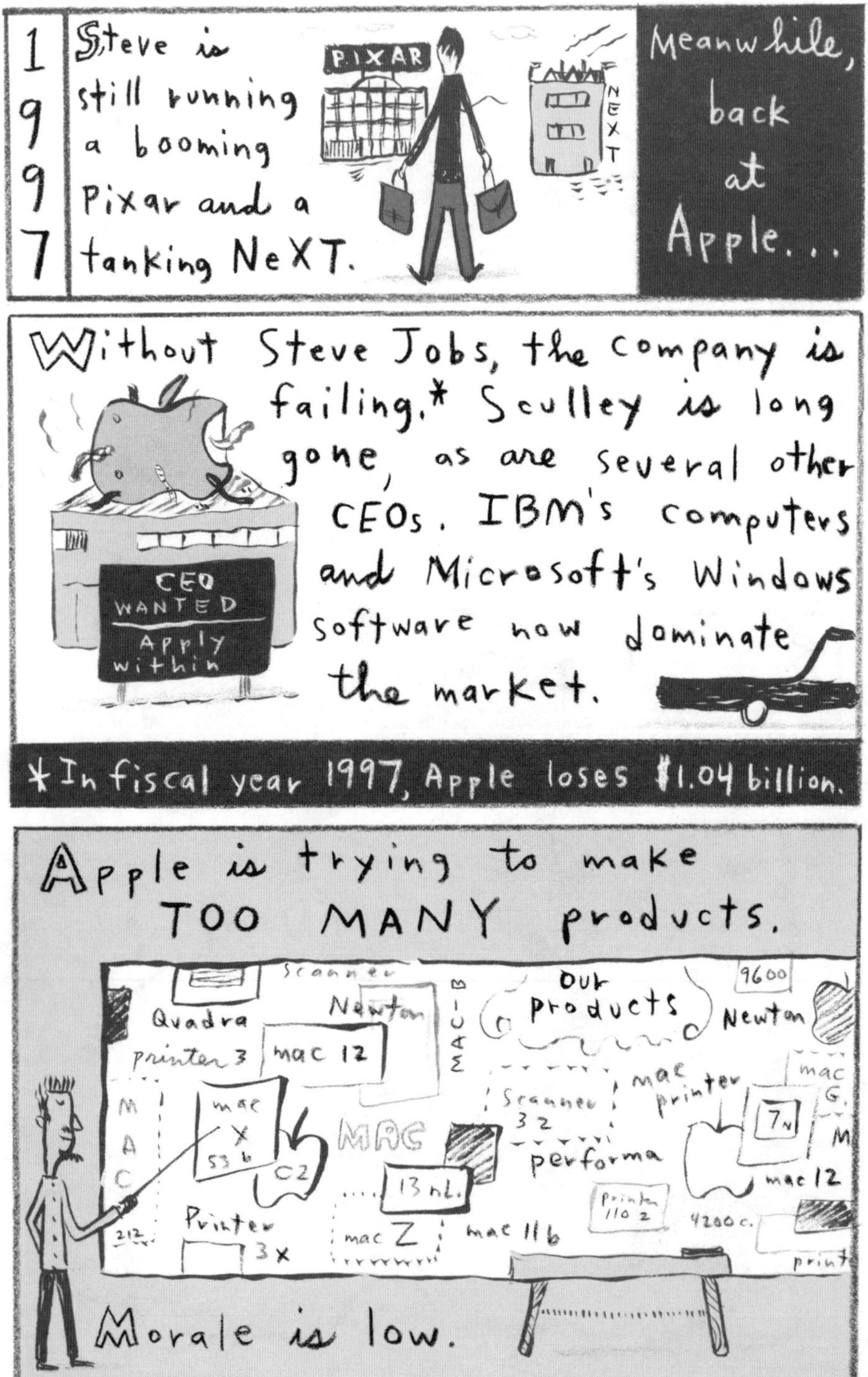
1997
Steve is still running a booming Pixar and a tanking NeXT.
PIXAR
NEXT
Meanwhile, back at Apple...
Without Steve Jobs, the company is failing.* Sculley is long gone, as are several other CEOs. IBM's computers and Microsoft's Windows software now dominate the market.
CEO WANTED
Apply within
* In fiscal year 1997, Apple loses $1.04 billion.
Apple is trying to make TOO MANY products.
Our products
Quadra
Newton
printer 3
mac 12
MAC-B
9600
Newton
MAC
mac X 53 b
Scanner 32
mac printer
7N
MAC
performa
C2
13 nL.
mac 12
Printer 3x
mac Z
mac IIb
Printer 110 2
4200 c.
212
Morale is low.

1996 Apple pays $429 million cash plus 1.5 million shares to Steve

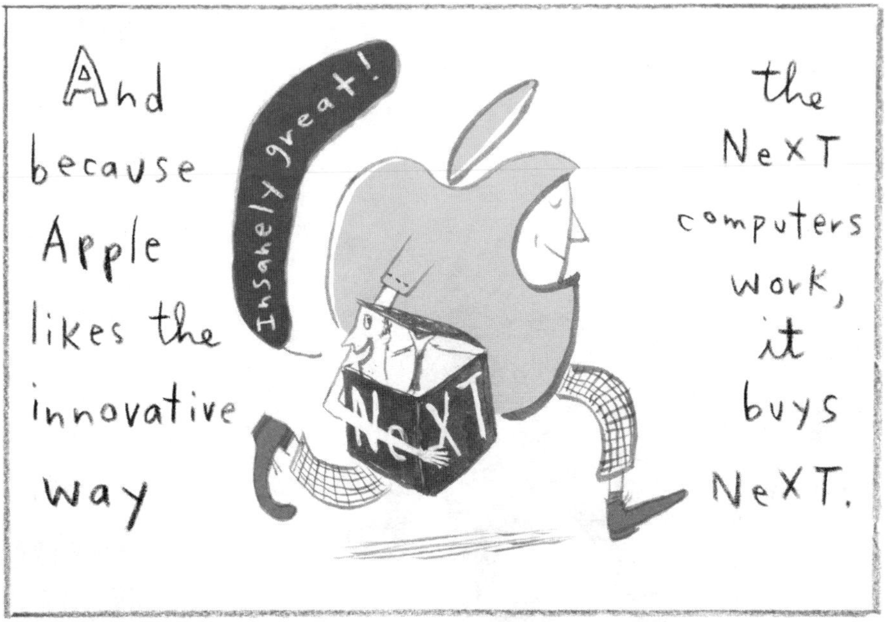
And because Apple likes the innovative way
Insanely great!
NeXT
the NeXT computers work, it buys NeXT.

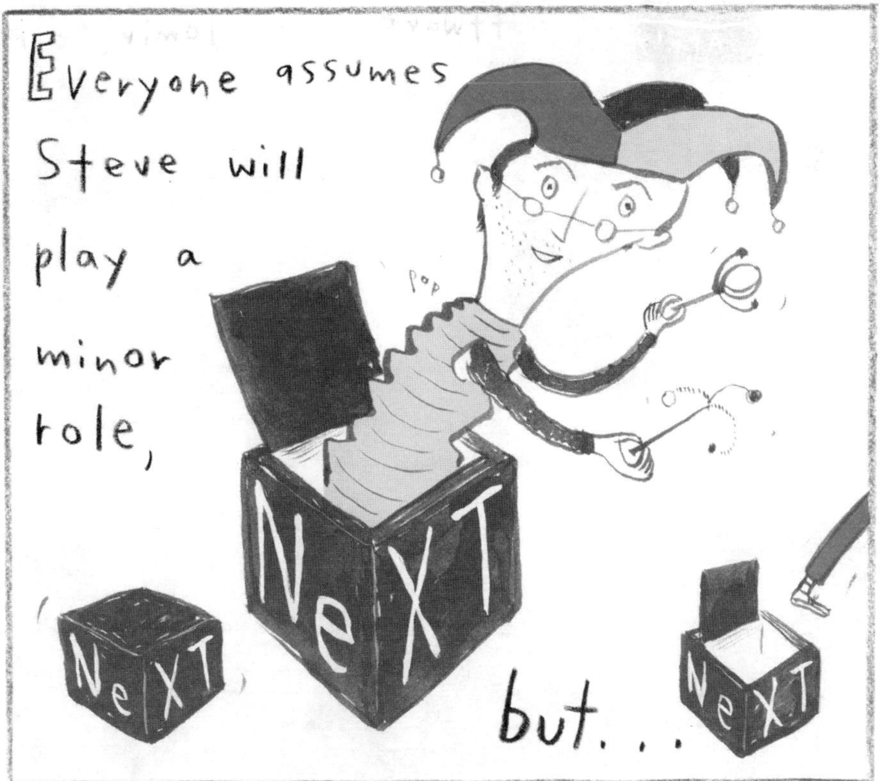
Everyone assumes Steve will play a minor role,
pop
NeXT
NeXT
NeXT
but...
NeXT

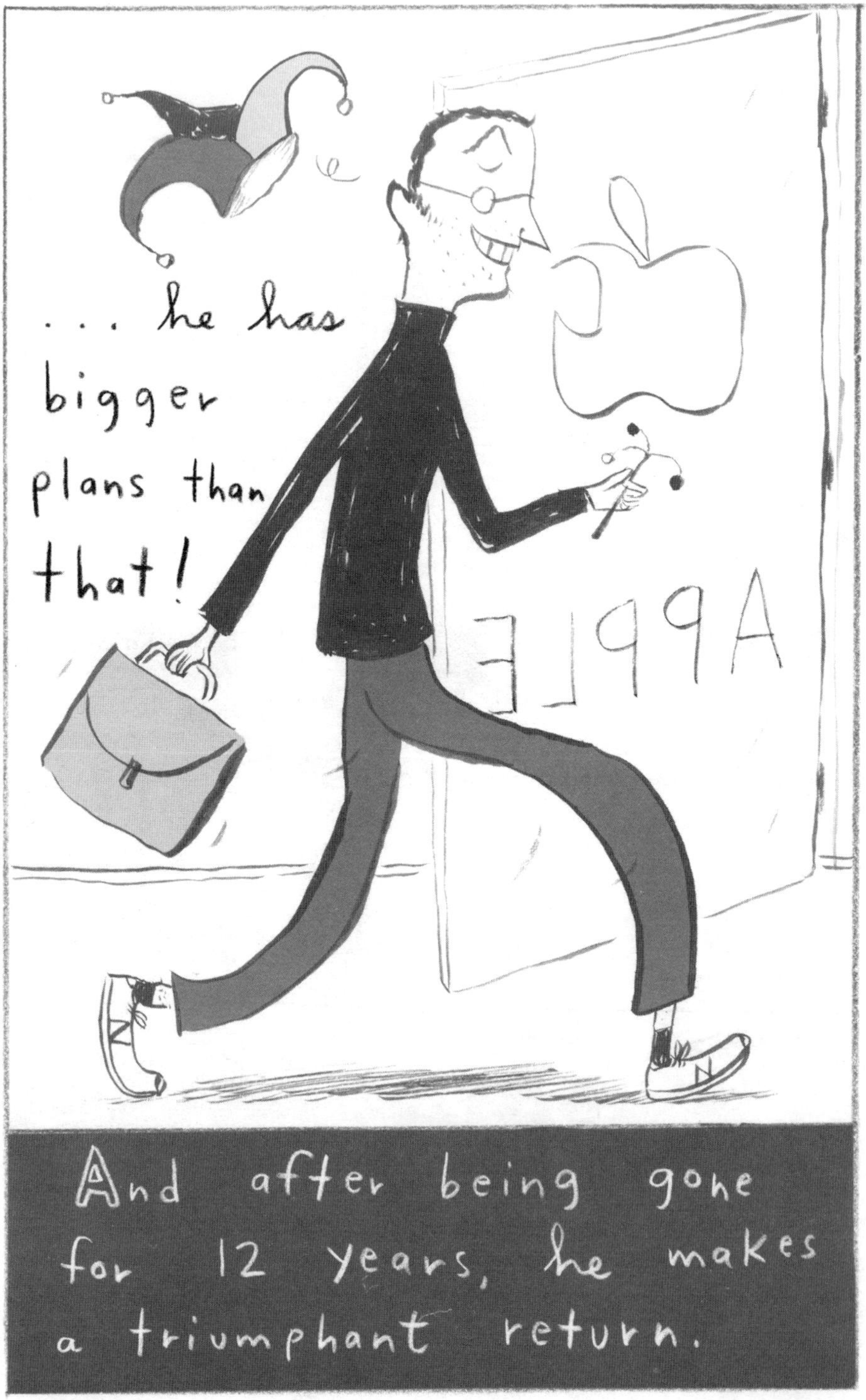
. . . he has bigger plans than that!
APPLE
And after being gone for 12 years, he makes a triumphant return.

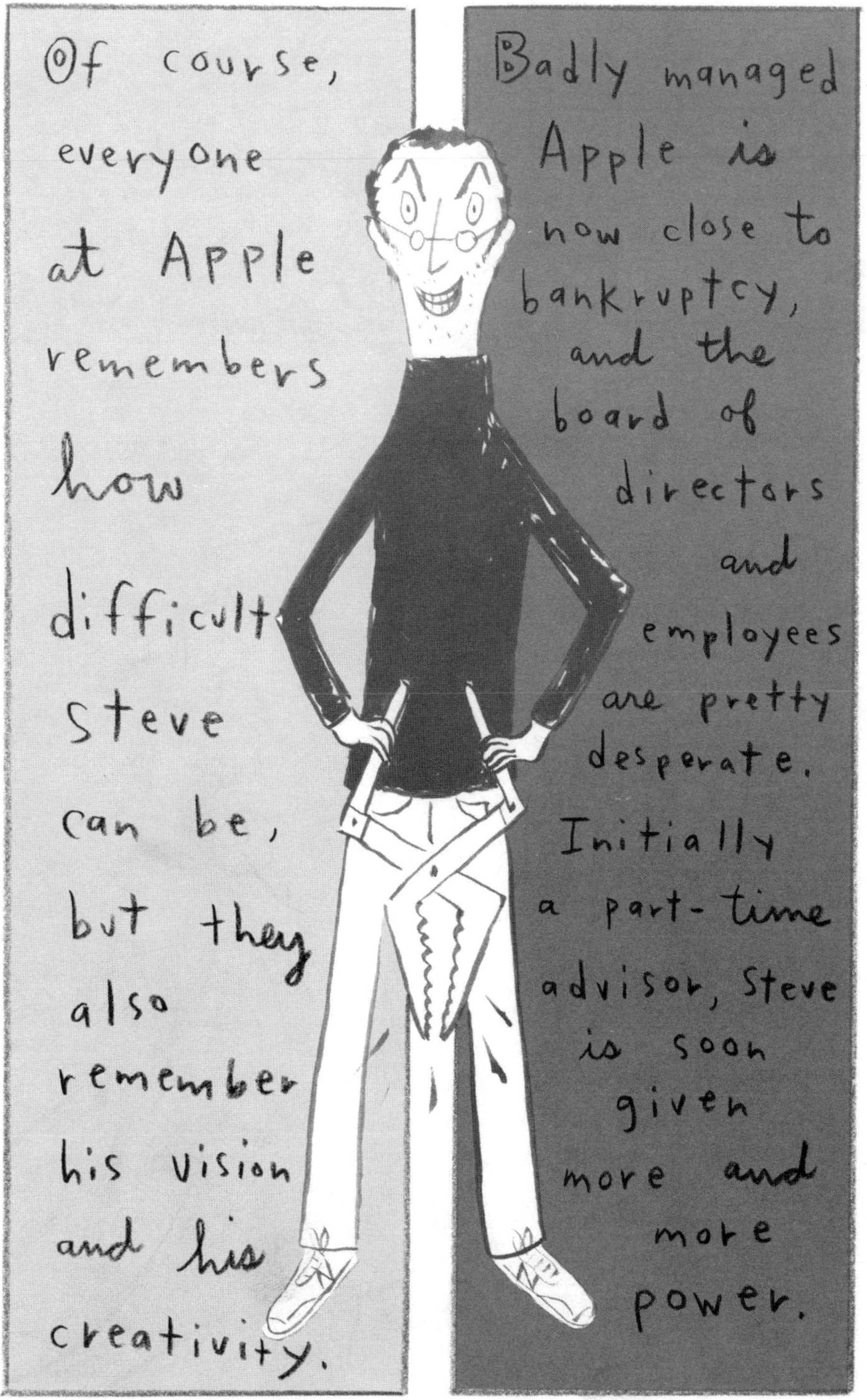
Of course, everyone at Apple remembers how difficult Steve can be, but they also remember his vision and his creativity.
Badly managed Apple is now close to bankruptcy, and the board of directors and employees are pretty desperate. Initially a part-time advisor, Steve is soon given more and more power.

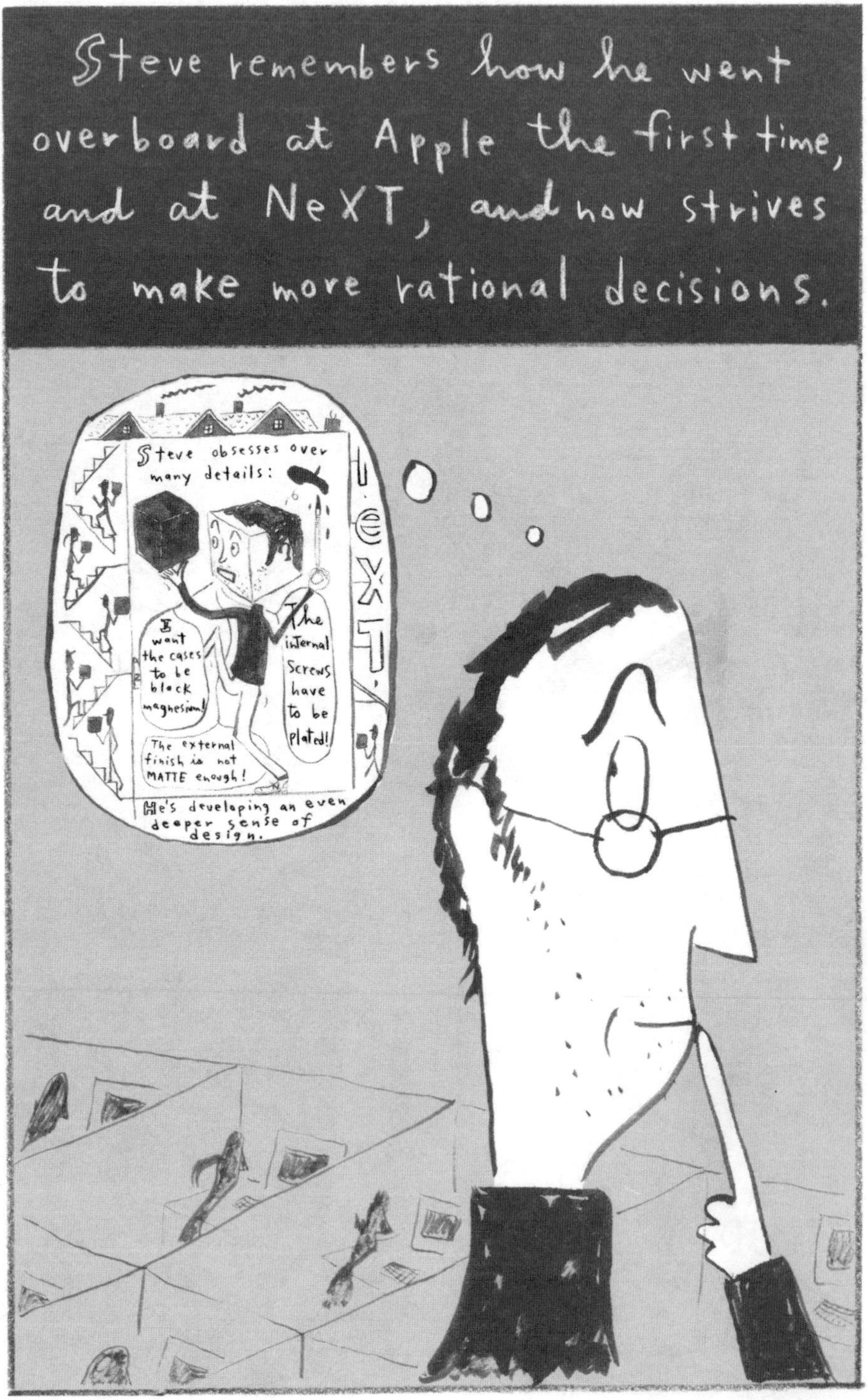
Steve remembers how he went overboard at Apple the first time, and at NeXT, and now strives to make more rational decisions.
Steve obsesses over many details:
I want the cases to be black magnesium!
The internal screws have to be plated!
The external finish is not MATTE enough!
He's developing an even deeper sense of design.
NeXT

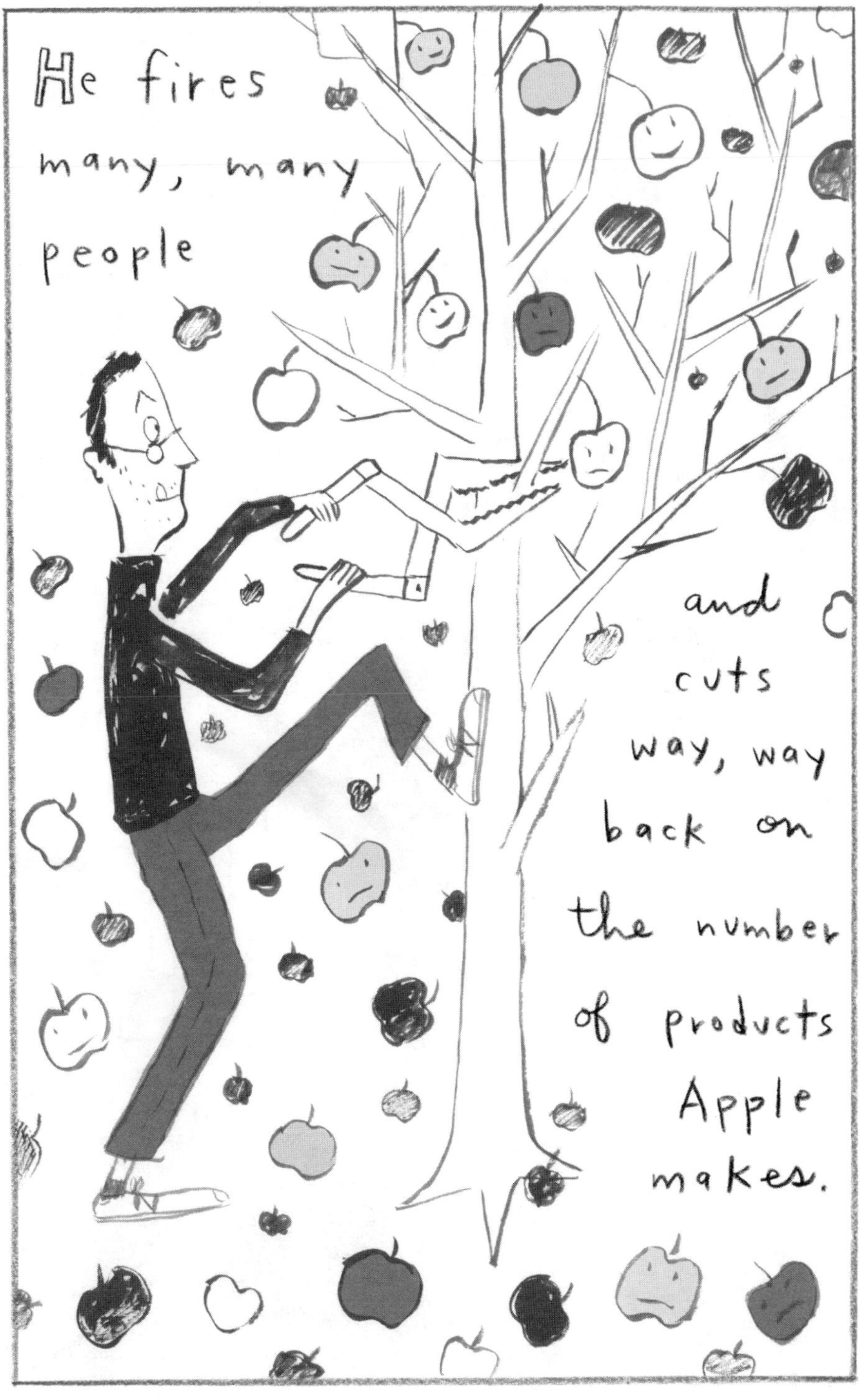
He fires many, many people
and cuts way, way back on the number of products Apple makes.

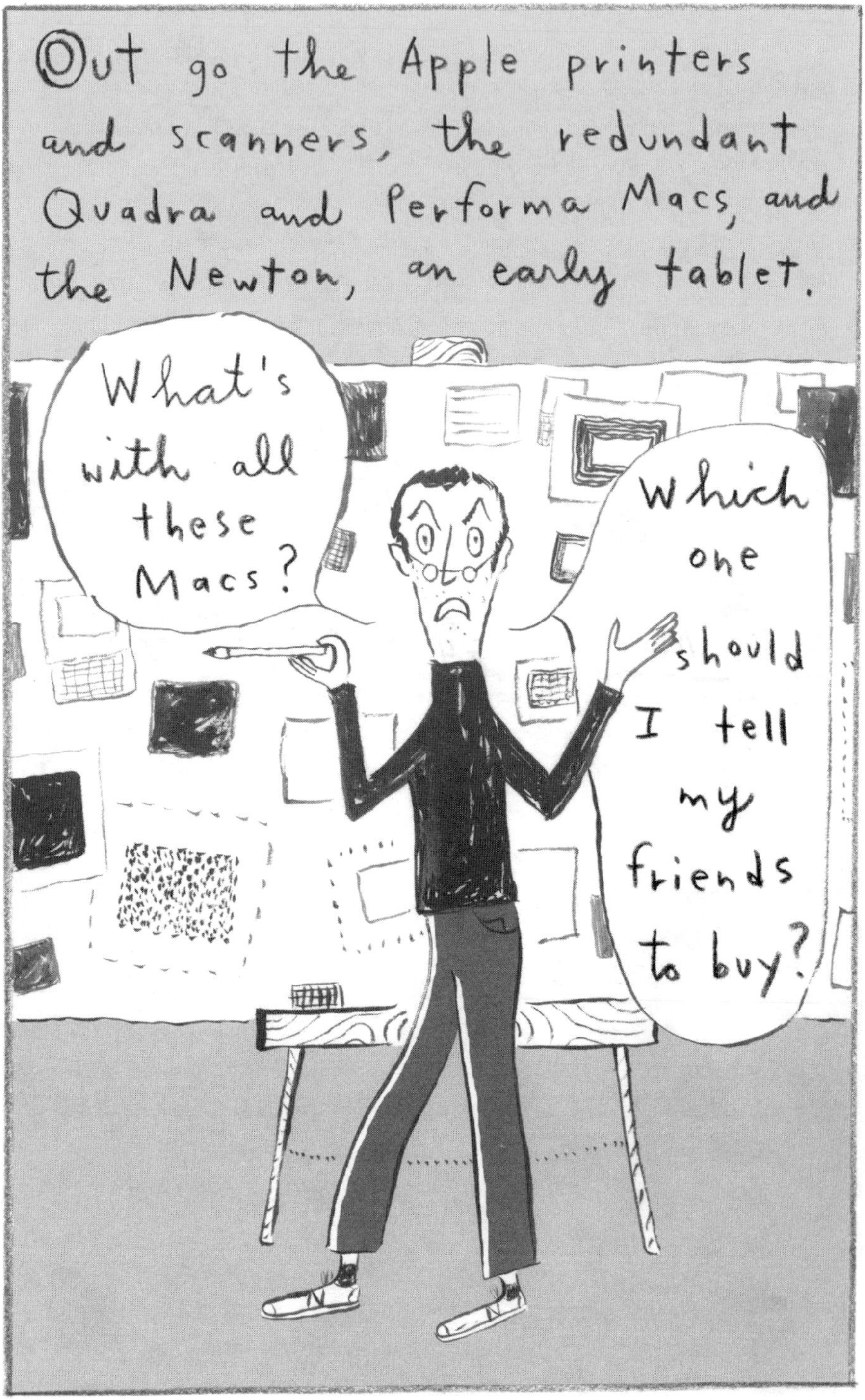
Out go the Apple printers and scanners, the redundant Quadra and Performa Macs, and the Newton, an early tablet.
What's with all these Macs?
Which one should I tell my friends to buy?

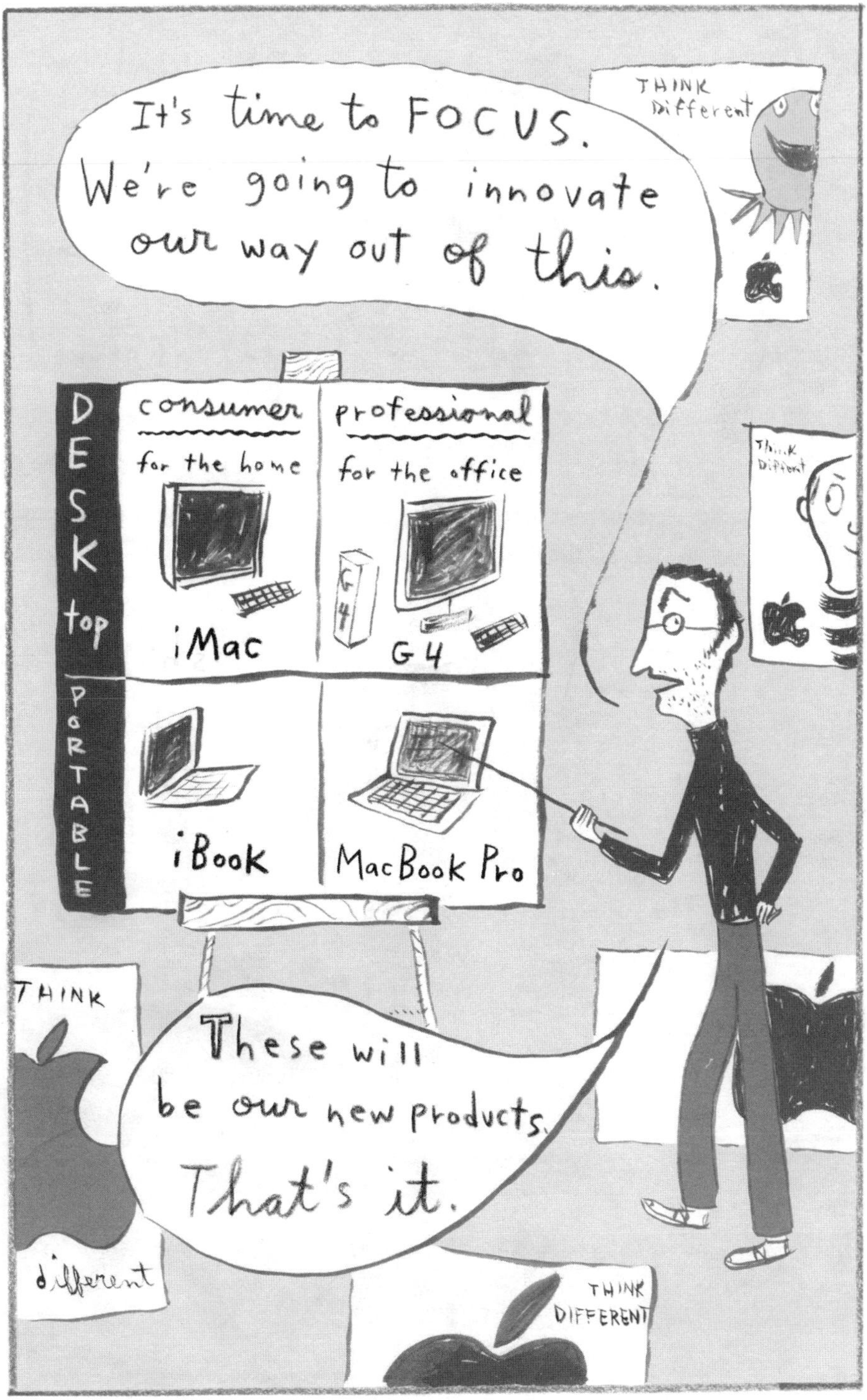
It's time to FOCUS. We're going to innovate our way out of this.
THINK Different
Think Different
DESK top
PORTABLE
consumer
for the home
iMac
professional
for the office
G4
G4
iBook
MacBook Pro
THINK
different
These will be our new products. That's it.
THINK DIFFERENT

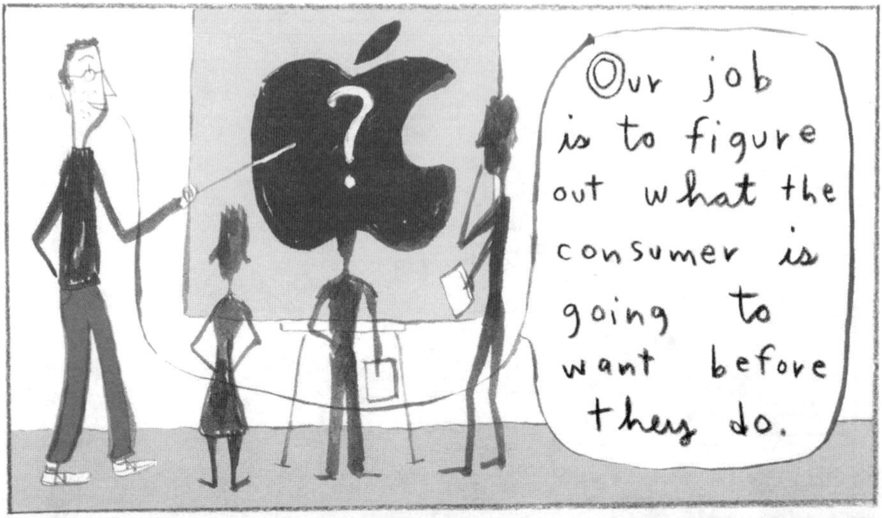
Our job is to figure out what the consumer is going to want before they do.

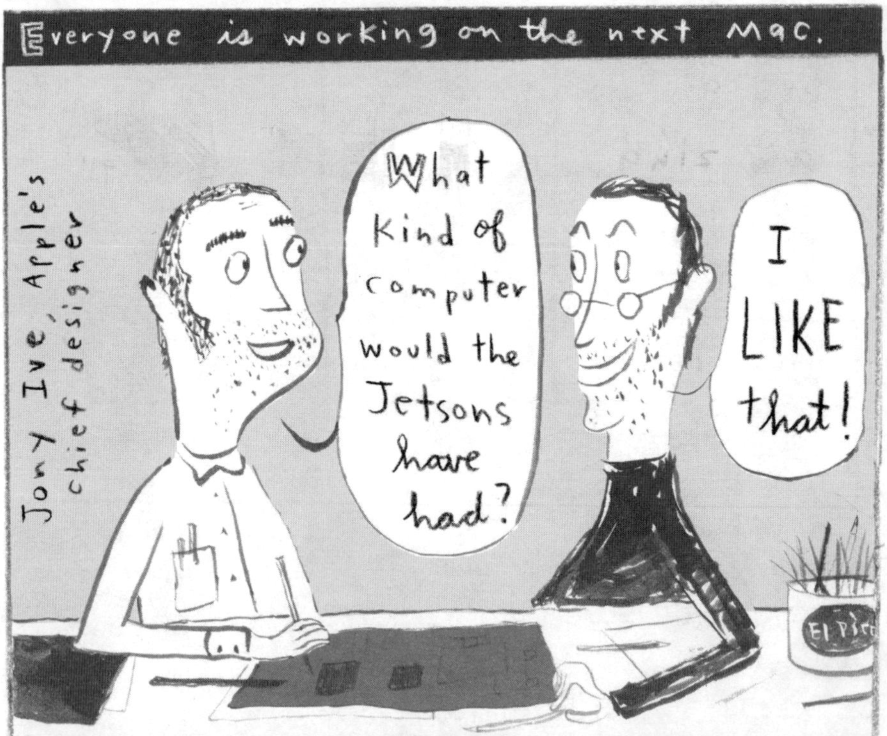
Everyone is working on the next Mac.
Jony Ive, Apple's chief designer
What kind of computer would the Jetsons have had?
I LIKE that!

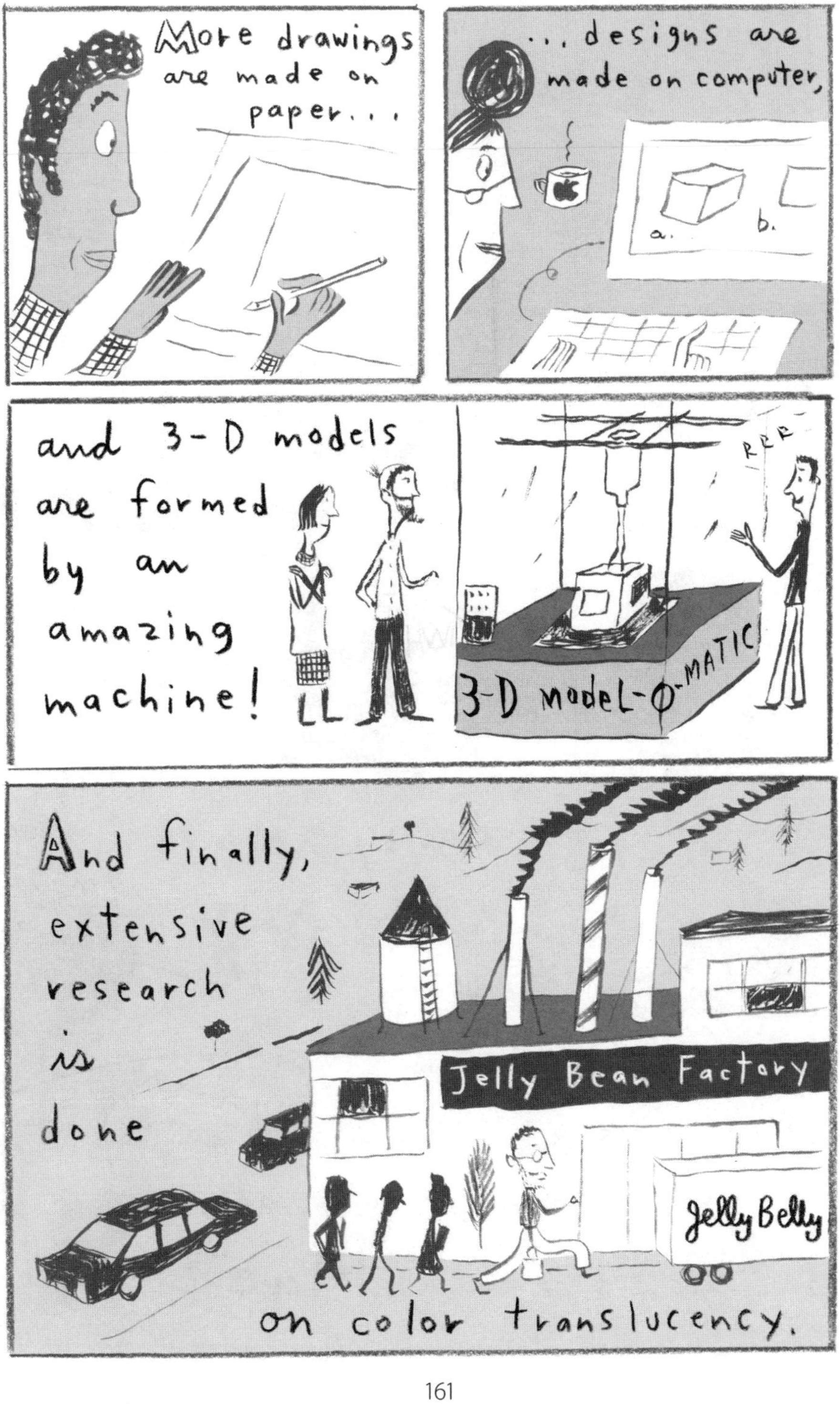
More drawings are made on paper...
...designs are made on computer,
a.
b.
and 3-D models are formed by an amazing machine!
RRR
3-D MODEL-O-MATIC
And finally, extensive research is done
Jelly Bean Factory
Jelly Belly
on color translucency.

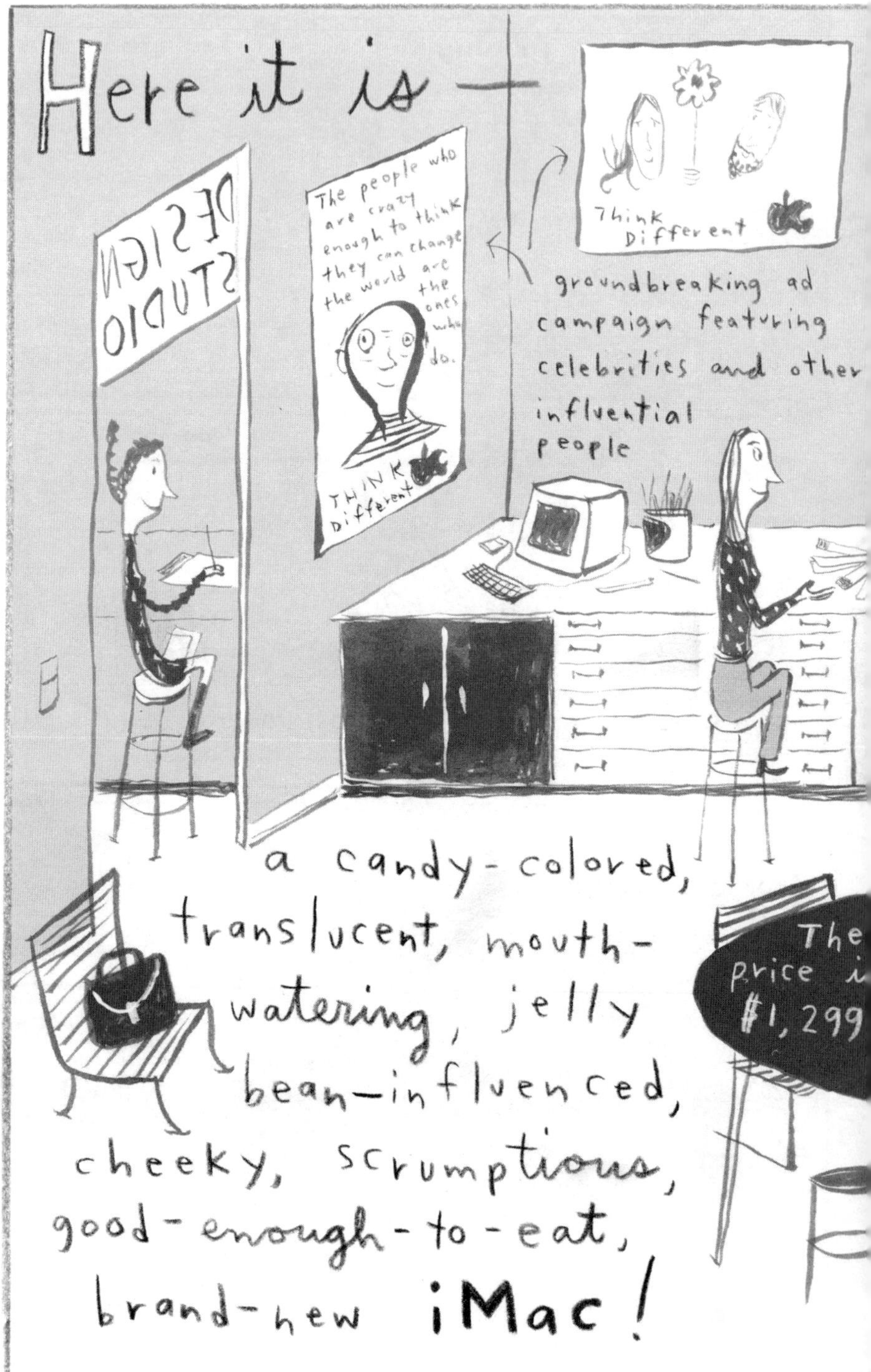
Here it is –
DESIGN STUDIO
The people who are crazy enough to think they can change the world are the ones who do.
THINK Different
Think Different
groundbreaking ad campaign featuring celebrities and other influential people
a candy-colored, translucent, mouth-watering, jelly bean-influenced, cheeky, scrumptious, good-enough-to-eat, brand-new iMac!
The price i
$1,299

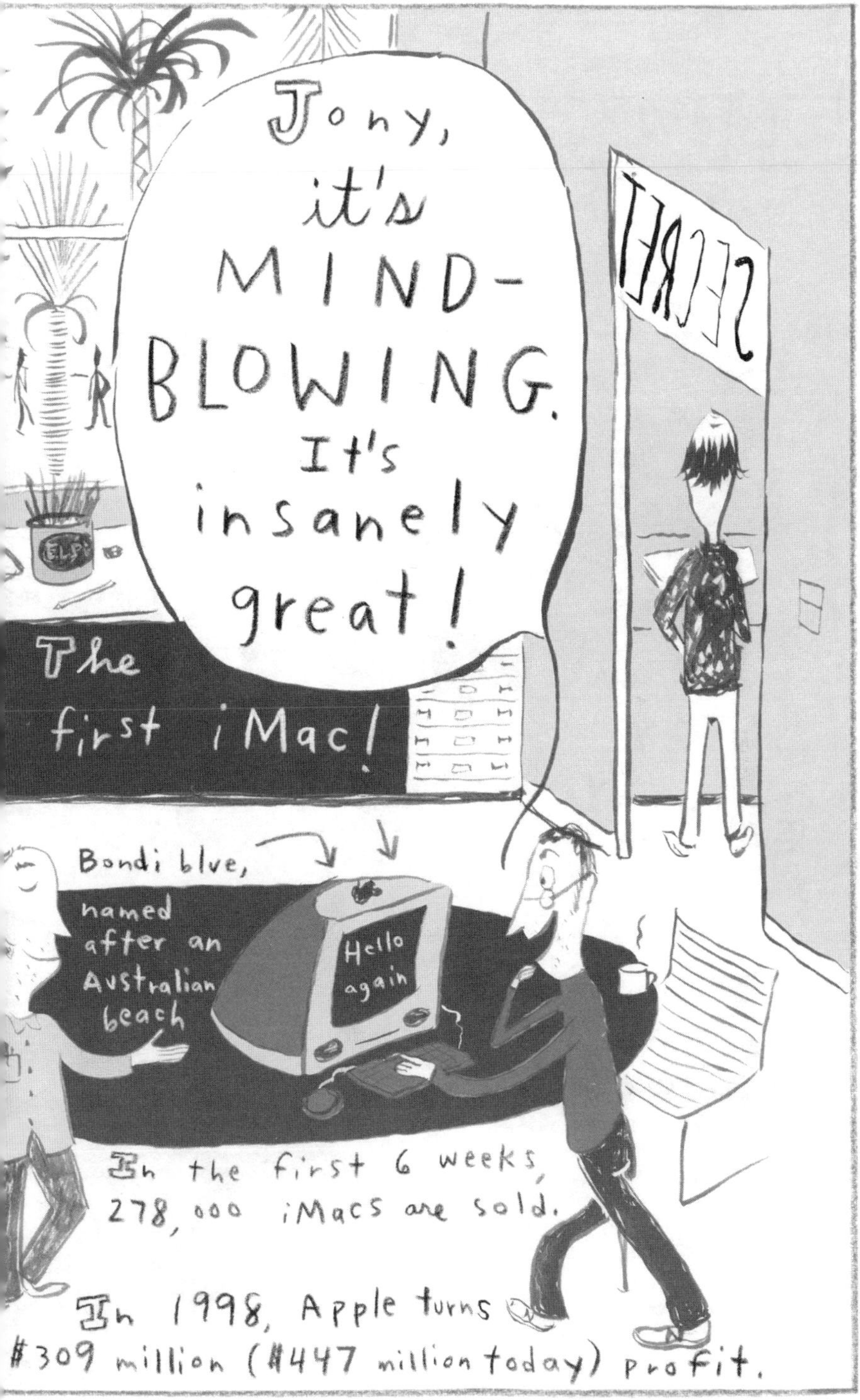
Jony, it's MIND-BLOWING. It's insanely great!
SECRET
The first iMac!
Bondi blue, named after an Australian beach
Hello again
In the first 6 weeks, 278,000 iMacs are sold.
In 1998, Apple turns $309 million ($447 million today) profit.

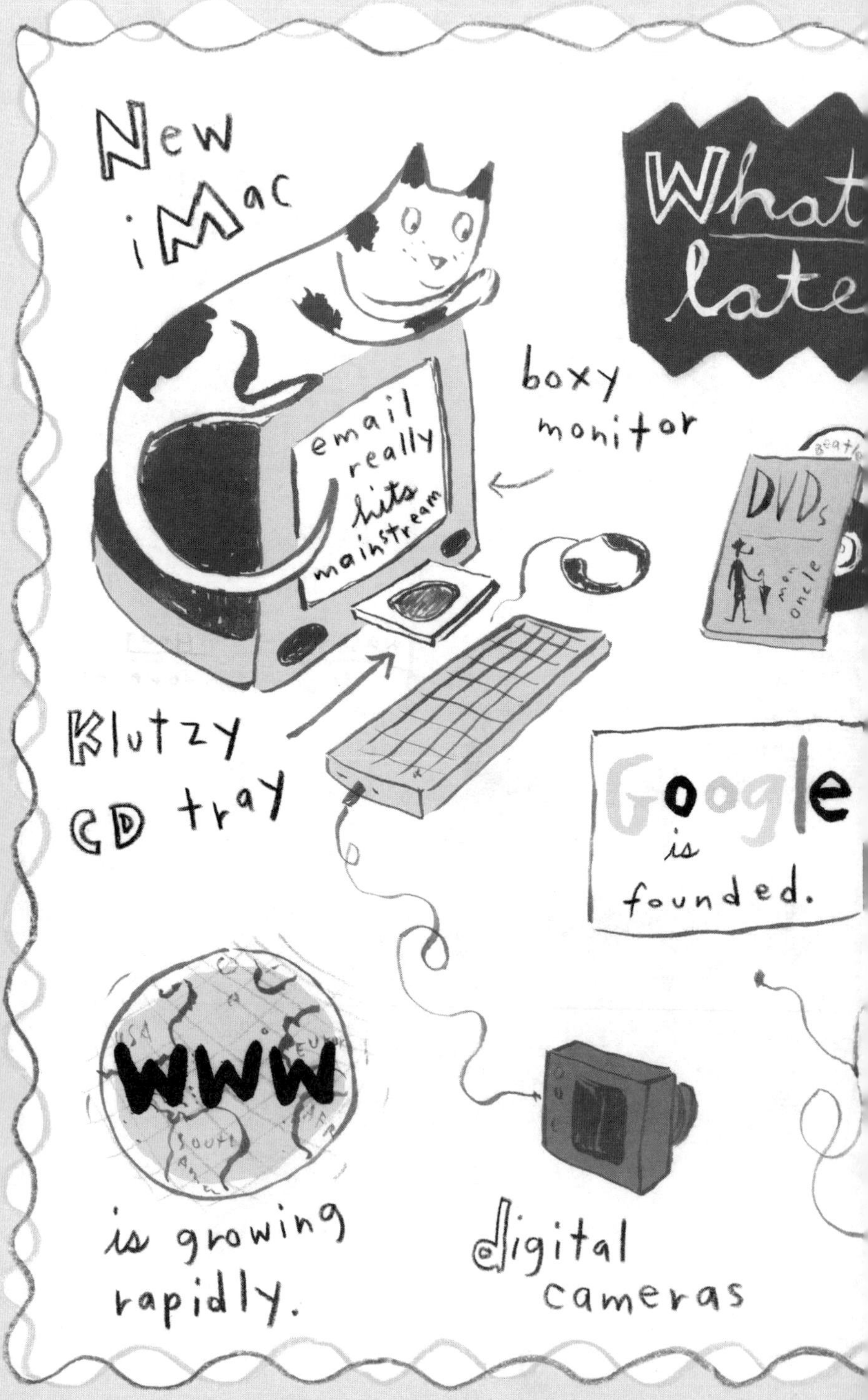
New iMac
email really hits mainstream
boxy monitor
Klutzy CD tray
What late
DVDs
mon oncle
Google is founded.
WWW
is growing rapidly.
digital cameras

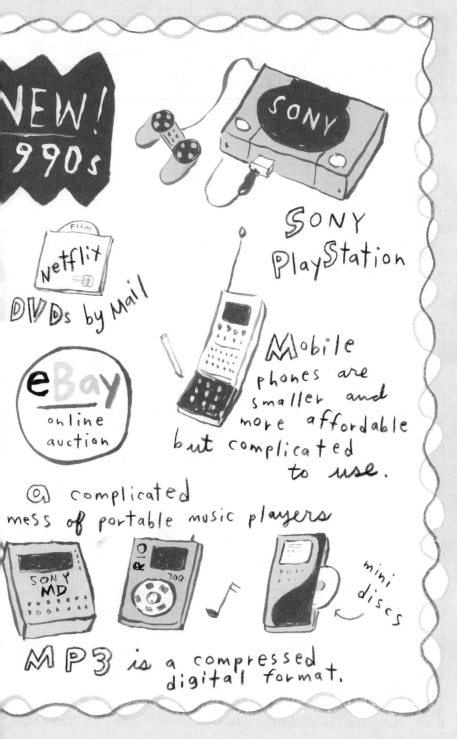

NEW!
990s

SONY PlayStation

netflix
FILM
DVDs by Mail

eBay
online
auction

Mobile phones are smaller and more affordable but complicated to use.

@ complicated
mess of portable music players

SONY MD

RIO 300

♪

mini discs

MP3 is a compressed digital format.

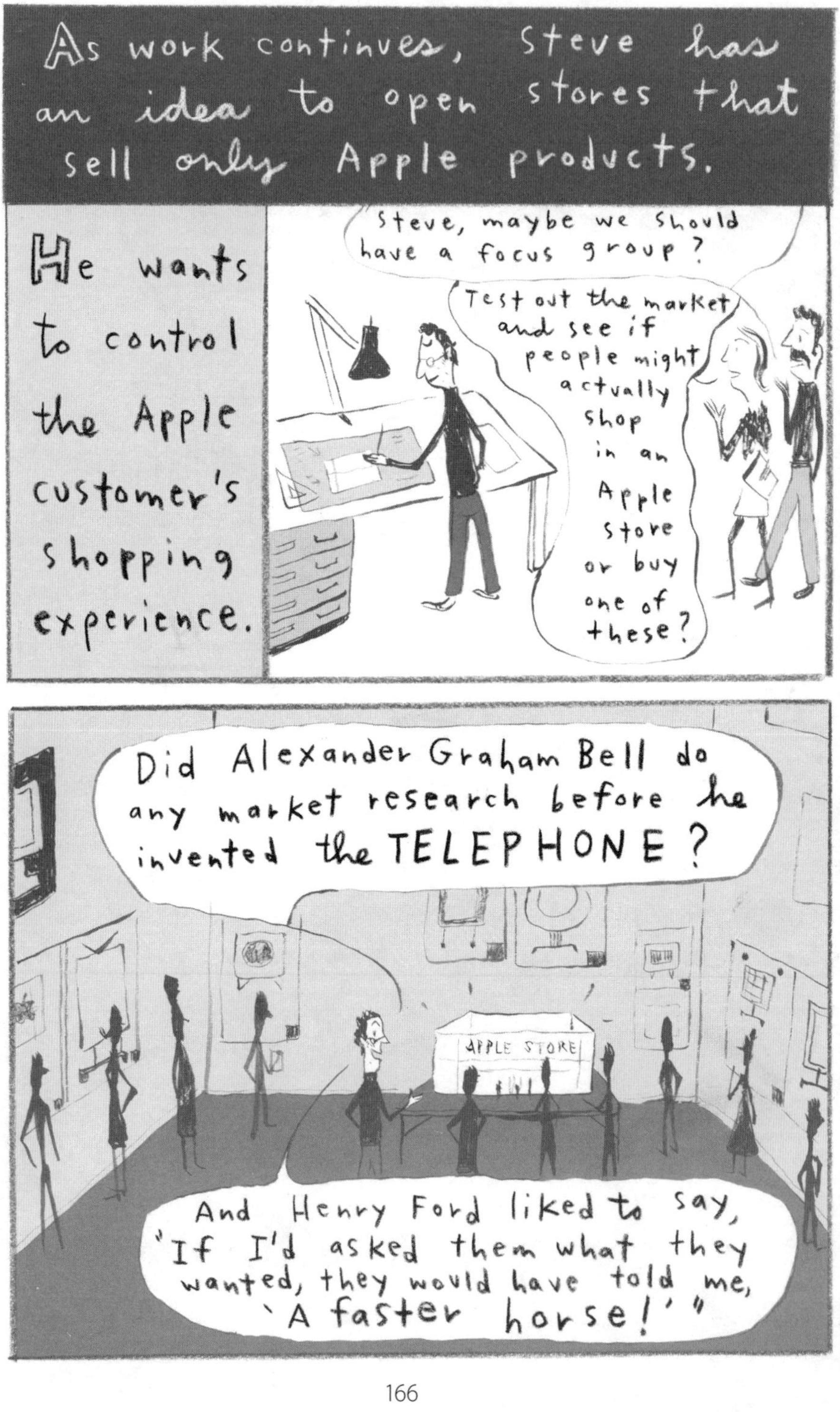
As work continues, Steve has an idea to open stores that sell only Apple products.
He wants to control the Apple customer's shopping experience.
Steve, maybe we should have a focus group?
Test out the market and see if people might actually shop in an Apple store or buy one of these?
Did Alexander Graham Bell do any market research before he invented the TELEPHONE?
APPLE STORE
And Henry Ford liked to say, "If I'd asked them what they wanted, they would have told me, 'A faster horse!'"

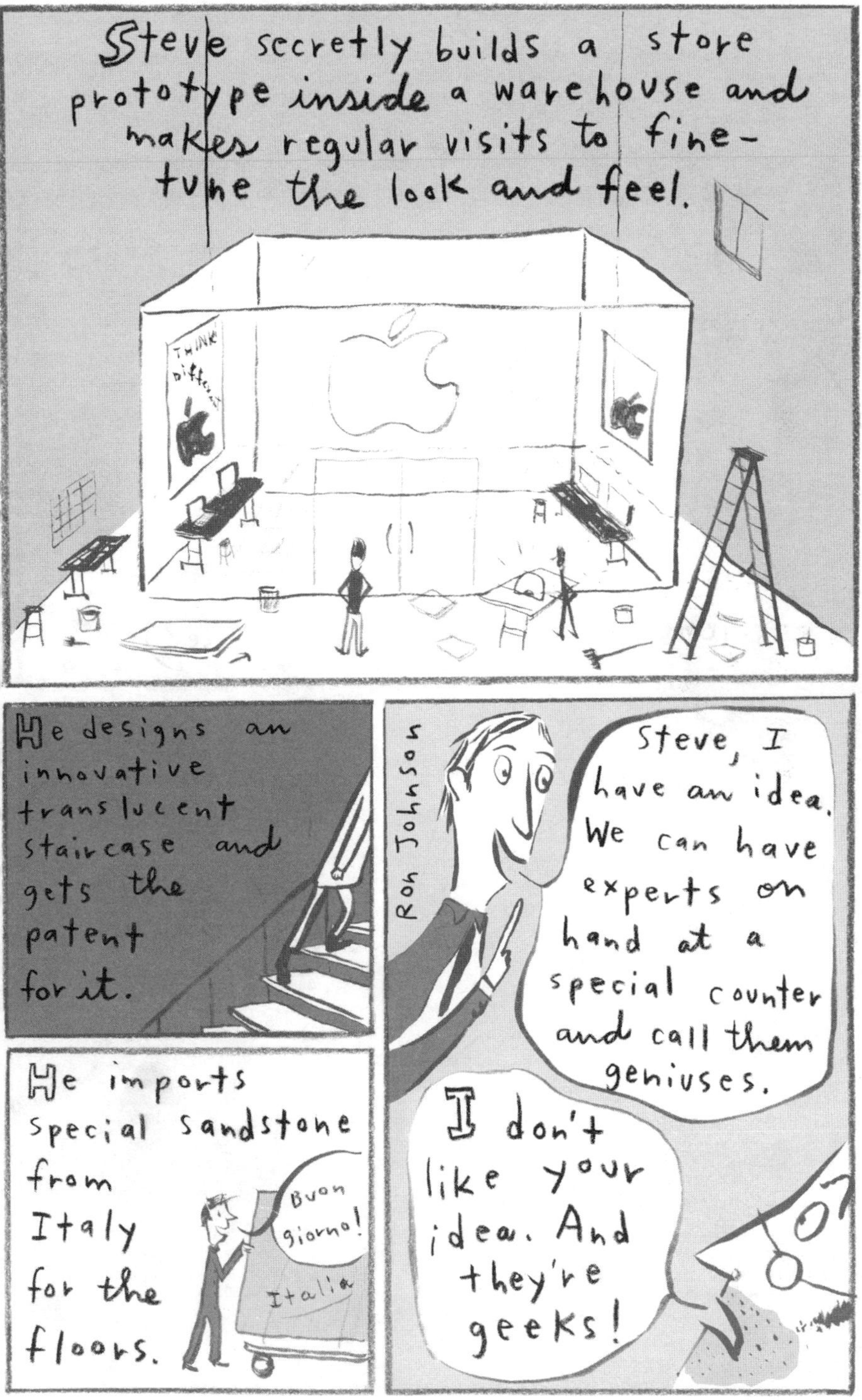
Steve secretly builds a store prototype inside a warehouse and makes regular visits to fine-tune the look and feel.
THINK different
He designs an innovative translucent staircase and gets the patent for it.
Ron Johnson
Steve, I have an idea. We can have experts on hand at a special counter and call them geniuses.
I don't like your idea. And they're geeks!
He imports special sandstone from Italy for the floors.
Buon giorno!
Italia

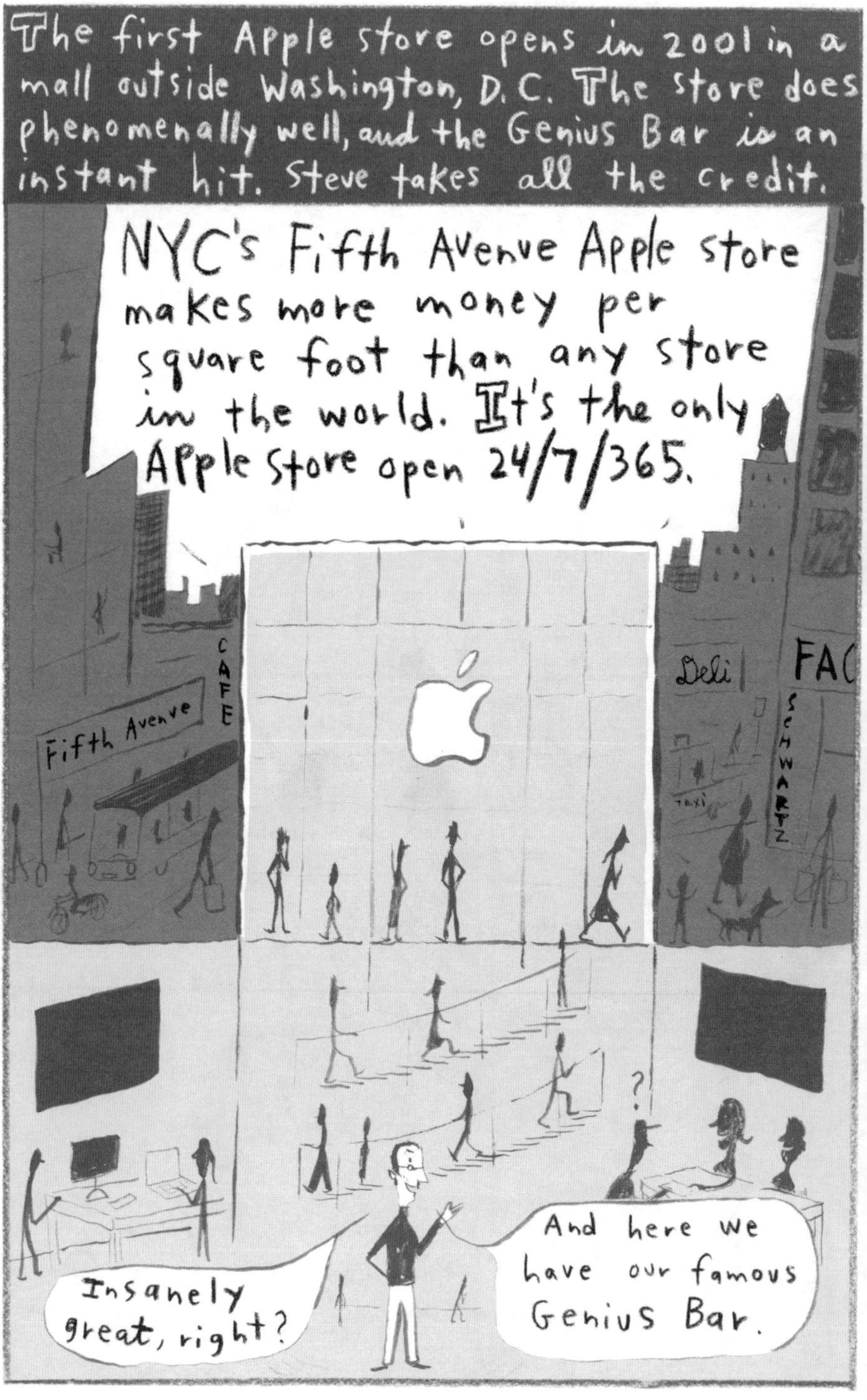
The first Apple store opens in 2001 in a mall outside Washington, D.C. The store does phenomenally well, and the Genius Bar is an instant hit. Steve takes all the credit.
NYC's Fifth Avenue Apple store makes more money per square foot than any store in the world. It's the only Apple store open 24/7/365.
CAFE
Fifth Avenue
Deli
FAC
SCHWARTZ
TAXI
?
Insanely great, right?
And here we have our famous Genius Bar.

Chapter

12

Expansion

(2000 - 2004)

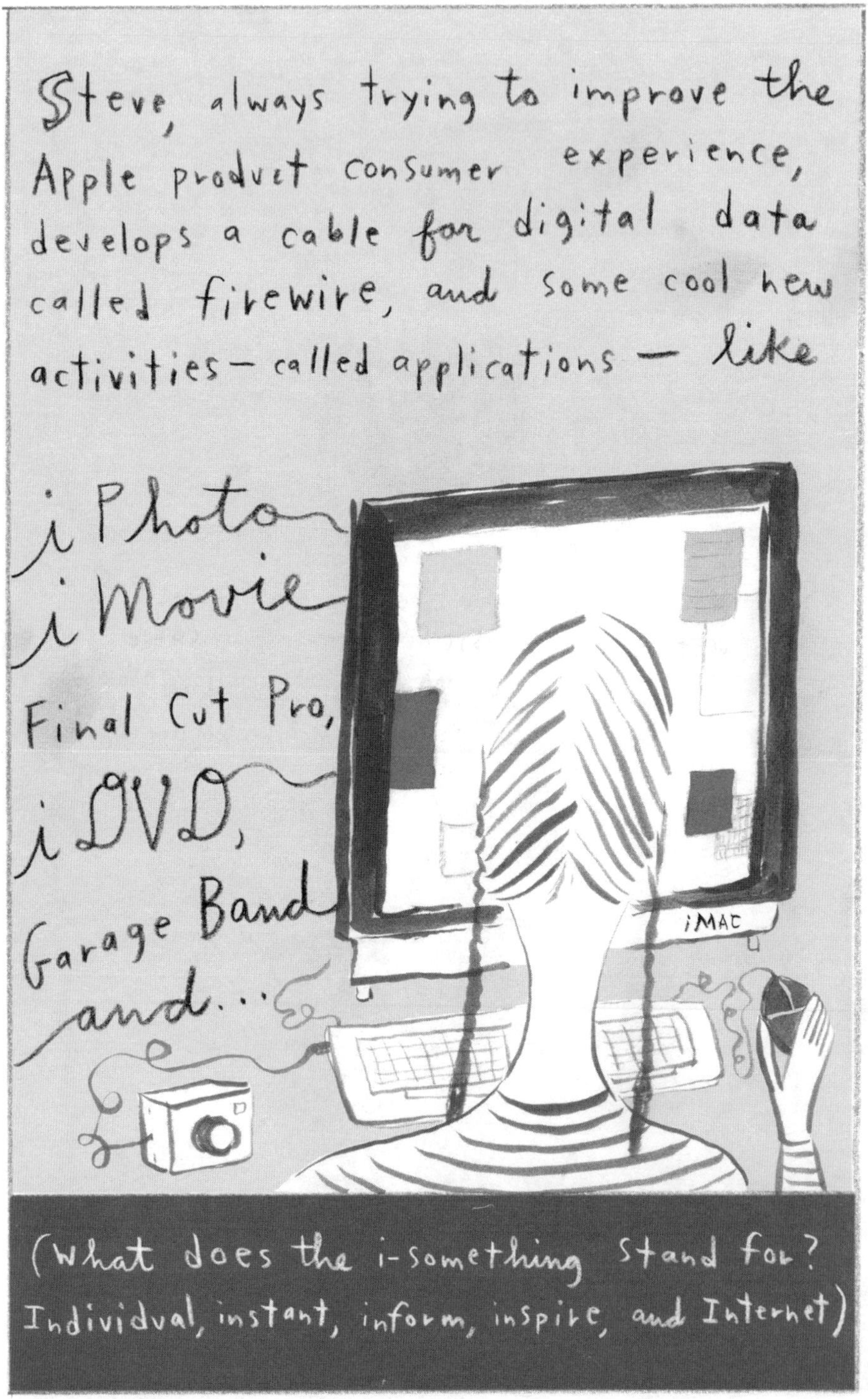
Steve, always trying to improve the Apple product consumer experience, develops a cable for digital data called firewire, and some cool new activities—called applications—like
iPhoto
iMovie
Final Cut Pro,
iDVD,
Garage Band
and...
iMAC
(What does the i-something stand for? Individual, instant, inform, inspire, and Internet)

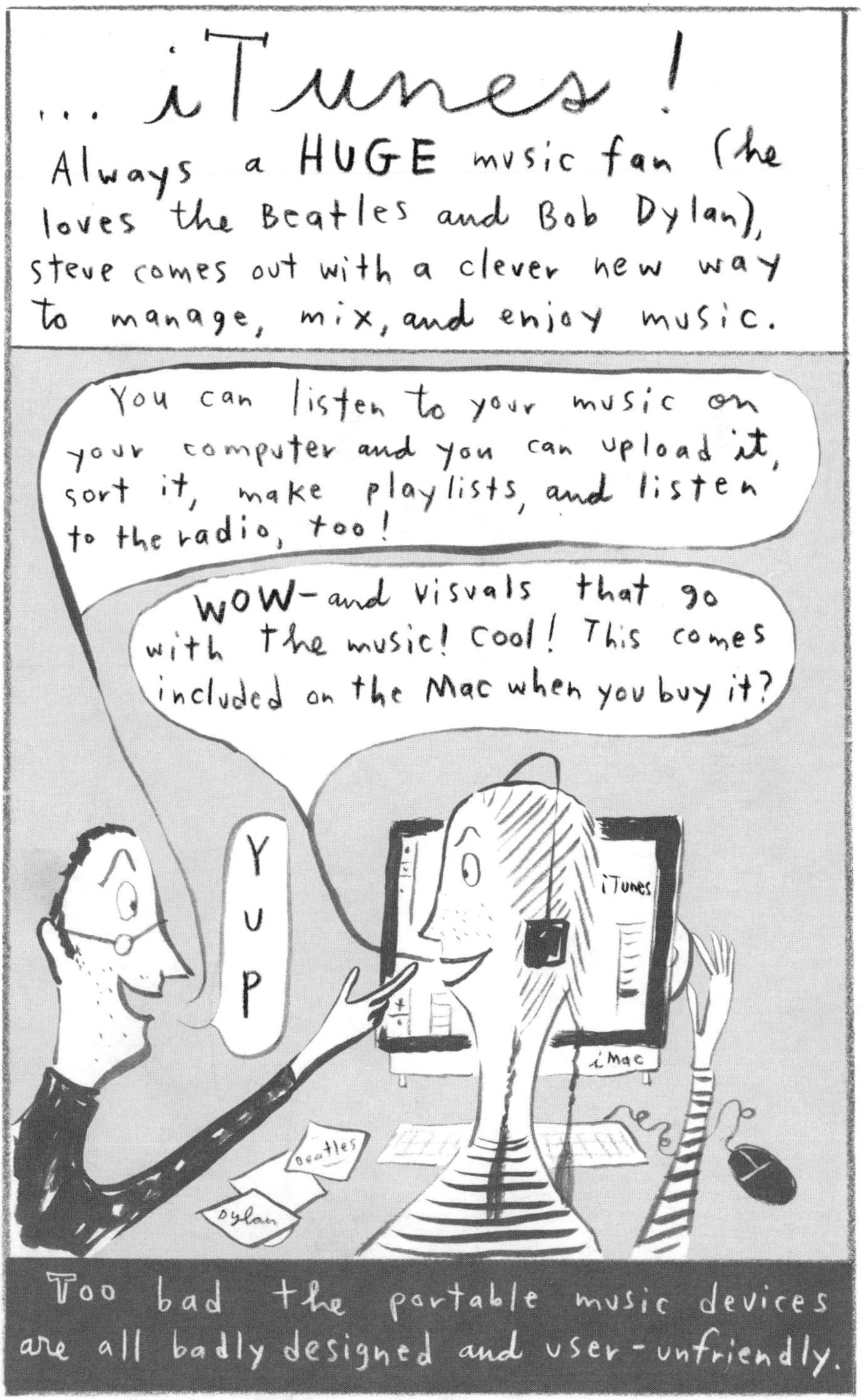
... iTunes!
Always a HUGE music fan (he loves the Beatles and Bob Dylan), steve comes out with a clever new way to manage, mix, and enjoy music.
You can listen to your music on your computer and you can upload it, sort it, make playlists, and listen to the radio, too!
WOW- and visuals that go with the music! Cool! This comes included on the Mac when you buy it?
YUP
iTunes
iMac
Beatles
Dylan
Too bad the portable music devices are all badly designed and user-unfriendly.

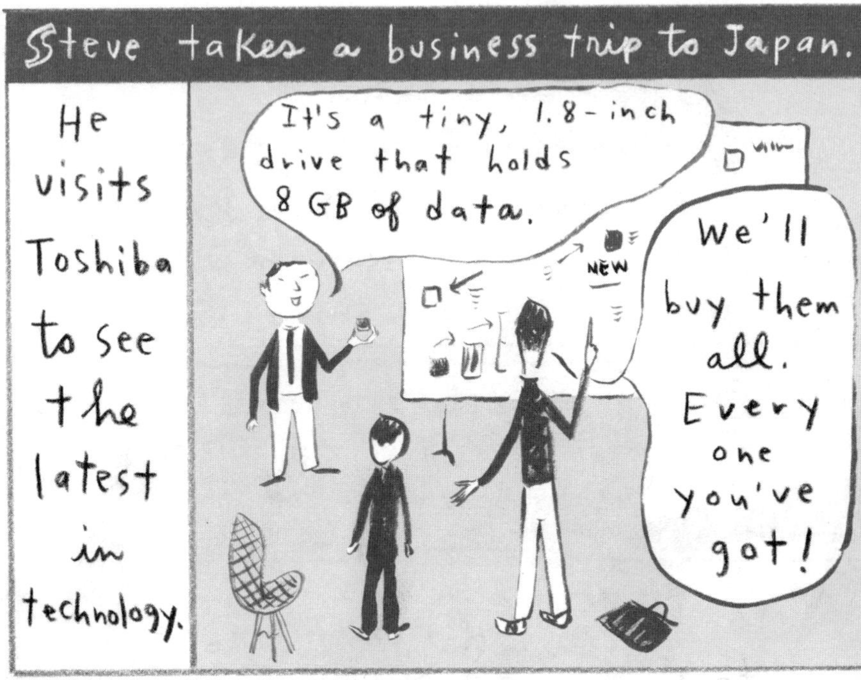
Steve takes a business trip to Japan.
He visits Toshiba to see the latest in technology.
It's a tiny, 1.8-inch drive that holds 8 GB of data.
NEW
We'll buy them all. Every one you've got!

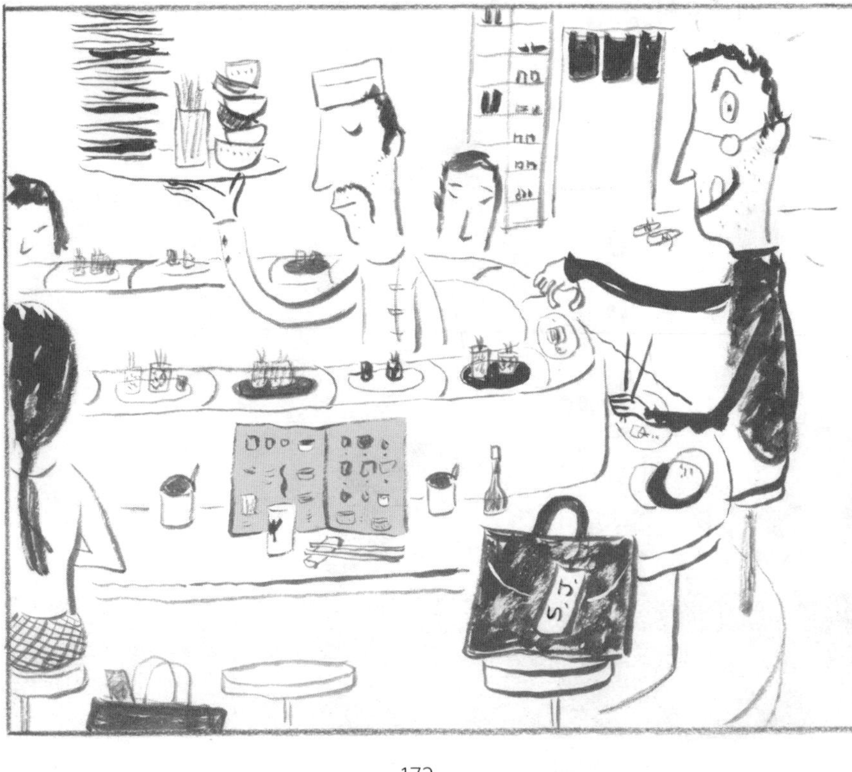
S.J.

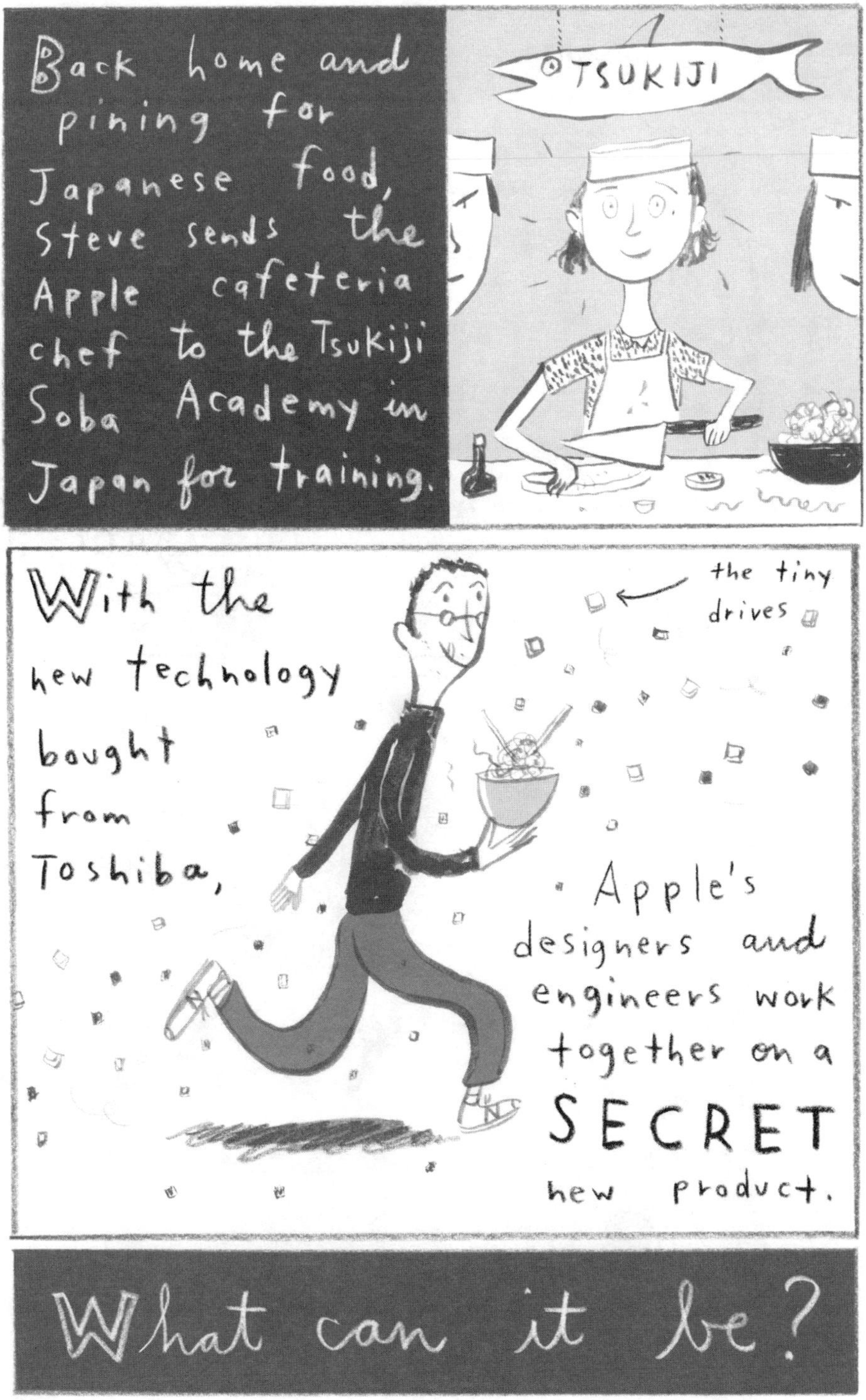
Back home and pining for Japanese food, Steve sends the Apple cafeteria chef to the Tsukiji Soba Academy in Japan for training.
TSUKIJI
With the new technology bought from Toshiba,
the tiny drives
Apple's designers and engineers work together on a SECRET new product.
What can it be?

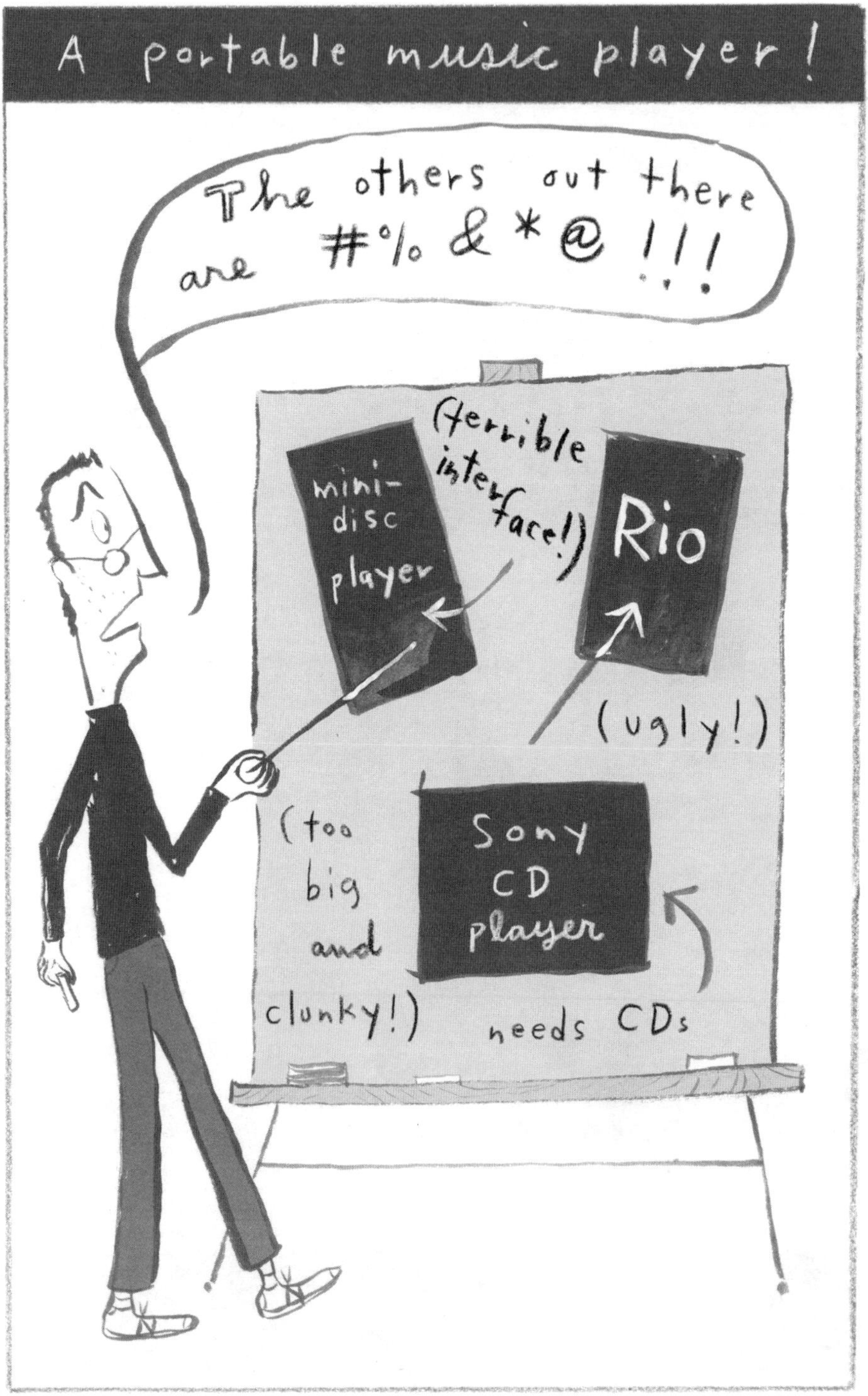
A portable music player!
The others out there are #%&*@!!!
mini-disc player
(terrible interface!)
Rio
(ugly!)
Sony CD player
(too big and clunky!)
needs CDs

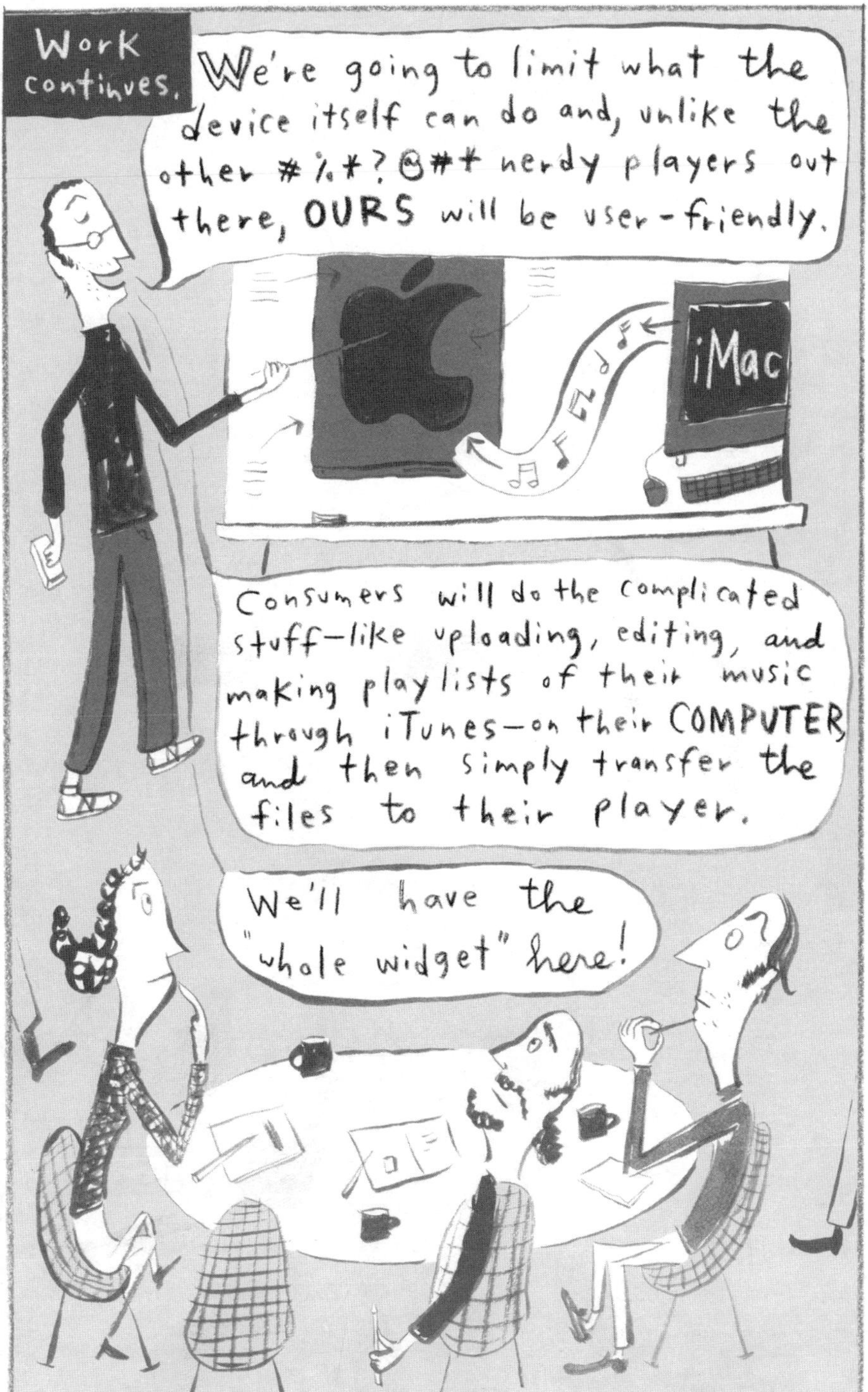
Work continues.
We're going to limit what the device itself can do and, unlike the other #%*?@#* nerdy players out there, OURS will be user-friendly.
iMac
Consumers will do the complicated stuff—like uploading, editing, and making playlists of their music through iTunes—on their COMPUTER, and then simply transfer the files to their player.
We'll have the "whole widget" here!

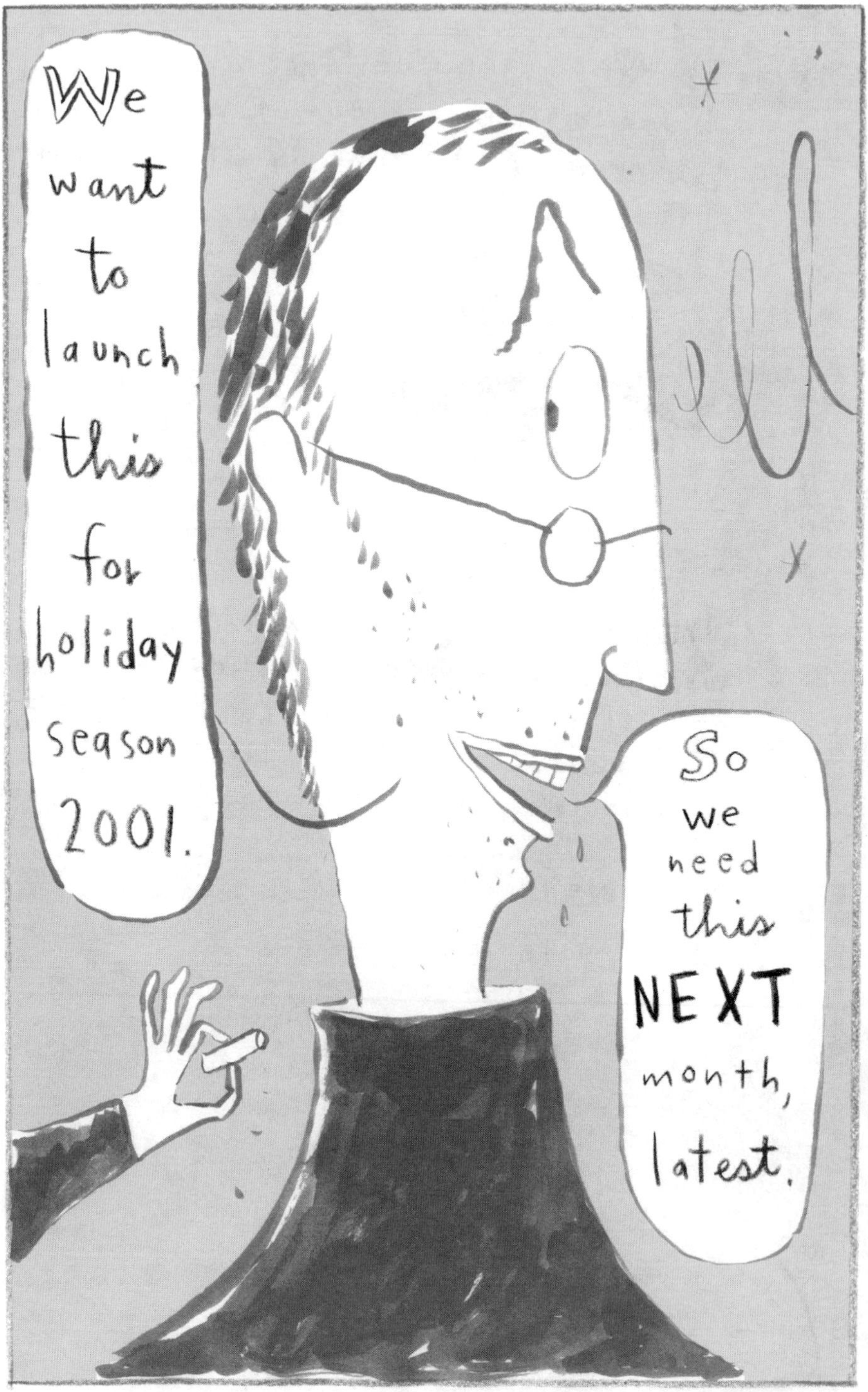
We want to launch this for holiday season 2001.
So we need this NEXT month, latest.

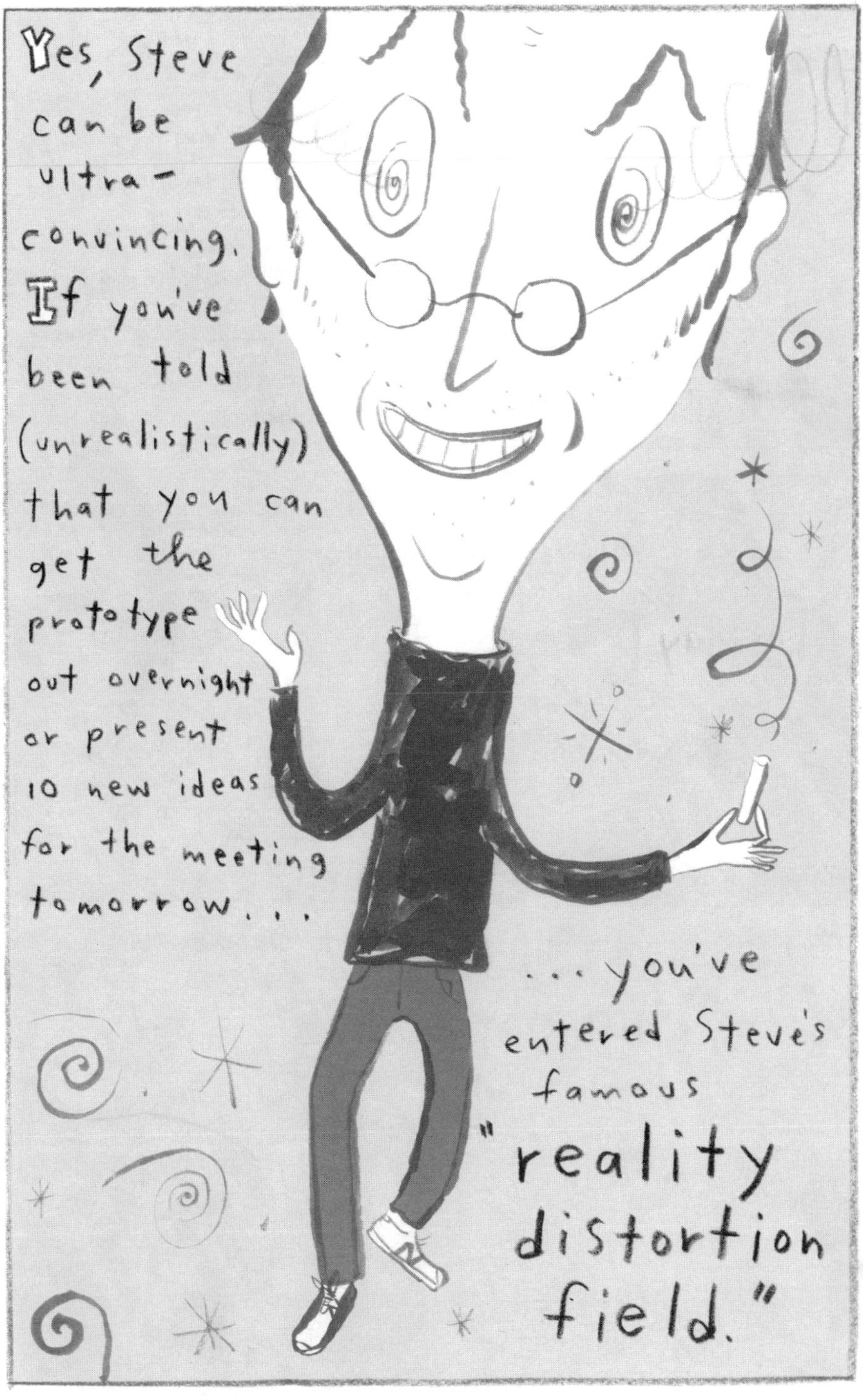
Yes, Steve can be ultra-convincing. If you've been told (unrealistically) that you can get the prototype out overnight or present 10 new ideas for the meeting tomorrow...
...you've entered Steve's famous "reality distortion field."

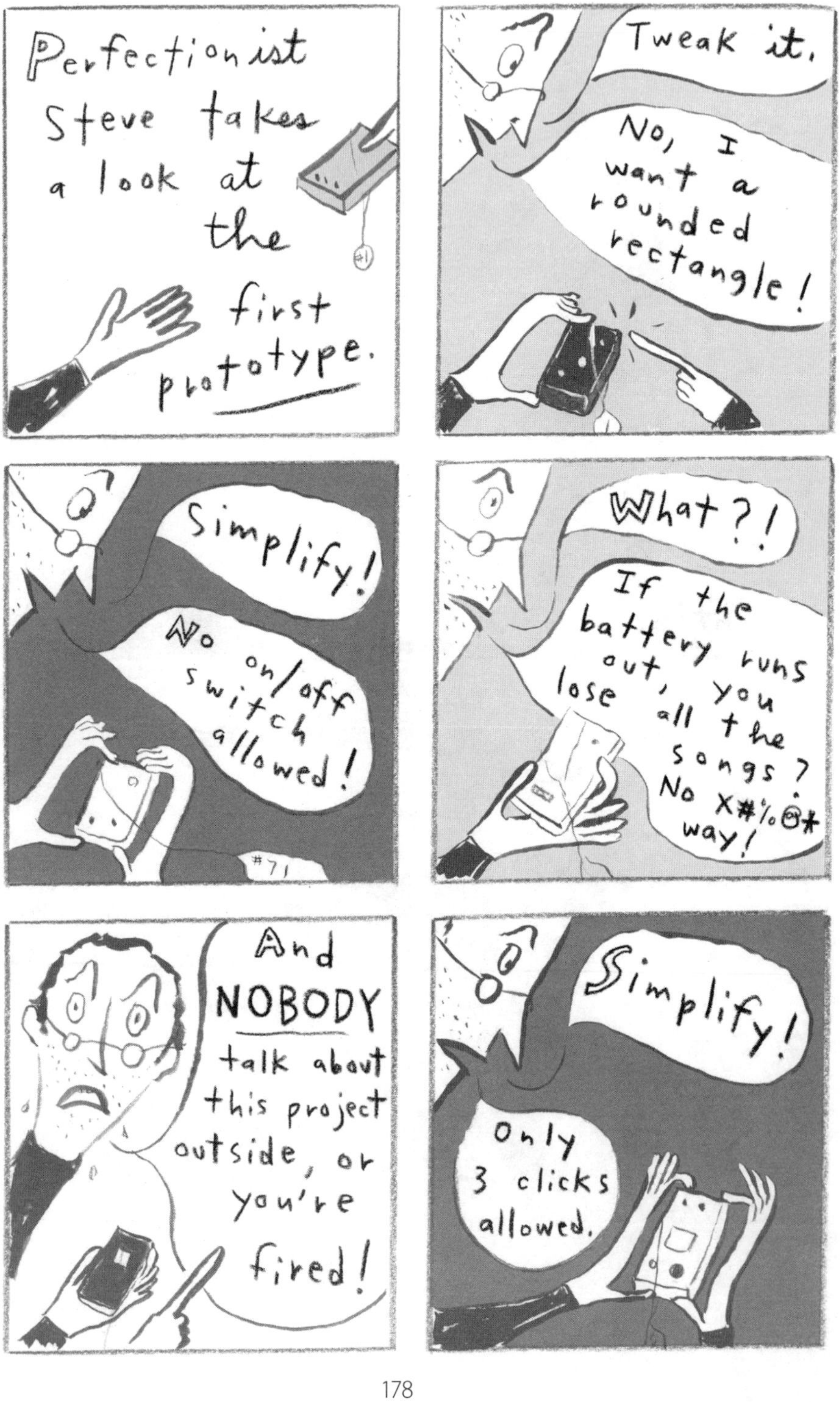

Perfectionist Steve takes a look at the first prototype.
#1
Tweak it.
No, I want a rounded rectangle!
Simplify!
No on/off switch allowed!
#71
What?!
If the battery runs out, you lose all the songs? No X#%@* way!
And NOBODY talk about this project outside, or you're fired!
Simplify!
Only 3 clicks allowed.

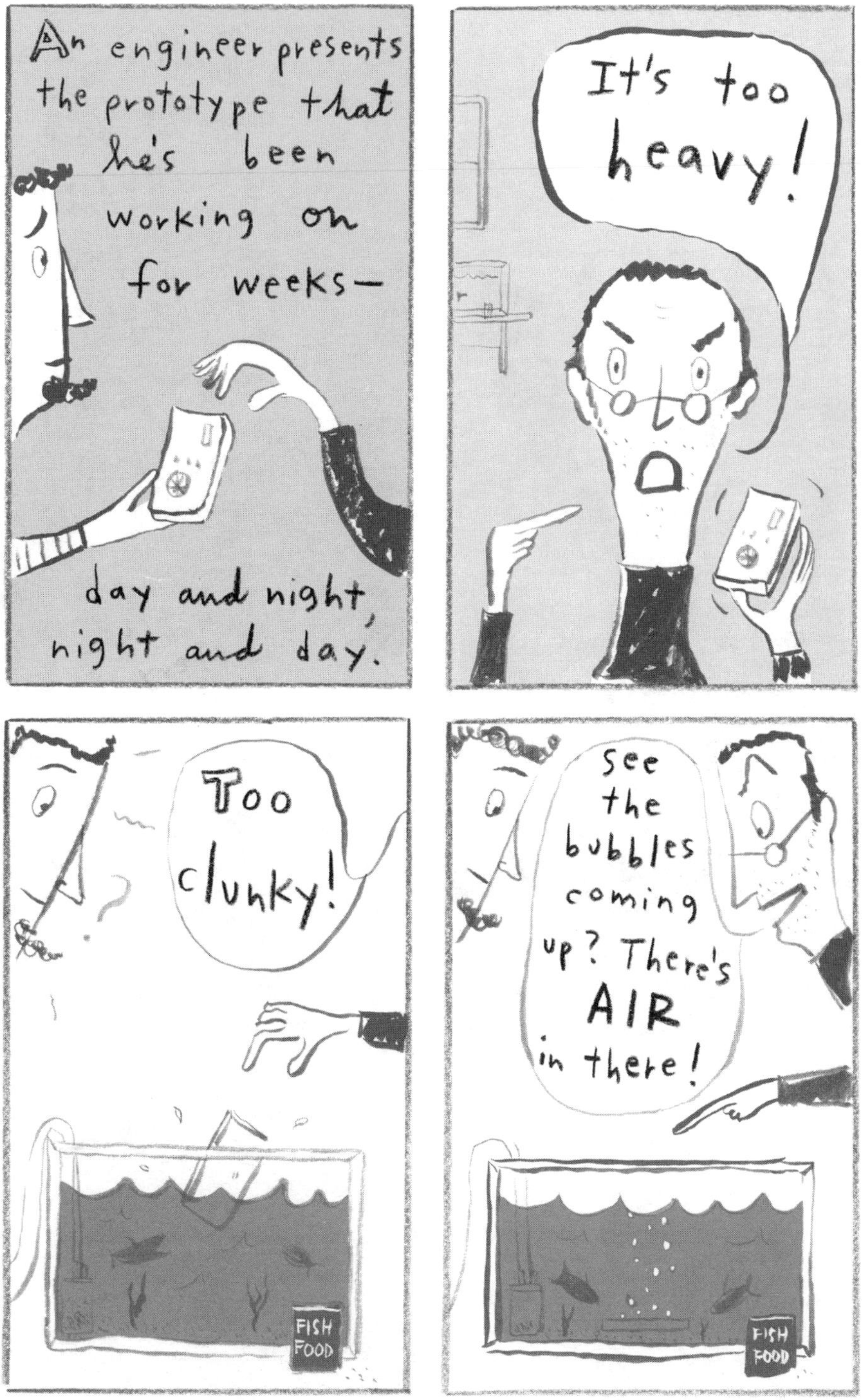

An engineer presents the prototype that he's been working on for weeks—
day and night, night and day.
It's too heavy!
Too clunky!
See the bubbles coming up? There's AIR in there!
FISH FOOD
FISH FOOD

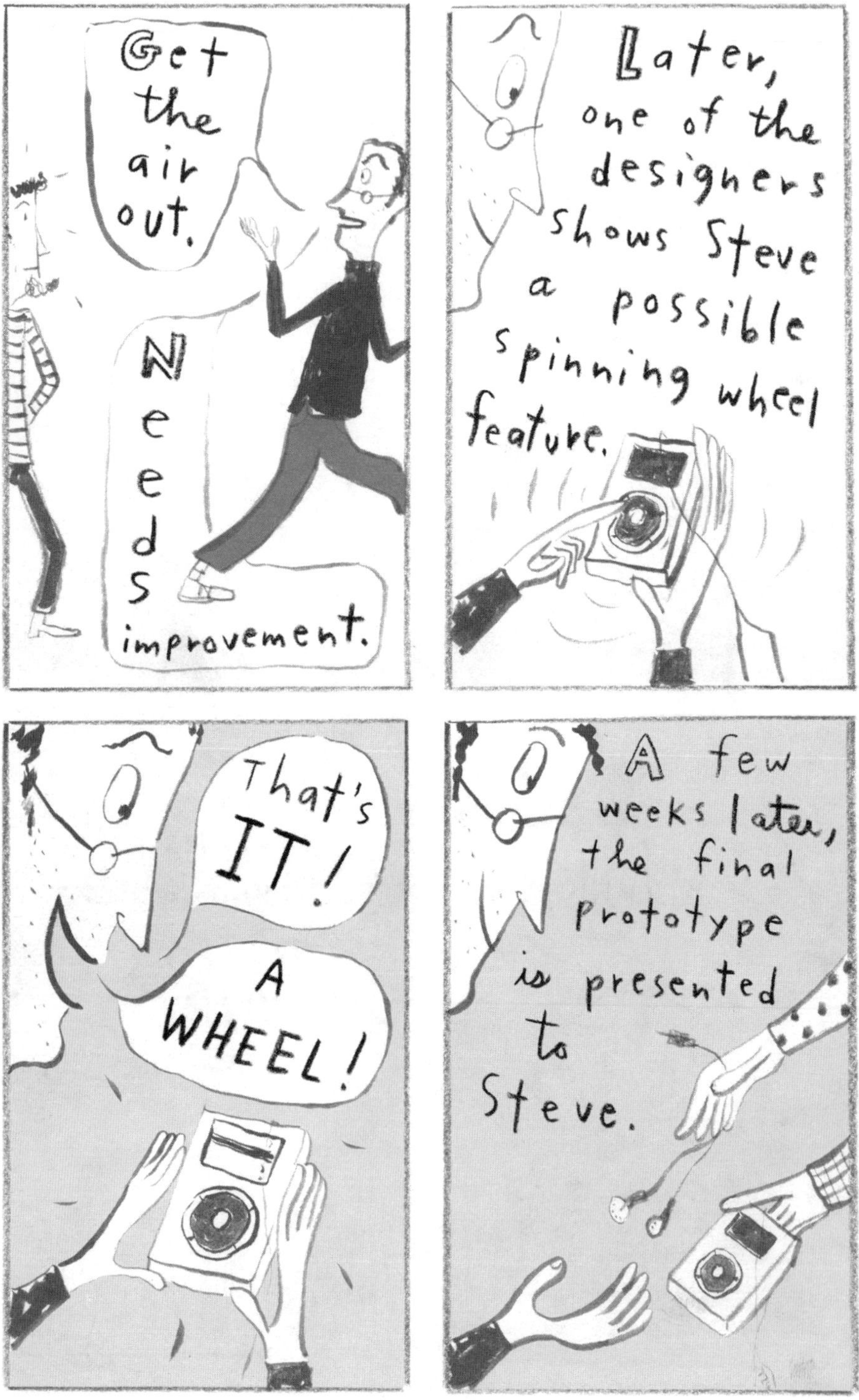
Get the air out.
Needs improvement.
Later, one of the designers shows Steve a possible spinning wheel feature.
That's IT!
A WHEEL!
A few weeks later, the final prototype is presented to Steve.

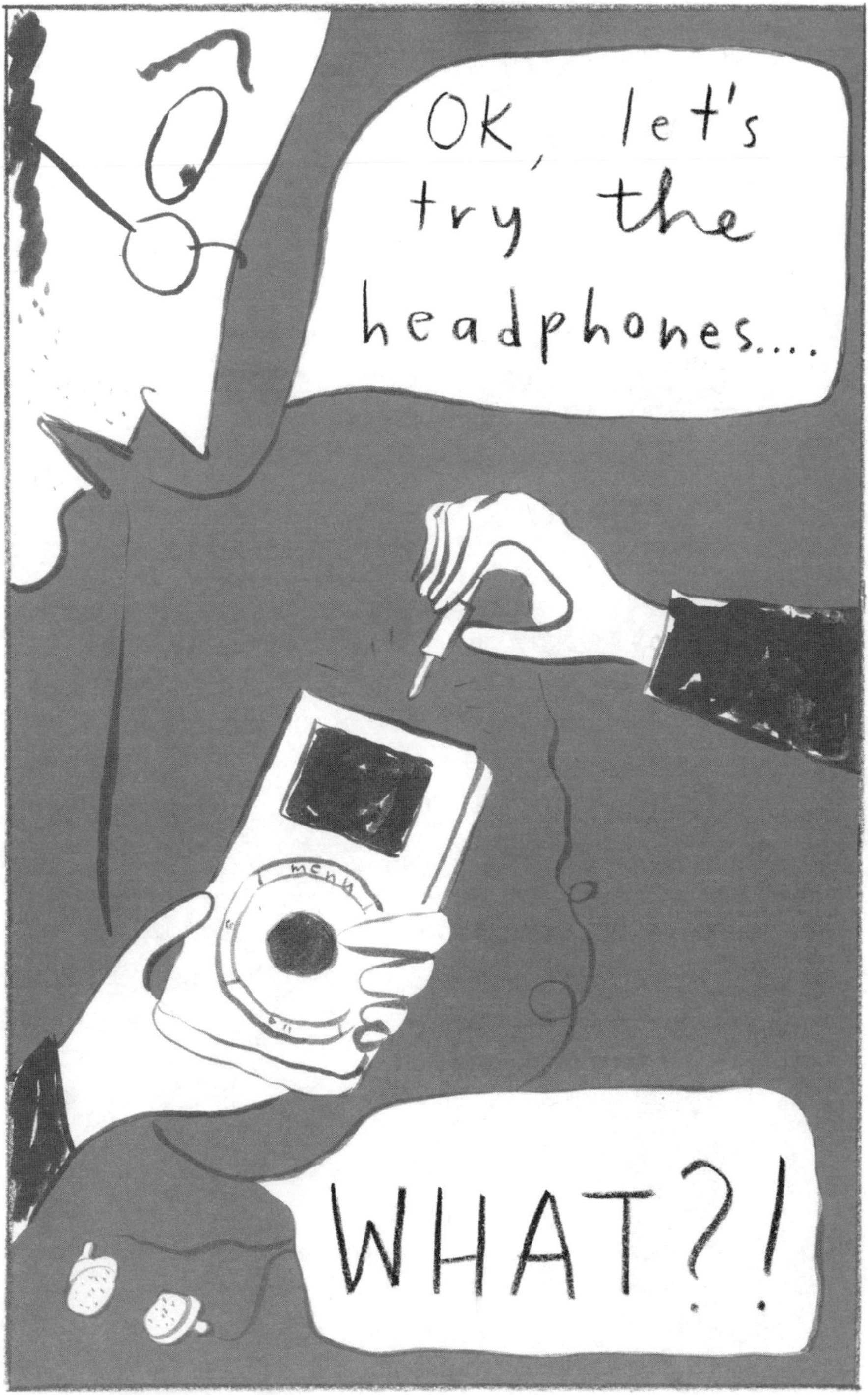
OK, let's try the headphones....
menu
WHAT?!

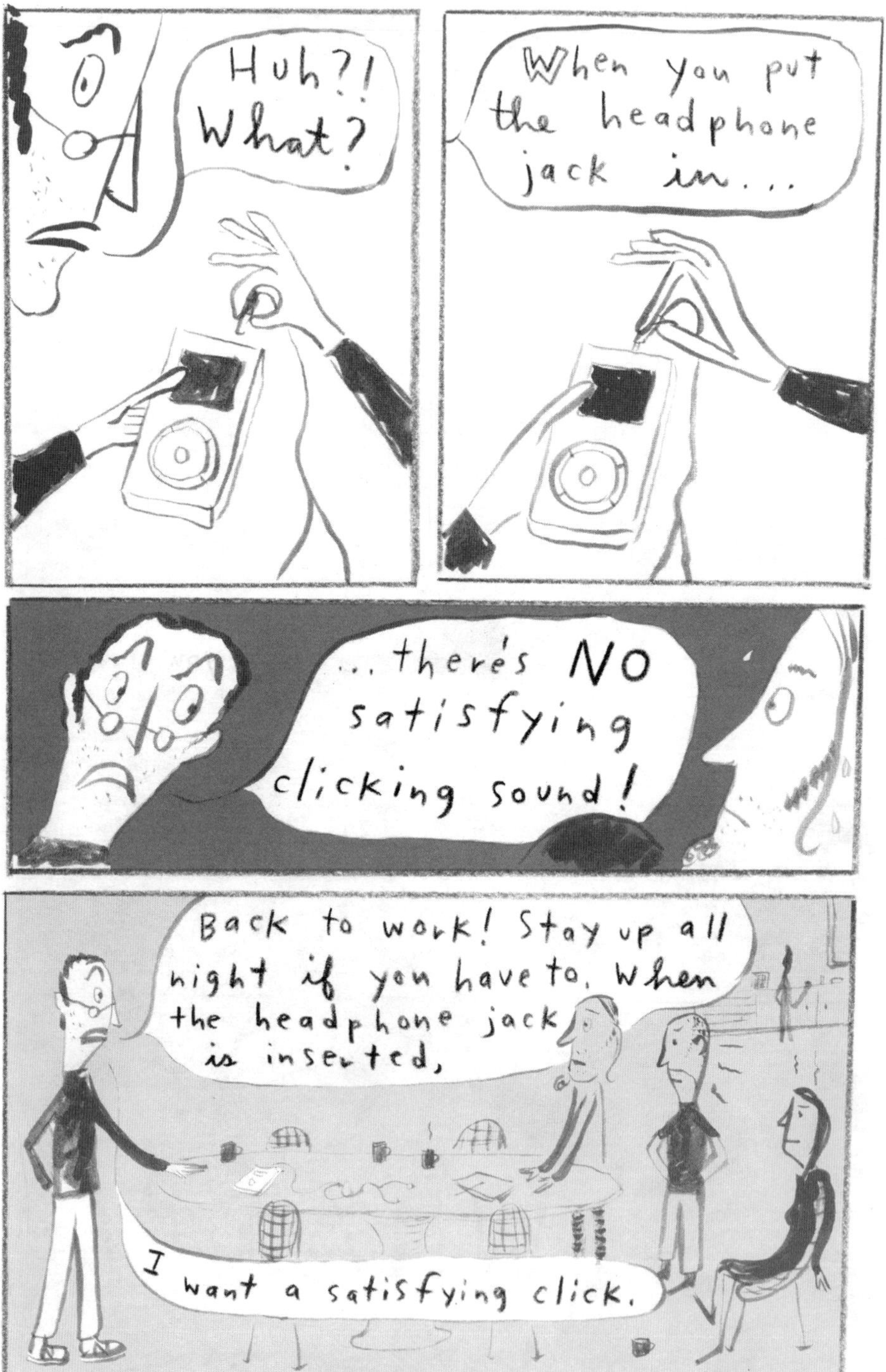
Huh?! What?
When you put the headphone jack in...
...there's NO satisfying clicking sound!
Back to work! Stay up all night if you have to. When the headphone jack is inserted,
I want a satisfying click.

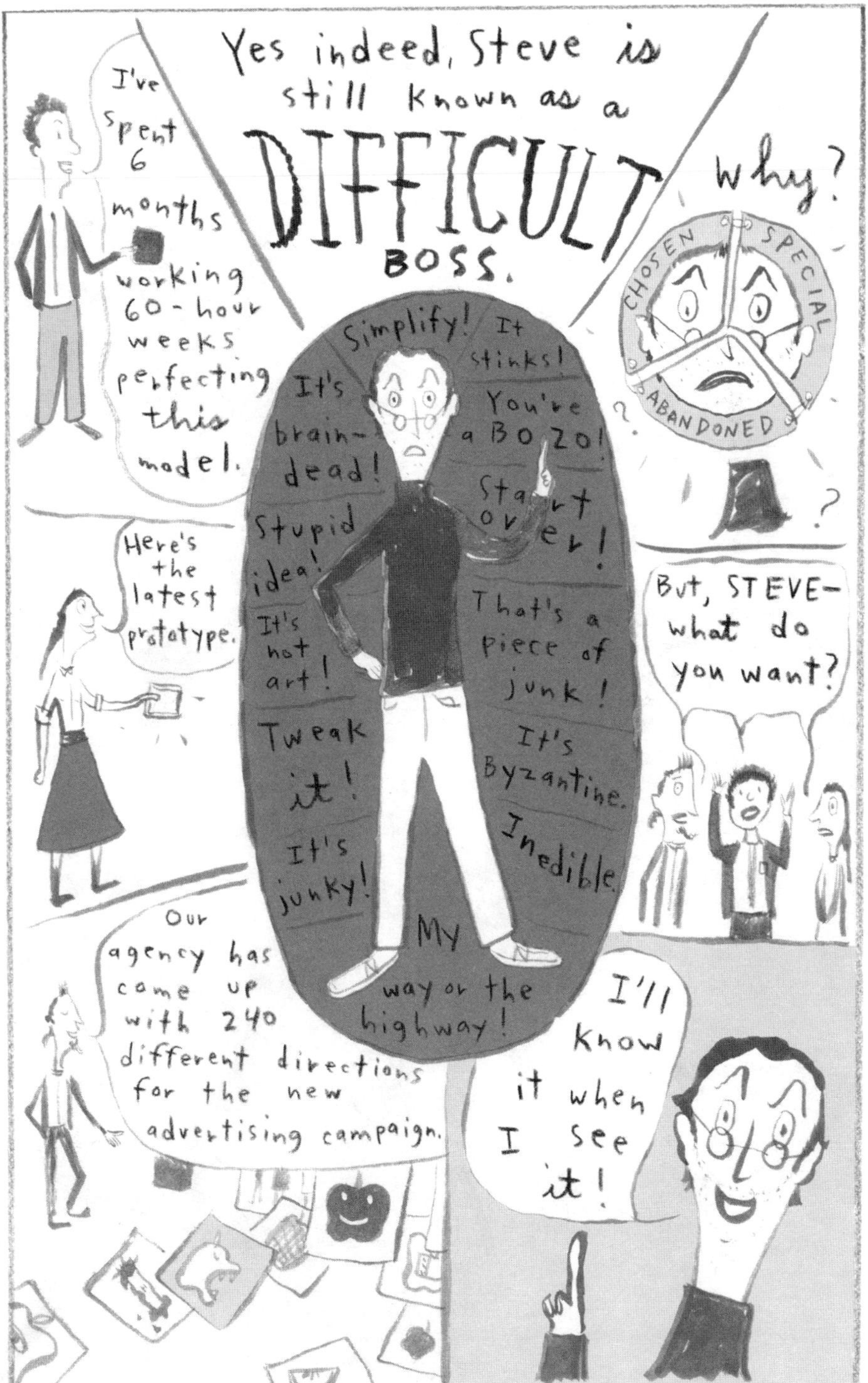

Yes indeed, Steve is still known as a DIFFICULT BOSS.
I've spent 6 months working 60-hour weeks perfecting this model.
Why?
CHOSEN
SPECIAL
ABANDONED
Here's the latest prototype.
Simplify!
It stinks!
It's brain-dead!
You're a BOZO!
Start over!
Stupid idea!
That's a piece of junk!
It's not art!
Tweak it!
It's Byzantine.
It's junky!
Inedible.
My way or the highway!
But, STEVE– what do you want?
Our agency has come up with 240 different directions for the new advertising campaign.
I'll know it when I see it!

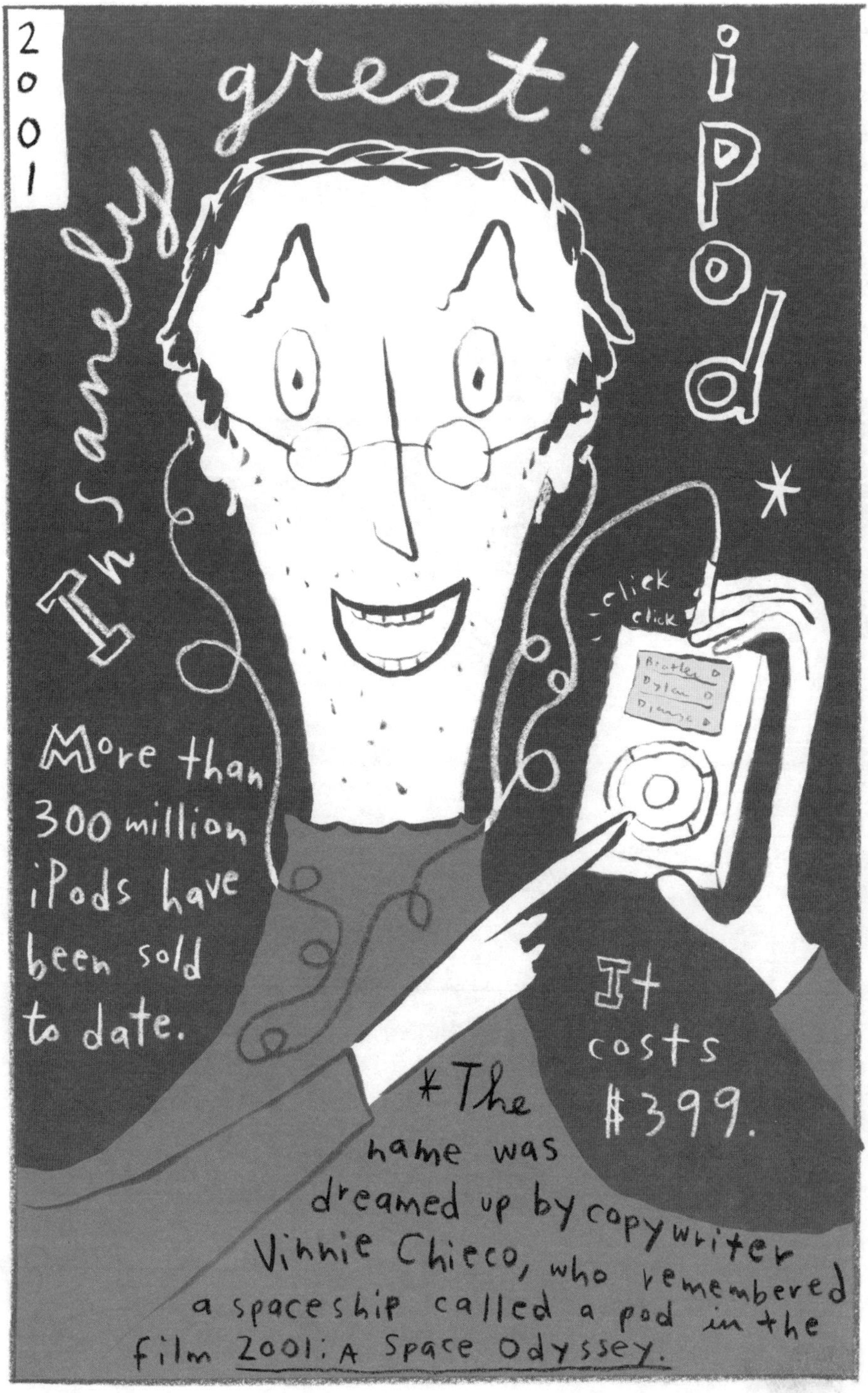
2001
Insanely great!
iPod*
click click
Beatles
Dylan
More than 300 million iPods have been sold to date.
It costs $399.
*The name was dreamed up by copywriter Vinnie Chieco, who remembered a spaceship called a pod in the film 2001: A Space Odyssey.

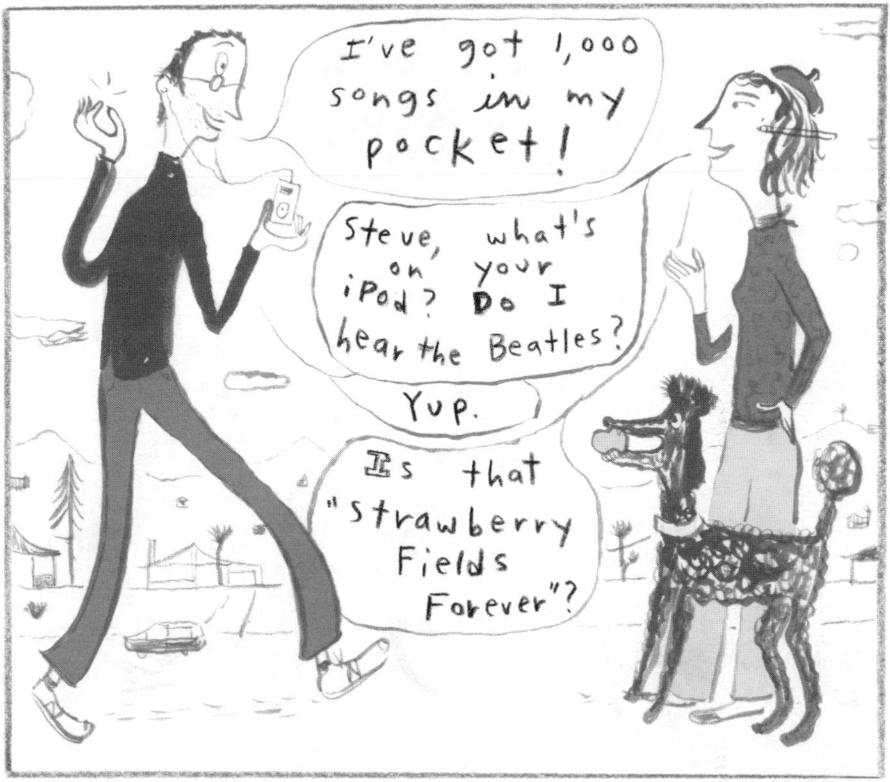
I've got 1,000 songs in my pocket!
Steve, what's on your iPod? Do I hear the Beatles?
Yup.
Is that "Strawberry Fields Forever"?

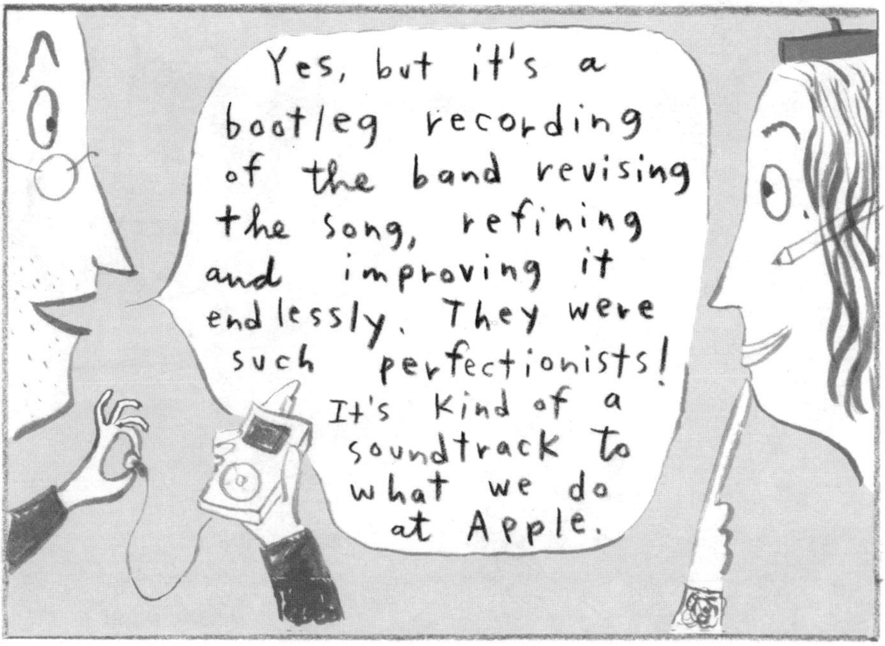
Yes, but it's a bootleg recording of the band revising the song, refining and improving it endlessly. They were such perfectionists! It's kind of a soundtrack to what we do at Apple.

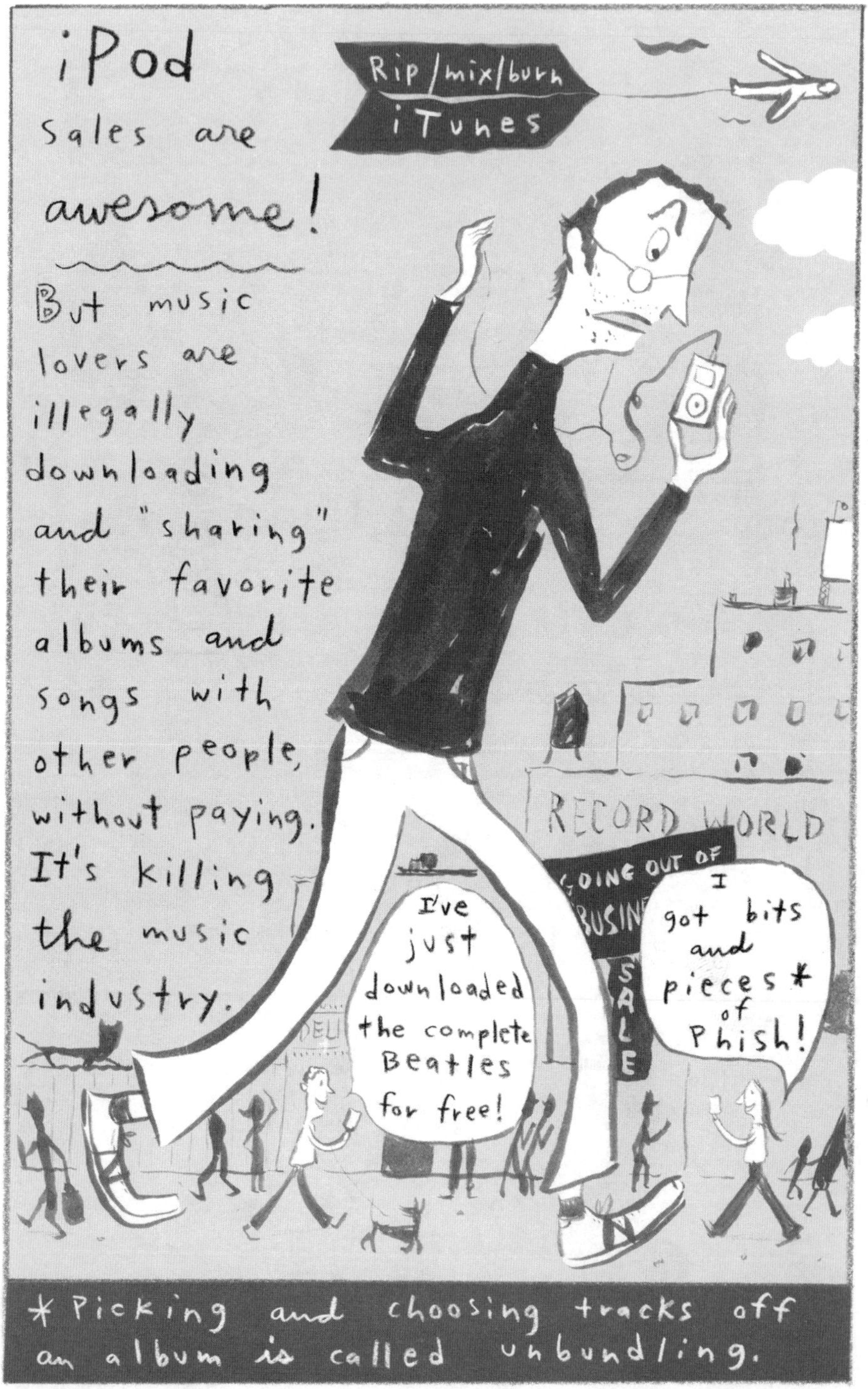
iPod sales are awesome!
Rip/mix/burn iTunes
But music lovers are illegally downloading and "sharing" their favorite albums and songs with other people, without paying. It's killing the music industry.
RECORD WORLD
GOING OUT OF BUSINE
SALE
DELI
I've just downloaded the complete Beatles for free!
I got bits and pieces* of Phish!
* Picking and choosing tracks off an album is called unbundling.

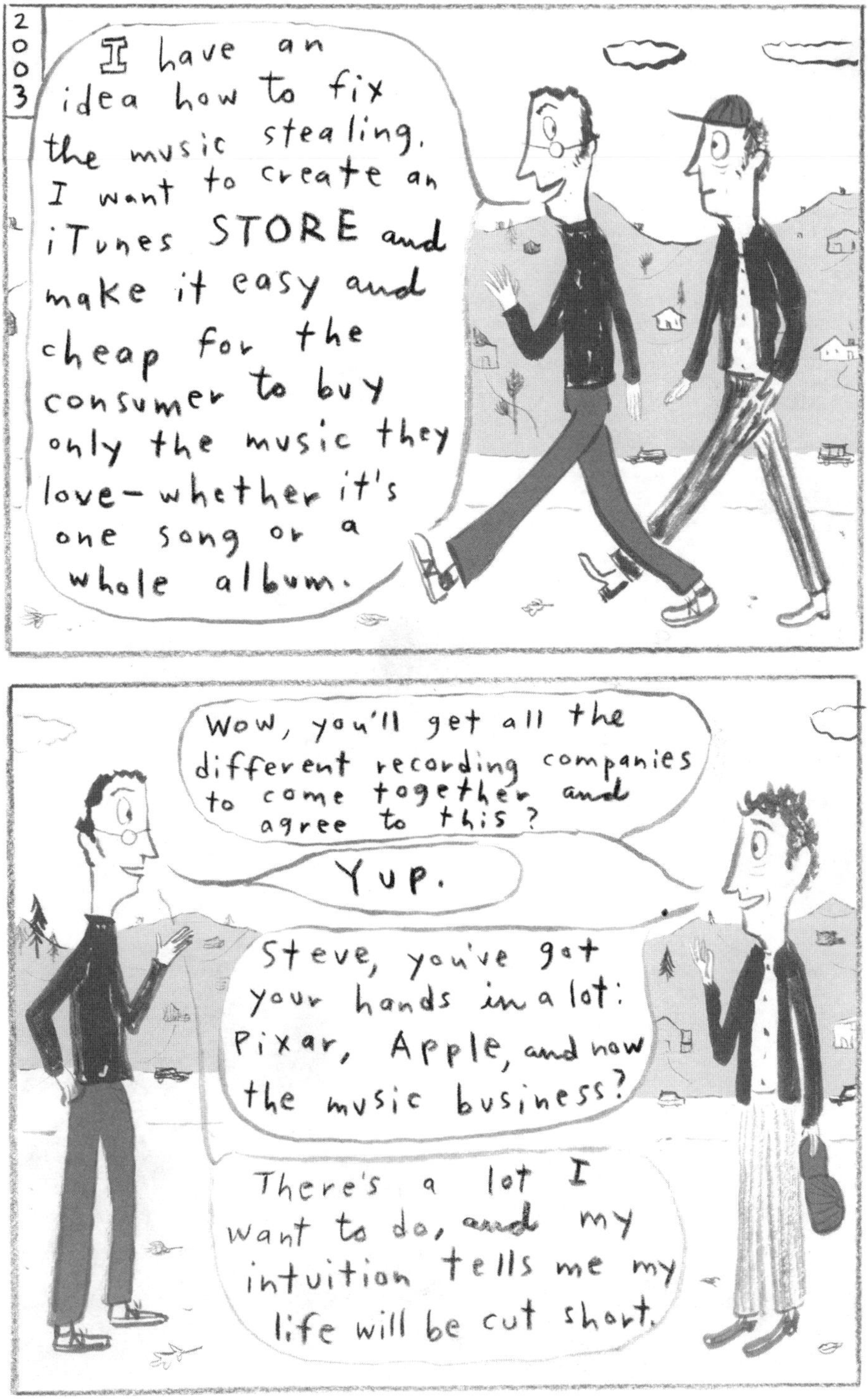
2003
I have an idea how to fix the music stealing. I want to create an iTunes STORE and make it easy and cheap for the consumer to buy only the music they love– whether it's one song or a whole album.
Wow, you'll get all the different recording companies to come together and agree to this?
Yup.
Steve, you've got your hands in a lot: Pixar, Apple, and now the music business?
There's a lot I want to do, and my intuition tells me my life will be cut short.

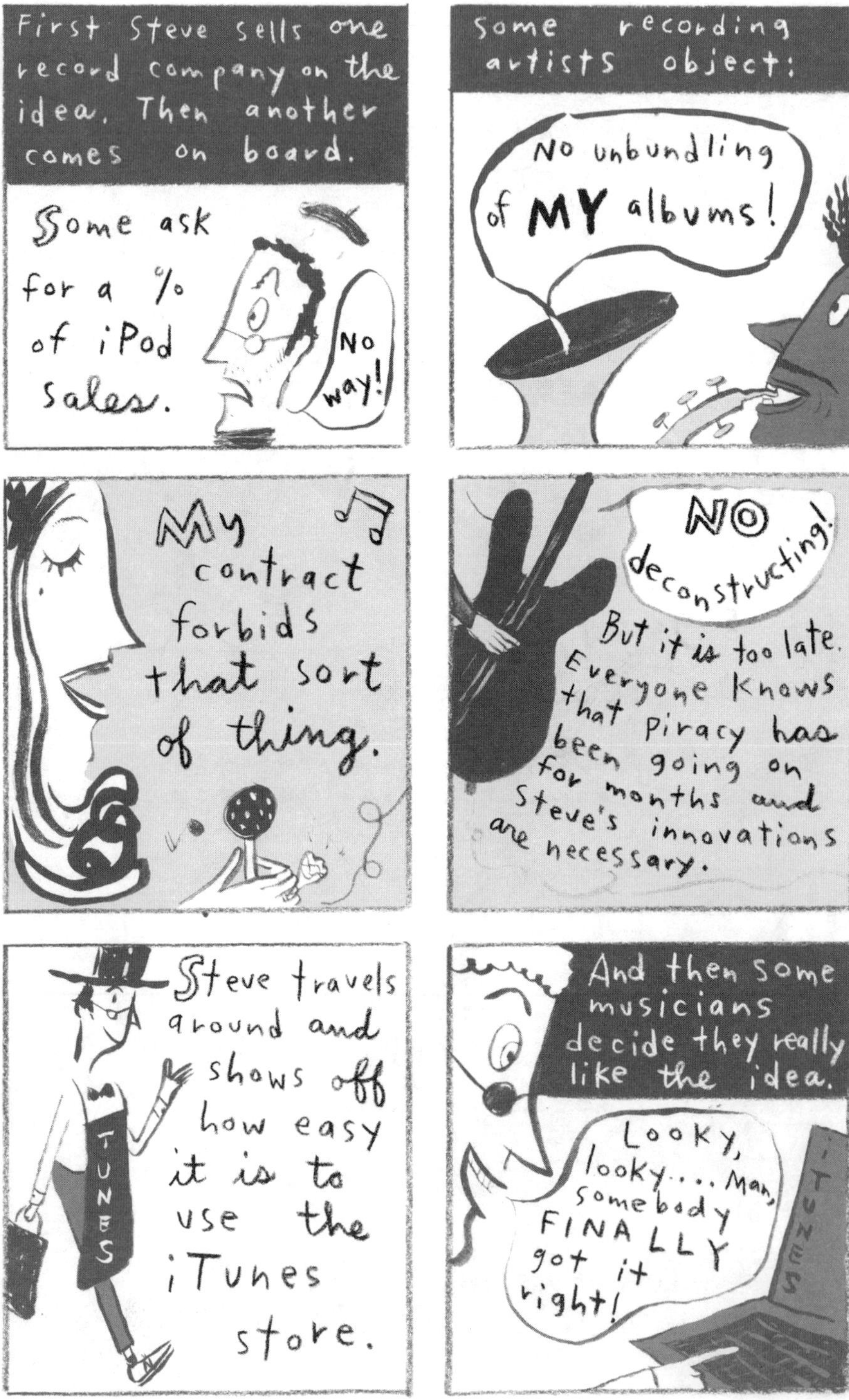

First Steve sells one record company on the idea. Then another comes on board.
Some ask for a % of iPod sales.
No way!
Some recording artists object:
No unbundling of MY albums!
My contract forbids that sort of thing.
NO deconstructing!
But it is too late. Everyone knows that piracy has been going on for months and Steve's innovations are necessary.
Steve travels around and shows off how easy it is to use the iTunes store.
iTUNES
And then some musicians decide they really like the idea.
Looky, looky... Man, somebody FINALLY got it right!
iTUNES

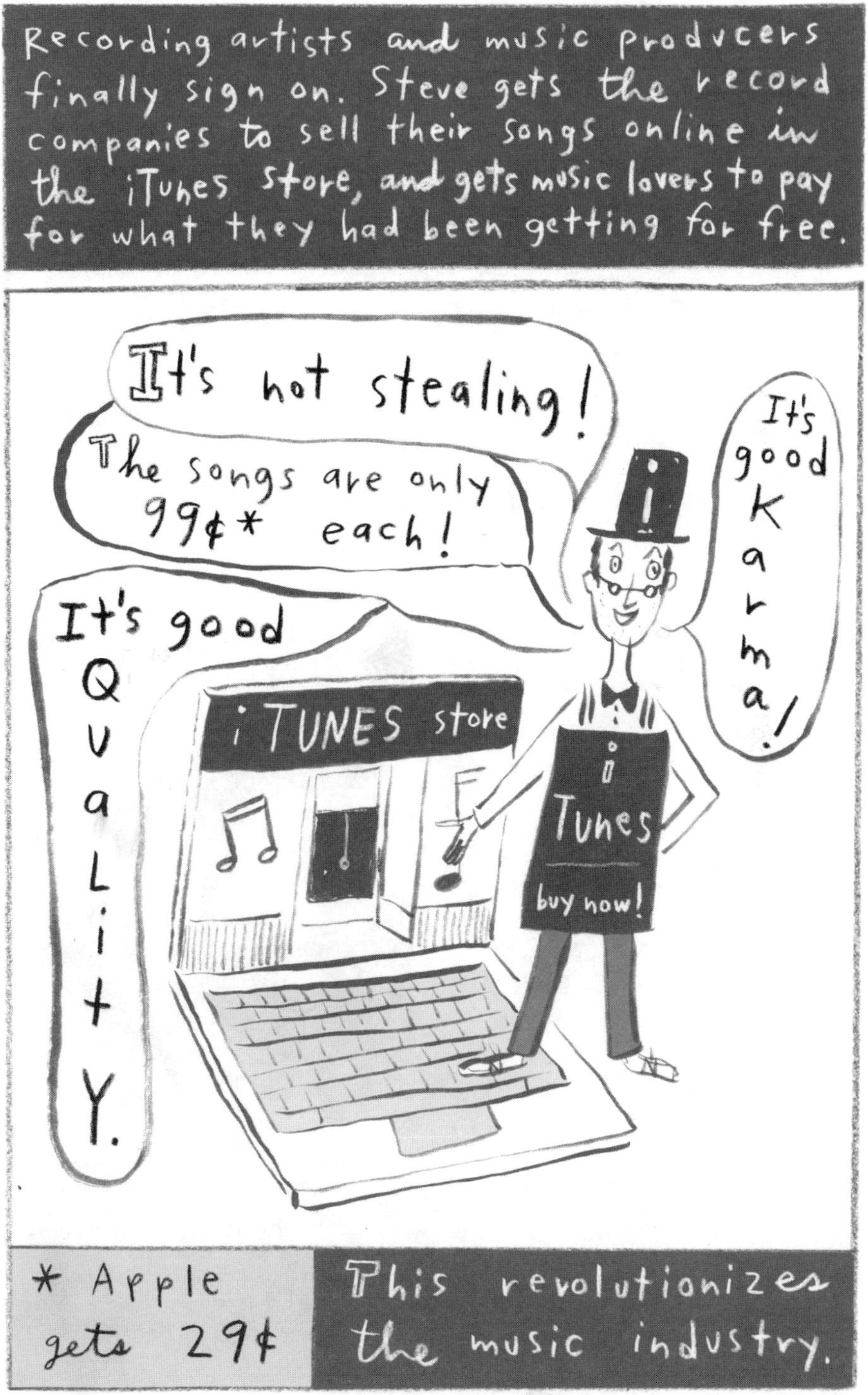
Recording artists and music producers finally sign on. Steve gets the record companies to sell their songs online in the iTunes store, and gets music lovers to pay for what they had been getting for free.
It's not stealing!
The songs are only 99¢* each!
It's good Karma!
It's good QuaLitY.
iTUNES store
iTunes buy now!
* Apple gets 29¢
This revolutionizes the music industry.

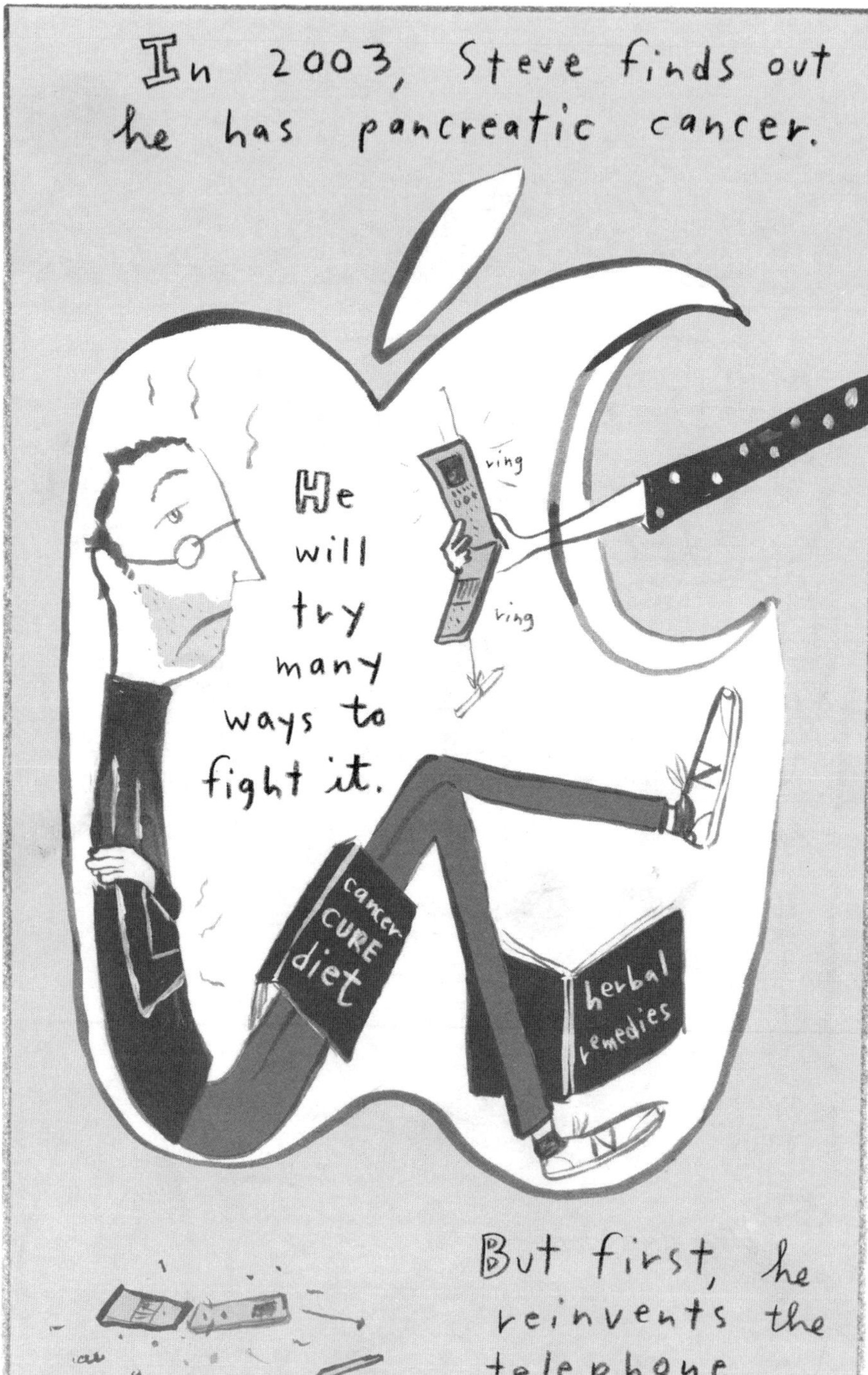
In 2003, Steve finds out he has pancreatic cancer.
ring
ring
He will try many ways to fight it.
cancer CURE diet
herbal remedies
But first, he reinvents the telephone.

Chapter

13

COMPUTER

Refined
DESIGN
(2004-2011)

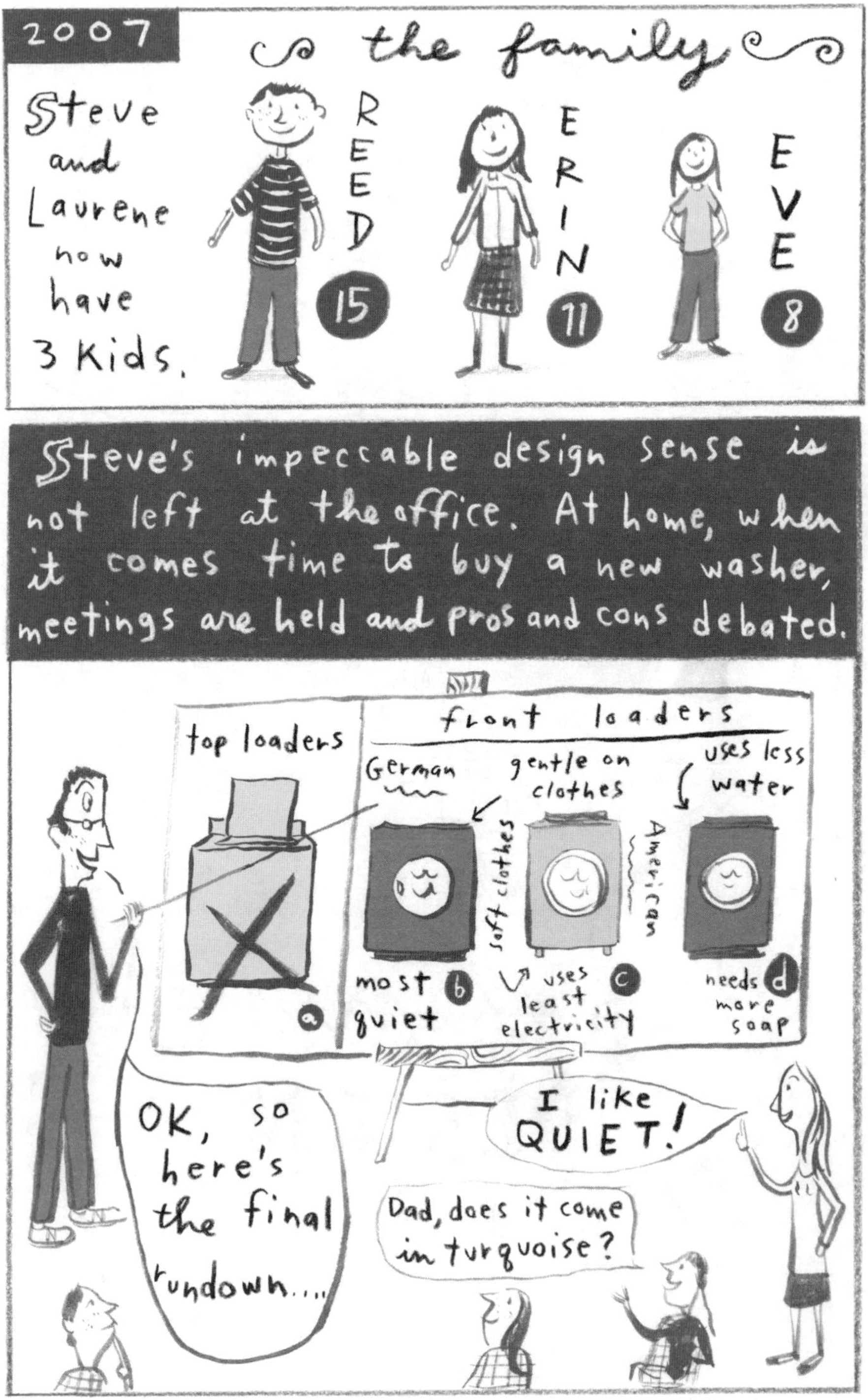

2007
the family
Steve and Laurene now have 3 Kids.
REED 15
ERIN 11
EVE 8
Steve's impeccable design sense is not left at the office. At home, when it comes time to buy a new washer, meetings are held and pros and cons debated.
top loaders
a
front loaders
German
gentle on clothes
uses less water
soft clothes
American
most quiet
b
uses least electricity
c
needs more soap
d
OK, so here's the final rundown....
I like QUIET!
Dad, does it come in turquoise?

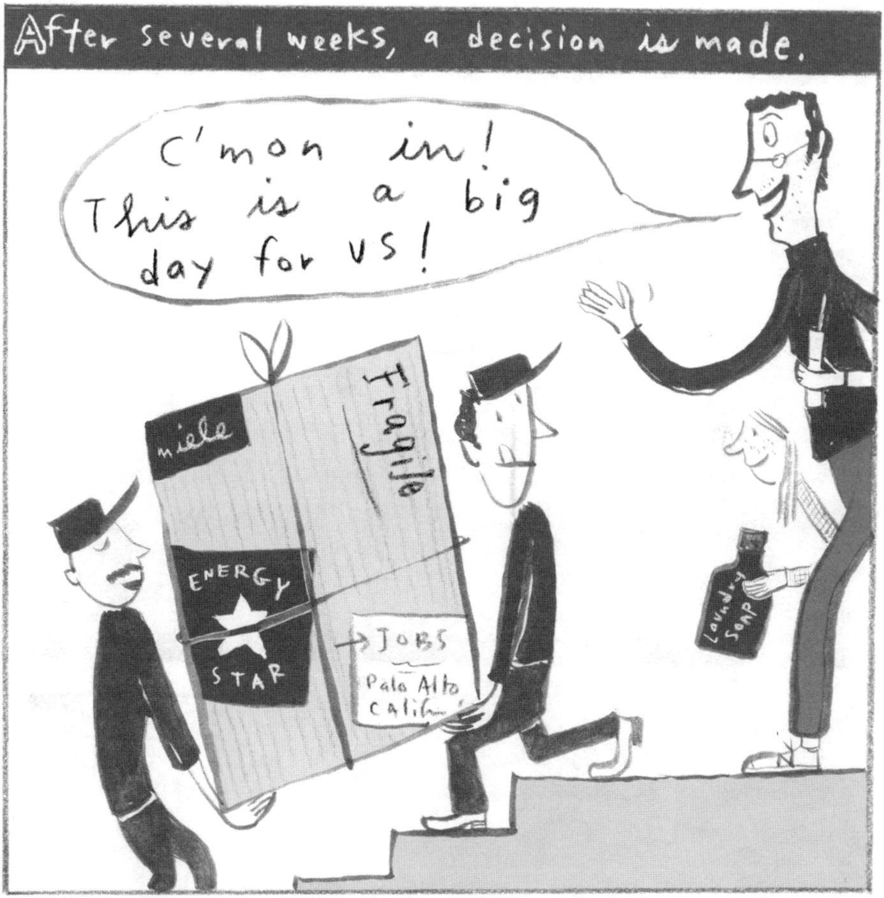
After several weeks, a decision is made.
C'mon in! This is a big day for us!
miele
Fragile
ENERGY STAR
JOBS
Palo Alto
Laundry SOAP

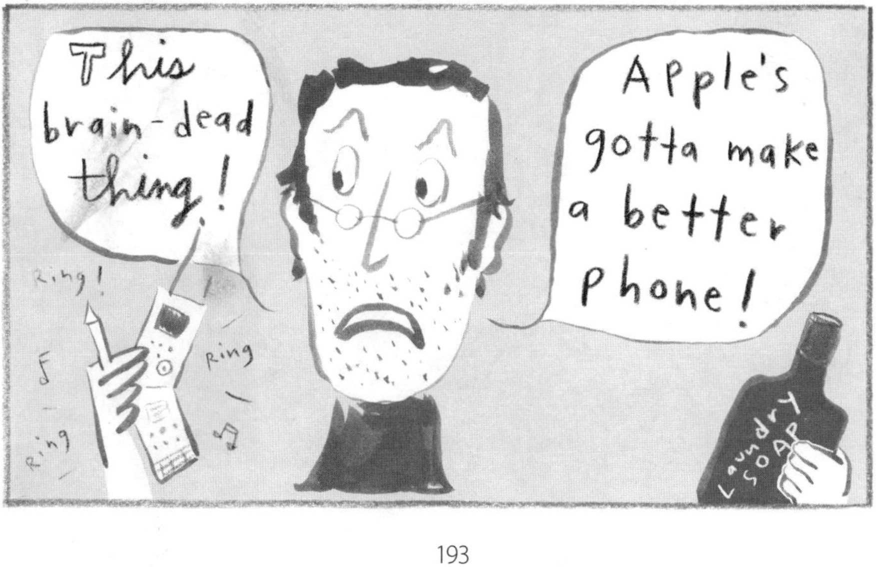
This brain-dead thing!
Apple's gotta make a better phone!
Ring!
ring
Ring
Laundry SOAP

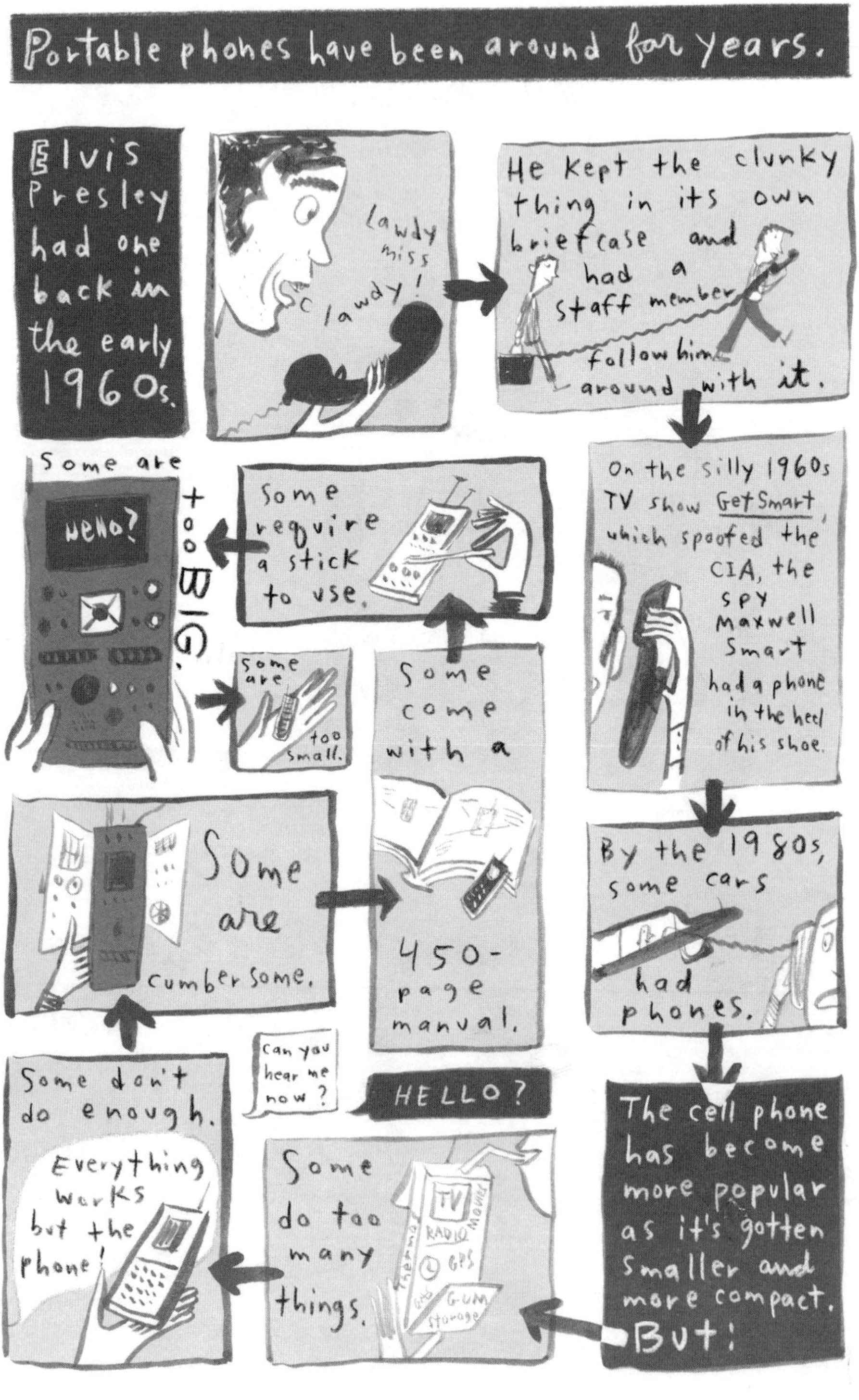
Portable phones have been around for years.
Elvis Presley had one back in the early 1960s.
Lawdy miss Clawdy!
He kept the clunky thing in its own briefcase and had a staff member follow him around with it.
On the silly 1960s TV show Get Smart, which spoofed the CIA, the spy Maxwell Smart had a phone in the heel of his shoe.
By the 1980s, some cars had phones.
The cell phone has become more popular as it's gotten smaller and more compact. But:
Some do too many things.
TV
RADIO
MOVIES
GPS
GUM
Storage
HELLO?
Can you hear me now?
Some don't do enough.
Everything works but the phone!
Some are cumbersome.
Some come with a 450-page manual.
Some require a stick to use.
Some are too BIG.
HELLO?
Some are too small.

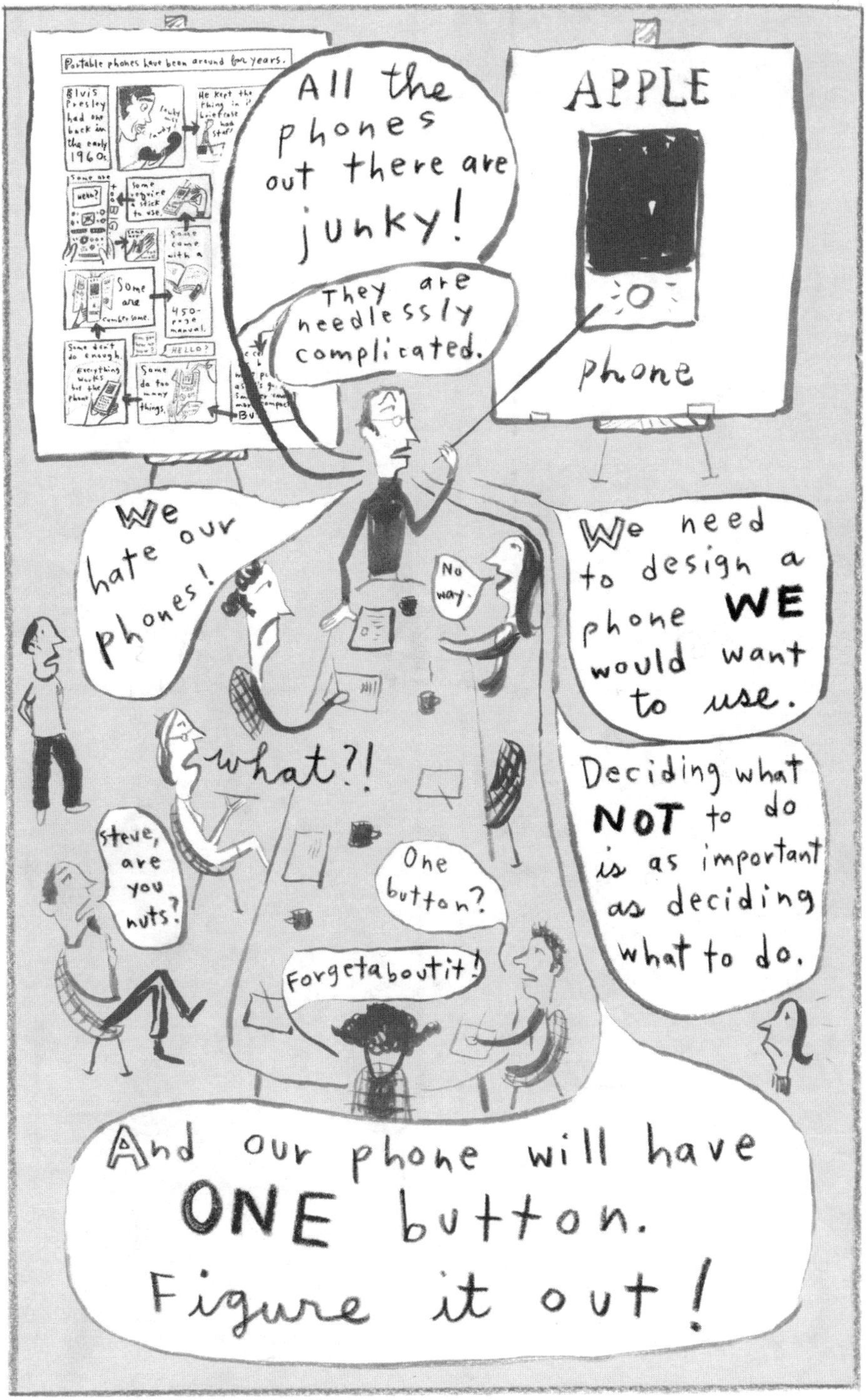

Portable phones have been around for years.
Elvis Presley had one back in the early 1960s.
He kept the thing in a briefcase
Some are
Some require a stick to use.
Some come with a
450-page manual.
Some are cumbersome.
Some don't do enough.
Everything works but the phone
HELLO?
Some do too many things.
All the phones out there are junky!
They are needlessly complicated.
APPLE
phone
We hate our phones!
No way.
We need to design a phone WE would want to use.
what?!
Deciding what NOT to do is as important as deciding what to do.
steve, are you nuts?
One button?
Forgetaboutit!
And our phone will have ONE button. Figure it out!

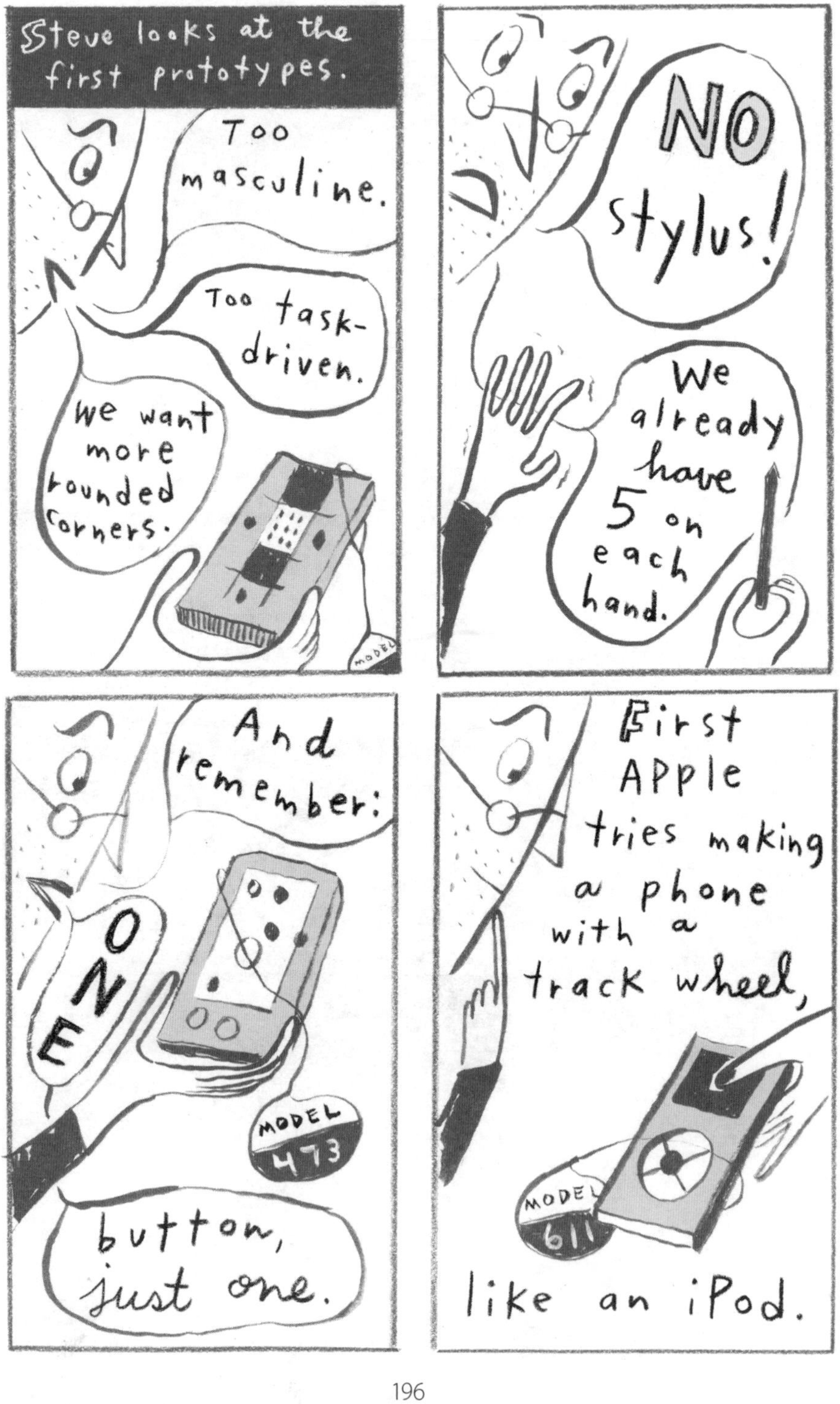
Steve looks at the first prototypes.
Too masculine.
Too task-driven.
We want more rounded corners.
MODEL
NO stylus!
We already have 5 on each hand.
And remember:
ONE
button, just one.
MODEL 473
First Apple tries making a phone with a track wheel,
MODEL 611
like an iPod.

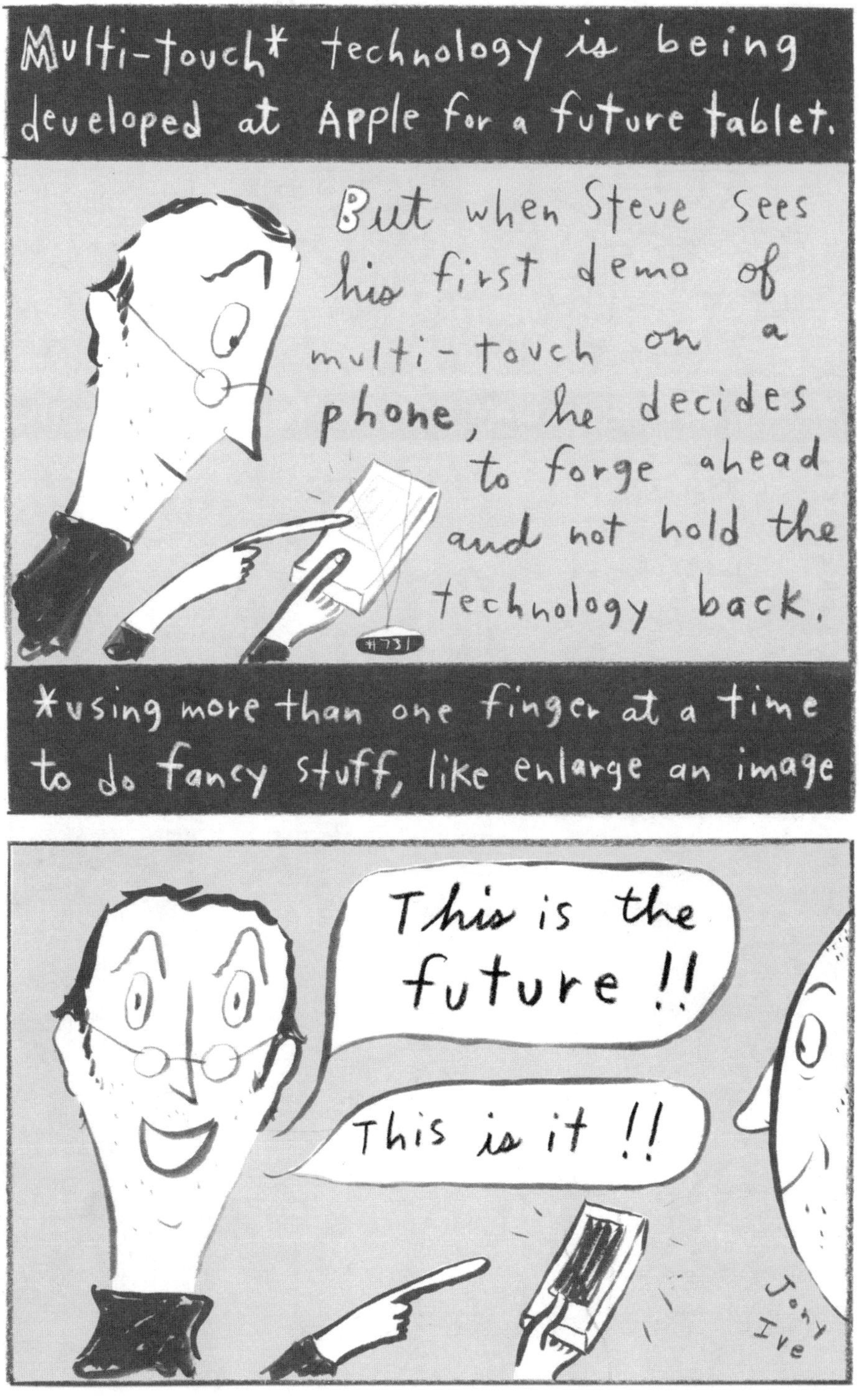
Multi-touch* technology is being developed at Apple for a future tablet.
But when Steve sees his first demo of multi-touch on a phone, he decides to forge ahead and not hold the technology back.
#731
*using more than one finger at a time to do fancy stuff, like enlarge an image
This is the future!!
This is it!!
Jony Ive

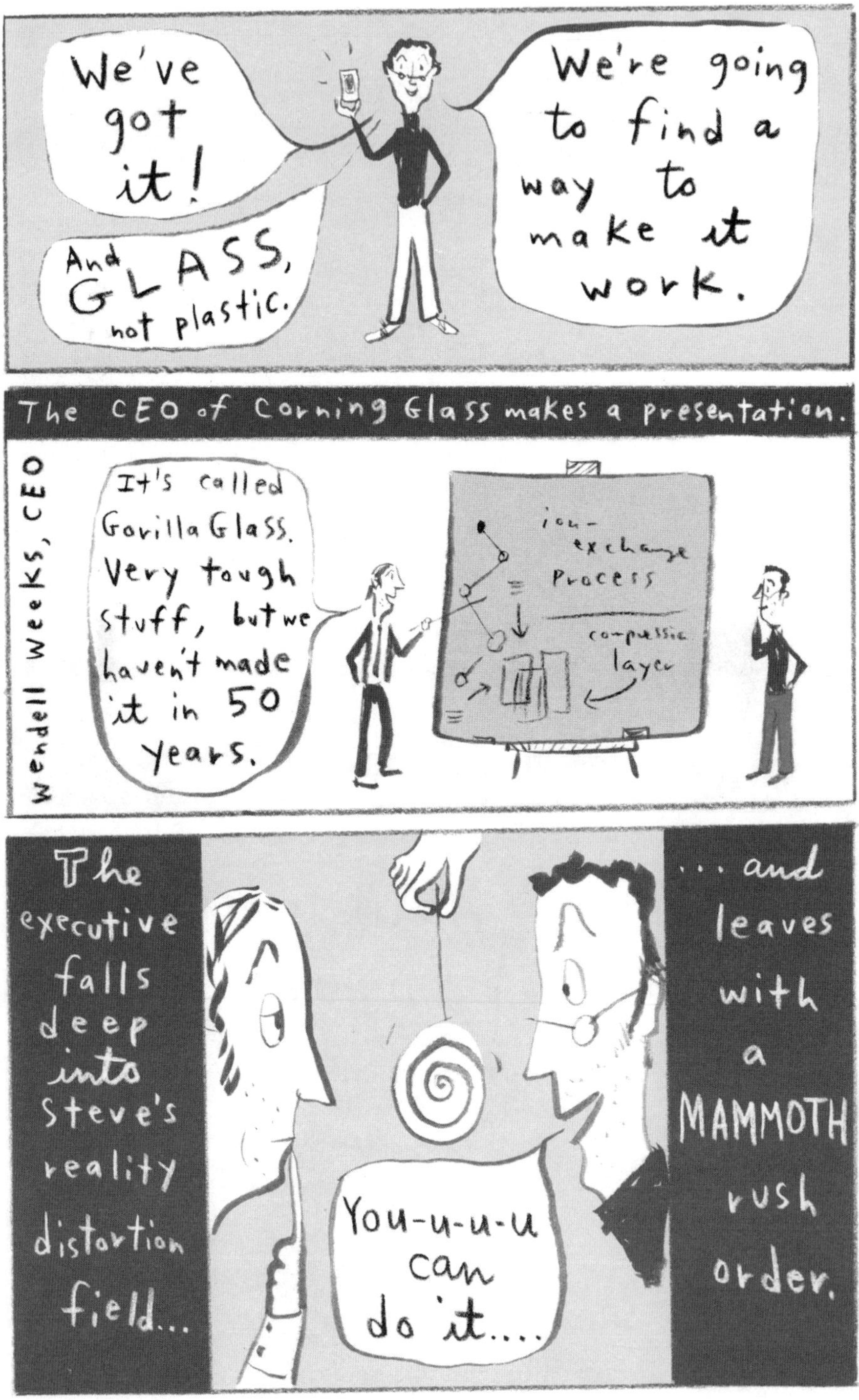
We've got it!
And GLASS, not plastic.
We're going to find a way to make it work.
The CEO of Corning Glass makes a presentation.
Wendell Weeks, CEO
It's called Gorilla Glass. Very tough stuff, but we haven't made it in 50 years.
The executive falls deep into Steve's reality distortion field...
You-u-u-u can do it....
... and leaves with a MAMMOTH rush order.

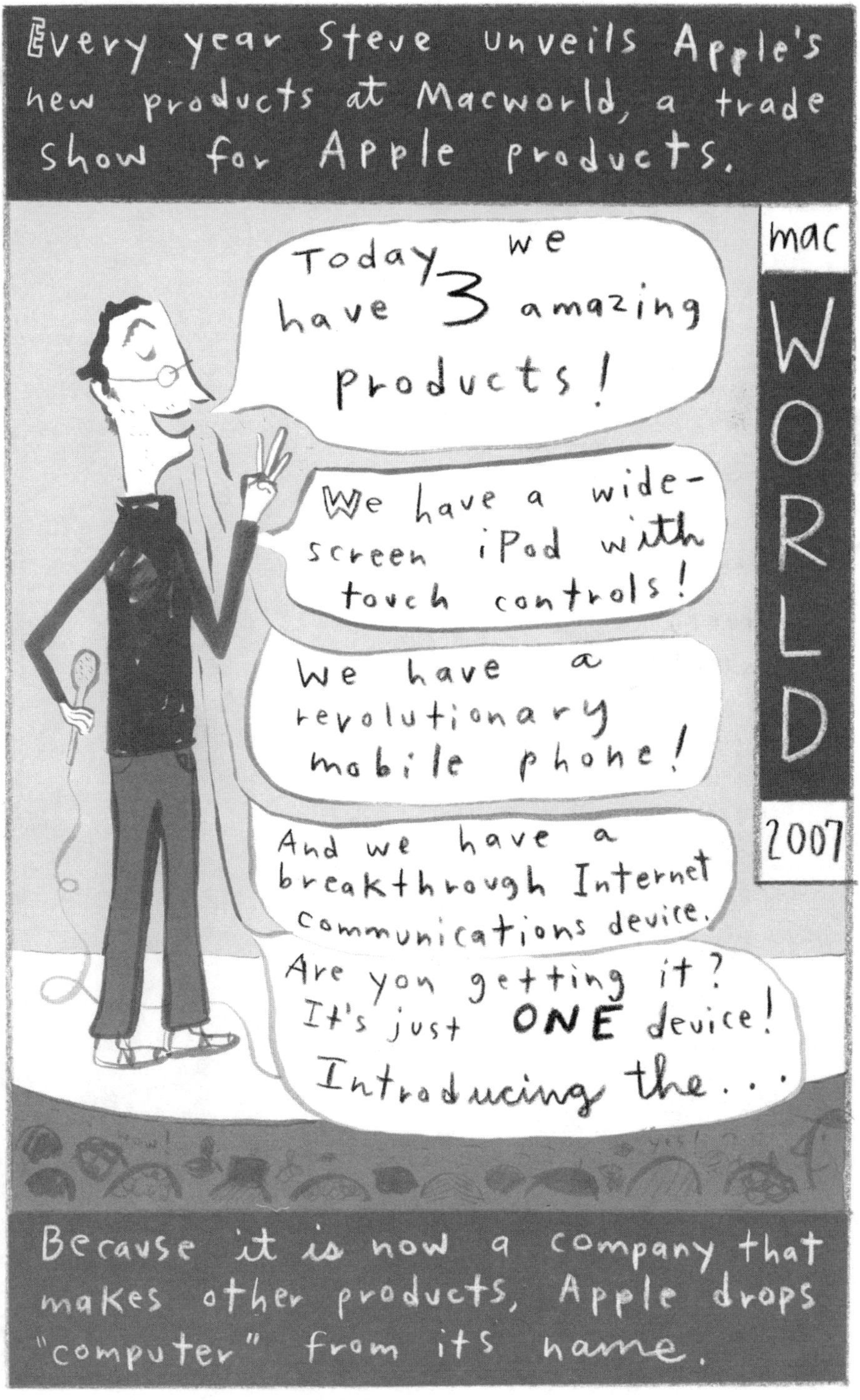
Every year Steve unveils Apple's new products at Macworld, a trade show for Apple products.
mac WORLD 2007
Today we have 3 amazing products!
We have a wide-screen iPod with touch controls!
We have a revolutionary mobile phone!
And we have a breakthrough Internet communications device.
Are you getting it? It's just ONE device! Introducing the...
Because it is now a company that makes other products, Apple drops "computer" from its name.

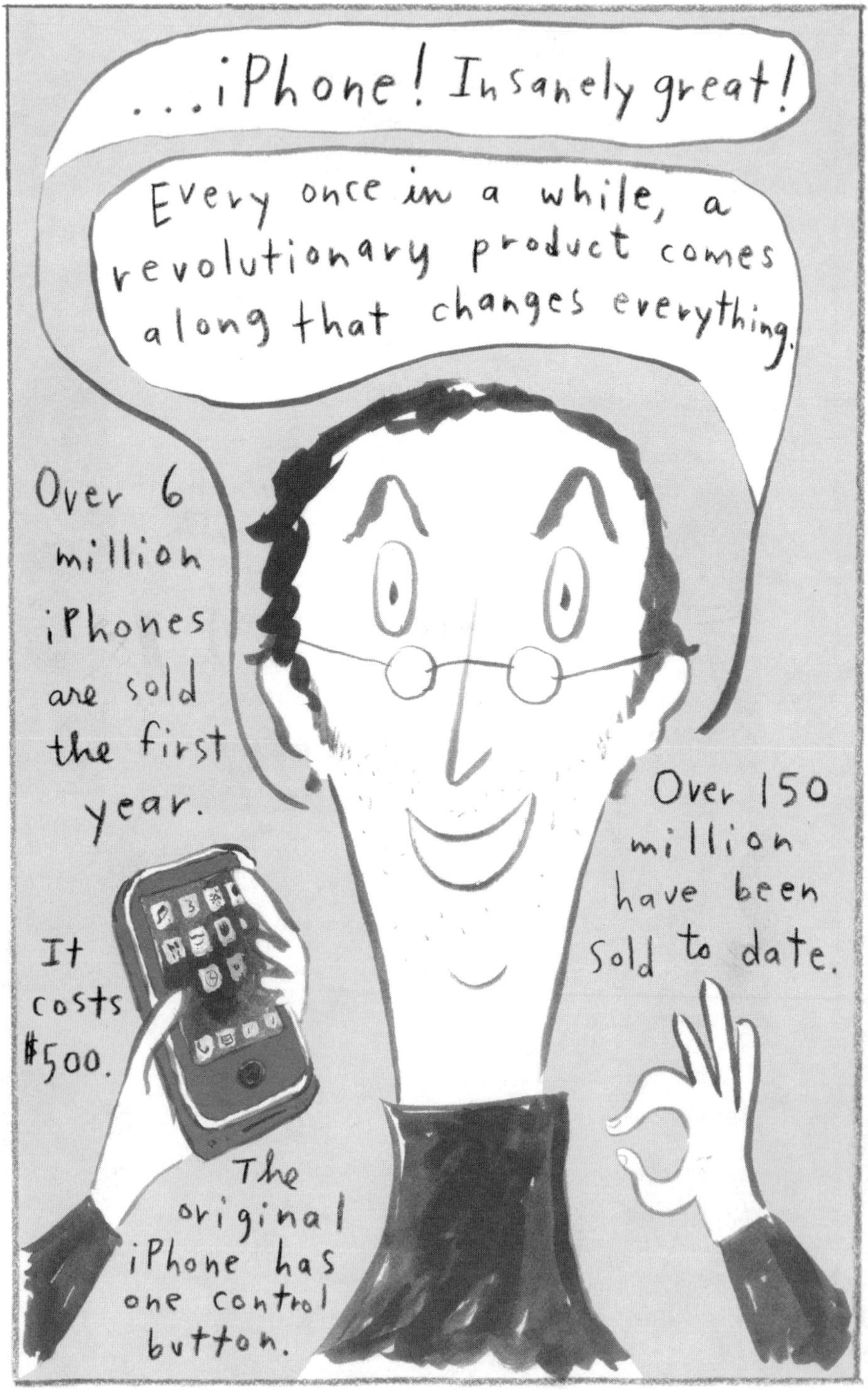
...iPhone! Insanely great!
Every once in a while, a revolutionary product comes along that changes everything.
Over 6 million iPhones are sold the first year.
Over 150 million have been sold to date.
It costs $500.
The original iPhone has one control button.

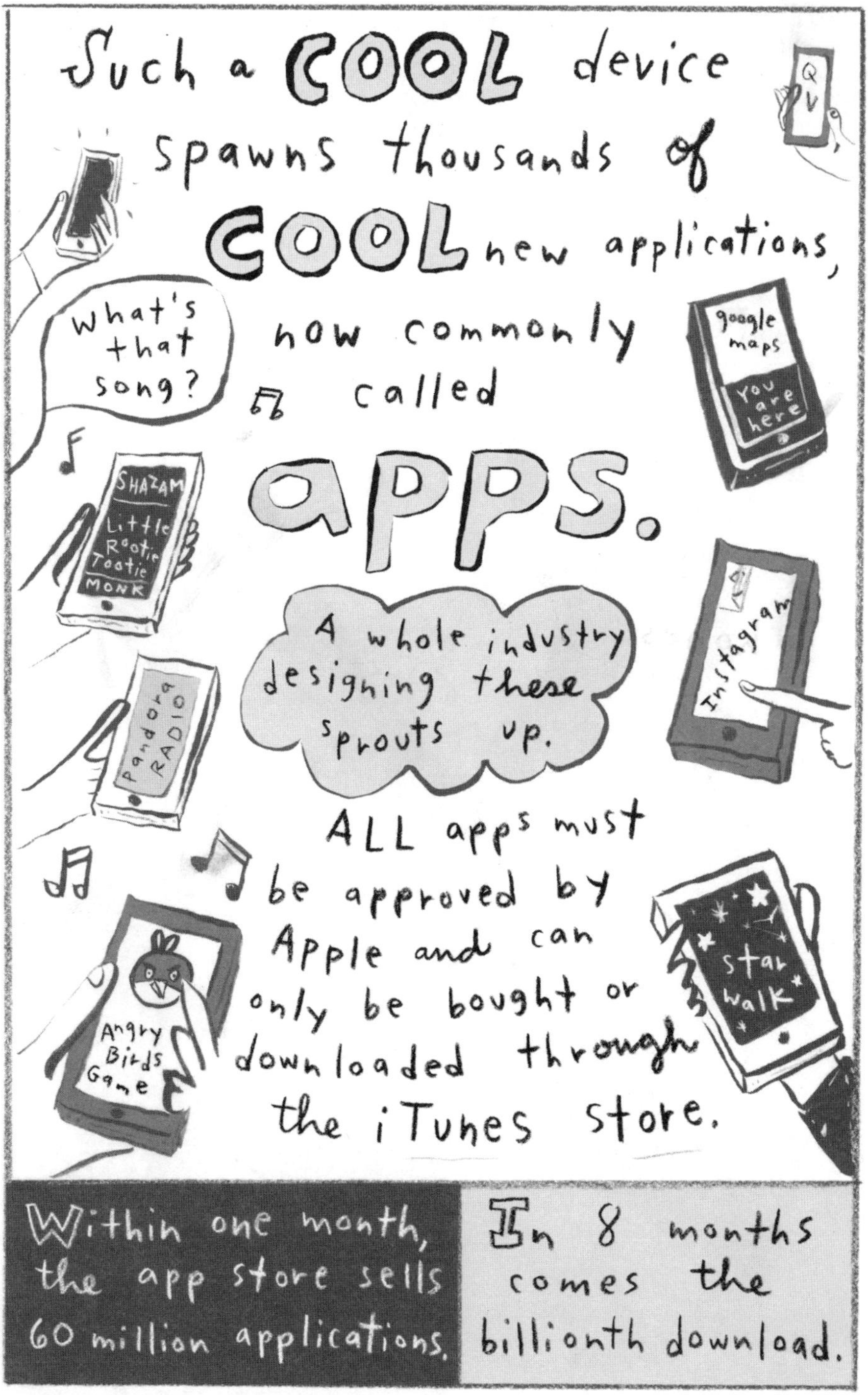

Such a COOL device spawns thousands of COOL new applications, now commonly called apps.
Q V
what's that song?
google maps
You are here
SHAZAM Little Rootie Tootie MONK
A whole industry designing these sprouts up.
Instagram
Pandora RADIO
ALL apps must be approved by Apple and can only be bought or downloaded through the iTunes store.
Angry Birds Game
star walk
Within one month, the app store sells 60 million applications.
In 8 months comes the billionth download.

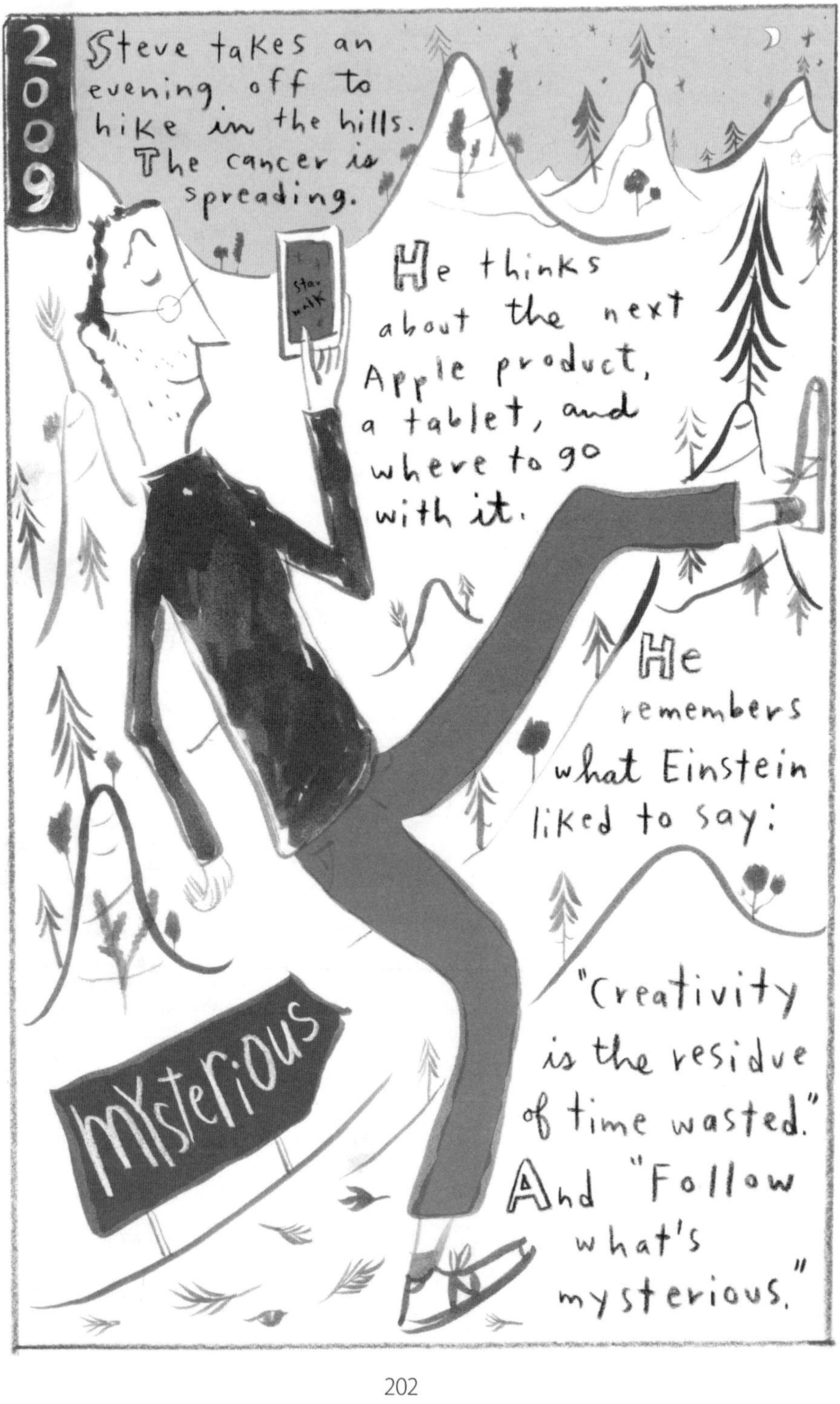
2009
Steve takes an evening off to hike in the hills. The cancer is spreading.
He thinks about the next Apple product, a tablet, and where to go with it.
Star walk
He remembers what Einstein liked to say:
"Creativity is the residue of time wasted."
And "Follow what's mysterious."
mysterious

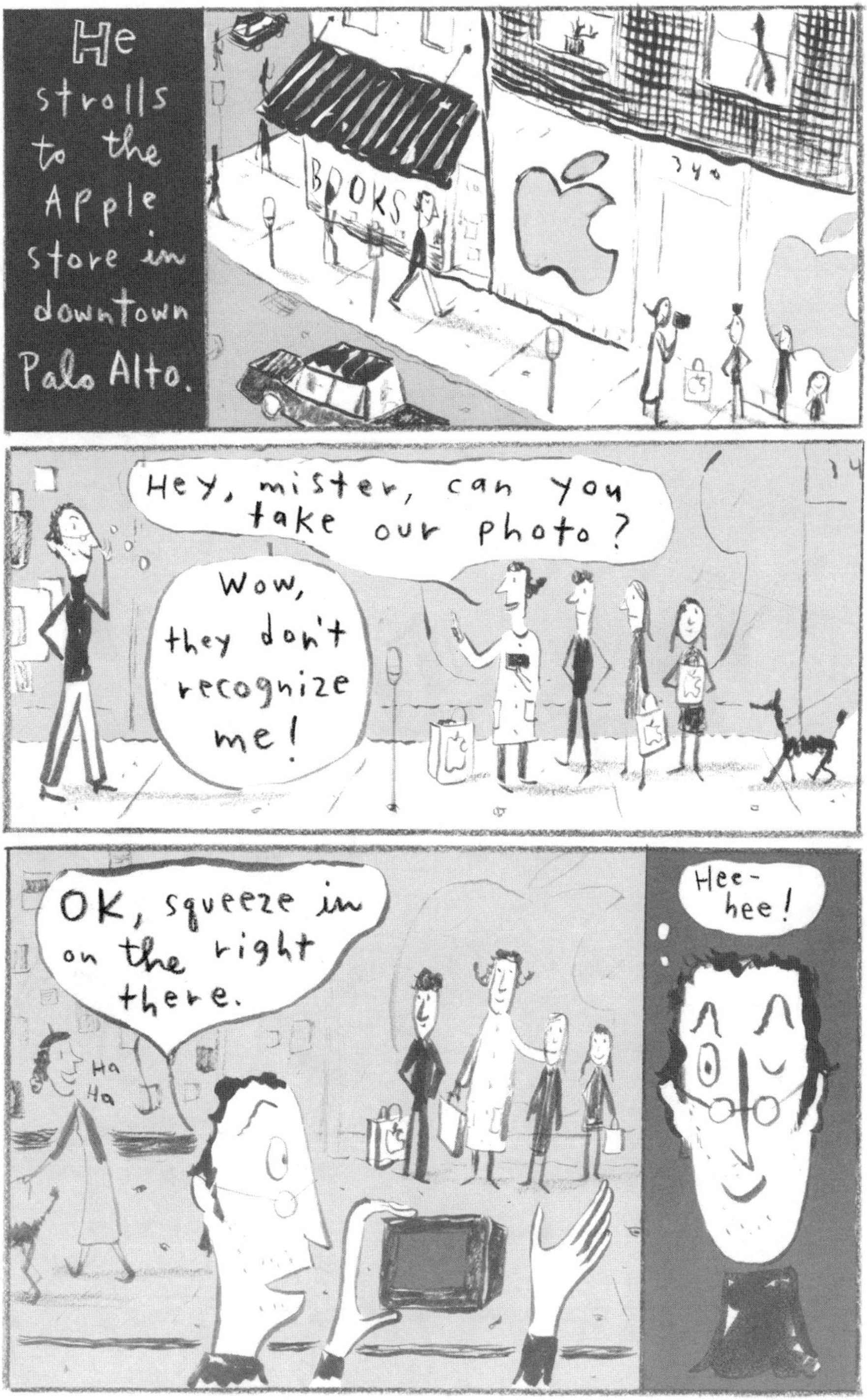
He strolls to the Apple store in downtown Palo Alto.
BOOKS
Hey, mister, can you take our photo?
Wow, they don't recognize me!
OK, squeeze in on the right there.
Ha Ha
Hee-hee!

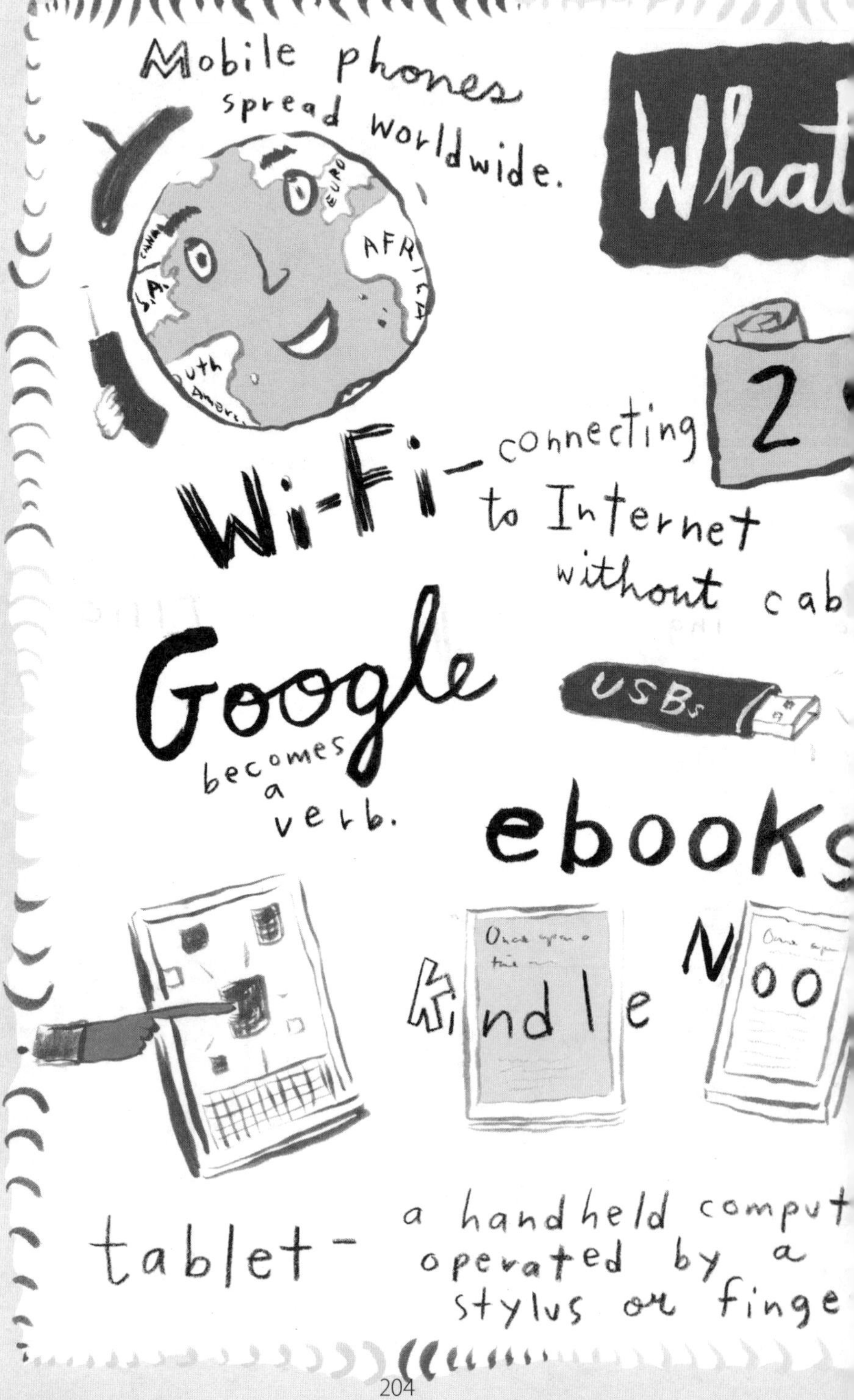

Mobile phones spread worldwide.
EURO
AFRICA
S.A.
What
2
Wi-Fi – connecting to Internet without cab
Google becomes a verb.
USBs
ebook
Kindle
Noo
tablet – a handheld comput operated by a stylus or finge

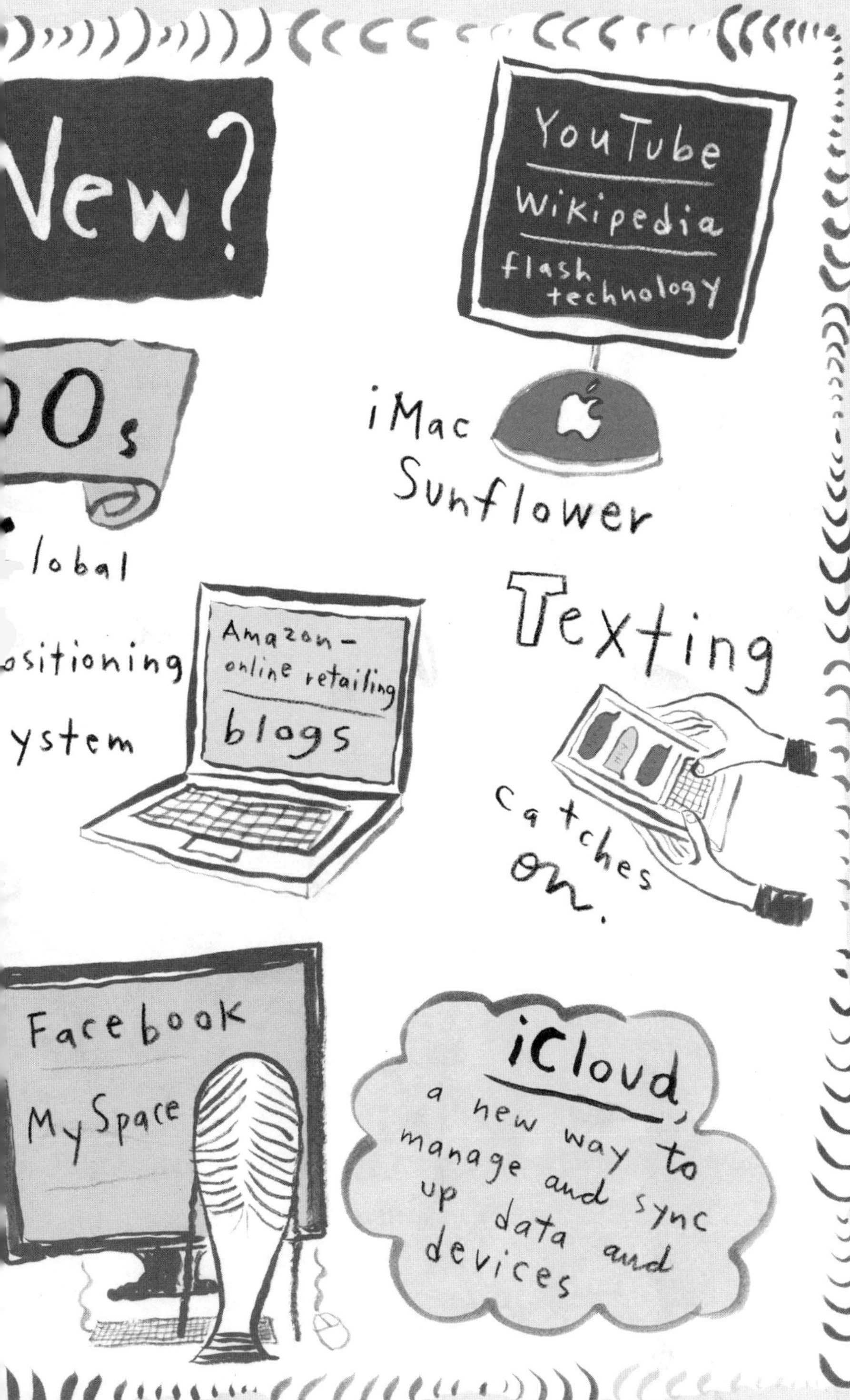
New?
YouTube
Wikipedia
flash technology
iMac
Sunflower
00s
lobal
ositioning
ystem
Amazon-
online retailing
blogs
Texting
catches on.
Facebook
MySpace
iCloud,
a new way to manage and sync up data and devices

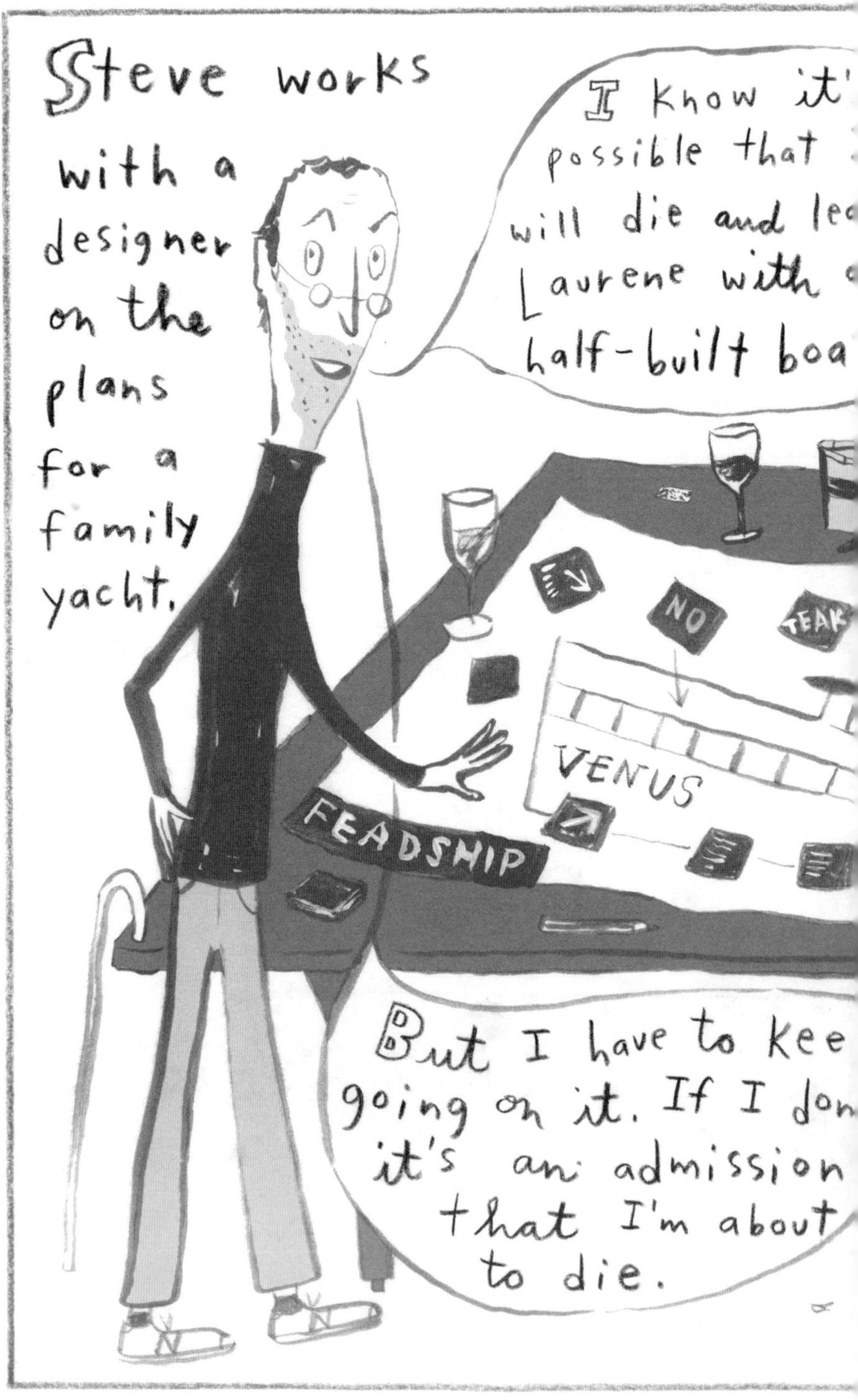
Steve works with a designer on the plans for a family yacht.
I know it's possible that I will die and leave Laurene with a half-built boat.
NO
TEAK
VENUS
FEADSHIP
But I have to keep going on it. If I don't, it's an admission that I'm about to die.

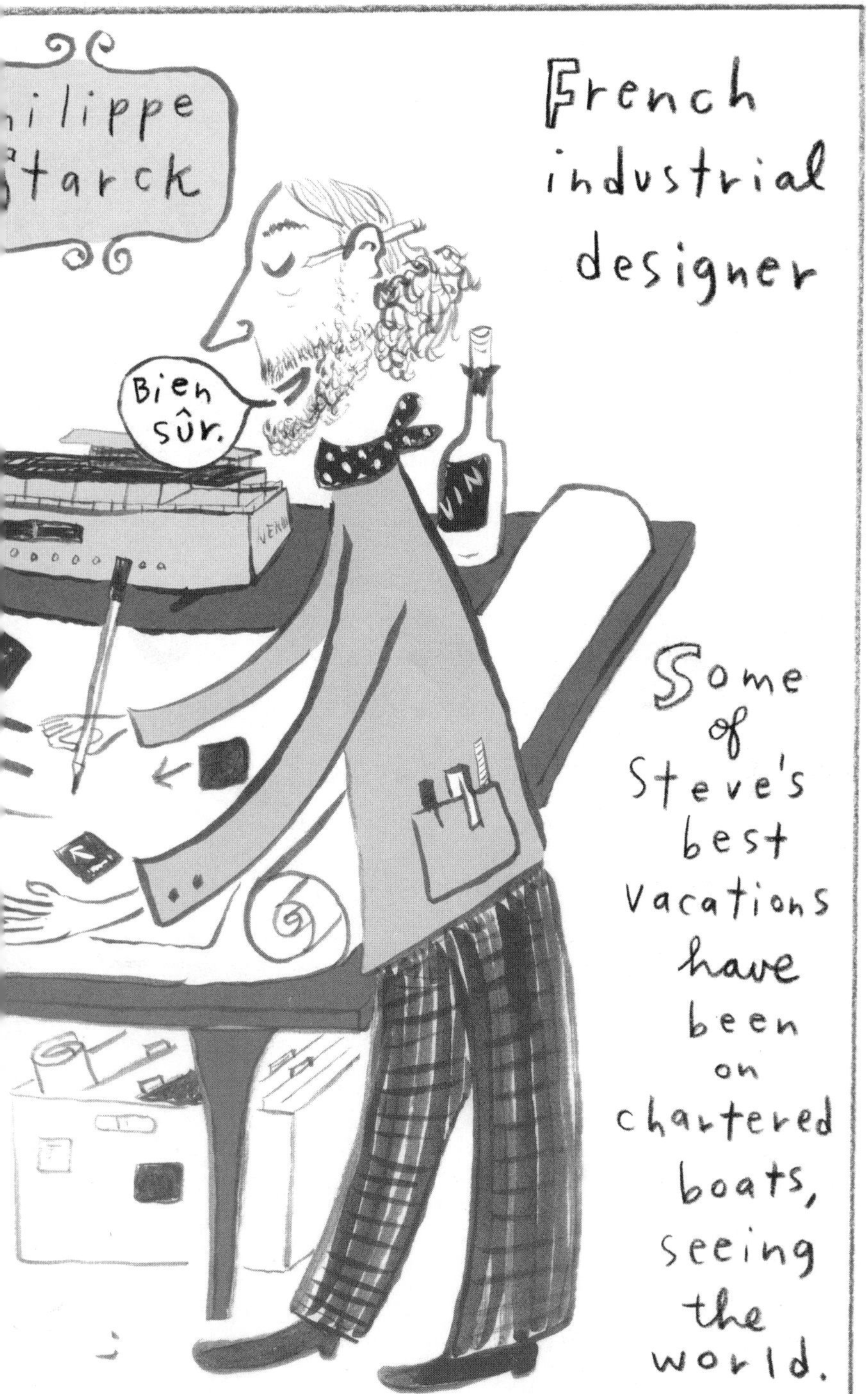
ilippe
tarck
French industrial designer
Bien sûr.
VIN
Some of Steve's best vacations have been on chartered boats, seeing the world.

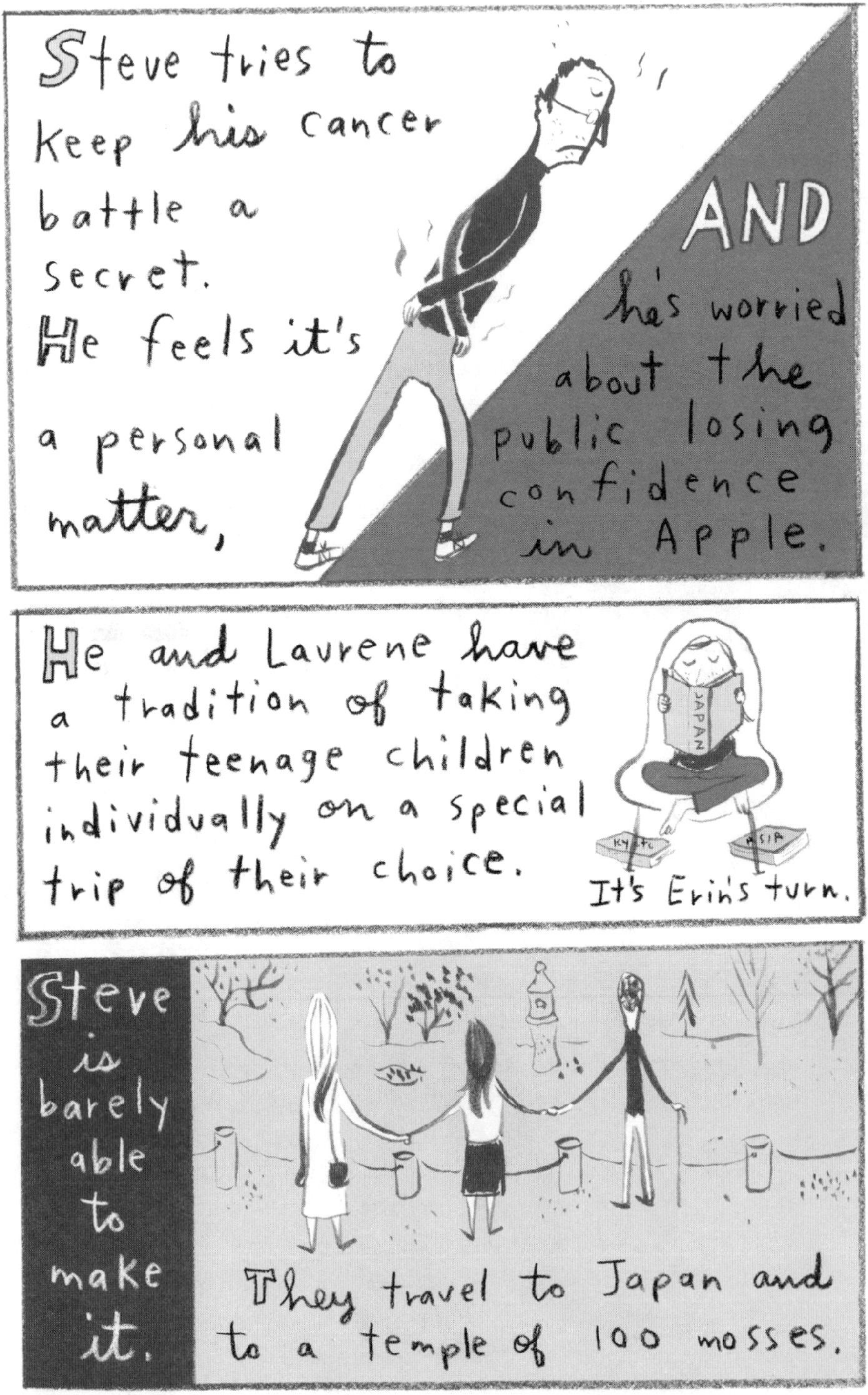
Steve tries to keep his cancer battle a secret. He feels it's a personal matter,
AND he's worried about the public losing confidence in Apple.
He and Laurene have a tradition of taking their teenage children individually on a special trip of their choice.
JAPAN
KYOTO
ASIA
It's Erin's turn.
Steve is barely able to make it.
They travel to Japan and to a temple of 100 mosses.

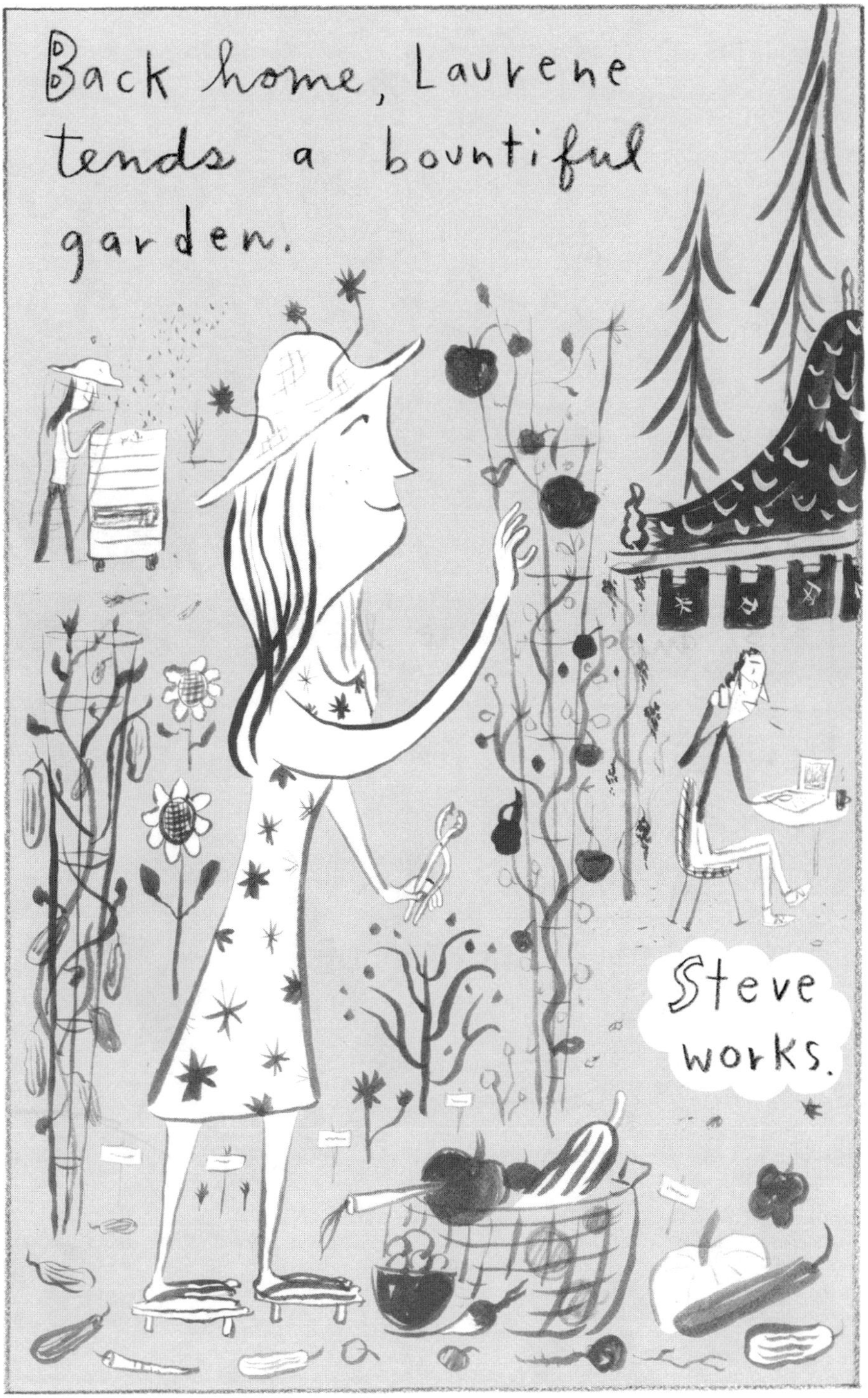
Back home, Laurene tends a bountiful garden.
Steve works.

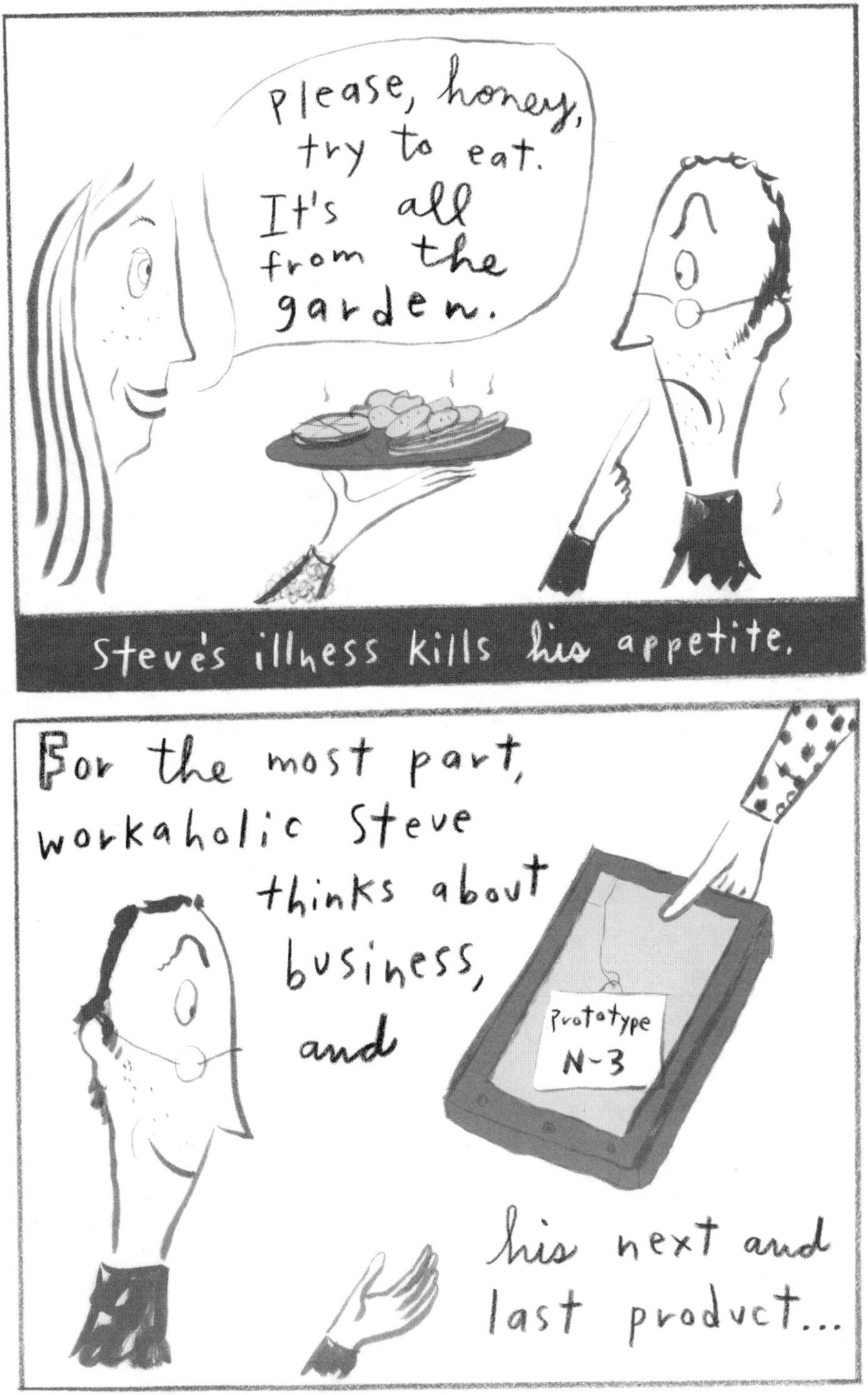
please, honey, try to eat. It's all from the garden.
Steve's illness kills his appetite.
For the most part, workaholic Steve thinks about business, and
prototype N-3
his next and last product...

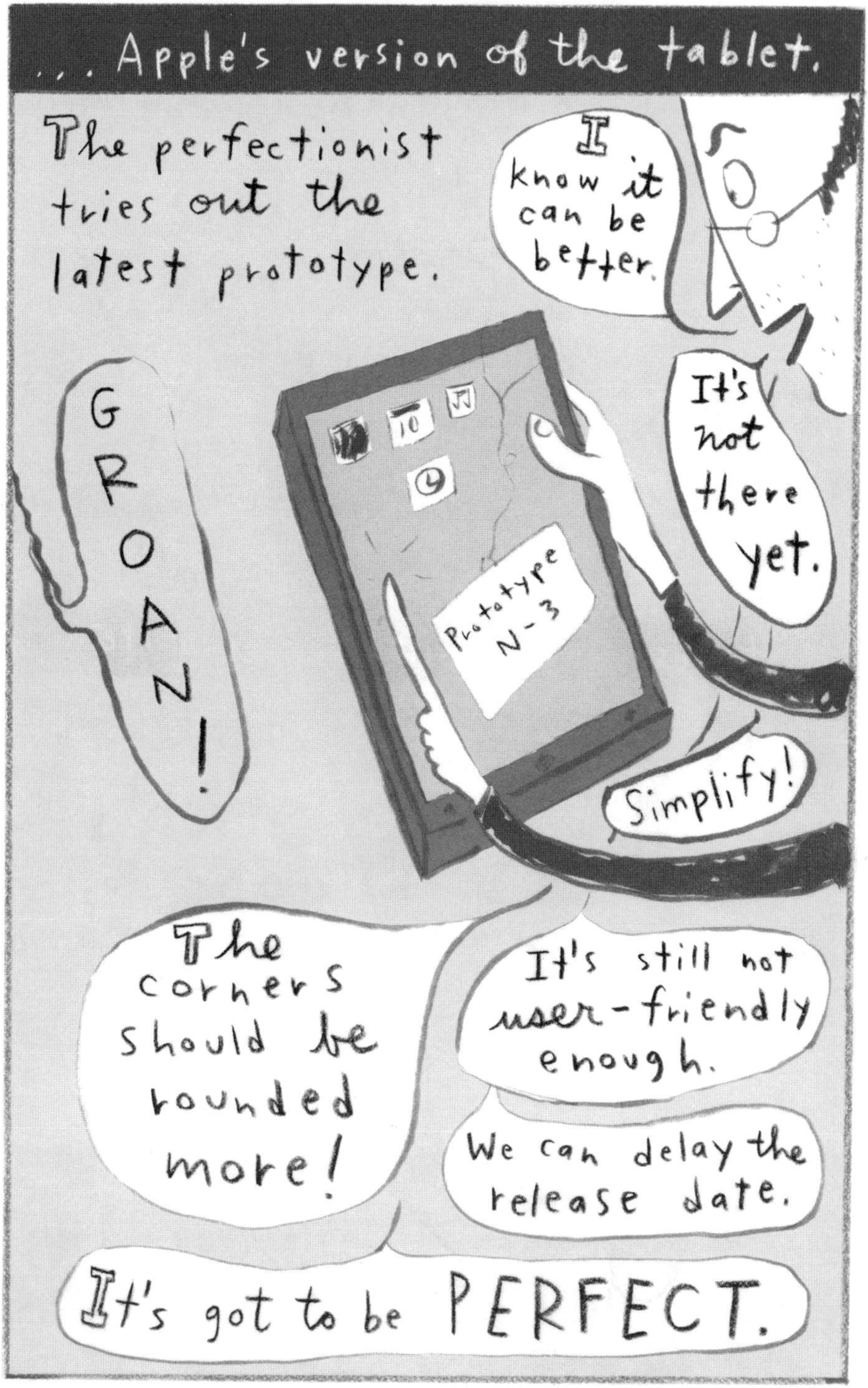

...Apple's version of the tablet.
The perfectionist tries out the latest prototype.
I know it can be better.
GROAN!
It's not there yet.
Prototype N-3
10
Simplify!
The corners should be rounded more!
It's still not user-friendly enough.
We can delay the release date.
It's got to be PERFECT.

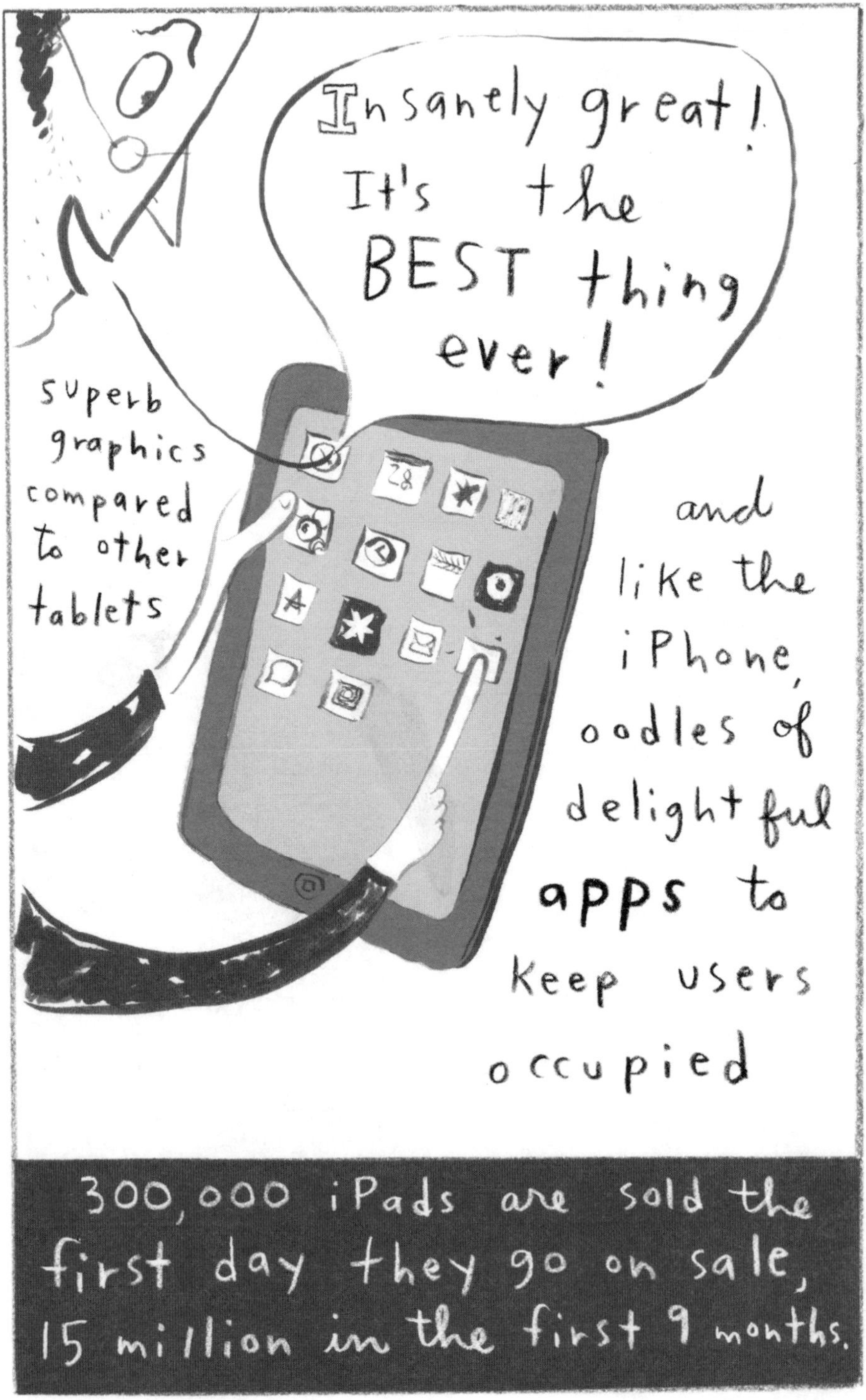

300,000 iPads are sold the first day they go on sale, 15 million in the first 9 months.

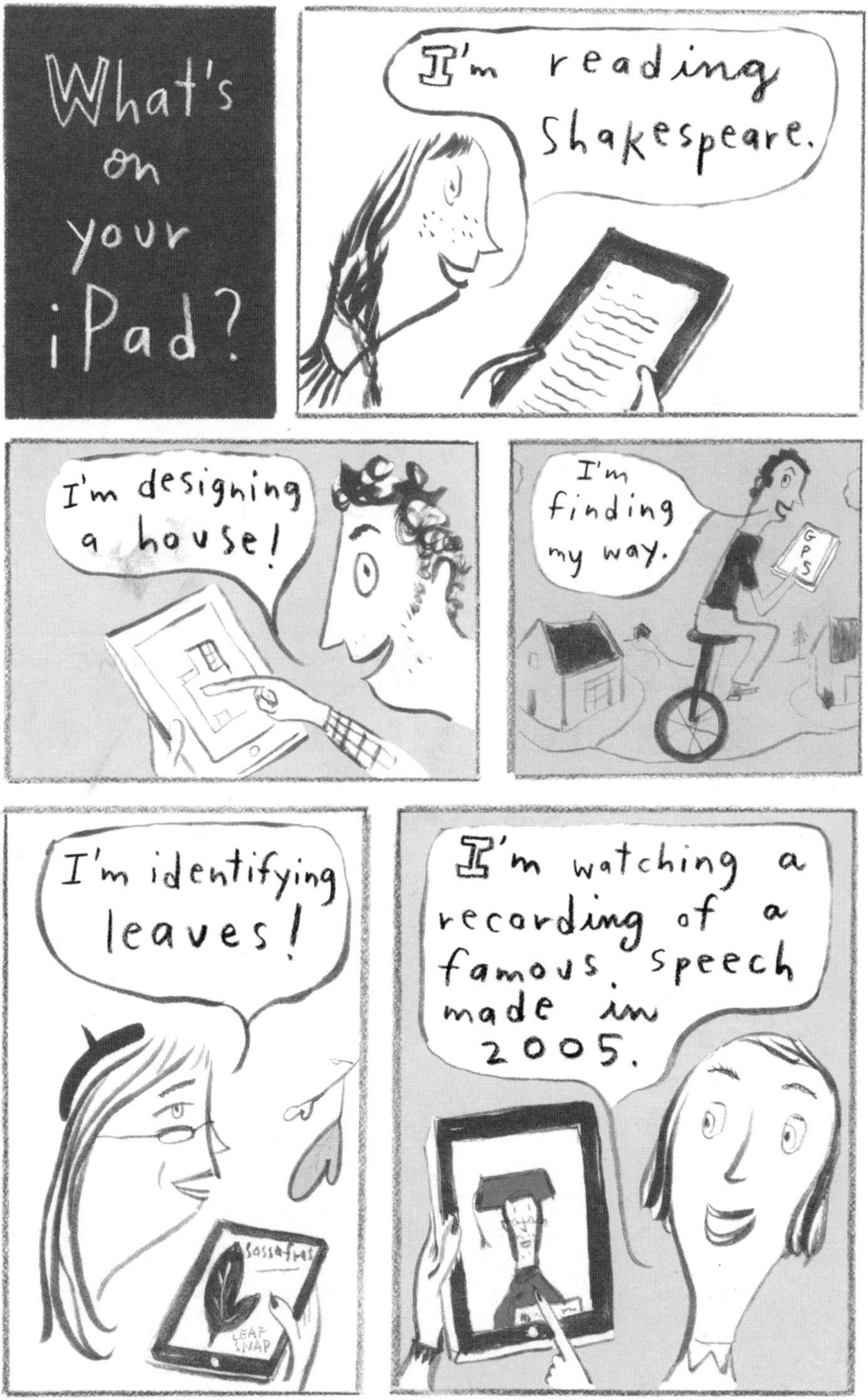
What's on your iPad?
I'm reading Shakespeare.
I'm designing a house!
I'm finding my way.
GPS
I'm identifying leaves!
Sassafras
LEAF SNAP
I'm watching a recording of a famous speech made in 2005.

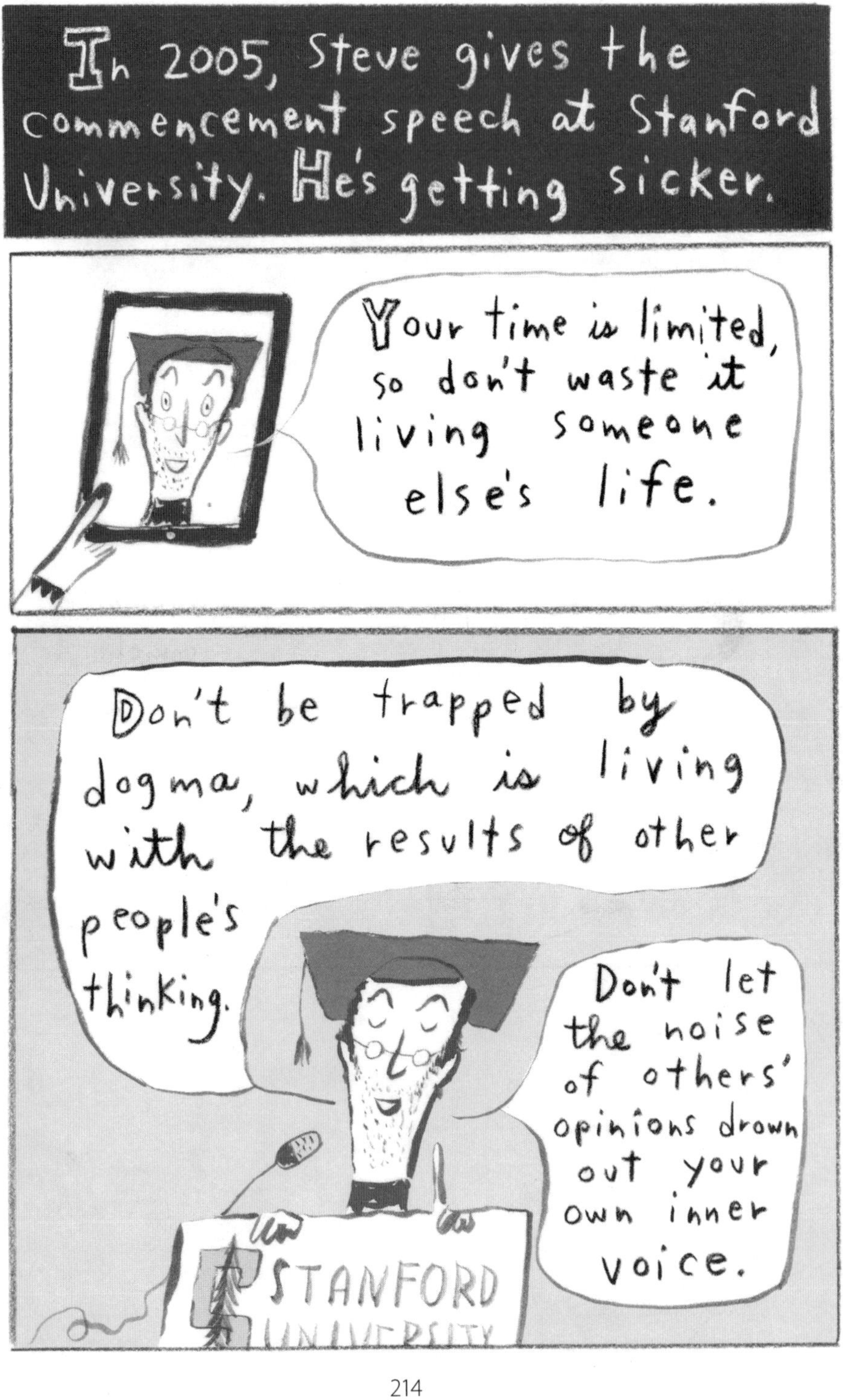
In 2005, Steve gives the commencement speech at Stanford University. He's getting sicker.
Your time is limited, so don't waste it living someone else's life.
Don't be trapped by dogma, which is living with the results of other people's thinking.
Don't let the noise of others' opinions drown out your own inner voice.
STANFORD

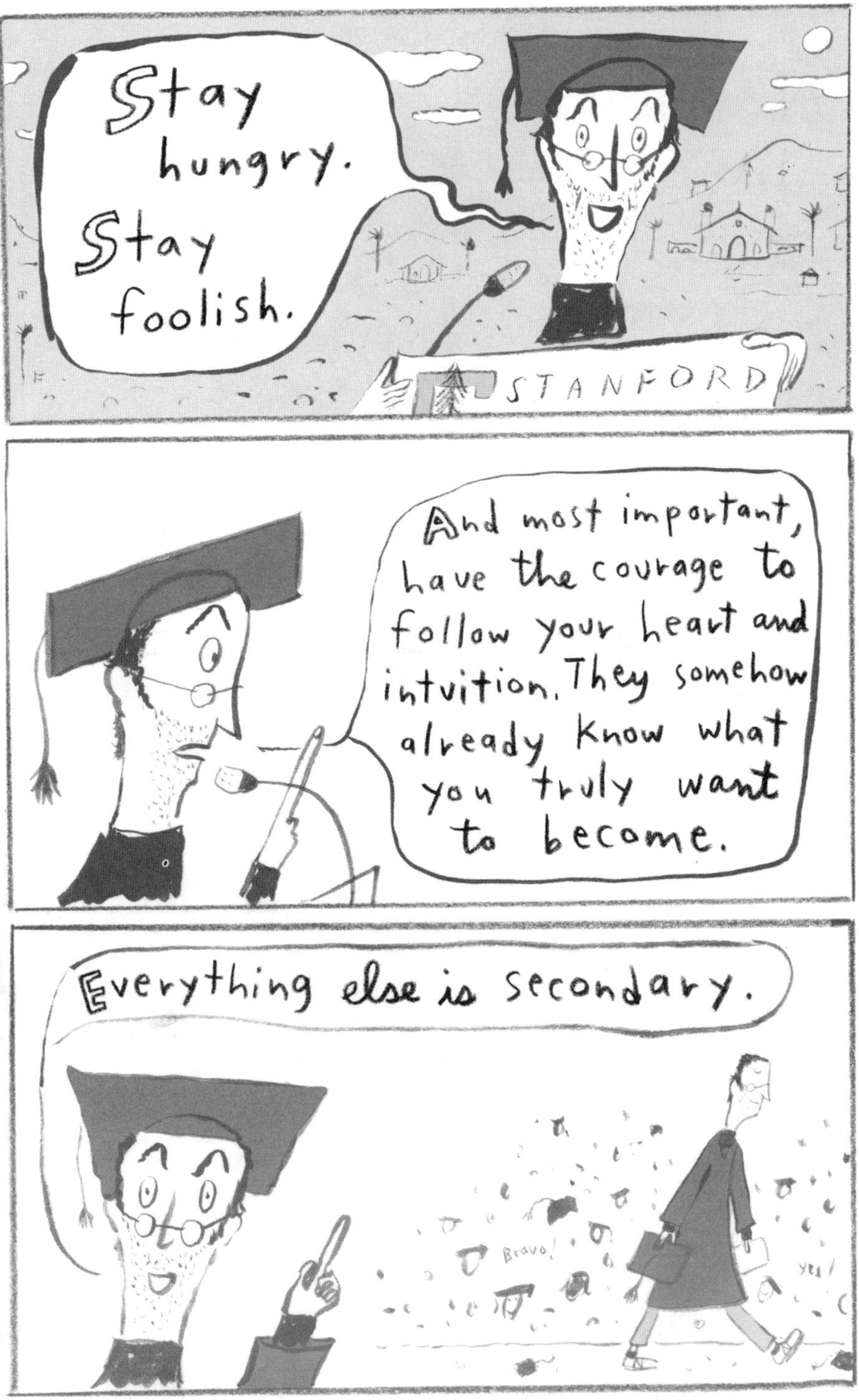
Stay hungry. Stay foolish.
STANFORD
And most important, have the courage to follow your heart and intuition. They somehow already know what you truly want to become.
Everything else is secondary.
Bravo!
yes!

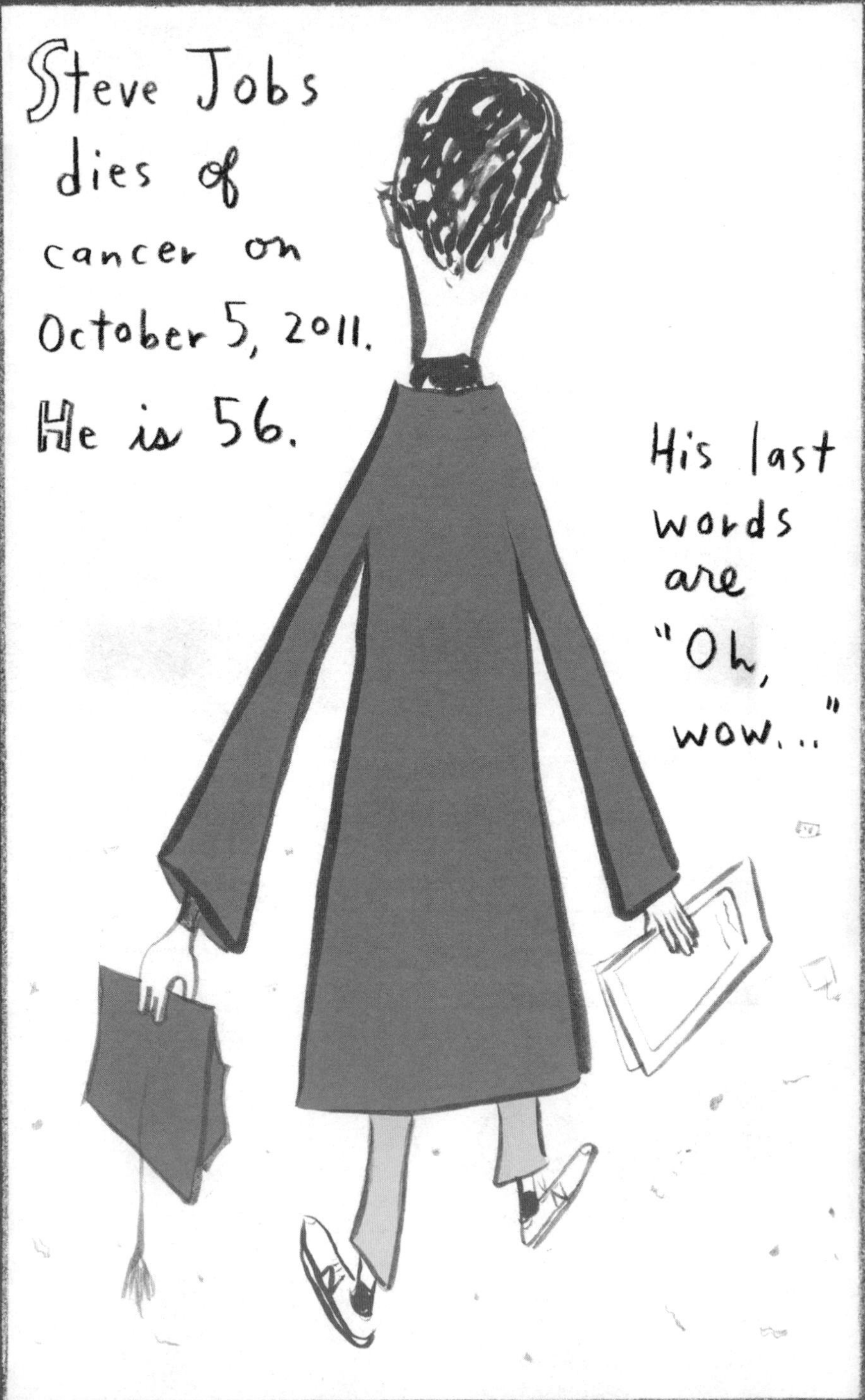
Steve Jobs dies of cancer on October 5, 2011.
He is 56.
His last words are "Oh, wow..."

Acknowledgments

Thanks to Anne, Lee, Rachael, and Stephanie at Schwartz & Wade Books; my agent, Brenda Bowen; David Biedny for a top-notch tech overview and history; Nick Sung for a terrific tour; my assistants, Ellspeth Tremblay and Dingding Hu; Isabelle Dervaux; Anne Silverstein; siblings Andrea and Sammy Recalde; the Bellport, New York, library; and my two favorite people in the world, Carl and Sam Friedberg.

Bibliography

The teetering stack of material I've accumulated to write and illustrate this book is over four feet tall! In the pile are books, DVDs, photographs, maps, clippings, sketches, printouts, and magazines, including old copies of *Popular Electronics, Popular Mechanics,* and *Mechanix Illustrated* from the 1960s and 1970s. More specifically:

Brown, David W. "In Praise of Bad Steve." *The Atlantic,* October 6, 2011, theatlantic.com/technology /archive/2011/10/in-praise-of-bad-steve/246242/.

Elliot, Jay. *The Steve Jobs Way: iLeadership for a New Generation.* Philadelphia: Vanguard Press, 2011.

Goldsmith, Mike, and Tom Jackson. *Eyewitness COMPUTER.* New York: DK Publishing, 2011.

Goodell, Jeff. "Steve Jobs in 1994: The Rolling Stone Interview." *Rolling Stone,* June 16, 1994, rollingstone.com/culture/news/steve-jobs-in-1994-the-rolling-stone-interview-20110117.

Isaacson, Walter. *Steve Jobs.* New York: Simon and Schuster, 2011.

Jobs, Steve. Macworld Expo keynote address, 2007, youtube.com/watch?v=-QZKy9FzR6k.

———. Stanford University commencement address, June 12, 2005, youtube.com /watch?v=VHWUCX6osgM.

Manjoo, Farhad. "Jobs the Jerk." *Slate,* October 25, 2011, slate.com/articles/technology /technology/2011/10/steve_jobs_biography_the_new_book_doesn_t_explain_what_made _the_.html.

Markoff, John. "Apple Computer Co-Founder Strikes Gold with New Stock." *New York Times,* 30 November 1995, nytimes.com/1995/11/30/us/apple-computer-co-founder-strikes-gold -with-new-stock.html.

———. *What the Dormouse Said: How the Sixties Counterculture Shaped the Personal Computer Industry.* New York: Viking, 2005.

Moritz, Michael. *Return to the Little Kingdom: How Apple and Steve Jobs Changed the World.* New York: Overlook Press, 2009. Kindle edition.

Morris, Betsy. "Steve Jobs Speaks Out." *Fortune,* March 2008, money.cnn.com/galleries/2008 /fortune/0803/gallery.jobsqna.fortune/.

Morrow, Daniel. Smithsonian Institution Oral History interview with Steve Jobs, April 20, 1995, americanhistory.si.edu/comphist/sj1.html.

———. "Steve Jobs interview: One-on-one in 1995." *Computerworld,* April 1995, computerworld .com/s/article/9220609/Steve_Jobs_interview_One_on_one_in_1995.

Richards, Mark, and John Alderman. *Core Memory: A Visual Survey of Vintage Computers.* San Francisco: Chronicle Books, 2007.

Rosenbaum, Ron. "Secrets of the Little Blue Box," *Esquire,* October 1971, historyofphonephreaking .org/docs/rosenbaum1971.pdf.

Sheff, David. "Steven Jobs." *Playboy*, February 1985, longform.org/stories/playboy-interview-steve
-jobs.

Triumph of the Nerds: The Rise of Accidental Empires. Ambrose Video, 2002.

Wolf, Gary. "Steve Jobs: The Next Insanely Great Thing." *Wired*, February 1996, archive.wired.com
/wired/archive//4.02/jobs.html?person=steve_jobs&topic_set=wiredpeople.

To further research this book, and especially for the pictures, I visited Silicon Valley and drove on the 101 Freeway and along El Camino Real. I visited the Computer History Museum in Mountain View, and went to Palo Alto and the Stanford Linear Accelerator Laboratory. I saw where Xerox PARC once was, and I got a glimpse of the suburban garage in Los Altos where Apple Computer was born, as well as the Jobs family house in Palo Alto. Back up north in the San Francisco Bay Area, I was given a tour of Pixar. (Thanks, NS!)

Notes

Any quotes not mentioned below in the source notes are made up, with an intent to communicate a sense of what I imagine was said.

"Here's to the crazy ones": advertising copy partly written by Steve Jobs.

Chapter 1
On growing up in the early days of Silicon Valley: Isaacson, 1–20, and Smithsonian interview.
On middle-school teacher Imogen Hill: *Playboy* and *Computerworld.*
On Larry Lang: *Computerworld* and Smithsonian interview.

Chapter 2
On building a frequency counter: *Playboy* and Isaacson, 17.

Chapter 3
On the blue box: *Esquire.*
On building the blue box: Moritz, Chapter 6: "The Little Blue Box," and *Triumph of the Nerds,* Part 1.
On selling the blue boxes: *Playboy* and Isaacson, 29–30.

Chapter 4
On being at Reed College: Isaacson, 33–41.
"If today were the last day": Stanford University commencement address.
"I'm going to find my": Isaacson, 45.
"Live each day as if": *Fortune.*
On meeting with Zen master Kobun: Isaacson, 48–50.

Chapter 5
"Don't take no" and "Pretend to be": Isaacson, 55.
On computer history: the Computer History Museum, Goldsmith, and Richards.
On choosing a company name: Isaacson, 63, and Moritz, Chapter 10: "Half Right."
"I don't think it would have happened without": *Playboy.*

Chapter 6
On Markkula: Isaacson, 75–78, and Moritz, Chapter 12, "Mercedes and a Corvette."
On the early days of Apple and first uses of Apple IIs: Moritz, Chapter 18, "Welcome IBM, Seriously."
"You should never start a company": Isaacson, 78.

Chapter 7
On Xerox PARC: *Triumph of the Nerds,* Part 3.

Chapter 8
"If it could save a person's": *Triumph of the Nerds,* Part 3.
"Do you want to spend the rest of": *Triumph of the Nerds,* Part 3.
"Good artists imitate": *Triumph of the Nerds,* Part 3. (Steve Jobs attributed this quote to Pablo Picasso.)
On being ousted from Apple: Isaacson, 194–210.
On NeXT: "It's not late": Isaacson, 236.

Chapter 9
    On finding his biological family and on meeting Laurene Powell: Isaacson, 250–283.

Chapter 10
    On the early days of Pixar: Isaacson, 238–249.
    "There's no yacht": *New York Times*.

Chapter 11
    "Which one do I tell": Isaacson, 337.
    "What kind of computer would the Jetsons": Isaacson, 352.
    "Did Alexander Graham Bell": Isaacson, 170.
    "Henry Ford liked to say": Elliott, 147.
    On the design of the first Apple Store: Isaacson, 368–377.

Chapter 12
    "There's no satisfying clicking": *Slate*.
    On the development of the iPod: Isaacson, 490–510.
    On tossing an iPod prototype into a fish tank: *The Atlantic*.
    "What's on your iPod?": Isaacson, 497.

Chapter 13
    On the history of cell phones and development of the iPhone: Elliott, 203–204.
    "The phone will have only one": Elliott, 23, and *Fortune*.
    On the design of the iPhone: Isaacson, 465–475.
    "This is the future!": Isaacson, 468.
    "Every once in a while a revolutionary product comes along": Macworld Expo
        keynote address.
    On appliance shopping: *Wired*.
    On designing the family yacht: Isaacson, 529.
    "Your time is limited": Stanford University commencement address.

About the Author

Jessie Hartland is the author and illustrator of the highly acclaimed graphic biography *Bon Appétit: The Delicious Life of Julia Child,* which the *New York Times* described as "bursting with exuberant urban-naïf gouache paintings and a hand-lettered text that somehow manages to recount every second of Child's life." Her illustrations have appeared in newspapers and magazines throughout the world, including the *New York Times, Bon Appétit, Martha Stewart Living, Real Simple,* and *Travel + Leisure.* She is also a commercial artist whose work can be seen on ceramics and fabric, as well as in advertisements and store windows. She lives in New York City with her family. Visit her at jessiehartland.com.